RUSSIA & ARABIA

RUSSIA & ARABIA

Soviet Foreign Policy toward the Arabian Peninsula

MARK N. KATZ

THE JOHNS HOPKINS UNIVERSITY PRESS
Baltimore and London

This publication was prepared under grants from the Rockefeller Foundation and from the Kennan Institute for Advanced Russian Studies of the Woodrow Wilson International Center for Scholars, Washington, D.C. The statements and views expressed herein are those of the author and are not necessarily those of the Rockefeller Foundation or the Wilson Center.

The Johns Hopkins University Press
701 West 40th Street
Baltimore, Maryland 21211
The Johns Hopkins Press Ltd, London

The paper in this book is acid-free and meets the guidelines for permanence and durability of the Committee on Production Guidelines for Book Longevity of the Council on Library Resources.

LIBRARY OF CONGRESS CATALOGING-IN-PUBLICATION DATA

Katz, Mark N.
  Russia and Arabia.

  Bibliography: p.
  Includes index.
  1. Arabian Peninsula—Foreign relations—Soviet Union. 2. Soviet Union—Foreign relations—Arabian Peninsula. I. Title.
DS228.S65K37   1985   327.47053   85-45046
ISBN 0-8018-2897-X (alk. paper)

Contents

Preface

I undertook this study because I believe the Arabian Peninsula is of great strategic importance to the West for its tremendous oil reserves. These lines are being written in 1985, when oil prices have been sagging, so it is easy to forget that this region possesses over 40 percent of the world's total known oil reserves and that these reserves will last well into the next century and even beyond at current rates of production. Few other countries' known reserves are expected to last nearly this long. More petroleum will undoubtedly be found in many areas of the globe, but unless new discoveries outpace depletion of existing fields, over time the world will become increasingly dependent on oil from the Peninsula.

The revolution in Iran and the Iran-Iraq war have only served to heighten Western concern over the stability of the Peninsula. Many fear that the Soviet Union intends to extend its influence over these vulnerable countries and that Soviet control of the Peninsula could lead to a substantial increase in oil prices, a reduced flow of oil, or even an outright cutoff of oil to the West.

Yet while there is heightened concern over Soviet influence in the Arabian Peninsula, relatively little detailed research has been done on actual Soviet foreign policy toward this vital region, and there has been little discussion of the opportunities and constraints Moscow faces in extending its influence there. This book examines these issues as well as the problems that Soviet efforts to gain influence in the Peninsula pose for the West, especially the United States.

Up until 1985, Kuwait was the only Gulf Cooperation Council state with ties to Moscow. On September 26, 1985, though, the USSR and Oman announced they would establish diplomatic relations. This was a surprising move considering that while the Soviet leaders have regularly exchanged friendly messages with the leaders of Saudi Arabia, the UAE,

Bahrain, and Qatar (with whom they do not have diplomatic ties yet) on various occasions such as national holidays, the death of old leaders, and the accession of new ones, I have nowhere seen in the public record evidence of any such exchange between the USSR and Oman. Indeed, the Soviets have been more critical of Oman than of any other GCC state due to the Sultan's permitting the U.S. to use military facilities in his country as well as the presence of a substantial number of British officers in his armed forces. Oman has also been one of the harshest critics of the Soviet Union within the GCC.

Why Oman suddenly agreed to this step is not clear. Perhaps the Sultan wished to signal his displeasure to Washington regarding his government's negotiations with the U.S. over American access to Omani military facilities. Whatever the reason, however, now that Oman has recognized the USSR, it would not be surprising if other GCC states did so as well. During the summer of 1985, there were several indications that this might soon occur: the Bahraini Prime Minister made two statements urging that his country and the other GCC states reconsider their position on diplomatic relations with the USSR; a Soviet journalist was allowed to visit the UAE; and one of Saudi King Fahd's sons, Prince Faysal (head of the Saudi Higher Council for Youth and Sports), visited Moscow in August and met with Soviet Deputy Foreign Minister Kornienko (the first official Saudi visit to Moscow since the Saudi Foreign Minister went there as part of an Arab League delegation in December 1982). Yet, it is not certain whether any of the other GCC states, especially Saudi Arabia, will actually establish diplomatic ties with Moscow. Even if they all do, this does not mean that these governments will become close friends of the USSR. Their concern about Soviet involvement in Afghanistan, the Horn of Africa, and South Yemen, as well as about Moscow's backing the domestic opponents of these conservative regimes, will serve as an obstacle to Soviet efforts to draw these nations away from the United States and the West.

The number of people who deserve thanks for giving me assistance in this project is immense. I am particularly grateful to the Rockefeller Foundation for awarding me an International Relations Fellowship, and to the Kennan Institute for Advanced Russian Studies (a component of the Smithsonian Institution's Woodrow Wilson International Center for Scholars) for awarding me a research grant. I am especially indebted to John Stremlau, currently the Foundation's acting director for international relations, not only for giving me advice and support generally, but also for lending me a shirt, tie, and jacket when my luggage got lost en route to a conference we were both attending in Bellagio, Italy. Thanks are also due to Herbert Ellison, Secretary of the Kennan Institute, both for assisting me and for taking the initiative in creating the Kennan research grant program designed specifically to aid younger scholars.

I thank Bruce MacLaury and John Steinbruner for allowing me to be a guest scholar and giving me the use of an office at the Brookings Institution throughout the term of my Rockefeller fellowship. I also benefited greatly from comments from many of my Brookings colleagues, including Raymond Garthoff, Christine Helms, Ed Hewett, Jerry Hough, Michael MccGwire, Thomas McNaugher, and William Quandt. As Brookings let me use an office while I had the Rockefeller fellowship, the Georgetown University Center for Strategic and International Studies let me use one while I had the Kennan research grant. At CSIS, I especially thank Amos Jordan, William Taylor, Thane Gustafson, Robert Neumann, Fred Axelgard, and Shireen Hunter.

During the research for this book, I visited Oman, Egypt, and North Yemen (December 1982–January 1983), the Soviet Union (December 1983–January 1984), and Saudi Arabia and Kuwait (April 1984). It is not possible to mention all the people I met on these trips, but several whom I met in the Middle East, Western Europe, and the United States deserve thanks. In Oman, the Ministry of Information arranged several interesting interviews for me, including ones at the Defense Headquarters near Muscat and at the base in Salalah. In Cairo I had a very enlightening talk with former Egyptian Foreign Minister Isma'il Fahmy as well as with scholars from the Al-Ahram Center for Political and Strategic Studies, the American University in Cairo, and Cairo University. I am particularly grateful to Muhammad Ezzeldin 'Abd al-Monim, Director of Research at the Egyptian Foreign Ministry's Diplomatic Institute, and to Ann Lesch, formerly of the Ford Foundation's Cairo office, for their views and for arranging several meetings for me. Thanks are also due to the Ford Foundation for the use of its guest flat in Garden City.

Before going to the Middle East the first time, I had a fascinating conversation with North Yemen's Shaykh Sinan Abu Lahum of the Bakil Confederation (who was formerly governor of Hodeida) and Colonel Dirham Abu Lahum (former governor of Ibb and member of the Presidential Council). There are many others Yemeni officials and scholars I met in Sanaa and in Washington who deserve thanks but who prefer to remain anonymous. Special thanks are due to Muhsin al-Aini (former Prime Minister of the Yemen Arab Republic and currently the YAR's ambassador in Washington) and Muhammad Abu Lahum, without whose assistance and advice I would not have learned nearly as much about North Yemen.

In Moscow, I had useful conversations with scholars at the Institute for the U.S.A. and Canada and the Oriental Institute. I also met with several scholars at the Oriental Institute branch in Leningrad and have benefited from talks with several Soviet diplomats and scholars in Washington.

I would like to express my great appreciation for meetings with the Saudi Minister of Foreign Affairs, Prince Sa'ud bin Faysal; the Director of Intelligence, Prince Turki bin Faysal; and the Minister of State for Foreign Affairs, Shaykh Muhammad Ibrahim Massoud in Riyadh. I also had a fascinating conversation with Khalid as-Sudairi, Director-General of the Office of Strategic Studies attached to the Council of Ministers, and Prince 'Abdallah bin Faysal bin Turki of the Royal Commission for Yanbu and Jubail. In addition, I learned much from talks with Dr. 'Abd al-Karim Hamadi, special adviser to the Secretary-General of the Gulf Cooperation Council, and several professors at King Sa'ud University in Riyadh. Thanks are also due to Khalid Tindan, Nizar al-Madani, and Hassan Nazer for making my visit to Saudi Arabia extremely worthwhile. I would like to thank the Saudi Embassy in Washington and the Ministry of Information in Riyadh for all their efforts on my behalf. Special thanks are due to Rihab Massoud, whose help and advice have been extremely valuable to me.

In Kuwait, I had extremely interesting talks with the then Minister of State for Cabinet Affairs (now retired) 'Abd al-'Aziz Hussain, then Foreign Ministry Undersecretary (now Minister of State for Cabinet Affairs) Rashid ar-Rashid, and several scholars at Kuwait University. I would also like to thank the Kuwaiti Embassy in Washington as well as the Ministry of Information in Kuwait for arranging my visit.

I was, unfortunately, unable to visit South Yemen. Nevertheless, I did have exchanges with several people who come from there or who have visited Aden frequently, including the People's Democratic Republic of Yemen Ambassador to the United Nations, 'Abdallah al-Ashtal, Fred Halliday of the London School of Economics, Maxine Molyneux of Essex University, and Sultan Ghalib Al-Quaiti, who now resides in Saudi Arabia.

I would also like to thank several officials of the U.S. Department of State and the U.S. Information Agency who were extremely helpful in providing introductions, sharing their views, and offering their hospitality both abroad and in Washington. I am particularly grateful to Ronald Neumann for all his help and advice.

In addition, I also received helpful comments, criticisms, suggestions, and assistance from many other people, including William Griffith of MIT, J. E. Peterson of the Middle East Institute, Malcolm Peck of Meridian House International, former Deputy Assistant Secretaries of State Joseph Twinam and William Crawford, Charles Tripp of the Graduate Institute of International Studies in Geneva, former Soviet diplomat Vladimir Sakharov, Yahya Sadowski of the University of California at Berkeley, Manfred Wenner and Lealan Swanson of the American Institute for Yemeni Studies, J. B. Kelly, Mordechai Abir, Ursula Braun, Stephen Page, and many others who prefer not to be mentioned by name.

Finally, I would like to thank my five research assistants, Justin Burke, Miranda Cox, Thomas Firestone, Geoffrey Hathaway, and Susan Keats, for all their hard work. Jim Hitselberger and Steven Riskin, both former Brookings research assistants, were also very helpful. In addition to giving me essential lessons on how to operate a personal computer, my wife, Nancy Yinger, provided enormous support and encouragement through all stages of the research and writing. None of the individuals or organizations mentioned here are responsible for the statements and opinions expressed in this book. These, as well as any errors and omissions, are solely my responsibility.

I have used the Library of Congress system for transliterating Russian words except that sometimes in the text I have substituted the commonly accepted English forms of well-known names and words. Similarly for Arabic, more common names and words appear in their generally accepted English usage. Otherwise, out of the array of Arabic transliteration systems, I have employed the older version used by the U.S. Foreign Broadcast Information Service. Those who understand the language will know the Arabic spelling, while those who do not will avoid having to puzzle over symbols that are meaningless to them.

Abbreviations

ACDA	Arms Control and Disarmament Agency
ALF	Arab Liberation Front [Saudi]
ANM	Arab Nationalist Movement
ARAMCO	Arabian-American Oil Company
ATUC	Aden Trades Union Congress
BNLF	Bahrain National Liberation Front
CIA	Central Intelligence Agency
CMEA	Council for Mutual Economic Assistance
CPSU	Communist Party of the Soviet Union
DLF	Dhofar Liberation Front [Omani]
FLOSY	Front for the Liberation of South Yemen
GCC	Gulf Cooperation Council
NDF	National Democratic Front [North Yemeni]
NDFLOAG	National Democratic Front for the Liberation of Oman and the Arab Gulf
NLF	National Liberation Front [South Yemeni]
OAPEC	Organization of Arab Petroleum Exporting Countries
OPEC	Organization of Petroleum Exporting Countries
PDRY	People's Democratic Republic of Yemen [South Yemen]
PFLO	Popular Front for the Liberation of Oman
PFLOAG	Popular Front for the Liberation of the Occupied Arab Gulf [1968–71]
	Popular Front for the Liberation of Oman and the Arab Gulf [1971–74]
PLO	Palestine Liberation Organization
PRC	People's Republic of China
PRF	Popular Resistance Force [North Yemeni]
PSP	People's Socialist Party [South Yemeni]

RDF	Rapid Deployment Force
SACP	Saudi Arabian Communist Party
SAL	South Arabian League [South Yemeni]
SAM	surface-to-air missile
SANLF	Saudi Arabian National Liberation Front
SSM	surface-to-surface missile
UAE	United Arab Emirates
UAR	United Arab Republic
UPAP	Union of Peoples of the Arabian Peninsula [Saudi]
UPONF	United Political Organization—National Front [South Yemeni]
USSR	Union of Soviet Socialist Republics
YAR	Yemen Arab Republic [North Yemen]
YPUP	Yemen People's Unity Party [North Yemeni]
YSP	Yemeni Socialist Party [South Yemeni]

RUSSIA & ARABIA

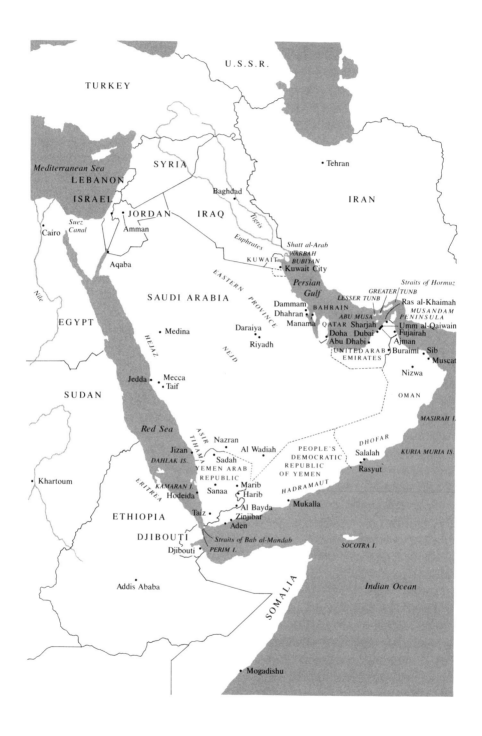

Introduction

The Arabian Peninsula consists of eight countries. Six of them—Saudi Arabia, Kuwait, Bahrain, Qatar, the United Arab Emirates (UAE), and Oman—are ruled by pro-Western monarchs and together form the membership of the Gulf Cooperation Council (GCC). The other two—North Yemen and South Yemen—experienced revolutions in the 1960s. The South has an avowedly Marxist-Leninist government and is closely allied to the USSR. In the North there is a non-Marxist military regime, but the central government has also had to contend with strong tribal and leftist forces. The Peninsula is bordered by the Persian (or Arab) Gulf to the east, the Indian Ocean to the south, the Red Sea to the west, and Iraq and Jordan to the north.

The primary reason the Peninsula is important to the West is oil. In 1984 the United States imported 35 percent of its oil, Western Europe 70 percent, and Japan 95 percent. Saudi Arabia alone is the second or third largest oil producer in the world, depending on whether it chooses to produce more or less than the United States in any given year. The UAE, Kuwait, Qatar, and Oman also produce significant amounts of oil, and they have the capacity to produce much more. Saudi Arabia, which pumped 4.7 million barrels per day in 1984, has in the past produced double this amount.[1]

More significant, these five countries possess 42.9 percent of the world's known oil reserves. Of all the countries that are currently producing oil, only a few now have proven reserves of forty or more years at current rates of production: Mexico, Iran, Iraq, Saudi Arabia, Kuwait, the UAE, and Libya.[2] Additional oil will undoubtedly be found in many countries, but unless new discoveries greatly exceed the depletion of existing fields, as time goes by the world will come to depend more and more heavily on these seven countries—five of which are on the Persian Gulf.

Much of this Persian Gulf region, though, is in turmoil. In early 1979, when the pro-Western Shah of Iran was overthrown by the Islamic revolutionary forces of the Ayatollah Khomeini, the price of oil leaped dramatically. Oil prices rose again after the outbreak of the Iran-Iraq war in September 1980. Soon thereafter, Iran succeeded in blockading Iraq's oil exports via the Gulf, Syria halted Iraqi exports from transiting the pipeline through its territory to the Mediterranean, and so Iraqi exports were reduced by over two-thirds the prewar level via a vulnerable pipeline to Turkey. The Islamic government of Iran is now hostile to the West, and the radical, pro-Soviet government of Iraq has been so in the past. Both have worked to raise the price of oil as high as possible.

All this has increased the importance to the West of the GCC countries. Saudi Arabia in particular has worked to keep oil prices moderate and supplies sufficient in order to protect the economies of the West; the present Saudi government believes that its own economic and military security would suffer if the West experienced an economic collapse, which rapidly rising petroleum prices could cause. If forces hostile to the West ever come to control Saudi Arabia, at a minimum oil prices could be expected to rise sharply, since there is currently no other oil exporter with the Saudis' market force to increase production and keep prices down. At worst, vital supplies could be denied altogether to the United States, Western Europe, and Japan.

Yet while Saudi Arabia and the other GCC states are of such importance to the West, they are also vulnerable in many ways. Their being among the last few absolute monarchies left in the world raises questions about their internal strength. The relatively small populations of these countries also make them vulnerable to outside attack. In addition, the Straits of Hormuz, through which most of their oil must pass, could be blockaded, as Iran has threatened to do.

Because of the Arabian Peninsula's vital importance and its vulnerability, many in the West have come to fear that the Soviet Union will try to extend its influence there. Some have seen the Soviet friendship with Iraq, military presence in South Yemen and Ethiopia, and invasion of Afghanistan as evidence of a Russian plan to first surround the region and then take control of it.

Before their 1917 revolution, the Russians had a strong influence in northern Iran and even then had attempted to establish a presence in the

Peninsula. They sent naval vessels to the Persian Gulf, tried to ally with the Saudis, subsidized a steamship line from Odessa to the Gulf, and like Germany, had plans to build a railroad through the Middle East with a terminus at Kuwait.[3] These prerevolutionary efforts to establish their own presence or reduce British influence, however, were largely unsuccessful, as were Soviet efforts in the late 1920s and early 1930s to make friends and form an anti-British alliance with King 'Abd al-'Aziz ibn Sa'ud, who united Saudi Arabia, and Imam Yahya of Yemen.[4] Also, in the negotiations held by Soviet and Nazi officials in 1940, the Germans recognized the area "in the general direction of the Persian Gulf . . . as the centre of the aspirations of the Soviet Union"[5] though precisely what this meant was not specified.

Yet though the Russians failed to gain much influence either at the turn of the century or in the 1920s and 1930s, they have been much more active since the 1950s and especially since the two Yemeni revolutions in the 1960s. Now as well as nearly a century ago, the West has been concerned that Russia may try to eliminate Western influence and gain a warm water port on the Gulf or the Indian Ocean to which the Russians would have overland access (this has been less a concern regarding the Peninsula than regarding Iran or Pakistan), and since the 1917 revolution, by the general Soviet desire to see Marxism spread to all countries of the world. The West's main concern now, though, is that the Soviets want to gain control over the Peninsula's oil.

There are two theories about why the Soviets might want to do this. The first is that oil consumption in the USSR and Eastern Europe will exceed domestic production and that Moscow will want to control Persian Gulf oil to meet its own and its allies' needs. The second is that the Soviets want to govern this region's oil in order to control the supply to the West or even deny access altogether. Both deserve further examination.

In April 1977 the Central Intelligence Agency (CIA) predicted that Soviet oil production would decline and that the USSR and Eastern Europe would have to import 3.5–4.5 million barrels per day of oil by 1985.[6] This study and similar ones later increased speculation that to obtain the oil it needed the USSR would seek to take control of the oil-rich Persian Gulf region. Other studies, however, forecast that the USSR would be able to produce enough oil for its own needs and thus would not have to import massive quantities of oil. In 1981 the Defense Intelligence Agency predicted that Soviet oil production would rise gradually through 1985, remain steady through the end of the 1980s, and rise again in the

1990s.[7] A subsequent study by David Wilson found that the CIA had underestimated the ability of the Soviets to substitute natural gas for oil. He also predicted that while Soviet oil production would grow very slowly and oil consumption would continue to rise (though also slowly) in the 1980s, the main effect would be to cut Soviet oil exports, not to force Moscow to import petroleum.[8]

At present it seems that the later, more optimistic predictions are more accurate. In 1983, far from importing petroleum, the USSR actually exported 3.6 million barrels per day (b/d) of oil. Indeed, the USSR is the world's largest oil producer, and in 1983 its production was 12.5 million b/d while its consumption was only 9.1 million b/d. In addition, the Soviets have oil reserves of 60–80 billion barrels (about 9 percent of the world's total) and natural gas reserves of over 1,200 billion cubic feet (41 percent of the world's total).[9] At current rates of production, known Soviet oil reserves will last only about fourteen years, but additions to oil reserves through new discoveries in Siberia are keeping pace with the depletion of older fields in the western USSR.[10]

Yet the Soviets do have important problems with regard to oil. They have admitted that they face serious difficulties in extracting oil from the Tyumen region of western Siberia, which supplies over half the USSR's oil; these difficulties include the cold climate, shortages of machinery and spare parts, poor-quality equipment, lack of infrastructure, and low labor productivity. In addition, the Soviet Union lacks the technology for the complex, difficult extraction processes it increasingly needs. In 1984, for the first time since World War II, Soviet oil production declined slightly over the previous year's level to 12.2 million b/d. This has led some to predict that Soviet oil exports will drop substantially by the end of the decade.[11] These are, however, problems of production that Moscow can ameliorate in time by improving its own management and technology as well as by importing Western technology. Indeed, if the United States is really afraid that the Soviets might attempt to take control of the Gulf because they could not pump enough oil domestically, it should definitely make this complex oil-drilling technology available to Moscow instead of trying to restrict it as Washington has been doing.

Another problem Moscow faces is that its communist allies (mainly in Eastern Europe) produce much less oil than they consume. In 1983 they produced 405,000 b/d but consumed 2.4 million. Much of the Soviet Union's oil exports have traditionally gone to its socialist allies, but the Soviets have apparently limited these exports to 1980 levels so they can sell most of the rest to the West for hard currency. Thus Eastern Europe has had to buy oil from the Middle East or other countries that require hard currency payments, which has undoubtedly contributed to its economic problems. But as Jonathan Steele pointed out, Eastern Europe is hardly likely to invade the Persian Gulf—nor are the Soviets likely to do so on its behalf.[12] The Soviet attitude toward the Eastern European countries seems to be to provide them with oil to a certain extent, but then to let them either limit their oil consumption or reorient their economies so as to export more goods to the West and thereby earn the hard currency to buy oil.

Although the USSR might conceivably want to control the Persian Gulf to obtain the region's oil for its own use, it now has enough oil for its own and much of its allies' needs through the medium term and perhaps the long term as well. The Soviet Union thus has no urgent need to seek control of the Persian Gulf for this reason as the proponents of this theory speculate.

Whether the other theory, that the USSR wants to control Persian Gulf oil in order to regulate or even deny the West's access to it, is true is difficult to tell. There is not enough evidence to prove the theory true, but the absence of such evidence does not prove it false either. The Soviets have not publicly admitted that this is their intention, nor are they likely to do so. As I mentioned earlier, many point to Soviet military involvement in Ethiopia and South Yemen, alliance with Iraq, and invasion of Afghanistan as part of a plan to first surround the Gulf and then seize control of it. Others see Soviet military involvement in each of these countries not as part of a larger design, but as individual instances where the Soviets took advantage of local conditions to extend their influence. Even if these moves were part of a grand design, the design was apparently faulty in that it did not anticipate the anti-Soviet insurrections in Afghanistan and Ethiopia. Marxist governments in Kabul and Addis Ababa have been unable to defeat the rebels after many years, even with the help of over 100,000 Soviet soldiers in Afghanistan and at times over 10,000 Cuban troops plus Soviet advisers in Ethiopia. Iraq gladly receives Soviet military assistance, especially now that Iranian troops are in its territory, but Baghdad has suppressed the local communists and has carefully guarded its independence from Moscow. Only in South Yemen is Soviet influence strong and armed opposition to the government absent, but South Yemen has so far been unsuccessful in its attempts to export revolution to its neighbors.

Still, it is not difficult to imagine what the Soviets could do if they controlled the Persian Gulf's oil. The United States currently imports only 3 percent of its oil from the Gulf, but Western Europe imports 28 percent and Japan over 50 percent;[13] as I pointed out earlier, this dependence is likely to increase in time. While the United States may be able to do without Gulf oil, Western Europe and Japan could not easily do so. If the Soviets controlled the flow of oil from the Persian Gulf, they could threaten to cut off oil supplies to Western Europe and Japan, thus forcing these nations to choose between economic collapse (which would also greatly weaken their defense capabilities) and reorienting their foreign policies to favor Moscow rather than Washington. The Soviets would surely want to see them end their military alliances with the United States. It is possible, then, that through controlling the Persian Gulf's oil, the USSR could induce Western Europe and Japan to cease cooperating with America and to pursue friendship with the USSR. In a world where Western Europe and Japan had become "Finlandized" or even allied to the USSR, America would have few strong allies to rely on.

But would this actually happen? Could the Soviets ever take control of the Gulf? Even if they did, could Moscow really succeed in detaching the United States from its Western European and Japanese allies? Although politicians, officials, scholars, and journalists might argue either way, in truth these questions cannot be answered with confidence. Yet because it is conceivable that this could happen, America, Western Europe, and Japan should rightly be concerned about Soviet influence in the Gulf and the Peninsula. For even if the Soviets do not have any sort of master plan to control the Gulf, their efforts to weaken Western influence there and enhance their own, even on a haphazard basis when an opportunity they did not create happens to arise, could lead to Soviet control of the Gulf and to a host of problems that the Western alliance would definitely not want to confront.

Yet even if the Soviets actually intend to gain control of the Arabian Peninsula and the Persian Gulf, how could they do so? The several options include a direct Soviet invasion, Soviet support for an invasion from a neighboring country, promotion of Marxist revolution or other measures to overthrow the present governments, and building good relations or even alliances with the governments already in power.

The "worst case" would be a direct Soviet invasion. The forces of the GCC would hardly be sufficient to fend off the military might of the USSR. Invading the Peninsula, however, would be an extremely difficult undertaking for the USSR. The Peninsula does not border directly on the Soviet Union, and so this operation would not be nearly as easy for Moscow as launching the invasions of Hungary, Czechoslovakia, or Afghanistan. Further, since the Arabian Peninsula is so vital to Western interests, the United States and its allies might well decide to contest an attack by the USSR. A Soviet invasion of the Peninsula, then, could lead to a direct superpower clash; this is something the Soviets have sought to avoid because a favorable outcome for the USSR cannot be guaranteed and such a conflict might escalate into a nuclear war.

The Soviets could attack Iran, which does border on the USSR and which the West might be neither willing nor able to defend as it would the Peninsula, but as the Soviet experience in Afghanistan has demonstrated, exercising full control over Iran might not be possible even after many years. In addition, if it is the USSR's aim to control all the Persian Gulf's oil, the conquest of Iran alone would not allow Moscow to halt the flow of oil from the Arabian countries of the Gulf. Even if the Soviets blocked the Straits of Hormuz, the Peninsula states could build oil pipelines bypassing them through Oman on the Indian Ocean. The Soviets would clearly be in a good position to disrupt these pipelines or invade the Peninsula if they first conquered Iran, but such an act could lead the Peninsula states to invite a strong Western military presence into their territory to defend them against this greater Soviet threat.

Because of the distance between the USSR and the Arabian Peninsula, the risk of wider conflict with the United States, and the uncertain prospects for success, a direct Soviet invasion of the Peninsula does not seem likely. A Soviet invasion of Iran just for the purpose of controlling Persian Gulf oil does not seem likely either, since Iran could prove difficult to subdue and conquering it alone would not give the Soviets control over all, or even most, of the region's oil.

While attacking the Peninsula might lead to a wider superpower conflict, if such a conflict were already taking place the Soviets might indeed want to attack the Peninsula. But if this conflict was a worldwide nuclear war, the Soviets might not be in a position to send forces to this region, since these forces may be destroyed first. If there were a protracted, nonnuclear conflict in Western Europe, the USSR would probably see halting the flow of oil from the Gulf to the West as an urgent priority in order to weaken their opponents, but it would have to be careful about husbanding its military forces in order to fight in Western Europe, keep a substantial reserve on the Chinese border, and still have sufficient strength to defeat both indigenous and Western forces in the Gulf—not an easy task. What the Soviets might do regarding the Gulf during a wider conflict with the West is, of course, highly speculative to comment upon, since a nuclear war or war in Europe appears extremely unlikely.

In the absence of such a conflict, a Soviet-backed invasion of the Peninsula by one of Moscow's allies seems as unlikely as a direct Soviet invasion of the Peninsula, primarily because such an attack would also risk Western intervention and possibly wider conflict with the West. Indeed, several of Moscow's allies would not be willing or able to mount an invasion of the Peninsula even if Soviet forces were also involved. The radical Iraqi government has at times been hostile toward the Arab monarchies, but since the outset of the Iran-Iraq war, and especially since Iranian troops crossed into Iraq, Baghdad has relied heavily on Saudi Arabia and the other GCC states for vital economic and financial assistance. Iraq neither desires nor is in a position to attack them now, and even if it were Iraq would want to do so for its own sake, not on behalf of the Soviets. Iran might try to invade the Peninsula in order to spread Islamic revolution there, but this would not be in Soviet interests since the Tehran government is as anti-Soviet as it is anti-American. In addition, Iran must first accomplish the difficult task of defeating Iraq if it is going to have the best opportunity and a maximum of its forces available for invading the Peninsula. An invasion from Marxist Ethiopia would be difficult to launch even with Soviet and Cuban support, since the invasion force would have to cross the Red Sea and at present Addis Ababa has been unable to bring the coastal region of Eritrea under its control owing to insurgency there. An invasion of Saudi Arabia or Oman from Marxist South Yemen would have to cross hundreds of miles of desert and would be very difficult to mount. Finally, any invasion or threatened invasion of the GCC states with or without Soviet support could lead them to invite Western military assistance or even protective intervention.

Yet if the USSR and its allies are unlikely to invade the Peninsula because of the difficulties and risks involved, there are other policies that the Soviets have used in the past and undoubtedly will use in the future to gain influence in the Peninsula. If successful, these policies could also lead to Soviet control over Persian Gulf oil, but they do not have the same disadvantages as mounting an invasion. Supporting an insurrection in one of these countries might lead the government it is directed against to seek Western military assistance, but it would not have the same risk of a superpower clash as a direct invasion. Further, because of the domestic unpopularity in the United States since Vietnam of becoming heavily involved in fighting insurgents, the U.S. government might not be able to give much assistance to a country facing such insurgency. None of the governments on the Peninsula is democratic, it is uncertain how much domestic support they command, and there have been previous attempts to overthrow most of them. A successful insurrection brought to power a Marxist government in South Yemen, defeating the attempts of the British to hand power over to a pro-Western government there when the country became independent. But as the failure of the Marxist insurrection in neighboring Oman demonstrated, supporting insurgency does not always succeed, especially if the West (in this case Britain) manages to success-fully help suppress it.

Befriending governments already in power has the advantage of being a peaceful policy designed to persuade countries to voluntarily distance themselves from the West and draw closer to the USSR. Should such a policy appear to be succeeding, the West would be ill advised to attempt to reassert its influence by force, since this would only induce these states to seek Soviet protection and could increase Soviet influence. Ordinarily, then, Soviet diplomatic success in winning friends would not result in a superpower confrontation. The USSR has succeeded in befriending the noncommunist governments of North Yemen and Kuwait and instituting military relations with them. Most of the other GCC states, including Saudi Arabia, have expressed disappointment with the U.S. and apprecia-tion for the USSR on certain issues, particularly the Arab-Israeli conflict. Nevertheless, the Soviets have so far failed to establish even diplomatic relations with Saudi Arabia and the rest of the GCC (except Kuwait). Kuwait and North Yemen have also limited their relations with the USSR and definitely do not want Soviet influence to grow.

Invasion of the Peninsula is not a policy the Soviets have pursued in the past, nor is it likely they will pursue it in the future. But promoting revolution and befriending governments already in power (even when they are conservative ones) are policies that Moscow has pursued in the past to gain influence in the region, and both have met with a certain degree of success. In examining Soviet foreign and military policy toward the Arabian Peninsula, then, I will concentrate on how the Soviets have attempted to gain influence through these two policies, why they have achieved what success they have, why these policies have so far largely failed in the GCC countries, and what the prospects are for Soviet success in either promoting revolution or befriending governments in power. I

11

shall examine in particular Soviet involvement in armed conflicts and Soviet military and economic assistance relationships where these have been present. In addition, I shall discuss Soviet attitudes and policies toward established governments and toward opposition groups in each country, the views of the USSR held by each of the Arabian Peninsula governments and these countries' policies toward a number of regional and international issues.

As we will see, the extension of Soviet influence in the Arabian Peninsula has been seriously hindered because the Soviets have attempted (or at least have been so perceived by the GCC governments) to pursue both policies at the same time. Because the Soviets have supported Marxist guerrillas as well as relatively inactive Marxist groups espousing revolution, most of the conservative GCC governments fear that the Soviets would take any opportunity to overthrow them despite Moscow's claims about the benefits of friendship with the USSR. Yet contrary to what is commonly believed, the Soviets have not strongly supported Marxist revolution in the Arabian Peninsula. The revolution in which the Soviets had the heaviest military involvement was the one in North Yemen, which turned out to be non-Marxist. There was a successful Marxist revolution in South Yemen, but Moscow did not give much support to the Marxists there until after they came to power. Marxist insurrections in Oman (1965–75) and North Yemen (1979–82) also failed, as did the plans of Marxists in Saudi Arabia and Bahrain.

Simply because the Soviets have had limited success in extending their influence to the Peninsula in the past, however, does not mean the West should be complacent about the future. It is important to understand under what conditions a concentrated Soviet effort either could help a Marxist revolution succeed or could persuade any of the established governments to ally with Moscow or at least become less friendly with the West. Finally, I shall offer some thoughts on what this means for the West. For while the importance of the region and its oil supplies has led Western (particularly American) foreign policy makers to plan for countering the less likely threat of a Soviet invasion by creating the Rapid Deployment Force, they have paid little attention to these less dramatic but more likely contingencies.

North Yemen

The Yemen Arab Republic (YAR), or North Yemen, occupies a strategic position on the southwestern corner of the Arabian Peninsula bordering oil-rich Saudi Arabia to the north and east and Marxist South Yemen to the south. North Yemen is also one of the nations bordering on the Straits of Bab al-Mandab, through which pass all ships in transit from the Mediterranean to the Indian Ocean, and vice versa, through the Suez Canal and the Red Sea. Both Yemens have the lowest per capita income of the Arabian Peninsula countries, but North Yemen appears to have the largest population of them all—a fact of grave concern to the YAR's northern neighbors, which already contain large numbers of Yemeni workers. Unlike the wealthier nations of the Gulf Cooperation Council, North Yemen does not have great supplies of oil or other mineral resources (though a promising oil discovery was made in 1984), and the YAR economy is highly dependent on expatriate workers' remittances and foreign aid.

Although it signed a treaty of friendship with Moscow in 1964 and a treaty of friendship and cooperation with it in 1984, North Yemen is the only truly nonaligned nation in the area. Currently, South Yemen and Ethiopia are closely allied to the Soviet Union as well as to each other and Libya through the tripartite agreement of 1981. Saudi Arabia is linked to the United States, and Somalia, Sudan, Egypt, and Oman have allowed the U.S. to use military facilities for its Rapid Deployment Force. Djibouti allows France to station forces on its territory. Finally, Oman, the UAE, Qatar, Bahrain, Kuwait, and Saudi Arabia all recently formed the Gulf Cooperation Council.

While many of these alliances cannot be seen as permanently fixed, as both superpowers' changing relations with Egypt, Sudan, Ethiopia, and Somalia during the 1970s have shown, that North Yemen has not entered a military alliance with any outside or regional power has tended to make it an arena where many nations compete for influence. Among those that have sought to gain influence there since the 1962 revolution are the Soviet Union, the United States, the People's Republic of China, the United Kingdom, Egypt, Saudi Arabia, South Yemen, and to a lesser extent Iraq, Syria, and Libya.

A complicating factor in this competition for influence is that since the 1962 revolution and even the end of the Yemeni civil war in 1970, the YAR government has never been fully in control of North Yemen; indeed there are several divisions within Yemeni politics. In the northern part of the YAR, the great Bakil and Hashid tribal confederations are very powerful and are armed. In the southern part, particularly in the area bordering on South Yemen, the leftist National Democratic Front (NDF) has fought against YAR forces. Within the YAR army, on which successive military regimes since 1974 have been based, there have also been disputes. The weakness of the central government in Sanaa has allowed outside powers to seek influence in North Yemen through forces resisting the government. Saudi Arabia has supported the northern tribes while South Yemen has aided the NDF. But both the tribes and the NDF are coalitions of forces that also have competing interests, and attempts to influence them from outside have not always been successful.

The two often contradictory aims of Soviet foreign policy toward the countries of the Arabian Peninsula—support for the government in power and support for revolutionary movements to overthrow conservative governments—have both met with some success in North Yemen, but neither has worked completely. The Soviet Union enjoyed good relations with the highly conservative and autocratic Imamate regime in Yemen, with which it first established relations in 1928. From 1955 right up to the outbreak of the revolution on September 26, 1962, Moscow gave the regime political, economic, and military support. Throughout the civil war between Egyptian-backed republican and Saudi-backed royalist forces, the Soviets consistently supported the republic and gave it crucial military assistance after Egyptian forces withdrew from Yemen in 1967 and the royalists appeared on the verge of victory. However, when the survival of the republic was assured, it became clear that the revolution in North Yemen was not a radical one, unlike the revolution in South Yemen. Although the USSR has cooperated with each successive government in Sanaa since the revolution and since 1979 has provided substantial military assistance to the government of Colonel Salih, the YAR government has sought to limit North Yemen's dependence on the USSR.

North Yemen's wariness of the Soviets stems from Sanaa's perception that the USSR has, at least indirectly, supported Marxist revolution in the YAR through its support of South Yemen. North Yemen fought border wars with South Yemen in 1972 and 1979 and with the South Yemeni–armed NDF sporadically from 1978 to 1982. Yet even though Moscow has supported its opponents, successive Sanaa governments have actively sought Soviet military and economic assistance. Indeed, part of the reason Soviet foreign policy has been more active in the YAR than any other country of the Arabian Peninsula except South Yemen has been that the North Yemenis themselves have wanted Soviet involvement in their country.

After an overview of the history of North Yemen, I shall examine Soviet involvement in North Yemen's various conflicts, Soviet-YAR military and economic relations, Soviet policy toward and involvement in YAR internal politics, and Soviet and YAR attitudes toward various foreign policy questions.

HISTORICAL OVERVIEW

Yemeni history and civilization stretch back at least a millennium before the birth of Christ. The ancient empire of Saba (or Sheba) was based here, and it was from Yemen that the biblical Queen of Sheba went out to visit King Solomon. At various times before the coming of Islam, empires based on what is now North Yemen ruled over South Yemen, parts of Saudi Arabia, Oman, and beyond. On several occasions, however, Yemen was occupied by foreign powers, including the Ethiopians and the Persians.[1]

Islam first came to Yemen during the lifetime of the Prophet Muhammad. Later Yemen was divided by the Sunni-Shia split that divided the Moslem world elsewhere too. In the southern part of North Yemen, the Tihama plain along the Red Sea coast, and what is now South Yemen (the People's Democratic Republic of Yemen—PDRY), the Shafei branch of Sunni Islam came to predominate (Shafei is one of the four legal schools accepted by Sunnis; it is different from the Hanbali school, which predominates in Saudi Arabia). In the northern part of North Yemen, the population adhered principally to the Zaidi branch of Shiite Islam (the

Zaidi branch of Shiism differs from the Shiism practiced in Iran). This division of the North Yemeni population has continued right up to the present. Although there are no accurate statistics, it is believed that North Yemen is equally divided between Zaidis and Shafeis, with the Shafeis perhaps having a slight majority.[2] Although relations between the two communities are not hostile, the division is an important one because political authority has traditionally been held by the Zaidi Imams until the 1962 revolution. The leaders of the YAR have also been predominantly Zaidi, and this has sometimes been a source of discontent among the Shafeis.

In 1538 the Ottoman Turks invaded Yemen and soon expanded their control throughout most of it.[3] The Turks, however, had much trouble in keeping the Yemenis subdued. In 1635 Yemeni forces defeated the Turks and an independent Zaidi state arose. The Zaidi Imam ruled what is now North Yemen and by 1658 had extended his authority throughout what is now South Yemen and the Dhofar province of Oman. This was the most recent period in Yemen's history when a united Yemeni state existed, for in 1728 Lahej (the western area of present-day South Yemen) broke free of the Imam's rule. Areas farther east also asserted their independence from the Imam. By the beginning of the nineteenth century, even the Tihama, which is part of present-day North Yemen, was no longer under the Imam's control.[4] By the time the British took Aden in 1839, the Imam was in no position to stop them.

Yemen in the nineteenth century saw increasing foreign encroachments. The British expanded their presence in the South Yemeni sultanates, and Saudi, Egyptian, and Turkish forces became involved in North Yemen. The Turks sought to reassert their control throughout the Arabian Peninsula. In 1849 they occupied portions of the Tihama coast, and in 1872 they moved into Sanaa and the Yemeni interior. This second Turkish occupation lasted until 1918, when the Ottoman Empire broke up completely at the end of World War I. Before this, in March 1914, the Anglo-Turkish Convention was ratified; it included an agreement on a border between the two parts of Yemen. No Yemeni was a party to this agreement, and later the border became a source of dispute between independent North Yemen and the British in the South. Even now it is a source of friction between the two Yemens, since only part of the border was ever delimited on the ground.[5]

As before, the Yemenis did not submit easily to Turkish rule, and the Zaidi Imams led numerous revolts against them. This was especially true under Yahya bin Muhammad al-Mutawakkil, who became Imam in 1904. Even before the collapse of their empire at the end of World War I, the Turks signed a treaty with Yahya in 1911 granting him autonomous power in the Zaidi regions while the Turks continued to govern the Shafei areas.[6] After the war Yemen became independent, and Yahya set about consolidating his own rule in the Zaidi region as well as trying to expand it to the whole of what he regarded as the traditional domain of the Imams.

Imam Yahya was successful in this effort insofar as he united the territory of what is now North Yemen firmly under his rule. He took control of the Shafei areas of southern North Yemen, seized the Tihama from the Idrisis (who ruled in the Asir, the ethnically Yemeni area just north of Yemen in what is now Saudi Arabia), and put down several revolts by Zaidi tribes during the 1920s.[7] However, he failed to extend his authority to the Asir, which the Saudis also claimed. Conflict broke out between Saudi Arabia and Yemen in November 1933, and in April 1934 Saudi armies under Prince Sa'ud and Prince Faysal invaded Yemen. Prince Faysal's army penetrated as far south as Hodeida, and in May 1934 the two countries signed an agreement whereby Yemen agreed to Saudi control of the Asir and Saudi forces withdrew from Yemen.[8] Similarly, when Yahya tried to extend his control south of the Anglo-Turkish border, the British struck back with air attacks against North Yemeni positions. Britain and Yemen signed an agreement to respect the frontier in February 1934, though its provisions were subsequently disputed. Yahya also objected to the extension of British influence in the southern protectorates during this period; until then the British were mainly interested only in Aden itself.[9]

Because of his troubles with Britain, Imam Yahya sought the support of foreign powers in the 1920s. In 1926 Yemen signed a friendship treaty with Italy, and on November 1, 1928 it signed a ten-year treaty of commerce and friendship with the Soviet Union. The Soviets, who at this time had relations with 'Abd al-Aziz Ibn Sa'ud, also established relations with Yemen partly to counter the British presence on the Peninsula. The Soviets were able to export a limited amount of goods to Yemen at this time, including kerosene, soap, sugar, wood products, and agricultural machinery. Soviet trade missions were established in Sanaa and Hodeida, and Soviet doctors, journalists, and on one occasion a film crew were also sent to Yemen. Nevertheless, by the mid-1930s Soviet interest in Yemen declined. Although the 1928 treaty was extended for another ten years in 1938, Moscow recalled the entire Soviet mission to Yemen that year, and relations were not restored until 1955. Certain members of the Soviet mission refused to go back to Moscow and fled elsewhere; those who did return were reportedly executed in Stalin's purges soon thereafter.[10]

Yahya kept his country neutral during World War II and isolated from foreign influence throughout his rule, though he did join the Arab League in 1945, established relations with the United States in 1946, and joined the United Nations in 1947.[11] The Imam was assassinated in February 1948 in a coup attempt launched by 'Abdallah al-Wazir (who aspired to become Imam himself) and other opponents of the regime known as the "Free Yemenis" who were based in Aden. The coup was crushed by Yahya's son Crown Prince Ahmad, who then became Imam.[12] Friction between Imam Ahmad and the British soon grew concerning rising British influence over the sultans of the South, British refusal to recognize Ahmad's claims to South Yemen, the activities of the Free Yemenis in Aden, whom Ahmad feared the British supported, and finally Britain's plans to create a South Arabian Federation out of Aden and all the sultanates, which would then be even less amenable to Sanaa's influence. Frontier incidents increased, and as in the 1920s, North Yemen sought foreign support for its position. Imam Ahmad joined with President Nasser of Egypt (whose relations with Britain were also deteriorating) and King Sa'ud of Saudi Arabia (who was unhappy with Britain's opposition to his claim to the Buraimi Oasis in eastern Arabia) in the anti-British Jidda Pact signed April 21, 1956.[13] Diplomatic relations were also renewed with the Soviet Union in October 1955 and established with the People's Republic of China in August 1956.[14] The U.S., USSR, and China all began to give aid to Yemen in the late 1950s.

Soviet-Yemeni relations, dormant since 1938, suddenly became active again. They began with a meeting between the Soviet ambassador to Egypt and the acting Yemeni Foreign Minister in Cairo during October 1955. On October 31, 1955 a five-year treaty of friendship was signed that came into force March 30, 1956. On March 8, 1956, the two countries signed a trade agreement that apparently included secret clauses for arms deliveries.[15] Yemen's ties with the socialist countries were also strengthened by the visits of Ahmad's son, Crown Prince Muhammad al-Badr, to the Soviet Union and Eastern Europe in the summer of 1956 and to Eastern Europe, the Soviet Union, and China at the end of 1957.

Soon after the merger of Egypt and Syria into the United Arab Republic (UAR) in February 1958, Imam Ahmad linked Yemen with them in a more loosely knit federation called the United Arab States. This federation involved no loss of sovereignty to the Imam. Its main benefit to

Ahmad was that Nasser did not also turn against him during Egypt's growing polemic with Saudi Arabia and call for the overthrow of the monarchy. Ahmad never intended to transform Yemen on the revolutionary
pattern of Egypt. However, strains developed between Nasser and
Ahmad, and soon after Syria withdrew from the UAR in late 1961, Imam
Ahmad published a poem criticizing Nasser's policies and ideas as incom-
patible with Islam. Nasser responded by terminating the United Arab
States on December 26, 1961, and by having his propaganda apparatus
virulently attack the Imam's regime.[16]

Nasser's enmity was not the only threat the Imam faced. In March
1955 Ahmad's brother Prince 'Abdallah tried unsuccessfully to make himself Imam with the aid of some officers.[17] In addition, when Ahmad went
to Rome in April 1959 to undergo medical treatment, he left Crown
Prince Badr in charge. Badr, who was attracted to Nasser's ideas of Arab
socialism and to "progressive" ideas generally, began a series of
"reforms" that included inviting Soviet and Egyptian military advisers to
Yemen. Rebellions within the army and among the tribes soon erupted,
and Badr had to pay large sums to the northern tribes to restore order
among them as well as to quell the army. When Imam Ahmad suddenly
returned to Yemen in August 1959, he put an end to Badr's reforms and
attempted to take back the money Badr had paid to tribal leaders. When in
late 1959 Ahmad invited the paramount shaykh of the Hashid and the
chief's son to visit him under a safe-conduct in order to settle their differences, Ahmad had them both killed. This angered the northern tribes,
which revolted in 1960.[18] Added to these problems, three army officers
attempted to assassinate Ahmad in March 1961; though struck by five bul-
lets, the Imam survived.[19]

Despite the growing opposition he faced, Ahmad was not overthrown
but died in his sleep on September 18, 1962. The next day the *ulema* proclaimed Badr Imam, and he immediately announced several reforms,
including the creation of a forty-member consultative council, half of
whom were to be elected by the people. However, on September 26, Badr
was overthrown in a coup led by Col. 'Abdallah as-Sallal, whom Badr
had freed from Ahmad's prison in 1955 and had only just appointed army
chief of staff.[20] Badr is something of a tragic figure, since his commitment
to modernization and reform alienated the traditional supporters of the
Imamate but gained him little respect among the internal and external
opponents of the regime who wanted to see the Imamate destroyed and
replaced by a republic like Nasser's Egypt. Though the leaders of the

newly proclaimed Yemen Arab Republic declared that he was dead, Badr escaped the attack on his palace, fled north, and rallied the royalist forces to fight.

Thus began the Yemeni civil war, which dragged on until mid-1970 and which will be examined later. Since the 1962 revolution, the YAR has had a succession of leaders who have striven to maintain their authority, strengthen the power of the central government, and weaken the influence of other internal as well as external forces. As-Sallal, who proclaimed the YAR and became its first president, proved to be a weak leader. Nasser sought to dominate the politics of the YAR, and he was easily able to do so, since the Egyptian army presence in Yemen reached as high as 70,000 men compared with the republican forces of only some 7,500. Nasser also managed to frustrate the republicans' attempts to seek sufficient backing from other powers, including the USSR, that would have allowed them to be less dependent on Egypt. Since no other country was willing to provide them with such assistance, they had no choice but to rely on the Egyptians, because they were not strong enough to defeat the Saudi-backed royalist forces on their own. Nasser frequently interfered in the YAR's leadership struggles and detained many republican leaders in Cairo. President as-Sallal remained in Egypt from September 1965 to August 1966, then was flown back to Sanaa because Nasser was angry that the YAR Prime Minister, General Hassan al-Amri, was attempting to break free of Egyptian influence.[21]

Yet even though Nasser had detained him, as-Sallal was too dependent on the Egyptians to survive their withdrawal from Yemen in the fall of 1967 after their defeat by Israel in the Six Day War. On November 5, 1967, while he was in Baghdad about to leave for the USSR, al-Sallal was overthrown and a Republican Council was set up with 'Abd al-Rahman al-Iryani as its chairman.[22]

Al-Iryani was North Yemen's first and so far only civilian president. His period in office saw the YAR fend off the royalist advance that almost captured Sanaa, the dissolution of the royalist forces, and the 1970 peace with most of them and Saudi Arabia that brought the war to an end. While the YAR's ties with Saudi Arabia improved, its relations with South Yemen worsened, and in 1972 there was a border war between the two Yemens. Once the fighting was over, however, the Sanaa and Aden governments announced an agreement to unite the two Yemens into one country. In domestic politics, a constitution was promulgated in 1971, and in March of that year elections were held for a Consultative Assembly. The al-Iryani government, though, was not strong and was unable to assert its authority over contending forces. The tribal leaders, who dominated the Consultative Assembly, were relatively powerful at this time. They sought a conservative, pro-Saudi, and pro-Western orientation for North Yemen. Other somewhat more leftist forces advocated that North Yemen be oriented more toward South Yemen, the other radical Arab states, and the socialist countries. Al-Iryani himself was not a forceful leader, and he alternately appointed conservatives and liberals to the post of prime minister. On June 13, 1974, al-Iryani was deposed in a military coup led by Lt. Col. Ibrahim al-Hamdi.[23]

Al-Hamdi, who styled himself Chairman of the Command Council, sought to increase the authority of the central government over the tribes. In his campaign against them, al-Hamdi moved first against the Bakil and then against the Hashid. In October 1975 al-Hamdi dissolved the Consultative Assembly, which was a bastion of tribal influence—its chairman had been Shaykh 'Abdallah al-Ahmar, chief shaykh of the Hashid. Yet while al-Hamdi sought to limit the influence of the conservative shaykhs internally, his foreign policy was strongly pro-Saudi, and the period of his rule saw deteriorating relations between Moscow and Sanaa. North Yemen did not produce oil, but the steep rise in oil prices beginning in fall 1973 brought large flows of money into the YAR via increased remittances from Yemenis working in the oil fields and greater economic assistance from oil-rich Arab states.[24]

In March 1976 a coalition of leftist groups formed the National Democratic Front (NDF). Al-Hamdi tolerated this group because it shared his goal of weakening the tribes. The tribes launched several rebellions against him, and although they did not succeed in regaining the powerful role they had enjoyed before, al-Hamdi did compromise with them to the extent of appointing three shaykhs onto the Command Council in September 1977.[25]

On October 11, 1977, al-Hamdi and his brother were assassinated in Sanaa. Lt. Col. Ahmad Hussein al-Ghashmi, who was up to then a member of the Command Council and the armed forces chief of staff, became chairman of a newly reconstituted Command Council. The assassination came at a time when relations between the two Yemens were about to improve through a visit to Aden by al-Hamdi (which would have been the first visit by a YAR leader to the PDRY). South Yemeni media blamed Saudi Arabia and "forces opposed to unity" for al-Hamdi's death—a charge Saudi Arabia strongly denied. Other sources state that al-Hamdi's death was arranged by al-Ghashmi, who simply wanted to seize power for himself.[26]

Al-Ghashmi's brief rule was marked by a continued pro-Saudi and pro-Western orientation, cool relations with the Soviet Union, and continued attempts at cooperation with South Yemen's moderate leader, Salim Rubayyi 'Ali. Internally, al-Ghashmi was opposed not only by the tribes, but also by the NDF and other army officers. Major 'Abdallah 'Abd al-'Alim, a Shafei officer from southern North Yemen who had been a close colleague of al-Hamdi and who was commander of the paratroop forces, had been retained by al-Ghashmi (a Zaidi) as a member of the Command Council. But in May 1978, when al-Ghashmi's hand-picked legislature abolished the Command Council and elected al-Ghashmi President, Major al-'Alim and some of his forces staged a rebellion in the Hajariyah region near the PDRY border. According to press reports, the rebels were defeated and al-'Alim fled to South Yemen, where he later joined forces with the NDF.[27]

Shortly thereafter, on June 24, 1978, al-Ghashmi was killed when a bomb exploded in his office. The bomb was brought by a South Yemeni emissary in his briefcase; when he opened the case, both he and al-Ghashmi were killed. Two days later, Salim Rubayyi 'Ali was ousted and immediately executed by a pro-Soviet faction in Aden led by 'Abd al-Fattah Isma'il. The new PDRY leadership said that 'Ali had caused the death of al-Ghashmi in collusion with Saudi Arabia and the United States and at the same time was attempting to bring about a right-wing coup in Aden. The plot, they claimed, was discovered by Isma'il and other "loyal" forces, who then ousted 'Ali. According to press reports, what actually happened was that 'Ali, who was opposed to dependence on the USSR and favored closer ties to the West and conservative Arab states, was cooperating with al-Ghashmi and had agreed to return Major al-'Alim and his associates to North Yemen for trial. The emissary he sent to Sanaa (al-Ghashmi seemed to believe he would bring al-'Alim back with him) was intercepted by the forces of Isma'il and replaced with another emissary who unknowingly carried the bomb. As soon as al-Ghashmi was killed, Isma'il blamed the killing on 'Ali (who, it was publicly known, had sent an emissary to Sanaa), accused 'Ali of plotting a coup in Aden as well, and thereupon had him arrested and executed. What role, if any, the Soviet Union, Cuba, and East Germany played in these events has never been verified, though some accused these nations of complicity.[28] As a result of these events, relations between North and South Yemen deteriorated sharply. Sanaa called for Arab League sanctions against Aden, and at an emergency meeting held in Cairo July 1–2, the League's Council decided to impose political and economic sanctions against South Yemen. However, only fifteen of the League's twenty-two members attended the meeting, and the sanctions were not observed by the seven mainly radical states not attending.[29]

A four-man Presidential Council was immediately formed in Sanaa after al-Ghashmi's death; one of its members, Lt. Col. 'Ali 'Abdallah Salih, rapidly gained power, and on July 17 he was elected President by the legislature and also became commander-in-chief of the armed forces. Salih had previously been one of the main supporters of al-Hamdi and had helped al-Ghashmi crush al-'Alim's revolt. Salih's rule received the acquiescence of the tribes, which had opposed al-Ghashmi for removing their leaders from the Command Council, to which they had been appointed by al-Hamdi just the month before his death. Salih appointed some tribal leaders as members of the Constituent People's Assembly (North Yemen's legislature has undergone several name changes and has been relatively powerless under military rule), including Shaykh 'Abdallah al-Ahmar. Nevertheless, there was opposition to Salih's rule, and abortive coup attempts were made in both September and October 1978. When Salih ordered the execution of al-'Alim and thirty other officers (most of whom had fled to Aden) on August 10, 1978, relations between Salih and the NDF began to grow more confrontational.[30]

As a result of increased NDF activity and tension between Sanaa and Aden, the two Yemens again clashed in February 1979. The fighting ended less than a month later, and the two governments again agreed to unite. The NDF, however, was not defeated, and it conducted an insurrection against the Salih government in southern North Yemen. Salih's other opponents included elements of the army, some Shafei tribes in the southern YAR who objected to Zaidi rule as well as Saudi influence, and the conservative Zaidi tribes (some of which formed an Islamic Front with Saudi backing), who feared Salih's cooperation with Moscow and Aden.[31]

Salih was finally able to crush the NDF insurgency in the summer of 1982. Since then he has continued his balancing efforts both externally and internally. Salih has worked to build good relations with Washington, Moscow, Riyadh, and Aden. Several meetings between YAR and PDRY leaders have taken place and projects leading toward unity between the two countries have been agreed upon, though actual unity does not appear likely to take place. He has also worked to strengthen his authority internally and has added to his titles that of Chairman of the General People's Congress (a body designed to unite representatives from different groups within North Yemen in support of Salih). In May 1983 Salih was unanimously reelected President by the legislature for four more years.[32] How long he will stay in power remains to be seen, but that he has done so since 1978 despite the various forces opposed to him indicates that he is not unskilled at preserving his authority.

SOVIET INVOLVEMENT IN CONFLICT

North Yemen has experienced several conflicts since the birth of the republic in 1962. These were the civil war (1962–70), the border wars with South Yemen in 1972 and 1979, and the intermittent NDF insurgency from 1978 to 1982. The degree of Soviet involvement in each of these will be examined here.

The Civil War

The most serious of these four conflicts was the Yemeni civil war, which is also the conflict the Soviets became most heavily involved in. For examining the Soviet role in the Yemeni civil war, it is useful to divide the war into two periods: (1) from September 1962 until June 1967, when Egypt played a large role in the conflict and Soviet foreign policy was limited to aiding Egyptian efforts, and (2) the period after June 1967 until the end of the war, when Egypt pulled out of Yemen after its defeat in the June 1967 war and the USSR took a direct role in support of the YAR.

After the coup of September 26, 1962, the first foreign government to recognize the Yemen Arab Republic was the Soviet Union on September 28; Egypt followed a day later on September 29.[33] During the course of the war, the number of Egyptian troops in North Yemen reached as high as 70,000.[34] This was more than enough to dominate the weak YAR government, which did not have nearly as many troops of its own. The USSR furnished the arms and equipment for both the UAR and the YAR armed forces. However, Soviet foreign policy priorities soon became apparent in the way it armed the latter. Before the coup, the USSR shipped arms directly to Imam Ahmad; after it this direct Soviet-Yemeni arms link ceased, and instead the Soviets delivered arms to Egypt and Egypt decided which ones would go to the YAR.[35] Thus began a pattern that was to last until the Egyptians left.

On October 1, 1962, Khrushchev cabled his greetings to the new YAR leaders, signaling his personal interest in the new republic. However, with the onset of the Cuban missile crisis in October 1962, Soviet attention to events in Yemen waned.[36] The Cuban missile crisis may have done much to convince the Soviets that it was in their best interests to confine their role to supporting Nasser's intervention in Yemen and not to become directly involved themselves. Direct Soviet involvement not only would have been difficult given the relative inaccessibility of Yemen, but it would have risked an American military response, whereas Egyptian intervention did not. The YAR leadership sent a delegation to Moscow in November 1962 to seek direct Soviet aid, but it was disappointed. By December 1962 the USSR had agreed to provide the YAR with economic assistance and had sent several hundred agricultural, technical, and military advisers to the YAR.[37] These last did not engage in combat but instead were limited to aiding the Egyptians as well to working on military construction projects.

Little Soviet economic assistance reached the YAR in 1963, but one Soviet project that did have military significance was the completion of a modern airport near Sanaa. This not only allowed weapons to be delivered directly from Egypt to the Yemeni capital instead of first to Hodeida on the coast and then to the interior, but also allowed the Egyptians an air base from which to bomb royalist positions. Until the airport's completion in September 1963, Egyptian-manned heavy Tupolev bombers had to fly missions from bases in upper Egypt.[38]

Nasser and as-Sallal had at first hoped that the Yemeni revolution would spread to Saudi Arabia and the rest of the Peninsula, but by early 1963 it became clear that the republican forces were having difficulty defeating the royalists even in Yemen. Several efforts were then made to seek a negotiated end to the war. In April 1963, the UAR, Saudi Arabia, and the YAR reached an agreement that Saudi Arabia would stop supporting the royalists and the UAR would withdraw its troops from Yemen. United Nations observers were sent to oversee the arrangement, but the proposed settlement failed because the royalists, who were not a party to the agreement, refused to abide by it, and because neither Saudi Arabia nor Egypt stopped supporting its allies.[39]

Fearing that Nasser was about to abandon his support for the YAR, as-Sallal toured several Arab and socialist countries in June 1963 seeking direct aid for Yemen, but he was unsuccessful. Nasser insisted that all foreign aid for the YAR be channeled through Cairo, thus allowing him to keep much of this aid for Egypt.

In March 1964 Saudi-Egyptian relations began to improve, and a resumption in diplomatic ties (broken in October 1962) was announced. As-Sallal's fears that Egypt might abandon him were renewed, so he visited Moscow March 16–24, 1964, and attempted to obtain direct Soviet assistance. The Soviets signed a treaty of friendship with him to replace the 1955 treaty signed with the Imamate; this new treaty was valid for five years and called for automatic renewal every five years thereafter unless terminated by either side. The Soviets also signed economic, technical, and cultural agreements in which they promised several aid projects, including the construction of a road between Hodeida and Taiz. The 1964 treaty of friendship did not contain any military consultation or assistance clauses as do many more recent Soviet treaties of friendship and cooperation with Third World nations, but a secret military aid agreement was reportedly signed by the two sides. However, the Soviets apparently did not deliver the arms it called for until after the Egyptians withdrew from Yemen.[40] As-Sallal also met with Khrushchev when the latter visited Cairo in May 1964, but he was unable to persuade him to increase Soviet aid to the YAR.[41]

In 1964 and 1965 the republican war effort stagnated. Dissension within republican ranks grew owing to Shafei resentment of Zaidi dominance of the government, general Yemeni dislike of Egyptian control over YAR politics, and as-Sallal's apparent lack of ability. Nasser grew to fear that the war could not be won, and in August 1965 he met with King Faysal in Jidda, where they signed an agreement whereby Egypt pledged to withdraw all its forces by September 1966 and Saudi Arabia promised to end its support to the royalists. A plebiscite was to be held by November 1966 in which the Yemenis would decide what form of government they desired. A conference among all Yemeni parties would be held at Harad, inside North Yemen, in November 1965 to decide on a provisional government until the plebiscite. Both the U.S. and the USSR expressed their approval of this agreement.[42] But with Nasser seemingly about to withdraw from Yemen, the Soviets began to take a more direct interest in the YAR. In late 1965 and early 1966, some Soviet and Czech arms were sent directly to the YAR (the first such direct shipment since the revolution). The Soviets also reportedly urged the YAR not to compromise over the retention of republican government in Yemen and suggested that the Egyptians work to build up the strength of the YAR army.[43]

The effort to bring the war to an end did not succeed. Republicans and royalists were unable to agree on the form of a provisional government. Further, when the British announced on February 22, 1966 that they would leave Aden by 1968, Nasser changed his mind about leaving North Yemen so that he could help the pro-Egyptian Front for the Liberation of South Yemen (FLOSY) come to power.[44] Although Egyptian forces in North Yemen had been reduced to 20,000 by May 1966, their level rose again to 60,000 the following November. A renewed UAR offensive took place and peace efforts were stalled.

With Egypt's renewed commitment to remain in Yemen came Cairo's desire to prevent the Soviets from gaining influence in Sanaa. During Kosygin's visit to Egypt in May 1966, the UAR government tried to prevent the YAR Prime Minister, Gen. Hassan al-Amri, from meeting with him. Upon Kosygin's insistence, the meeting did take place, and Kosygin reportedly proposed that the Soviet Union arm and equip a YAR army of 18,000 men and that East Germany also supply military equipment to the YAR. The Egyptians, however, opposed this, and so the Soviets dropped the proposal.[45] Al-Amri persisted in his efforts to obtain arms directly from the USSR as well as to assert YAR independence from Egypt in foreign and domestic policies during the summer of 1966. These moves by al-Amri and his political allies so incensed Nasser that he returned President as-Sallal to Sanaa in August 1966 after detaining him in Cairo since September 1965. Al-Amri ordered Yemeni troops to the airport to prevent as-Sallal from landing, but stronger Egyptian forces moved in to ensure that he did.[46]

Until the June 1967 war, the Soviets did not really attempt to establish a direct military relationship with the YAR and provided economic assistance only in coordination with Egypt.[47] China, by contrast, did not route its economic aid for Yemen through Cairo but sent it directly to Sanaa instead, much to Nasser's annoyance. China, however, did not send military aid to the YAR.[48] Although the Soviets and the Chinese appeared to be competing in the amount of economic aid they supplied to North Yemen, neither the Egyptians nor the Russians had to fear that the Chinese would gain influence there via military aid.

Throughout this first portion of the war, Soviet commentary on military operations was fairly meager. In a statement about Soviet political and economic aid along with the "help of arms" Khrushchev said "everyone knows . . . the role played by this support in the struggle of the peoples of the UAR, Indonesia, Yemen, and other countries against the colonialists."[49] Soviet Third World specialist Georgi Mirsky also wrote in a *New Times* article that "weapons made by Soviet workers were used to defeat the colonialists . . . in the Yemeni mountains";[50] this statement, however, did not indicate what role the Soviet government played in transferring these weapons to Yemen. In the spring of 1965 Radio Moscow referred to Soviet assistance to a number of countries including "Yemen in 1962"[51] but not in the years after that. Occasional references were also made to the presence of Egyptian troops in the YAR at the YAR's request. Nasser was given credit for all peace initiatives, and the Saudis were blamed for their failure.[52] Soviet commentary on the royalists was uniformly negative and that on the republicans generally positive, but some articles about the latter did note that there were differences among republican leaders and that the YAR had not succeeded in carrying out reforms in agriculture or in constructing a state-run economy.[53]

Although the Soviets supported the YAR, their main concern was Egypt. Nasser wanted to ensure that Egypt remained in control of events in the YAR. The Yemenis, not surprisingly, sought to assert their independence from Egypt by turning toward others, including the Soviet Union. Unwilling to risk losing Nasser as an ally, the Soviets were unreceptive to YAR requests for direct Soviet military assistance.

The Arab-Israeli war of June 1967 had a dramatic impact on the conflict in Yemen. One of the immediate effects was that anti-Soviet sentiment arose in Yemen, as elsewhere in the Arab world, for what was perceived as Soviet failure to support the Arabs adequately.[54] More important, Nasser lost the will to continue the expensive and domestically unpopular war that seemed to have become "Egypt's Vietnam." As-Sallal once again sought to establish a direct arms supply relationship with the Soviets, since the Egyptians were about to withdraw. On August 1, 1967, as-Sallal sent his deputy premier to Moscow to seek Soviet military and economic assistance that would come to the YAR direct and not via Cairo. This time the Soviets agreed and quickly sent a military delegation to Sanaa to judge what the YAR needed (at this time the YAR army had only 7,000 men).[55] There were press reports that the Soviets offered military aid to the YAR in exchange for the air base near Sanaa that the Egyptians had previously used, but the Soviets denied this. Whether or not these reports were true, the Yemenis did not grant the Soviets a base or military facilities on their territory, but they did succeed in obtaining some Soviet military aid.[56]

At the Khartoum Conference held August 29 to September 1, 1967, Nasser agreed to withdraw all his troops from Yemen before the end of the year in exchange for King Faysal's promise to cut off support to the royalists and to give Egypt financial assistance to help make up for Cairo's losses from the June war and the closure of the Suez Canal. This agreement between Egypt and Saudi Arabia, which was made without the participation of either the Yemeni republicans or the royalists, was immediately denounced by as-Sallal. Apparently believing himself in a strong position with the promise of Soviet weapons to come, as-Sallal called for the rejection of the Khartoum Agreement and refused to negotiate with the royalists. This stance only served to undermine his already weak position, since other republican leaders were calling for negotiations with the royalists. Significantly, the Soviets also called for negotiations between the two sides and praised the Khartoum Agreement.[57] Having lost both internal and Egyptian support, as-Sallal was overthrown on November 5, 1967, while in Baghdad en route to Moscow for the celebration of the fiftieth anniversary of the Russian Revolution. Expressing no regret at as-Sallal's downfall, Moscow immediately moved to establish close ties with the new al-Iryani government.[58]

Once as-Sallal had been ousted, Soviet military aid began to arrive. In mid-November 1967, twenty-four MiG-19s arrived in the YAR, followed shortly thereafter by some Ilyushin bombers and supplies of small arms.[59] Al-Iryani's civilian Prime Minister, Muhsin al-Aini, announced that the USSR had now agreed to supply the YAR with the weapons it had promised in 1964, thus confirming that there had been a Soviet-YAR arms agreement then and that the Soviets had failed to honor it until late 1967.[60]

With the Egyptian troops rapidly leaving Yemen, the royalists saw their opportunity to finally defeat the republic. Royalist forces surrounded the capital in early December 1967, thus beginning the siege of Sanaa. By December 18, the situation appeared so bleak that the civilian al-Aini resigned as prime minister so that General al-Amri could take the position and organize the republic's defenses. The Soviets also helped by mounting an airlift to Sanaa, flying some ten thousand pounds of food and weapons into the capital over a period of three weeks.[61] About forty Soviet technicians and pilots were also present, and Soviet pilots even flew combat missions for the YAR in MiGs—the first time Soviet pilots were engaged in combat in a nonaligned country.[62] However, after the royalists shot down one MiG with a Soviet pilot, the Russians were withdrawn and Syrians flew the Soviet aircraft instead. Despite these efforts, the Soviets appeared doubtful at first whether the republic would survive. The Soviet embassy staff (along with the embassy staffs of all other countries except China) was evacuated from Sanaa early in the siege.[63] It was reported that Brezhnev canceled a trip to Cairo in January 1968 so that he would not be there when the YAR was overcome by the royalists.[64]

The republicans finally broke the siege on February 8, 1968, and the royalist forces never fully recovered from the defeat. The republicans owed their survival to the royalists' failure to press the attack against Sanaa during Ramadan (which came in December that year) when the republicans were weakest; defections among the tribal forces that the royalists had assembled; the Soviet airlift and Soviet air support (since the royalists had no air force, the small fleet of Soviet aircraft was able to control the skies); the help of National Liberation Front (NLF) units from South Yemen, which had recently come to power in Aden; and al-Amri's policy of arming the urban citizenry with Soviet weapons and organizing them into a Popular Resistance Force (PRF) to assist the regular YAR army.

During the siege of Sanaa, the Saudis came to fear that a large-scale Soviet presence was building up in North Yemen, and so on January 4 Radio Medina warned that Saudi Arabia would resume its support to the royalists if the Soviets did not stop aiding the republicans.[65] As the royalist cause foundered, the Soviet line changed from urging negotiations between the antagonists to criticizing the royalists after their defeat.[66]

During the spring of 1968, the YAR government faced a threat from the left. The PRF units, which contained many Shafeis from southern North Yemen, had come under the influence of the radical wing of the NLF. In late March 1968, PRF units attempted to seize a shipload of Soviet arms in Hodeida but were prevented by the YAR army and tribal forces. Fearing the radical NLF might gain strength in the North, al-Amri began to give support to the pro-Nasser FLOSY, which had been defeated in Aden (many FLOSY members, however, escaped to North Yemen and set up bases from which they sought to overthrow the NLF); this did much to sour relations between the two Yemeni governments.

According to Richard Bissell, the Soviets did not oppose al-Amri's efforts to crush the PRF because Moscow feared that the NLF and PRF were pro-Chinese. From Moscow's point of view, a pro-Peking government in Aden was undesirable, but another one in more populous North Yemen would have been even more so. The Soviet writer L. N. Kotlov made clear in his 1971 book that Moscow was disappointed at the defeat of the left in North Yemen. He did not identify the PRF as pro-Chinese, but he did see the forces who defeated them as conservative tribal shaykhs.[67] This latter view that the Soviets were disappointed at the defeat of the left seems more plausible, since the level of Soviet military aid to the YAR dropped considerably after the siege of Sanaa. It was reported that an arms agreement was reached in August 1968 when the royalist forces again approached Sanaa (the royalists then shot down another MiG, which they claimed had a Soviet pilot).[68] However, when al-Amri visited Moscow in early October 1968, he was unable to obtain the level of military and economic assistance he wanted.[69] A deterioration in relations was noticeable when Radio Sanaa announced shortly after al-Amri's return that Soviet-YAR ties would remain strong "as long as these relations continue to be based on respect for our policy and sovereignty and as long as the USSR continues to appreciate the aims of the agreements we concluded with it in the various fields without any conditions."[70]

The only noteworthy Soviet military activity in the Yemeni civil war after 1968 was the visit of Soviet warships to Hodeida in January 1969 and again in January 1970. Economic assistance to ongoing projects was continued (the Hodeida-Taiz road was completed during the summer of 1969), but no significant new Soviet aid commitments were made.[71] In February 1970, when the remaining royalist forces launched their last offensive and seized the town of Sa'da near the Saudi border, Soviet military advisers reportedly recommended that the YAR react harshly, but this advice was rejected in favor of a more conciliatory approach in order not to alienate Saudi Arabia, with which North Yemen was attempting to develop friendly relations. Peace talks between the republicans and royalists began in Jidda in March 1970, royalist leaders (except for the royal family) were allowed to return to Sanaa in May, and the YAR established diplomatic relations with both Saudi Arabia and the United Kingdom (which had also supported the royalists) in July.[72] By the end of the war the "revolutionary" government in Sanaa had become relatively conservative, seeking expanded aid from and friendly ties with the West and the conservative Arab states as well as with its traditional supporters among the radical Arab and socialist states.

Soviet involvement in the Yemeni civil war after the June 1967 war is noteworthy, because although the Soviets thought the YAR was important enough to warrant direct (but limited) Soviet military participation to save it from defeat, once its survival was assured the Soviets were unwilling to remain involved. This was not a case of the Soviets' being expelled from a country as they were in Egypt and Somalia later, for the YAR government sought additional Soviet assistance that Moscow did not give. One reason for this Soviet behavior may have been that the USSR was willing to make a short-term, low-cost effort to help the republic stave off defeat but did not want to become involved in the republicans' efforts to defeat the royalists as Egypt had been for so long without success. Further, continued Soviet military involvement in North Yemen may have led the Saudis or even the West to strongly aid the royalists; without this Soviet involvement, Saudi Arabia seemed content to honor its agreement with Egypt and not do so. In addition, while North Yemen actively sought Soviet economic and military assistance, it was also seeking aid from the West and conservative Arab governments—the Sanaa government was clearly not going to become Marxist or become so pro-Soviet as to justify greater Soviet assistance. Finally, as North Yemen was becoming more conservative, South Yemen was becoming more radical, and the Soviets were becoming engaged in a competition with China for influence in Aden. As tension between North and South Yemen grew—partly because of the large number of the NLF's opponents who had fled to the North and who sought to overthrow the NLF from there—the Soviets did not want to alienate Aden by giving Sanaa military aid that the NLF would consider threatening. Outwardly, the Soviets preferred not to support either Yemen against the other—a policy they would adhere to later when clashes between North and South took place.

The 1972 War

At the beginning of 1972, both the Sanaa and the Aden governments were struggling to assert their authority over their countries. Each also gave a certain amount of support to the internal opponents of the other regime. Large numbers of FLOSY members were present in the North, and many of them worked in the YAR government including, 'Abdallah al-Asnaj, who had become YAR Foreign Minister.[73] The NLF, for its part, aided radical Shafei groups, including former PRF elements, opposed to the more conservative YAR regime; one of these groups was called the Yemeni Revolutionary Resistance Fighters.[74] Despite attempts to seek unity made by both governments, there were strong forces who opposed it, particularly the Zaidi tribes of North Yemen.

The event that began the fighting was the killing in South Yemen of Shaykh 'Ali bin Naji al-Ghadir and sixty-five of his men on February 21, 1972. The then YAR Prime Minister, Muhsin al-Aini, claimed that the Aden government had paid these men "to commit hostile acts against the Sanaa government" but that when they failed the South Yemenis murdered them.[75] PDRY Prime Minister 'Ali Nasir Muhammad admitted that the shaykh and his followers had been killed by South Yemeni forces, but he claimed they were saboteurs from North Yemen who had entered the PDRY under Saudi-American direction.[76] A meeting of the Bakil and Hashid tribes of North Yemen was held, and they "decided to declare war on the PDRY."[77] The YAR opposed this move by the tribes, fearing that a conflict might escalate and outside powers become involved, but Sanaa was unable to block them, and fighting took place along the border.[78]

The immediate Soviet reaction to this crisis was to state that outside forces ("imperialism, Zionism, and Arab reaction") had provoked the conflict and were the only ones to benefit from it. The Soviets also called for a rapid settlement of differences through negotiations.[79] This was the tone of most Soviet commentary about the conflict.[80] In a Radio Moscow broadcast on March 21, however, it was stated that while "imperialist quarters" had been unable to influence the YAR leaders, subversion against South Yemen was being carried out by "mercenary groups which are generously armed by American and British intelligence." Both Yemens were then called upon to "frustrate the intrigues of imperialism and reaction."[81] In other words, though the YAR leadership was not to blame, the Soviets saw the PDRY and not the YAR as the victim of aggression and thus supported Aden. Yet while most Soviet statements indicated that the USSR was neutral in the conflict, Soviet actions definitely favored South Yemen. The London *Sunday Telegraph* reported in March that the USSR was supplying MiG-21s to the PDRY and that two hundred South Yemeni pilots were being trained in the USSR.[82]

Sporadic fighting took place through mid-May and then stopped, though relations between the Yemens were still tense. On July 2 the YAR reestablished diplomatic relations with the United States—the first Arab country to do so after the June 1967 war[83]—and allowed the United National Front of South Yemen (an umbrella organization of Aden's opponents) to be formed in Sanaa on August 20.[84] But despite these moves toward the West and against South Yemen, Sanaa was careful not to blame Moscow for Aden's actions. In July the YAR Information Ministry criticized an anti-Soviet article published in the biweekly *Sawt al-Yaman* and warned it against "publishing anything which could harm the friendly relations between Yemen and the Soviet Union."[85] Al-Aini also denied a press report in August that the YAR was going to expel Soviet advisers working in the YAR.[86]

Serious fighting broke out along the border again on September 26, and this time the armies of both the YAR and the PDRY were involved. Each side blamed the other for causing the conflict. On October 8, YAR forces captured Kamaran Island from the PDRY.[87] Both sides agreed to a cease-fire arranged by the Arab League on October 13, though fighting continued until October 19. Soon after this, the prime ministers of both Yemens signed a peace accord and an agreement on unification in Cairo on October 28. This was followed by a further unification agreement signed by the presidents of both North and South in Tripoli, Libya on November 28.[88] Unification did not take place, but there was relative peace between the two Yemens for several years.

Soviet commentary on the autumn fighting was much the same as it was earlier: blame for the conflict was assigned to the United States and Saudi Arabia, but not to either Yemen. The Soviets praised the Arab League's mediation effort and the cease-fire, deplored the fighting that continued afterward, hailed the peace and unification accords, and proclaimed the agreements a victory over imperialism.[89] As before, however, on the level of actions it appeared that the Soviets favored South Yemen. A ship with Soviet arms bound for Hodeida reportedly changed course after the fighting broke out and later went to Aden instead.[90]

The YAR government appeared to be less convinced of Soviet goodwill during this round of fighting. On October 3 a Beirut paper cited YAR sources as saying that Soviet advisers based in the South were involved in raids against the North and that the YAR would soon expel its Soviet advisers.[91] The next day a YAR spokesman stated that the North had shot down three MiGs belonging to the PDRY.[92] Even after the fighting ceased, al-Aini told the Middle East News Agency "that the south is receiving unlimited air and ground military aid from the Soviet Union."[93] He also revealed that the YAR had not received any weapons or spare parts from the Soviets since 1970.[94]

Nevertheless, the North Yemenis did not go very far in criticizing the Soviets. Al-Aini carefully pointed out that Soviet arms aid to Aden did not mean the Soviets were helping Aden "to commit aggression."[95] The Sanaa government did not expel Soviet advisers, and on October 5

Sanaa's *Ath-Thawrah* praised Soviet-YAR cooperation even though fighting was still going on.[96]

The Soviets did give military aid to South Yemen during the 1972 border war, but at the same time they made a special effort to retain good relations with North Yemen. They blamed the United States and Saudi Arabia for the fighting and did not excoriate the YAR government. Moscow did not want to drive Sanaa into breaking relations with the USSR and relying even more heavily on the West and conservative Arab states. Similarly, the Sanaa government felt it important to retain Soviet friendship even when YAR leaders themselves admitted that Aden was receiving Soviet military assistance and using it against the North. Sanaa probably calculated that breaking relations with the Soviets would only lead Moscow to support Aden even more, whereas continued friendly ties would induce the Soviets to seek a negotiated settlement—which is exactly what the Soviets did through supporting the Arab League mediation efforts.

The 1979 War

Tension between the two Yemens grew again as a result of the assassination of North Yemen's al-Ghashmi in June 1978, which South Yemen was involved in. The new YAR leader, Colonel Salih, also thought that Aden had supported the two coup attempts against him in September and October 1978. There were also several reports issued by the PDRY-backed NDF describing battles between YAR armed forces and "the peoples armed revolutionary forces" inside North Yemen from November 1978 through the beginning of 1979.[97] In addition, the Salih government gave support to anti-PDRY organizations based in the North.[98] With all this going on, it was not surprising that fighting broke out along the border on February 24, 1979.

There have been several accounts about the level of fighting that actually took place in the 1979 war. The YAR claimed that South Yemeni armed forces—not just NDF units—attacked North Yemen and that the PDRY was using MiG-2ls, heavy artillery, and missiles. Further, the YAR charged that Cuban and East German advisers had participated in the PDRY attack (Aden denied this allegation).[99] The YAR government also charged that Cuban and Ethiopian forces were involved in the fighting, and President Salih stated that there were "foreign forces exceeding 14,000 soldiers" in the PDRY, but he did not specify what countries they were from.[100] Kuwait's *As-Siyassah* reported that 2,700 Cuban soldiers and 150 Soviet military experts had been airlifted from Ethiopia to South Yemen over a three day period in early March.[101]

The U.S. Department of State made little comment on the use of Soviet, Cuban, East German, or Ethiopian armed forces in the conflict, but it estimated that the invasion force consisted of two or three PDRY brigades as well as NDF units.[102] On the scope of the conflict, the State Department said:

> The fighting between North and South Yemen grew from border inci-
> dents in January and early February to cross-border, offensive opera-
> tions by South Yemeni units against the North Yemen towns of
> Qatabah and Bayda. Harib, another town in North Yemen, also fell to
> the South and there was fighting in the Wazaiyyah area. Fighting con-
> tinued (including strikes by South Yemeni aircraft) despite an Arab
> League cease-fire on March 3. South Yemeni forces did not withdraw
> from their positions but consolidated their positions and by March 6,
> after more fighting, they had moved 30 kilometers past Bayda and
> Qatabah toward the main north-south road linking Sanaa and Taiz.[103]

These reports were disputed by Lt. Col. John J. Ruszkiewicz, U.S. military attaché in Sanaa at the time of the 1979 war, who stated that the actual level of fighting was not as great as this. He believed that the YAR government, on the one hand, had exaggerated the level of conflict in order to convince the U.S. government to supply arms directly to North Yemen instead of through Saudi Arabia (which Sanaa complained did not deliver) as well as to procure a range of modern American weapons that it had not been able to obtain before. The Carter administration, on the other hand, had also exaggerated the seriousness of the conflict in order to dem-onstrate American resolve to defend the region shortly after the Iranian revolution toppled the pro-Western Shah.[104] Steps taken by the Carter administration to assist the YAR included the announcement on February 28, 1979, that the United States would speed up delivery of a $100 million arms package already ordered by Sanaa and another announcement on March 9 that the President was invoking emergency legislation to send the YAR, without the consent of Congress, a further $390 million arms pack-age including twelve F-5E jet fighters and sixty-four M-60 tanks. Most of the arms, however, would first be sent to Saudi Arabia, which had pur-chased them, and the Saudis would transfer them to Yemen. In addition,

Carter ordered the USS *Constellation* from the Philippines to sail for the Arabian Peninsula.[105]

Relatively few American arms had reached North Yemen, however, when the fighting stopped. Under Arab League auspices, a cease-fire was announced March 3 but was disregarded. Another cease-fire was observed on March 16, both PDRY and NDF forces began withdrawing on March 18, and they completed their withdrawal the following day. As occurred after the 1972 conflict, an agreement to unite the two Yemens was reached on March 30 by Salih and Isma'il in Kuwait. Also as before, little actual progress was made toward unification.[106]

Although the United States backed the YAR, the public reaction of the USSR was not to support the PDRY but to blame the United States and Saudi Arabia for the conflict and to encourage the two Yemens to settle their conflict through negotiations. The very first Soviet media reaction to the outbreak of hostilities was a TASS bulletin that summarized several contradictory reports, including a PDRY Foreign Ministry statement that YAR forces had crossed the border but had been repulsed, an NDF communiqué from Aden saying that its forces had captured four towns in the YAR, and a report from Cairo that the YAR had accused the PDRY of attacking it before the Arab League.[107] On February 28, Radio Moscow called for both Yemens to end the fighting but cited a Jordanian newspaper to the effect that U.S. arms shipments to the YAR had caused the conflict—thus indirectly indicating Soviet disapproval of the YAR.[108] Further commentary condemned the U.S. announcement that it would send arms to North Yemen and praised the Arab League mediation effort.[109] Another commentary harshly criticized the United States for sending the *Constellation* to the area after a cease-fire had been agreed upon March 3 (which did not hold), and accused the United States of trying to increase tension through this action.[110] The announcement that U.S. military advisers would go to the YAR was also seen as a U.S. attempt "to torpedo" the peace talks.[111] The Soviets also reported that Washington was greatly displeased when a cease-fire and troop withdrawal did occur, since this reduced tension and thereby hurt American interests.[112] At no time did the Soviets directly criticize the YAR or accuse it of aggression.

The Soviets denied the *As-Siyassah* report that Cuban troops and Soviet advisers had been airlifted from Ethiopia to South Yemen,[113] but the Soviets did take some actions that definitely benefited Aden. In March 1979 the Soviets delivered to the PDRY fifteen MiG-23, ten MiG-21, and ten Su-20 fighter aircraft, as well as other weapons, all as grants.[114] While it is not clear whether these weapons arrived in time to be used in the fighting, according to the State Department there were eight hundred to a thousand Soviet advisers (half of whom were military), five hundred to seven hundred Cuban advisers (also half of whom were military), and one hundred East German advisers (primarily concerned with internal security) in the PDRY while the fighting was going on.[115] In the months following the end of the 1979 war, the Soviets took further actions to support the PDRY militarily, and in October 1979 Moscow and Aden signed a treaty of friendship and cooperation.[116]

The YAR government did denounce alleged Cuban, East German, and Ethiopian involvement in the conflict, but it was careful not to criticize the USSR directly. President Salih stated that Aden had started the war "in the interests of a dubious international strategy" but did not mention the Soviets by name.[117] Indeed, the YAR Information Minister said on March 1 while the fighting was still going on that Sanaa regarded the USSR as "a friendly state and is anxious to maintain friendship with it."[118] There were no reports in 1979 as there were in 1972 that the YAR was about to expel Soviet advisers. Once again, both the USSR and North Yemen found it important to see good bilateral relations continue even though both were involved in actions (Soviet support to the PDRY, YAR receipt of assistance from the United States and Saudi Arabia) that the other objected to.

After the conflict was over, and perhaps as a condition for the PDRY's withdrawal from YAR territory, Salih made some changes in his government that gave it a somewhat leftist image. One of the most significant was that the pro-Saudi, anti-PDRY, and antiunity 'Abdallah al-Asnaj lost the post of foreign minister on March 21 and was replaced by Hassan Makki, who was regarded as a "leftist" (al-Asnaj was, however, appointed political adviser to Salih). Further, Salih began negotiations with the NDF over what role they might play in the government.[119] Fearing this change to the left in Sanaa as well as the efforts toward unity being made, Saudi Arabia reportedly slowed down dramatically the transfer of American weapons to the YAR. In June 1979, al-Asnaj flew to Washington to try once again to persuade the United States to send arms directly to Sanaa, but he failed. It was widely reported at this time that the Central Intelligence Agency expected Salih's regime to collapse within six months owing to the increased activity of his opponents within the army and among the rebels since the end of the fighting.[120] Because he could not obtain American weapons either from Washington or Riyadh, Salih turned toward the Soviets. Moscow obliged him readily, and Soviet arms reached the YAR by the end of 1979. As a result of this, Saudi-YAR relations deteriorated markedly.[121]

The NDF Insurgency

Unlike North Yemen's three earlier wars, the NDF insurgency was hardly noticed in the West. The National Democratic Front came into being in 1976 when several small leftist groups in the YAR joined forces. These groups represented a variety of often conflicting ideologies but were composed primarily of Shafeis from the southern YAR opposed to the dominance of the conservative Zaidi tribes to the north. Al-Hamdi allowed the NDF to grow partly because they supported his policy of weakening tribal influence on the central government.[122]

The NDF's political demands at this time were permission for political parties and unions to form and operate legally, creation of a Consultative Council in which leftist forces would be represented, the release of political prisoners, and other social reforms. It also called for unity with South Yemen and denounced Saudi influence in the YAR.[123] The NDF did not advocate revolution at this time, but it did want YAR internal and external policies to be transformed in a leftist direction. The NDF's relations with the central government were not bad during al-Hamdi's rule, but they deteriorated sharply when al-Ghashmi came to power. The NDF organized a large meeting in Sadda in March 1978 during which al-Ghashmi's "one-man rule" was denounced. The NDF also objected to his pro-Saudi orientation and his detaining leftists.[124] The NDF, however, was far from being unified, and in August 1978 an NDF statement admitted that its political activity had been "frozen" since April 1978 pending the resolution of differences among its leadership.[125]

During the latter part of 1978, the NDF gained strength through the defection of YAR army officers dissatisfied with Salih's rule. As was mentioned before, Major al-'Alim fled with an entire battalion of paratroopers to Aden and reportedly joined the NDF after his abortive rebellion near Taiz in May 1978. Following the abortive coup attempts in September and October 1978, a large group of officers opposed to Salih, known as the "13 June Front" fled south; after meetings held from December 25, 1978, through January 5, 1979, Radio Aden announced that this group had decided to join the NDF.[126] Fighting between Salih's forces and the NDF took place from November 1978 through early 1979, and NDF units were heavily involved in the 1979 border conflict between North and South.

PDRY and NDF forces had fought well in the 1979 war and had succeeded in penetrating YAR territory near the border. These forces pulled back as a result of the cease-fire agreement, but the NDF remained in a strong political position while Salih had been weakened. The NDF began to increase its demands and now sought ministerial posts within the Sanaa government. Thus began a long series of intermittent negotiations between Salih and the NDF interspersed with fighting that lasted from mid-1979 until mid-1982.

In June 1979 Salih began talks with the NDF over what role the latter could play in the government, but by the following month the talks were deadlocked and fighting was reported in August.[127] Soon thereafter negotiations were renewed, and in early 1980 Salih and the NDF seemed on the point of resolving their dispute. The NDF announced in February 1980 that an agreement had been signed calling for a cease-fire and for a coalition government with five NDF ministers to rule in Sanaa. Release of political prisoners, free elections, and unity with the South were also to occur. At the same time, the PDRY reportedly agreed to reduce its backing of the NDF and withdraw some South Yemeni army units from the border.[128]

Neither Salih nor the NDF, however, was really willing to adhere to the agreement. The PDRY government did appear to reduce its support to the NDF, but in early 1980 NDF fighters moved in large numbers into southern YAR and took control of several towns, where they removed the shaykhs from power and ruled on South Yemeni lines.[129] For his part, Salih apparently had no intention of sharing power with the NDF but instead sent his army to confront it.[130] As a result, fighting increased in 1980, and the NDF accused Saudi Arabia of subverting the Salih-NDF agreement and attempting to increase its own influence by "spreading Wahabism to destroy Yemeni identity."[131]

Another cease-fire was reached after the new PDRY President, 'Ali Nasir Muhammad, who had overthrown Isma'il in April 1980, visited Sanaa at the end of August 1980. The NDF also agreed to suspend its clandestine radio broadcasts in exchange for permission to publish a newspaper (*Al-Amal*) under YAR government auspices.[132] The cease-fire, however, was quickly broken, and heavy fighting was reported in November and December. The NDF fought not only the YAR army but also the Islamic Front—a tribal force backed by Shaykh 'Abdallah al-Ahmar of the

40

Hashid and supported by Saudi Arabia.[133] At this time NDF forces were on the defensive, and in January 1981 Kuwait's *Al-Watan* reported that the NDF had been defeated "once and for all" and had withdrawn to the PDRY.[134]

This was not the case, however, since the NDF soon renewed its activity in southern YAR. Cease-fires reported in July and then August 1981 were followed almost immediately by reports of fighting, which was especially heavy in the autumn.[135] After his visit to Moscow October 26–28, Salih went to Damascus and met with several opposition figures, but apparently no agreement was reached.[136] In November, Salih and 'Ali Nasir Muhammad met in Kuwait when, according to an NDF source, the PDRY President signed a cease-fire agreement with the YAR on behalf of the NDF.[137] That 'Ali Nasir Muhammad did so indicates the subordinate relationship of the NDF leadership to the Aden government. In addition, then YAR Prime Minister 'Abd al-Karim al-Iryani revealed in December 1981 that the YAR and PDRY had agreed a year earlier "not to support any military, political or press activity directed against the other."[138]

The November 1981 cease-fire appeared to offer some hope for seeing the conflict finally end, since it involved the PDRY as well as the NDF, but instead it gave way to the heaviest fighting yet. 'Ali Nasir Muhammad was either unwilling or unable to halt the NDF's activity or to stop his own government from supporting the NDF. While 'Ali Nasir Muhammad seemed to prefer a peaceful solution to the conflict, two of his powerful rivals in Aden—Defense Minister Salih Muslih Qasim and First Deputy Chairman of the Council of Ministers 'Ali 'Antar—were said to advocate full PDRY support to NDF military activities.[139] As a result Salih decided to seek military victory over the NDF, and in January 1982 he dismissed several high-level officers who reportedly advocated a less forceful approach in order not to provoke PDRY retaliation.[140] By March the fighting had become very heavy, and according to the *Washington Post*, two Su-22s supplied to the YAR by the USSR were shot down by NDF antiaircraft weapons that also came from the Soviet Union—a circumstance that did not please the Sanaa government.[141]

Despite heavy casualties, YAR forces kept fighting and the NDF was again on the defensive. In mid-March, NDF General Secretary Sultan Ahmad 'Umar said that the NDF "would give up the regions it held around Ibb, in the center, and at Al-Bayda' and Ar-Rawtha, in the southern part of the country, if the government freed 4,000 political prisoners and granted political and labor freedom."[142] Following mediation by the

Palestine Liberation Organization, a cease-fire came into effect April 3, but it quickly broke down.[143] The NDF claimed this was because of the Sanaa government's "refusal of Front proposals."[144] According to YAR officials, though, the truce was broken by the NDF when it captured the town of Juban six miles from the PDRY border.[145]

The NDF was suffering from other problems besides the YAR offensive. In an interview published in Beirut's *As-Safir* March 28, Sultan Ahmad 'Umar admitted that the 13 June Front had left the NDF and that the NDF was trying to persuade it to rejoin.[146] In addition, heavy rains caused a series of flash floods in the western region of the PDRY adjacent to the border at the end of March 1982, which made South Yemeni support to the NDF extremely difficult. When the YAR army launched its final offensive in May 1982, it was aided by 6,000 northern tribesmen and locally recruited militia. Of the 5,000 NDF fighters remaining, up to 1,000, along with several NDF leaders, defected to the YAR. A final cease-fire was reached by Salih and 'Ali Nasir Muhammad a few weeks after the fighting was over.[147] The NDF insurgency was finally ended and has shown no signs of reemerging up to the present.

The Soviets had made relatively little comment about both the 1972 and 1979 border wars but made almost none at all about the NDF insurrection. The Soviets did cite an NDF communiqué at the beginning of the 1979 war stating that the NDF had captured several towns in the North,[148] but apart from this the Soviets remained silent about the NDF's involvement in conflict with YAR forces in both the 1979 war and the later insurrection. Instead, the Soviets frequently lauded their good relations with North Yemen, sent and received messages and delegations, and generally portrayed Soviet-YAR relations as close. Salih met with Brezhnev in October 1981 to negotiate about arms while the fighting was going on.

Whether or not the Soviets gave direct aid to the NDF is difficult to establish. The Soviets never admitted to doing so, and the NDF has never claimed to receive direct Soviet support. The NDF, however, did receive Soviet arms from the PDRY and to a lesser extent from Libya and Syria, but the degree to which the Soviets were involved in or approved of these arms transfers is uncertain. As was mentioned before, 'Ali Nasir Muhammad seemed to oppose PDRY military support to the NDF's attempt to overthrow Salih whereas his rivals Qasim and 'Antar supported it. In the internal PDRY power struggle (in which the NDF issue was only a part), Moscow supported 'Ali Nasir Muhammad and so apparently did not strongly support the NDF's actions. This policy may have resulted from a

Soviet assessment that the NDF's prospects for ultimate success were poor.

The Sanaa government also said very little about the role of the Soviets or about the insurrection throughout most of the conflict. YAR statements about both the USSR and the PDRY spoke mainly of friendly and cooperative relations; the NDF was not mentioned at all. However, at the end of the conflict in May 1982, the YAR made its displeasure public. In an interview published in *Le Monde* May 7, 1982, Prime Minister al-Iryani charged that the "Yemen People's Unity Party" (founded in March 1979 and apparently the Marxist-Leninist political wing of the NDF; al-Iryani used the terms YPUP and NDF interchangeably, though it seems doubtful that the party represented all the factions within the NDF) was "a 100 percent Marxist-Leninist party comparable to those which have taken up arms against the El Salvador government"; that it had its headquarters in and received arms from Aden; and that its guerrillas operated in the YAR. Al-Iryani also charged that three of the YPUP leaders were also "full members" of the ruling Yemeni Socialist Party's (YSP) Politburo in Aden—a charge that was apparently not true.[149] In addition, the YAR recalled its ambassador from Moscow in early May, reportedly in protest over Soviet aid to the rebels.[150]

Characteristically, Sanaa did not go far in its criticism of the Soviets. A spokesman at the YAR embassy in Moscow immediately denied that the Ambassador had been recalled "due to deteriorating relations" and asserted he had only returned home "on a working visit."[151] Similarly, while al-Iryani criticized PDRY aid to the NDF in his *Le Monde* interview, he insisted that the USSR was not involved: "They assure us they have no contacts with the guerrillas and we have no reason not to believe them."[152] Both Salih and al-Iryani further denied that there was any tension in Soviet-YAR relations soon thereafter.[153]

Of North Yemen's four conflicts, the Soviet Union was most heavily involved in the first one—the civil war. The USSR mainly confined itself to assisting Egypt in this conflict, but when Egypt withdrew the Soviets themselves became directly involved, though only to a limited extent and for a short time. North Yemen has used mainly Soviet weapons in its three other conflicts as well. In these later conflicts, the Soviets adopted a public stance of noninvolvement but took actions that aided the YAR's opponents more than the YAR. Yet Moscow and Sanaa have both worked to maintain good relations even after North Yemen has, always cautiously, indicated its displeasure over Soviet aid to Aden. Part of the reason North Yemen does not distance itself from the Soviets despite the hostile actions of Moscow's South Yemeni allies is that the YAR wishes to continue receiving Soviet military assistance.

THE MILITARY ASSISTANCE RELATIONSHIP

Soviet military aid to North Yemen began before the revolution when in November 1956 a Soviet ship brought fifty antiaircraft guns and other small arms from Czechoslovakia. By August 1957 eight shiploads of weapons had arrived, including some thirty T-34 tanks and other weapons.[154] These weapons were fairly old, and Imam Ahmad hid key parts to many of them for fear his army might use the weapons against him. They were, however, the first modern arms introduced into the country, and North Yemen's armed forces have relied mainly on Soviet weaponry ever since. As of July 1984, the YAR's inventory of Soviet arms included 500 T-54/55 and 100 T-34 main battle tanks, an unspecified quantity of SA-2 and SA-7 surface-to-air missiles (SAMs), and 40 MiG-21, 10 MiG-17F, and 15 Su-22 combat aircraft. By contrast, the YAR possessed only 64 M-60 tanks, 11 F-5E fighters, and 4 F-5B trainers from the United States.[155]

Available figures on the value of Soviet arms transfers to Third World countries are notoriously imprecise, and the figures for the YAR are no exception. According to Hosmer and Wolfe, the value of Soviet arms transfers was less than $30 million in 1955–60, more than $30 million in 1961–64, less than $20 million in 1965–69, negligible in 1970–74, and about $420 million in 1975–80.[156] The U.S. Arms Control and Disarmament Agency (ACDA) gave somewhat higher figures, estimating the value of Soviet arms transfers at $32 million in 1964–73, $30 million in 1973–77, and $900 million in 1978–82. By comparison, the ACDA figures for the value of arms the YAR received from the United States were negligible in 1964–73, $26 million in 1973–77, and $230 million in 1978–82.[157]

The figures on Soviet military advisers in North Yemen are also imprecise. There have been Soviet military advisers there continuously since the mid-1950s despite the ups and downs in Soviet-YAR relations. Along with the first Soviet arms shipments to North Yemen in 1956–57 came about 35 Soviet military instructors and about 50 technicians from the USSR and Eastern Europe.[158] During the Yemeni civil war several hundred Soviet advisers helped both the Egyptian and the YAR forces.

The USSR also sent pilots to fly MiGs during the siege of Sanaa, but shortly thereafter the level of Soviet advisers was reduced. In the first half of the 1970s, their level fell from over 500 to about 100 in 1975. They remained at this level through 1979 but rapidly rose after that to 500, at which strength they have remained until the present.[159] In addition, through 1981 2,060 North Yemeni military personnel went to the USSR and Eastern Europe for military training.[160]

What has been the nature of the Soviet–North Yemeni arms relationship? As noted before, the Soviets supplied some arms to Imam Ahmad directly, but during the civil war they shipped them to the UAR instead of the YAR until the Egyptians withdrew in 1967. From 1969 to 1979 the YAR tried to obtain weapons from both East and West, but it was relatively unsuccessful until 1979. Not only was Sanaa unable to obtain new arms agreements with Moscow during this time, it was also unable to get the Soviets to deliver what they had promised in the 1960s. At first YAR leaders limited their public statements to praising past Soviet-YAR military cooperation, perhaps in an effort to remind Moscow about the present. President al-Iryani went to Moscow in December 1971 and discussed military assistance with the Soviets, but he failed to persuade them to continue deliveries.[161] During the 1972 border war, Sanaa began to openly criticize the Soviets for their neglect. In October 1972, al-Aini said that no new Soviet equipment had reached the YAR in three years.[162] Al-Iryani stated the following January that the USSR had stopped delivering weapons to both Yemens and was opposed to unity between them.[163] Rumors also circulated that Sanaa would expel all Soviet advisers.[164]

The number of Soviet military advisers in the YAR did decline, but not all left. In May 1973 the YAR Commander-in-Chief, Muhammad al-Iryani, went to Moscow in another attempt to obtain military assistance.[165] The USSR did agree to accept more YAR military officers for training in Soviet military academies, but the YAR still did not receive any weapons. The YAR Army Chief of Staff expressed the hope that "the Soviet friends will fulfill their commitment toward us."[166] In February 1974 he reiterated that promised Soviet arms had still not arrived.[167]

Soviet-YAR relations reached their lowest point during al-Hamdi's period in office, primarily owing to the arms issue. After being removed from the premiership in February 1975, al-Aini claimed that the visit of a Soviet military delegation to Sanaa he had arranged had been postponed by al-Hamdi and that suddenly a U.S.–Saudi arms package had arrived—the Soviets criticized this deal soon thereafter.[168] Lt. Col.

al-Ghashmi (not yet in power) said that the Soviets had not delivered any new weapons in a long time, that those Soviet weapons the YAR did possess were so old they ought to be "in the war museum" and that Soviet military experts would leave the YAR by September 1975.[169] Al-Hamdi himself announced on August 3 that Soviet-YAR relations were "frozen" and that the YAR had recently rejected a Soviet offer of MiG-21s. It was also reported in February 1976 that the YAR refused to accept a shipment of Soviet tanks and aircraft that had arrived in Hodeida; both these moves may have been a North Yemeni ploy to obtain better-quality weapons in larger quantities.[170] The following June, al-Ghashmi stated again that Soviet-YAR military relations were being suspended because the USSR had failed to deliver even spare parts for Soviet weapons North Yemen already owned.[171] Yet as before, the YAR did not expel Soviet military advisers. A YAR military delegation was received in Moscow by Marshal Grechko in November 1975, and despite his harsh words al-Ghashmi also received a Soviet military delegation in November 1976.[172]

Threats to expel Soviet military advisers having proved counterproductive, Sanaa abandoned its public criticism of the USSR over the arms issue. In April 1978 Marshal Ogarkov received the YAR Chief of Staff, and al-Ghashmi welcomed a Soviet military delegation to Sanaa in June shortly before his death.[173] After the assassination of al-Ghashmi and up to the subsequent conflict between the Yemens, several Soviet commentaries criticized U.S. arms transfers to the YAR for creating tension, but they did not criticize the YAR directly.[174] Similarly, the new YAR leader, Colonel Salih, condemned South Yemen but was careful not to criticize the Soviets. Even though Salih feared what the PDRY might do with its growing stockpile of Soviet weapons and sought American arms to counter Aden, in his public statements he merely said that the YAR sought to diversify its sources of arms, noted the YAR had Soviet ones, and complained that the U.S. weapons supply to the YAR was limited.[175] Even the anticommunist YAR Foreign Minister, 'Abdallah al-Asnaj, who averred that the YAR "could not fight communism on its own" said that the YAR had not expelled its Soviet advisers and had no intention of doing so.[176]

As was mentioned before, the U.S. announced that it would send a large arms package to the YAR via Saudi Arabia (which was paying for it), but Saudi Arabia held up the delivery of these weapons to the YAR partly because the conflict had ended, but also because Riyadh feared Salih's apparent move toward the left as well as the possibility that these weapons could be used to threaten the Saudis. Salih was disappointed over

Saudi and American unwillingness to aid him fully; this and his desire for modern arms to defend himself against both the PDRY and his internal opponents led to the YAR's signing a large arms deal with the USSR in the fall of 1979, which greatly surprised both Washington and Riyadh. This was presaged by an agreement with Poland in July 1979 for 200 T-55 tanks. In the Soviet-YAR arms agreements of September and November 1979, the USSR agreed to provide the YAR with 300 T-55s, 40 MiG-21s, 20 Su-22s, and an unspecified number of FROG SSMs and SA-2 SAMs. Unlike the U.S.–Saudi arms package, which was only partially delivered and very slowly at that, the entire Soviet arms package reportedly arrived between November 1979 and February 1980.[177]

Despite receiving Soviet weapons, Salih wanted to obtain American weapons as well. He continued to emphasize that the YAR sought to diversify its sources of arms. In a letter to President Carter in March 1980, Salih sought to assure him that the YAR was against communism but said that since the United States did not send enough arms, the YAR had accepted them from the USSR and that the YAR was still waiting to see what the U.S. would do.[178]

The obstacles to a direct U.S.–YAR arms relationship have been American unwillingness to provide arms on concessionary terms and the YAR's inability to pay full price for them. Saudi willingness to finance American arms for the YAR appeared to remove these obstacles, but when Saudi Arabia was no longer willing to do this, the U.S.–YAR military relationship foundered. The Soviets apparently offered weapons on more generous terms, but still not free—they expected to be paid for them. Nevertheless, the Soviets were responsive to the YAR's desire to obtain arms as cheaply as possible. Although in September 1981 the Soviets were reportedly asking Sanaa to pay its $630 million arms bill to the USSR, when Salih went to Moscow in October 1981 the Soviets agreed to cancel $265 million of the debt.[179] Salih later said that the YAR bought Soviet weapons partly because American arms were "very expensive."[180]

Yet despite the greater ease with which the YAR has been able to obtain Soviet weapons since the late 1970s and the increase in Soviet military advisers in the country, there is a definite limit to how far the YAR wishes to pursue military cooperation with the Soviet Union. In May 1983 Prime Minister al-Iryani stated that the 1964 USSR-YAR treaty of friendship that expired in 1984 would be renewed, but he added, "it is certain that when we renew the agreement . . . we shall not introduce any articles pertaining to security matters." In the Soviet-YAR treaty of friendship and cooperation signed by Chernenko and Salih in Moscow on October 9, 1984, there are no clauses referring to military assistance or mutual consultations in the event of a military threat.[181] The YAR does not intend to seek a close military relationship with a large Soviet presence as South Yemen has done.

Soviet commentary on the USSR-YAR military relationship has been extremely sparse over the years. The Soviets have referred to their military aid to the YAR in their annual greetings to the YAR leaders on the anniversary of the revolution (September 26), in joint communiqués and welcoming speeches when YAR leaders visit Moscow, and in other general commentaries about the YAR. However, the Soviets have given almost no hint as to the value and types of arms transfers or numbers of military advisers they send to the YAR.[182] The Soviets said little about their role in North Yemen's civil war when it was going on, but since then they have routinely taken credit for having "saved the republic." As mentioned earlier, the Soviets have also criticized U.S. arms transfers to the YAR as leading to tension in the area; they apparently believe that Soviet arms transfers to both Yemens do not.

Up until 1979, Soviet military aid to the YAR was not very large (this was true even during the siege of Sanaa, though the aid that was provided then was extremely important). The reason for this appears to be that although North Yemen has not become allied to the West or to conservative Arab states, it has not been willing to become closely allied militarily to the Soviets either. As long as Sanaa did not receive much military assistance from the West, there was little incentive for the Soviets to provide much either. The huge Soviet arms package to the YAR in 1979 is best explained as a Soviet reaction to the large U.S.-Saudi arms package earlier—Moscow wanted to prevent Sanaa from seeking to rely on the United States and Saudi Arabia exclusively and thereby become less amenable to Soviet influence. However, the USSR has built up South Yemen's armed forces to an even greater degree than North Yemen's. The PDRY has a military establishment somewhat larger than the YAR, even though the South's population is about one-quarter the size of the North's. The USSR has also sent more modern equipment to the PDRY, and there are 1,500 Soviet as well as Cuban and East German military advisers there.[183] Since the threat that the YAR has faced in its last three conflicts has either been the PDRY itself or forces supported by the PDRY, and since the Soviets have given substantial military assistance to Aden, the YAR government is naturally concerned about the degree of military support that Moscow gives to each Yemen. Similarly, there is undoubtedly a limit to how far the Soviets will militarily assist a state such as North Yemen that refuses to become closely aligned with the Soviets militarily, especially when that state is in conflict with another, such as South Yemen, that is so aligned.

THE SOVIET-YAR ECONOMIC RELATIONSHIP

The Soviet-YAR economic relationship has in one sense been the mirror image of the military relationship. Whereas the YAR received relatively little military aid from Moscow before 1979 in terms of value and relatively much since then, the Soviets gave North Yemen relatively more economic aid during the period 1955–64 but have been less generous since then. From 1954 to 1981, the USSR gave the YAR about $140 million in economic assistance, which is not much more than either the $135 million that the U.S. gave or the $130 million that China gave during this period (Eastern Europe also gave $40 million to Sanaa during these years).[184] The amount of economic assistance given by all of them, however, is small compared with what Saudi Arabia gives, which in 1981 was reported to be $250 million per year in support of the budget plus another $250 annually for development projects as well as payments believed made to various shaykhs, officers, and other leaders to secure Saudi influence.[185]

The USSR and North Yemen have also had a long trade relationship stemming from the late 1920s. Soviet-YAR trade grew from 4.4 million rubles in 1960 to 11.0 million in 1970, fell to 5.6 million in 1975, climbed to 20.6 million in 1977 and 48.1 million in 1980, but declined to 22.9 million in 1981 and 34.9 million in 1982.[186] Most of this trade consists of exports from the USSR to North Yemen, and very little of imports from the YAR to the USSR. Sanaa's trade with Moscow is small compared with its trade with the rest of the world; in the YAR fiscal year 1980–81, North Yemen's total imports were $2.1 billion.[187]

One area in which Soviet economic aid to the YAR has had a significant impact is education. From the 1960s up to the present, some 400 to 800 nonmilitary academic students have been in the USSR every year.[188] The Soviets have also sent a number of economic aid technicians to the

YAR over the years. In the mid-1960s there were over 600, but this figure had dwindled to 175 from the USSR and Eastern Europe in 1981.[189]

The most important Soviet economic aid projects in North Yemen were the construction of a port at Hodeida (completed in 1961), an airport near Sanaa (1963), a road from Hodeida to Taiz (1969), and a cement plant at Bajil (1973). In 1978 the USSR granted the YAR a loan of $38 million to expand the production capacity of the cement plant to 200,000 tons annually.[190] Other Soviet aid projects have included a hospital in Sanaa, several schools, various agricultural projects, a survey for water and other resources, a fish cannery, a building for Sanaa University, and other smaller projects.

The North Yemenis have not always been satisfied with the quantity and quality of Soviet economic assistance. For example, in September 1972, two articles appeared in Beirut's *An-Nahar* comparing Soviet and Chinese aid to the YAR. The Chinese were praised highly, but North Yemeni officials bitterly complained that the Soviets delivered less than they promised and demanded a political price for it; unsuccessful Soviet attempts to prevent President al-Iryani from making changes in the cabinet and to pressure the YAR to recognize East Germany instead of West Germany were cited. The Soviets were also accused of "cowardice" during the siege of Sanaa. In addition, "The Yemenis complain that up to the present time the Russians have yet to send them any equipment, military or otherwise, that was not defective—either lacking some fundamental part necessary for operation, or lacking spare parts essential for consumer maintenance."[191] In general, however, North Yemen has expressed gratitude for Soviet economic assistance while continually seeking to increase it.

Up to the early 1970s, Soviet economic assistance to the YAR formed a large share of all foreign aid received by North Yemen. As late as 1972, the Soviets claimed that their aid represented one-third of all foreign aid given to the YAR.[192] However, after the Saudi-YAR reconciliation of 1970, Saudi aid to the YAR began and soon outstripped all others. Neither the USSR nor any other country has attempted to compete with the Saudis by raising the amount of aid it gives. What this has meant is that North Yemen has come to have a large stake in maintaining good relations with the Saudis in order to keep receiving their money. Indeed, the desire for continued Saudi aid and the desire for political independence limit the extent to which North Yemen is willing to cooperate with the USSR even though Sanaa depends heavily on Moscow for military assistance.

THE SOVIETS AND YAR INTERNAL POLITICS

The Soviets have sought good relations with whoever happens to be the ruler of North Yemen. Once a leader is no longer in power, though, they have always moved quickly to establish good relations with the new leader. They have not made enemies of new rulers by expressing support or sympathy for old ones in those cases where they remained alive. In some instances the Soviets have expressed their dislike for the regimes of certain leaders after they have fallen even though Moscow hailed them and sought good relations with them while they were in power.

The most striking example of this was Soviet support for the Imamate and particularly for the somewhat pro-Soviet Prince Badr before the revolution, followed by instant Soviet condemnation of both after it. During the 1950s North Yemen was described as a "feudal" society, but Imam Ahmad was viewed as doing much to improve life and was praised for accepting aid from the socialist countries. Badr, who made two visits to the USSR while Crown Prince, was seen as a "well-known Arab statesman." When Imam Ahmad died, Khrushchev sent a message of condolence to Badr, and the Soviet government sent him its congratulations on his becoming the new Imam. Nevertheless, the USSR was the first country to recognize the new YAR. The Soviet media almost immediately began to expand on the horrors of the Imamate and accused Badr, so recently called a "progressive," of wanting to continue on his father's reactionary path. Soviet writers now claimed that the Imam and Badr had pursued friendship with the USSR only because as-Sallal and other "progressive" elements in the army had forced them to.[193] Yet while the Soviets portrayed the Imamate in such a negative light after the revolution, they did not deem it necessary to justify or apologize for supporting it.

This pattern has continued, though in a less dramatic form, for all the YAR rulers. As-Sallal was praised throughout his rule, but when he was ousted in November 1967 the new al-Iryani government was quickly welcomed.[194] The Soviets saw al-Iryani in a positive light when he was President, especially when he visited Moscow in December 1971, but they immediately recognized al-Hamdi after the June 13, 1974, "corrective step" that brought the military to power. Recently the Soviets have described the al-Iryani years from 1970 to 1974 as a time when reactionary, tribal elements dominated the country.[195] Although the foreign policy of both al-Hamdi and al-Ghashmi was relatively pro-Saudi, Moscow did not criticize them for this at the time. The Soviets sought to blame the assassinations of both on pro-Saudi and pro-Western forces. Indeed, the death of al-Ghashmi and the execution of Salim Rubayyi 'Ali in June 1978 elicited perhaps the longest and most intense Soviet coverage of events in the Yemens. For a full month after al-Ghashmi's death (which Sanaa blamed on Aden), the Soviets first denied South Yemeni involvement, and after 'Ali's execution they blamed al-Ghashmi's murder on him in conjunction with Saudi Arabia and the United States. The Soviets also exonerated the new Isma'il regime in Aden and expressed support for the new Salih government in Sanaa.[196] Yet though ever since their assassinations the Soviets have often described both al-Hamdi and al-Ghashmi as martyrs, *Izvestiia* noted that over the entire 1974–78 period (during which Soviet-YAR relations were poor) "imperialism and reactionary forces" caused "political instability."[197] The Soviets have portrayed Salih in positive terms so far, especially since his visits to Moscow in October 1981 and October 1984, but if he is overthrown they can be expected to embrace the new leadership. Finally, the Soviets have frequently made friendly statements about YAR officials whom they (rightly or wrongly) perceive as pro-Soviet, such as Muhsin al-Aini, who has served on various occasions as Foreign Minister and Prime Minister, but they have shown no attachment once they were ousted. Similarly, the Soviets criticized the anti-Soviet 'Abdallah al-Asnaj (Foreign Minister from 1975 to 1979) after Salih detained him in 1980 for allegedly conspiring to overthrow the government, but they did not express animosity toward him while he was in office.[198]

Concerning the forces opposed to the YAR government, *Pravda* once noted, "Although formally the activity of parties in the YAR is not allowed, a whole spectrum of political currents exists here."[199] Nevertheless, the Soviets have been extremely reluctant to comment on leftist opposition forces in the YAR. With regard to the NDF, the Soviets have done little more than acknowledge its existence. When al-Hamdi was killed in October 1977, Soviet media cited NDF statements claiming that the Saudis had arranged it.[200] At the outbreak of the 1979 war, the Soviets cited a Radio Aden report that the NDF had captured several North Yemeni towns, but the Soviets did not further publicize the NDF's role in this war or in its later struggle with the YAR government. In one article that did discuss its political nature, the members of the NDF were portrayed as supporters of the late al-Hamdi; the Marxist-Leninist aspect of the Front was not even mentioned.[201] This Soviet reluctance to discuss the NDF was unusual compared with the relatively large amount of coverage that

Moscow has given to other Marxist-Leninist groups in the Arabian Peninsula such as the Popular Front for the Liberation of Oman, the Bahrain
National Liberation Front, and the Saudi Arabian Communist Party. Yet
with the exception of the PFLO, the NDF has been more active and has
fought more than any of the other pro-Soviet liberation groups of the
Peninsula.

While the Soviets have not said much about the leftist opposition in
North Yemen, they have frequently commented on what they consider to
be the conservative opposition—the tribes. Soviet commentary on the
tribes has been uniformly negative. They blamed the tribes for the 1972
border war and accused them of working in the interests of the Saudis and
against cooperation with South Yemen. Though the Soviets knew that
al-Hamdi was pro-Saudi, they hailed him for having "succeeded in
removing the ruling shaykhs" from the YAR government.[202] The Soviets
warn that these forces will try to win back their power, but they note that
the YAR government is aware of the danger.

That the Soviets comment favorably on whatever leader is in power in
Sanaa—even though they denounce him once he is out of power—shows
that the USSR wishes to have good relations with existing YAR governments. Reluctance to support or even talk about the leftist opposition indicates that the USSR is unwilling to jeopardize its relations with the
existing government by supporting Marxist revolutionaries in North
Yemen. This has been true up to now and will probably remain so in the
near future. The Soviets, of course, would not be unhappy if the NDF or
another Marxist group did seize power in Sanaa, but they realize that the
Marxists have not been strong enough to take and hold power so far and
probably will not be so for some time. Yet while the Soviets are not anxious that the YAR become more "progressive" quickly, they are concerned that it not become more conservative either, and so they have
emphasized the dangers of tribal influence on the central government.

FOREIGN POLICY ISSUES

Aside from its quest for economic and military assistance from a wide
variety of sources including the U.S., the USSR, Western Europe, Eastern Europe, China, and other Arab states, North Yemen's primary foreign
policy concerns are its relations with its two immediate neighbors—South
Yemen and Saudi Arabia. North Yemen has also been concerned with a
number of foreign policy problems involving the Arab and Islamic

worlds, but the YAR has seldom been one of the major actors in these issues or had its interests seriously affected by them. Beyond the Middle East and the Horn of Africa, North Yemen has relatively little interest in world events and rarely comments on them unless they somehow affect the YAR or the Arab world generally. Thus, insofar as the YAR government is concerned with Soviet foreign policy, it is mostly in the context of its relations with Aden and Riyadh, to a lesser extent with regard to the Middle East and the Horn of Africa, and least of all with regard to the rest of the world.

Despite the fighting that has gone on between them, one of the continuing themes of foreign policy in both the YAR and the PDRY has been the quest for the unification of the two Yemens. Almost immediately after the 1972 and 1979 wars as well as the NDF insurrection, renewed activities regarding unity (joint meetings, work on a constitution, joint projects, and others) took place. In August-September 1983 this process went further than ever before when the Supreme Yemeni Council, consisting of top government officials from both sides, held its first set of meetings. Notwithstanding President al-Iryani's complaint in 1973 that the Soviets were opposed to Yemeni unity, they have generally issued statements supporting the steps toward unity that have been taken and encouraging further progress. As a practical matter, however, the Soviets would oppose unity if it meant that the PDRY would give up its Marxist-Leninist orientation. YAR insistence that a united Yemeni state be based on Islamic principles indicates that North Yemen would not be willing to adopt Marxism-Leninism as the price for unity.[203]

The actual prospects for unity between the Yemens appear fairly poor, not because outside forces oppose it as both Yemens have claimed, but because neither government has been willing to surrender power to the other. What the YAR government probably sees as the real value of efforts toward unity is the broadening and strengthening in the PDRY government of those who support peace and good relations with the YAR. The greater the extent of joint cooperation, joint projects, and intergovernmental contacts, the more the PDRY would stand to lose through conflict with the YAR and the more influence would be lost by those factions that advocate overthrowing the YAR government or supporting opposition movements like the NDF. Whether increased YAR-PDRY cooperation will indeed lead to this result is unclear—it has not been completely successful in the past—but this more limited goal is one the USSR can support. The USSR has consistently called for peaceful resolution of differences between the two Yemens mainly for fear that conflict between them might induce the YAR to turn toward the West.

Although it has occasionally been reported that Sanaa has called upon Aden to reduce its ties with Moscow,[204] the YAR government itself has been very circumspect in making statements about Soviet-PDRY relations. The YAR government has not criticized the Soviet-PDRY treaty of friendship and cooperation signed October 24, 1979; the YAR was hardly in a position to do so, since it signed a treaty of friendship in 1964 and a treaty of friendship and cooperation in 1984 with the USSR, though they did not explicitly call for military consultation and assistance as did the Soviet-PDRY treaty.[205] The YAR did object to the trilateral treaty of friendship and cooperation signed by the PDRY, Ethiopia, and Libya on August 19, 1981. The YAR Deputy Foreign Minister criticized the tripartite alliance because he saw it as paving the way for foreign intervention in the region.[206] The YAR also fears that it might become the target of the combined efforts of the tripartite alliance to attack or promote subversion against it.[207] Yet if the possibility exists for the PDRY to call upon Ethiopia and Libya under the tripartite treaty in a future conflict with the YAR, the possibility also exists for it to call upon the USSR under their treaty of friendship and cooperation. The YAR has raised its concern about the former possibility but has not yet done so about the latter, though both clearly exist.

With regard to Saudi Arabia, both the USSR and the PDRY have often warned the YAR against becoming too dependent on Riyadh, and Saudi Arabia has in turn frequently warned the YAR of the danger posed by both Aden and Moscow. Saudi Arabia opposed the republicans during the civil war, and even after the Saudi-YAR reconciliation of 1970 relations have not always been good. The Saudis have on occasion publicly stated their reservations about Yemeni unity and about the YAR's rapprochement with the USSR after the 1979 war (the Saudis fear that Yemeni unity would mean a Marxist government would rule both Yemens and would pose a greater security threat to the Kingdom than the PDRY does by itself).[208] There has also been tension over the border between the two countries, most of which is undefined.[209] The YAR government has also resented Saudi attempts to influence its policies as well as its involvement with certain northern tribes over which Sanaa wishes to assert its authority. On the whole, however, both have worked to maintain good relations with each other. As long as the YAR receives large-scale economic aid from Saudi Arabia and the other GCC states, the Soviets are not likely to succeed in drawing the YAR away from its close relationship with Riyadh. But as long as the YAR cannot obtain the level of military assistance it wants from Saudi Arabia and the West, Riyadh is unlikely to persuade Sanaa to end its military ties to Moscow. Yet even if Washington and Riyadh increased their military aid or Moscow increased its economic assistance, Sanaa would seek to preserve its political independence.

Like other Arab countries, North Yemen opposes Israel and supports the Palestinians and the Arab cause generally. The YAR has also criticized U.S. support for Israel, broken relations with Egypt for having signed the Camp David peace accords, and praised Soviet support for the Arabs. In joint communiqués issued after talks between Soviet and YAR officials, the similarity of the two governments' views on the Arab-Israeli conflict is often noted. During the 1973 Middle East war, the YAR participated in the Egyptian blockade of the Straits of Bab al-Mandab to prevent Israel from obtaining oil or other supplies via the Red Sea. Moscow and Sanaa also expressed concern over reports that Israel had occupied certain islands off the coast of the YAR.[210] North Yemen has also allowed the PLO to maintain a radio station in Sanaa, and it gave refuge to many PLO guerrillas after they were driven out of Lebanon by Israel and by Syrian-backed forces.[211] Nevertheless, the YAR has not been deeply involved in the Arab-Israeli conflict and has not allowed it to become an obstacle to relations with the United States. As was mentioned earlier, the YAR was the first Arab country to reestablish ties with Washington broken off during the 1967 Middle East war.

Both Sanaa and Moscow have called for the Red Sea and the Indian Ocean to be made "zones of peace" in which the forces of nonregional powers would be limited or banned. The two countries, however, have not always had similar ideas on what a zone of peace should be. For example, the YAR's al-Hamdi hosted a conference at Taiz in March 1977 that the presidents of South Yemen, Somalia, and Sudan also attended in order to discuss the transformation of the Red Sea into a zone of peace, ostensibly to counter a threat from Israel. However, both Ethiopia and the USSR objected to this plan because they claimed the nations involved would attempt to make the Red Sea an "Arab lake" and exclude Ethiopia through supporting the Moslem Eritrean separatists.[212] Like most other Arab countries, the YAR has supported Moslem Eritrean demands for separation from Ethiopia. In May 1977 the YAR allowed the Eritrean Liberation Front to open an office in Sanaa.[213] The Soviets had supported a Marxist Eritrean group when the pro-Western Emperor Haile Selassie ruled Ethiopia, but after the Ethiopian revolution brought a Marxist government to power in Addis Ababa, the Soviets switched their support. Nevertheless, the YAR and the USSR have not allowed their differing views on Eritrea and the formation of a Red Sea zone of peace to affect their bilateral relations.

When the Soviets invaded Afghanistan at the end of December 1979, most of the Arab world, including the GCC states, condemned them, while South Yemen openly defended Moscow. North Yemen, on the other hand, remained quiet. Sanaa did not denounce the Soviets, but a YAR delegation was sent to the Islamic Conference that met to discuss the invasion. Even the government-owned newspaper *Ath-Thawrah* asked President Salih why the YAR "did not have a clear stand" on this issue; Salih replied that YAR participation in the Islamic Conference showed what the country's position was, but that North Yemen would not be pushed to adopt the stands of others.[214] In other words, the invasion of Afghanistan was not important enough to the YAR that it would alter or cut its relations with the USSR as the Saudis were urging Sanaa to do.[215]

Regarding other regional issues, North Yemen has supported Iraq in the Iran-Iraq war, partly because Iraq is an Arab country fighting a non-Arab one and partly because Iraq has given economic assistance to the YAR in the past. According to press reports, the YAR assisted Moscow in transferring Soviet weapons to Iraq; the story was denied by the Soviets and seems implausible given the distance between North Yemen and Iraq.[216] Sanaa has expressed its disapproval of the U.S. Rapid Deployment Force and of the stationing of foreign troops in any of the countries of the region.[217] Salih has also praised the Brezhnev peace proposals for the Persian Gulf.[218] Unlike Saudi Arabia, the YAR has exhibited little concern for the condition of the Moslem population of the Soviet Union.

CONCLUSION

Since the end of the civil war, the primary threat to North Yemeni security has been South Yemen, and this will probably continue to be the case. Despite the YAR's inability to obtain the level of military assistance it wants from Saudi Arabia and the United States, it might appear short-sighted and self-destructive for North Yemen to rely heavily on the USSR for military assistance, since Moscow gives more assistance to the South, with which it is closely allied politically, ideologically, and militarily.

However, YAR leaders are convinced that building and maintaining friendly relations with the USSR is an important means of ensuring North Yemen's survival. The YAR government reasons that as long as good relations exist between Sanaa and Moscow, Moscow is less likely to support Aden when conflict between the two Yemens breaks out. Instead, the Soviets are more likely to support a peaceful solution to the conflict, as they did before. Although the Soviets did take some actions helping the South in previous conflicts, these actions were much more limited than they could have been.

Similarly, after the Ethiopian revolution, when two pro-Soviet governments were in power but came to fight each other over possession of the Ogaden region, Moscow attempted to arrange a compromise between the two. However, when the Somalis expelled the Soviets and abrogated their treaty of friendship and cooperation with the USSR in 1977, the Soviets no longer worked for a compromise but gave strong support to Ethiopia. Sanaa fears that if it also expelled Soviet advisers and ended friendship with Moscow because of Soviet support to South Yemen, the USSR might well give stronger military support to Aden in any future conflict between the Yemens. Unlike Somalia, which was attempting to seize territory from Ethiopia, North Yemen is seeking only to defend its territory from the South. If South Yemeni forces invaded the North with strong support from the Soviets, the YAR would be in a very difficult position. North Yemen's inability to obtain the arms it wants from the West and elsewhere compounds the problem from Sanaa's perspective, but even if it could obtain them, the YAR would still want to maintain friendly relations with the USSR for fear of what hostile ones might lead to.

North Yemen has certain obvious attractions for the Soviets. For the present, good Soviet-YAR relations serve to prevent Saudi and American influence from becoming predominant. YAR reliance on Soviet military equipment means that Sanaa is not likely to risk losing this assistance by attacking South Yemen. Indeed, part of the reason Moscow wants friendly ties with Sanaa is that these serve to protect Soviet interests in Aden. Over the longer term, establishment of a pro-Soviet government in Sanaa would put the USSR in a much better position to influence Saudi policy and perhaps even promote revolution within Saudi Arabia and the other GCC states. The weakness of the North Yemeni government also offers the Soviet Union an opportunity to see a pro-Soviet government come to power in Sanaa if North and South Yemen ever do unite—either peacefully or through force—since the better-organized party and government apparatus in Aden might be in a good position to spread its influence to the more populous but politically fractious North.

Nevertheless, there are also significant obstacles to the achievement of Soviet goals in North Yemen. While the PDRY government is better organized, South Yemen is too weak by itself to impose unity on the North, and if outside forces were brought in to help the South, North Yemen would turn to Saudi Arabia and the United States for military support—and might be more successful in obtaining it this time. If, on the other hand, the Yemens unite peacefully, there is no guarantee that the fractiousness of the North would not spread to the South. Even if a pro-Soviet government did come to power in Sanaa, the central government does not control all of North Yemen; the northern tribes would fight hard to prevent a Marxist government from extending its authority over them and, indeed, would seek to overthrow it. The Soviet Union does not want another anti-Soviet insurrection like that in Afghanistan, which could not easily be put down, especially since Saudi Arabia and the other conservative Arab states might seek a greater U.S. military presence to protect them if this occurred—another situation the Soviets would like to avoid.

On balance, Moscow and Sanaa both have stronger reasons for keeping their bilateral relations friendly than for allowing them to deteriorate. The Soviets also have an interest in restraining those elements in Aden advocating direct PDRY support for the overthrow of the Sanaa government, since this could provoke large-scale American and Saudi assistance to the YAR. Thus far, Moscow's interests have coincided with Sanaa's strategy of maintaining friendly relations with Moscow in order to dissuade the Soviets from pursuing policies inimical to the YAR. Yet should the NDF revive or another Marxist opposition group gain strength, this strategy might not succeed.

The possibility exists that domestic opposition to the Salih regime might be revived. His government is not a popular one and is backed mainly by the army. All political parties have been banned. That the central government is relatively weak provides the opposition with more of an opportunity to act effectively against it, provided the opposition can overcome its own weaknesses. While backed by Aden, the NDF did draw much support from within the YAR. Even though the NDF was defeated, the internal conditions that attracted people to it have not disappeared. These include Shafei dissidence, dislike for Salih within the army as well as other groups, and lack of economic development (though if the oil discovered in July 1984 leads to a major find, rapid improvement could be made in the economic realm).[219] Should a better-organized Marxist insurrection erupt, the YAR government could hardly rely on its new treaty of friendship and cooperation with Moscow to defend it or prevent Aden from supporting the opposition. In this sense the YAR's strategy of relying on Soviet friendship may prove to be a weak one in the long run.

South Yemen

2

South Yemen, or the People's Democratic Republic of Yemen, is the only nation ruled by a Marxist-Leninist party on the Arabian Peninsula or in the entire Arab world. Soviet influence is very strong in the PDRY, and in 1979 Moscow and Aden signed a treaty of friendship and cooperation. There are also Soviet, Cuban, and East German military advisers present in South Yemen. Of all the radical Arab states, South Yemen is unique because while the others have stressed their Arab nature and independence from the superpowers, Aden has put greater emphasis on its alliance with the pro-Soviet socialist states than on its membership in the Arab world. Not surprisingly, the other states of the Arabian Peninsula have often seen South Yemen as a threat to their security.

The PDRY, however, did not always have such a close relationship with the USSR or such a strong commitment to Marxism-Leninism. The National Liberation Front, which came to power after the British withdrew in November 1967, was not originally a Marxist organization, but a radical Arab nationalist one. There was a communist party in Aden—the People's Democratic Union—but it played almost no role in the revolution and in 1975 was absorbed by the Front. For its part, the Soviet Union gave little help to the NLF during the revolution and indeed appeared to favor its pro-Egyptian rival, the Front for the Liberation of South Yemen. Even when the radical wing of the NLF seized power from the moderate wing in 1969, the leadership was divided between pro-Soviet and pro-Chinese factions. It was only in 1978 that the staunchly pro-Soviet 'Abd al-Fattah Isma'il overthrew Salim Rubayyi 'Ali (who was regarded as being pro-Chinese and pro-Western), but in 1980 the more moderate 'Ali Nasir Muhammad in turn overthrew Isma'il.

An important question with regard to South Yemen is to what extent the USSR controls internal politics in the PDRY. Are leadership changes in Aden engineered by the Soviets to remove leaders who pursue policies Moscow disapproves of, or are these changes purely the result of internal power struggles the USSR does not control? The degree of Soviet influence over PDRY internal politics is important because it affects the extent to which South Yemen can pursue policies independent of the USSR. Although succeeding PDRY leaders have of their own volition invited an increasingly larger Soviet presence into the country, it is uncertain whether the South Yemenis could remove it now.

Another important question is to what extent the PDRY itself as well as the Soviet presence there represents a threat to the other countries of the Arabian Peninsula. South Yemen has at times had hostile relations with all three nations bordering it: it has fought two border wars with North Yemen, supported insurgents in both North Yemen and Oman, had clashes with the Saudis, and been hostile to Bahrain, Qatar, and the UAE when they became independent. Yet at times the PDRY has sought cooperative relations with its neighbors. Aden established diplomatic relations (but did not set up embassies) with Bahrain, Qatar, and the UAE in 1975 and with Saudi Arabia in 1976. South Yemen has also sought to improve relations with the North after each conflict, and in 1982 the PDRY and Oman normalized their hitherto very unfriendly relations. South Yemen's foreign policy toward its neighbors has fluctuated between hostility and cooperation; Aden's ultimate intentions toward them are unclear. Since taking power in 1980, 'Ali Nasir Muhammad has made strong efforts to have good relations with all the states of the Arabian Peninsula, but at present he is engaged in a serious struggle for power with his hard-line rivals. A new leader might decide to promote revolution as Aden has in the past.

Previous PDRY hostility toward its neighbors has not always been the result of offensive acts on Aden's part; it has sometimes been a defensive reaction to attempts by South Yemeni opposition groups based in Saudi Arabia and North Yemen to overthrow the Marxist regime in the late 1960s and early 1970s. Indeed, it was this defensive concern that contributed to South Yemen's increasing reliance on Soviet military aid. Nevertheless, it was during this period that Aden tried hardest to promote Marxist revolution throughout the entire Arabian Peninsula, thereby provoking its neighbors. Aden's support of the National Democratic Front insurgency in North Yemen, which ended only in 1982, shows that the PDRY has not abandoned its goal of promoting revolution when South Yemeni leaders think it might succeed. At the same time, Aden wants good relations with the conservative states of the Gulf Cooperation Council in order to receive money from them for economic development, especially since the Soviets have not been overly generous in giving assistance to the PDRY.

The Soviet Union has benefited from its close relationship with South Yemen. During the conflict between Ethiopia and Somalia over the Ogaden region, Moscow was able to use Aden as a transshipment point in sending Soviet arms and advisers to Addis Ababa. After the USSR lost the use of the Somali port of Berbera, it was able to transfer its activities to Aden. Even before this, Aden was used by Soviet naval and merchant vessels for refueling and repairs. The Soviet air force also has facilities in South Yemen. So far, South Yemen has proved a firmer Soviet ally than either Egypt or Somalia and does not have any significant internal opposition, as does the other Marxist state in the region, Ethiopia. Yet while the USSR has found South Yemen valuable in extending its military presence in the Indian Ocean area as well as facilitating its military involvement in the Horn of Africa, the Soviets have been extremely concerned about deemphasizing the threat from its presence in the PDRY toward the rest of the Peninsula. Indeed, the USSR has given little support to Aden in several of its conflicts with its neighbors.

In the past, the PDRY's attempts to spread revolution have hindered Soviet efforts to establish good relations with Saudi Arabia and the other conservative Arab Gulf states. At other times the Soviets have feared that South Yemen's efforts to establish good relations with these same states might lead Aden to distance itself from Moscow. Thus, both revolutionary and moderate leaders in Aden have posed problems for Moscow.

HISTORICAL OVERVIEW

Throughout the long history of the Yemens, the South has often been linked to the North, but the two have frequently been separated as well. On those occasions when the two were joined, the seat of power was usually in the North; seldom if ever has the South ruled the North. When the two have been separate, the South has existed not as a single unified state, but instead as a series of small sultanates. The last time there was a united Yemen was in the late seventeenth and early eighteenth centuries, and it was ruled by the Zaidi Imams of the North. One important difference between the two Yemens is that while the North has been and is now divided between Zaidi Shiites and Shafei Sunnis, the South is overwhelmingly Shafei Sunni. In 1728 the Sultan of Lahej (in the western part of South Yemen) broke away from the Imam's rule and became independent. Soon thereafter the Imam lost all control of South Yemen as numerous other sultans asserted their independence. This division of Yemen, then, preceded the arrival of the British in Aden.[1]

Except for a brief occupation of Socotra and Kamaran Islands and an abortive attack on Aden by the Portuguese in the early sixteenth century, South Yemen remained free from European colonial rule until the arrival of the British. When Napoleon invaded Egypt in 1798, the British feared that the French might then send forces by sea to invade India. In May 1799, British troops occupied Perim Island in order to control the Red Sea at the Straits of Bab al-Mandab. There being no fresh water on Perim, the British moved to Aden in September 1799 at the invitation of the Sultan of Lahej. In March 1800 they left Aden completely, judging that the French were not about to attack India after all.[2]

The British occupied Aden again in January 1839, and this time they stayed until 1967. The pillage by local Arabs of an Indian vessel flying a British flag shipwrecked near Aden was used as a pretext for the invasion, but the real reason was Britain's need for a station to service ships traveling to and from India.[3] Britain's primary interest was limited to Aden port, and the British did not seek to expand their rule into South Yemen as a whole. They did, however, wish to prevent other European powers from occupying any part of it, and so in 1857 the British occupied Perim to frustrate a French attempt to do so. The French did occupy one South Yemeni town in 1862 and planned to occupy more, but soon thereafter they allowed the British to buy out their position.[4]

With the opening of the Suez Canal in 1869, Aden's importance as a trade center as well as a refueling port rapidly expanded. At this time the Turks were expanding their control over North Yemen, and in 1872–73 they attempted to extend their influence to the sultanates of South Yemen (the earlier period of Ottoman rule in Yemen in the sixteenth and seventeenth centuries had included South Yemen). Both sides sent forces into the South Yemeni interior, but no fighting occurred. The weak Ottoman government agreed to regard certain South Yemeni tribes as inside the British sphere of influence. But as Turkish efforts to extend their rule south continued, along with the threat that France and Germany might obtain footholds along the coast, in 1886 the British began a policy of signing protectorate treaties with all the rulers of South Yemen (or South

Arabia, as the British called it).[5] These treaties served mainly to justify British intervention to keep foreign forces out. Although they did lead to greater British involvement in the affairs of the interior, especially in mediating disputes between rival tribes, the British left the local sultans almost completely in charge of their internal affairs. This was partly because the British authorities in India (who were then responsible for Aden and the protectorates and not the authorities in London) wanted to save money and partly because the British lacked interest in the rest of South Yemen beyond keeping others out and protecting Aden.

To put a stop to frontier incidents, the British and Turkish governments agreed in 1901 to establish a joint boundary commission. By May 1904 the commission had delimited the border from Bab al-Mandab to a point near the North Yemeni town of Harib, but it left the boundary to the northeast of this undefined. The Turkish government was dissatisfied with certain aspects of this agreement, but the British forced the Ottoman governor in Sanaa to accept it by threatening to cut off the supply lines to Turkish forces there. The Ottoman Sultan did not ratify the agreement until 1913, when his own influence in North Yemen had been considerably diminished by the young Imam Yahya, the future ruler of independent North Yemen.[6] This agreement dividing Yemen was not made with the consent of any Yemeni party, but there has been no other agreement to delimit the border. The shortcomings of the 1904 agreement have been a source of conflict between Sanaa and Aden ever since.

The Turks were allied with Germany during World War I, and in 1915 Turkish forces crossed the border and almost reached Aden itself. The British drove them back from positions threatening the port, but they remained in Lahej until the collapse of the Ottoman empire forced the Turks to abandon all their possessions in the Arab world.[7] After the war, there was tension along the frontier as Imam Yahya attempted to assert what he regarded as his rightful authority in the South Yemeni protectorates and the British attempted to stop him. In 1934 an Anglo-Yemeni treaty of friendship was signed in which both sides agreed to respect the status quo, but tension did not end, since both sides had different views regarding what the status quo was. Yahya was particularly enraged when, after control of South Yemen was passed from the India Office to the Colonial Office in 1937, the British implemented a policy of signing new treaties with all the protected states that provided for them to accept British advisers for their internal affairs. Yahya considered this an expansion of British authority beyond the 1934 status quo, and so he and later his son Ahmad continued their intermittent subversive efforts along the border up until the North Yemeni revolution in 1962.[8]

Despite Yahya's belief, this new series of advisory treaties (which was completed only in 1952) did not represent a major increase in British influence over the protectorates. The British still intended to keep expenditures down by relying on the local sultans as much as possible. This policy did indeed save money, but it proved extremely costly in the end. In the great wave of decolonization that took place following World War II, a difficult problem the British faced was that South Yemen was not a single unified state but a series of traditional sultanates plus the modern city of Aden (which like Hong Kong was a crown colony). In addition, London hoped to retain Aden as its primary military base for the Middle East/Persian Gulf area and did not want to grant full independence.

The long and complicated story of Britain's futile efforts first to remain in control of South Yemen and later to establish a viable pro-Western government there has been told in great detail already;[9] only the outline will be presented here. In 1954 the British proposed to the sultans of the western part of South Yemen (known as the Western Protectorate) that they form a federation, but the sultans rejected this plan because each feared the loss of his own authority within his territory. The British dropped the proposal, but by 1958 the Western Protectorate sultans themselves were calling for a federation and in 1959 it came into being (but South Yemen did not become independent). Events in the intervening years convinced the sultans that federation was in their interests. After the British and French failed to retake the Suez Canal from Nasser in 1956, it was clear that the British were no longer so strong in the Middle East. Agitation for independence grew stronger, especially within the city of Aden. There the Aden Trades Union Congress (ATUC) was founded and became powerful. Its leadership was dominated by North Yemenis (much of the labor force in Aden was from the North) who called not only for an end to British rule, but also for the unification of the two Yemens. Imam Ahmad also began a propaganda campaign calling for unity. The South Yemeni sultans wanted above all to avoid rule by Imam Ahmad and feared that the British might eventually abandon them. They reasoned that they would have a better chance to preserve their rule through a federation than as separate statelets.[10]

But not all the sultans wanted to join the South Arabian Federation, especially in the Eastern Protectorate, where the local rulers (who felt they had little in common with the Western Protectorate) hoped oil would soon be discovered, which would bring them revenues they did not want to share. Another difficulty was whether the city of Aden, which Britain ruled directly as a colony, would join the Federation. Several sultans feared that Aden's large population would allow the city to dominate the Federation and that the radicalism of the ATUC would spread to their territories. Similarly, many Adenis were afraid that the sultans would dominate the Federation and that the city's wealth would be heavily taxed to develop the impoverished interior. The British, for their part, wanted Aden to join the Federation, since neither the protectorates nor Aden separately seemed likely to form viable states and since they saw Aden's membership in the Federation as a way to ensure British control over the important military base there.[11]

A curious aspect of Britain's policy at this time was that while it insisted that Aden and the sultanates become federated, it also wanted the local governments involved to make the necessary decisions of their own accord. After much cajoling by the British, Aden's Legislative Council finally approved joining the Federation on September 26, 1962, but this decision was considered illegitimate by many residents of Aden for two important reasons. First, the electoral franchise in Aden was severely restricted; although native Adenis could vote, Arabs not only from the North but even from the protectorates were excluded. At the same time, Indians, Somalis, and others from the Commonwealth could vote. When the 1959 elections to the Council were held, Aden had a population of about 180,000, but only some 21,500 were registered to vote, and of these only about 5,000 actually did, since the ATUC had called for a boycott of the election.[12] Thus it was easy for the opponents of the British-sponsored Federation to argue that the Legislative Council's decision did not represent the true wishes of Aden's inhabitants.

Second, on the exact day of the vote to join the Federation the Yemen Arab Republic was declared in Sanaa. In the South this immediately increased popular support among Arab nationalists for unity with the North, since unity would mean rule not by an archaic Imam but by a revolutionary Arab republic instead. By contrast, rule by the North became even less appealing to the sultans and the Federation government.

Over the next few years, what little strength and appeal the Federation may have had deteriorated sharply. Soon after the revolution in the North, tens of thousands of Egyptian troops arrived in North Yemen to help the republicans fight the royalists; the Egyptians also armed and financed South Yemeni rebel groups. The rebels launched a terrorist campaign in which the British and the South Yemenis who cooperated with them became the prime targets. Several tribal revolts also broke out in the protectorates, including one in the Radfan Mountains on October 14, 1963—the date the Marxist government regards as the beginning of the South Yemeni revolution—which the Federation's troops could not defeat, necessitating the direct use of British troops.[13]

In October 1964 the Conservatives were defeated at the polls, and a Labour government came into office in London. The new Labour leaders put much less emphasis on attempting to strengthen the Federation and the sultans (a policy they identified with the Conservatives) and tried instead to work with the ATUC leaders. This policy did not succeed, however, because the ATUC leaders only had a power base in Aden, and the National Liberation Front, which was strong in the rural areas, insisted on a path of violent revolution without negotiations. In June 1965 the British outlawed the NLF, and the following September they dismissed the elected government of Aden (whose Chief Minister had called for the United Kingdom to recognize and negotiate with the NLF) and reinstituted direct British rule over Aden Colony.

In February 1966 the Labour government issued a White Paper on defense in which it announced that the South Arabian Federation would be granted independence by the end of 1968 and that the military base at Aden would be phased out by then. This announcement greatly disheartened the sultans, who increasingly feared that the British would abandon them. The Egyptians encouraged the rebels not to negotiate with the British but to fight on, since Nasser hoped to prevent the pro-British Federation from inheriting power and to promote a pro-Egyptian government instead. The rebels themselves continued to fight not only against the British and the Federation, but also against each other in a bitter struggle over which group would come to power.[14]

There were several competing independence movements in South Yemen. Beginning with the least radical, the Aden Association was founded in 1950 and strove for the independence of Aden Colony within the Commonwealth; many in this group opposed unity even with the protectorates. The Aden Association was the one political party that did not boycott the Aden Legislative Council elections; in 1955 it won three out of four and in 1959 eleven out of twelve elected seats available. This party drew its strength mainly from middle and upper class Adeni Arabs and had little following among the poorer residents of the city, especially the non-Adenis. When internal dissensions over the issue of joining the Federation erupted, the Association effectively collapsed in 1959.

Another group was the South Arabian League (SAL), also founded in 1950, which called for the independence of the South as a unitary state. The leadership of SAL came primarily from the ruling family of Lahej, the largest of the sultanates in the Western Protectorate. While it gained some popular support, the SAL's opposition to the Federation made the other sultans afraid that its real aim was to create a unitary state dominated by Lahej. At the same time, the SAL was regarded as "reactionary" by more radical nationalists. Egypt gave it some aid at first, but the SAL gradually came under the influence of Saudi Arabia. It did not develop a strong military wing and so was not a serious contender for power.[15]

A much more important group was what eventually became known as the Front for the Liberation of South Yemen (FLOSY). This group drew its support primarily from the unenfranchised Adeni laborers originally from the protectorates and North Yemen. It opposed the Federation and called for unity with the North. The group underwent several organizational changes. Originally the United National Front based in Aden, its boycott of the 1955 elections accomplished little. Several of its leaders were active in creating the ATUC in 1956, which held numerous political strikes in the colony. In 1962 the ATUC leadership created the People's Socialist Party. The PSP united with SAL in February 1965 to form the Organization for the Liberation of South Yemen. In January 1966 it split with SAL and joined with the NLF to become the Front for the Liberation of South Yemen. The NLF, however, left the Front in November 1966 and battled against FLOSY until independence.[16]

The National Liberation Front was formed in 1963 and drew its leadership from the Aden branch of the Arab Nationalist Movement (ANM). Like the ANM in Beirut, the NLF was originally pro-Nasser but became increasingly disaffected from him and turned toward Marxism instead. Unlike the ATUC (the predecessor of FLOSY), the NLF concentrated its efforts on organizing the poor tribesmen of the interior. The NLF also succeeded in building a military wing that was much more effective than the one FLOSY eventually set up. Because its operations were carried out primarily in the protectorates instead of in Aden and because its leadership was extremely clandestine, the British had little knowledge of the NLF and did not declare it illegal until June 1965, after the first NLF Congress had been held in North Yemen.[17]

Nasser had encouraged the PSP (later FLOSY) to unite first with SAL and then with NLF in the hope that the entire opposition could be controlled by pro-Egyptian elements. The more moderate NLF leader, Qahtan ash-Shaabi, agreed to this while in Cairo in January 1966 in order to obtain Egyptian arms and money, but the more radical NLF leaders in the field forced the NLF to withdraw from FLOSY in November.[18]

FLOSY had a less advantageous position than the NLF at the beginning of 1967, since the former's main support was in Aden while the latter's was spread throughout the interior. A series of events took place that weakened FLOSY even further. Nasser's defeat in the June 1967 Middle East war and subsequent withdrawal from North Yemen led to a severe reduction in Egyptian aid to FLOSY. Shortly thereafter, elements of the South Arabian Army (the Federation's army) mutinied and by autumn had almost completely joined forces with the NLF. In the summer of 1967 the NLF launched a military campaign in which it took over all the sultanates of the Western Protectorate; the sultanates of the Eastern Protectorate fell to it by October. Even the British themselves aided the NLF. Their enmity toward Nasser stemming from the Suez Canal crisis as well as his attempts to extend Egyptian influence over both Yemens was so great that they saw the NLF as being more acceptable than FLOSY simply because it was independent of Egyptian influence. That the NLF had Marxist leanings was overlooked. During the final battle between the NLF and FLOSY during the autumn of 1967, British forces on several occasions supported the former against the latter.[19]

The British government had moved up the announced date of independence for South Yemen first to January 1968 and then, as the situation deteriorated further, to November 1967. When the sultans of the interior were all overthrown, the Federation also collapsed, since its leadership had been composed of the sultans. In November 1967 the NLF finally agreed to hold talks with the British when authority had effectively passed to it. The last British soldiers left Aden on November 29, and on November 30 the NLF declared the independence of the People's Republic of South Yemen.[20]

The British did not achieve any of their aims during the South Yemeni conflict. From December 1963 (when a state of emergency was declared in Aden) until the end of the conflict, total British military casualties were 129 killed and 904 wounded.[21] These losses were hardly on the same scale as the approximately 50,000 Americans killed in Vietnam. It appears, then, that the British made a relatively weak effort to shape the outcome of the South Yemeni conflict, especially compared with their successful efforts against Marxist insurgency in Malaya and Oman. This failure, however, was due not to an insufficient military effort alone, but also to the political weakness of the successor government they were trying to create. The sultans of the Federation did not command the loyalty of the population of Aden or of the disaffected tribesmen of the interior. Also, the British did little to make the Federation more acceptable to the populace, as they did in Malaya by leaving the sultans there some authority in their own states but giving control of national policy to a democratically elected parliament. As it was, the Federation was unable to draw upon a sense of South Yemeni nationhood to counter the demand for unity with North Yemen made by both FLOSY and the NLF. Ironically, it was the NLF that led South Yemen into becoming a unitary state for the first time in its history when the differing policies followed by the two Yemeni governments made unity increasingly difficult.

When the NLF came to power, its ranks were divided into moderate and leftist factions. The moderates at first held the upper hand, since their leader, Qahtan ash-Shaabi, became President, Prime Minister, and Supreme Commander of the Armed Forces. But the leftists were active and called for nationalizing foreign capital, redistributing land, revamping the civil service and army along radical lines, and creating an armed militia of up to 150,000 men. Ash-Shaabi opposed these policies as being too radical, but the left was able to get them approved at the Fourth Congress of the NLF at Zinjibar in March 1968. Fearing the left, ash-Shaabi and the army (which particularly objected to the proposed imposition of political commissars on it) moved against the left the same month and arrested many of its leaders. Ash-Shaabi, however, did not control the whole country; the left was strong in the eastern part (Hadramaut), and a Maoist insurrection broke out there in 1968. Fighting occurred elsewhere too as FLOSY and SAL units, with the alleged support of Saudi Arabia and North Yemen, tried to take advantage of the NLF's divisions. In the Radfan Mountains, where the NLF first led tribesmen in the uprising of October 1963, a revolt broke out against the NLF. Ash-Shaabi was able to put down the left's insurrection in Hadramaut, but attacks from FLOSY, SAL, and various tribes continued. To strengthen his position against these other opponents, ash-Shaabi in April 1969 brought back into the government many of the leftist leaders he had defeated a year earlier.

The left, however, was by no means reconciled to ash-Shaabi and was soon able to take advantage of a split within the moderate camp to oust him. In June 1969, ash-Shaabi quarreled with his Interior Minister,

71

Muhammad 'Ali Haitham, and attempted to dismiss him. Haitham resisted and called upon his allies within the army as well as the left for support. On June 22 this combined opposition forced the resignation of ash-Shaabi and his cousin Faysal ash-Shaabi (who was Secretary-General of the NLF and had become Prime Minister in April 1969). A new five-man Presidential Council then came to power that included the Marxists Salim Rubayyi 'Ali, as its chairman, and 'Abd al-Fattah Isma'il, who became the new Secretary-General of the NLF. The more moderate Haitham became Prime Minister and a member of the Presidential Council, but he proved to be a weak figure who was unable to halt the large-scale purge of moderates from both the civil service and the army as well as the increasing Marxist orientation of the country. He was dropped from both his positions in August 1971, and was replaced by the Marxist Defense Minister, 'Ali Nasir Muhammad al-Hassani.[22]

One of the most difficult problems facing South Yemen after independence was the economy. Though Aden had been a thriving center of commerce under the British, the economy declined markedly in 1967–68 owing to the end of British contributions to the budget, the withdrawal of the military base with all its attendant expenditures, the closing of the Suez Canal during the June 1967 Middle East war (which led to a steep decline in the number of ships visiting Aden for bunkering services), and the flight of business capital from the country. The ash-Shaabi government undertook drastic measures such as reducing the salaries of civil servants by up to 60 percent and raising income tax rates on private sector earnings. His radical successors sought to completely transform the economy along socialist lines. In November 1969 the government nationalized all banks, insurance companies, and foreign firms with the exception of the British Petroleum Company's refinery at Aden (which was voluntarily transfered to the state in 1977 after years of operating below capacity). Western firms were even further discouraged from investing in South Yemen, and almost no aid was forthcoming from Western governments, who were increasingly alienated by Aden's revolutionary domestic and foreign policies. South Yemeni reliance on aid from the socialist countries, which had begun under ash-Shaabi, became even greater after him.[23]

Although the left was in control, serious differences over policy issues arose during the 1970s between 'Ali and Isma'il. Isma'il was pro-Soviet, advocated economic development according to the Soviet model, and favored the transformation of the NLF into a Soviet-style Marxist-Leninist party. 'Ali was pro-Chinese, opposed further reliance on the USSR, attempted to follow the Chinese model of development, and was critical of Isma'il's efforts to form a Marxist-Leninist party. 'Ali appeared to be more powerful in the mid-1970s, when he succeeded in establishing friendly relations with Bahrain, Qatar, and the UAE in 1975 and with Saudi Arabia in 1976. In 1977–78, though, Saudi-PDRY relations soured over South Yemen's support for Soviet-backed Ethiopia in the Ogaden war. On the domestic plane, 'Ali's efforts to foster radical economic development did not meet with success. Nor was he able to stop the 1975 unification of the NLF with the small communist Popular Democratic Union and the (Ba'thist) Popular Vanguard Party into a new organization headed by Isma'il called the United Political Organization-National Front (UPONF).[24]

By early 1978 'Ali's power had declined and his life came to an end in June 1978. Two days after YAR President al-Ghashmi was killed in his office by a bomb brought by a South Yemeni emissary, 'Ali was forced to resign and then was executed. He was accused of killing al-Ghashmi and of attempting a "counterrevolutionary" coup in Aden, though it appears that al-Ghashmi's death was actually arranged by Isma'il to provide a pretext for ousting 'Ali. With 'Ali out of the way, Isma'il presided over the transformation of the UPONF into the Yemeni Socialist Party in October 1978.[25]

Prime Minister 'Ali Nasir Muhammad immediately succeeded 'Ali as Chairman of the Presidential Council, but Isma'il was the strongman of the new regime. In December 1978 the Presidential Council was abolished and a Supreme People's Council was created with Isma'il as the Chairman of its Presidium; 'Ali Nasir Muhammad retained the post of Prime Minister. Under Isma'il, the PDRY's relations deteriorated with all its neighbors but improved with the USSR. On October 24, 1979, Moscow and Aden signed a treaty of friendship and cooperation.[26]

Isma'il was overthrown by 'Ali Nasir Muhammad in a bloodless coup on April 21, 1980. 'Ali Nasir Muhammad then became Chairman of the Presidium of the Supreme People's Council and Secretary-General of the YSP while retaining the post of Prime Minister. Isma'il later went into exile in the Soviet Union. Since then, the PDRY has worked to improve relations with all its neighbors while at the same time remaining closely allied to the USSR.

SOVIET INVOLVEMENT IN PDRY CONFLICTS

The conflicts that have taken place inside or along the borders of
South Yemen since World War II were the South Yemeni revolution,
clashes with Saudi Arabia, fighting with North Yemen as well as support
for North Yemeni insurgents, and skirmishes with Oman resulting from
the PDRY-supported insurgency there. The degree of Soviet involvement
in each of these will be examined here.

The South Yemeni Revolution

Even before serious agitation for independence began in South
Yemen in the late 1950s, Soviet writers had often condemned British colonial rule there. One of the links between the USSR and North Yemen
under the Imams was that both opposed "British imperialism" in the
South.[27] Nevertheless, the Soviets did not appear to pay much attention to
affairs in South Yemen until 1958 and 1959, when labor unrest in Aden,
tribal uprisings in the protectorates, and border clashes with North Yemen
all occurred at more or less the same time. The Soviets concluded then
that a national liberation struggle had broken out that was threatening Britain's position. Moscow also opposed the London-sponsored Federation,
which they saw as a means of continuing British rule.[28]

At first the Soviets did not appear to have any particular favorites
among the opposition groups or to recognize that there were serious differences between them. They even expressed support for the South Arabian League, though this was a "bourgeois-nationalist" organization.[29]
However, after the revolution in North Yemen and the rapid buildup of
Egyptian forces there, Moscow concentrated its praise on the organizations Nasser favored. Hence the Soviet press gave favorable coverage to
the National Liberation Front, the People's Socialist Party, the ATUC,
'Abdallah al-'Asnaj (the "radical" ATUC leader who would later become
YAR Foreign Minister and strongly anticommunist), and 'Abd al-Qawi
Makkawi (the Aden Chief Minister who was dismissed by the British in
1965 and who became leader of FLOSY soon thereafter).[30]

The Soviets gave political support to the two main opposition groups
in 1965 and 1966 when, with Egyptian encouragement, they cooperated
with each other and united in January 1966. However, when the NLF split
from FLOSY the following November, its relations with Egypt became
hostile, and the Soviets were forced to choose between the two rivals. Yet
instead of favoring the more Marxist-oriented NLF, in January 1967 the

Soviets began to publicly support the Egyptian-backed FLOSY. The NLF
was not criticized by name (indeed, it was hardly mentioned in the Soviet
press at all during this time), but Soviet emphasis on the importance of the
previous decision of the two organizations to unite showed that Moscow
disapproved of the NLF's withdrawal from FLOSY.[31] FLOSY welcomed
Soviet support, and in April 1967 its leader Makkawi effusively praised
"the Soviet Government for the positive and effective backing" of his
organization.[32]

By June 1967 the strength of the NLF had become increasingly
apparent. In addition, the lack of support for FLOSY outside Aden, combined with the cutback in Egyptian aid owing to Nasser's defeat by Israel
and his subsequent withdrawal from North Yemen, meant that FLOSY
was less able to challenge the NLF. The Soviet reaction to these developments was to portray FLOSY and the NLF as equals and to describe the
quarrel between them as beneficial only to the imperialists. Both were
called upon to settle their differences. When the NLF finally came to
power on November 30, 1967, the USSR immediately recognized the new
state. Yet even after independence, the Soviet press called for reconciliation between the two movements and paid tribute to FLOSY's contribu-
tion to the struggle for independence.[33] In later years the Soviets would
repeat the NLF's version of the South Yemeni revolution and would not
even acknowledge its previous support of FLOSY.

On the level of foreign policy actions, the fact that a large
Soviet-armed Egyptian army was in North Yemen meant that Soviet
weapons could easily be sent to the rebels in the South. The Soviets,
though, apparently did not become much involved in aiding the southern
rebels directly, but left this to the Egyptians. They did not send military
advisers or directly transfer large amounts of Soviet weapons as they did
in other Third World conflicts.[34]

The coming to power of the Marxist NLF, then, was not the result of
deliberate Soviet policy. As in North Yemen during the civil war, Soviet
aims in South Yemen were affected by the Kremlin's desire to maintain
and expand its friendship with Nasser's Egypt. The Soviets thus supported
both the NLF and FLOSY when Egypt did but became cool toward the
NLF after it left FLOSY. Even when Egypt and FLOSY were losing
influence over events in the South, the USSR called upon the NLF to end
its quarrel with the pro-Egyptian organization. Another Soviet motive
may have been to prevent what Moscow saw as a pro-Chinese Marxist
movement from coming to power. But whatever the reason, that the USSR

did not support the NLF in its rise to power meant that the NLF did not begin its rule as the firm Soviet ally that it later became.

Saudi Arabia and the Internal Opposition

The details of Saudi support to the NLF's opponents and fighting between South Yemen and Saudi Arabia are extremely sketchy, since both sides denied any aggressive actions on their own part and quite probably exaggerated the actions of the other side. In addition, there was no regular press coverage of the sporadic fighting that occurred.

The Saudis were extremely upset at the establishment of an avowedly Marxist regime on their border and so gave support to the large number of exiles that had fled from South Yemen. These included some of the former sultans, SAL units, and NLF dissidents. FLOSY also cooperated with the Saudis beginning in 1972, but before then it kept aloof from the incursions Riyadh supported.

One conservative force that was strong inside South Yemen was the army, especially those soldiers from the Aulaqi tribes whom the British had relied on heavily as armed levies before independence. They became disenchanted with the radicalism of the NLF and were instrumental in purging the left in 1968. However, when the left returned to power in the 1969 coup, it quickly purged the Aulaqis and replaced them with Dathina tribesmen who had been staunch supporters of the NLF (several top NLF leaders were also Dathina). Many of the Aulaqis then fled to Saudi Arabia or North Yemen. The Saudis provided the rebels with a training camp at Sharura (near the South Yemeni border post of Wadiah). In 1970 the Saudis also allowed them to broadcast the Voice of Free South Yemen from the radio station that up to then had been used by the North Yemeni royalists. Sporadic fighting organized by FLOSY and SAL took place in the Radfan Mountains and the Aulaqi strongholds during 1968 and 1969. After the leftist coup, a more organized attempt to invade and overthrow the Aden government was made in November 1969, but this was defeated in a battle at the frontier post of Wadiah.[35]

Beginning in 1970, exiles made several attempts to detach the Hadramaut and Mahra regions in the east from Aden and to set up an independent state there. A series of raids were made between October 1970 and June 1971, including one operation involving 500 to 700 rebels in February 1971. All, however, were defeated, as was a move into the Baihan region in the West during June 1971.[36] South Yemen was also capable of striking back. In the midst of reports of fighting inside South Yemen,

Riyadh claimed in March 1973 that two PDRY MiG-17s had attacked Saudi territory near Wadiah.[37]

The Saudi-sponsored rebels did not get very far, partly because beyond overthrowing the Aden government they did not offer a political program that would appeal to the South Yemeni populace, and partly because the exiles themselves were divided. By 1971 even Aden claimed that Riyadh was unhappy with the exiles' lack of activity and was threatening to cut off support to them unless they did something.[38] Up until 1972 FLOSY had not cooperated with the other exile groups, and its leader, Makkawi, even admitted having talks with the PDRY Defense Minister 'Ali Nasir Muhammad.[39] In 1972, though, FLOSY joined the others in an umbrella organization called the United National Front, which Makkawi headed.[40] But disputes among exile leaders continued, and although the Voice of Free South Yemen claimed great victories for several years, the rebels made no progress. Saudi Arabia ceased its support, and the rebel radio station stopped transmitting when Riyadh and Aden normalized their relations in 1976.[41]

Throughout this entire period, the Soviets made many statements strongly supporting the Aden government, denouncing its opponents, and blaming Saudi Arabia as well as the United States and Britain for the clashes. The Soviets did not portray the opposition as stemming from FLOSY[42] but always presented it as an attempt by the old sultans to regain their positions.[43] They also described the attempt to establish a separate state in Hadramaut and Mahra as a Saudi–American-backed plan to seize Aden's alleged oil reserves there.[44] When the left was fighting the Aden government in 1968, though, the Soviets had remained extremely quiet; only after the fighting was over in early 1969 did they once identify the left as the "Mao clique."[45]

The Soviets had already begun to provide some military assistance to South Yemen during these years, but it is not clear whether Moscow undertook specific actions to help Aden fight the Saudi-backed rebels. The PDRY leaders, however, appear to have become convinced that because of the public support Moscow gave them in these clashes, they should turn toward the USSR for aid, especially since Moscow was more capable of providing military assistance than Peking. In June 1970 Isma'il stated that there was a direct link between these attacks and PDRY requests for Soviet aid: "increased imperialist danger in this area will lead to requests for more assistance from the Soviet Union and the socialist bloc in order to be able to repulse imperialism and its local reactionary agents."[46] Even Salim Rubayyi 'Ali, who was later ousted and condemned for being anti-Soviet, in 1972 referred to the USSR as "a strategic ally" and called upon it "to give every means of support to defeat the imperialist-reactionary aggression against the PDRY."[47]

With relatively little effort, then, the Soviets were able to exploit the Saudi-PDRY clashes to draw South Yemen closer to them. Large-scale Soviet military assistance was not necessary, since the attacks of the Saudi-supported exiles never seriously threatened the Aden regime. They were big enough, however, to frighten the PDRY leaders into seeking increased Soviet military support. The Saudis also seem to have learned that their hard-line policy had failed, and so in later years they tried a soft-line approach to wooing Aden away from Moscow that proved a much more serious challenge to Soviet interests.

Clashes with Oman

South Yemen's skirmishes with Oman came about as a result of Aden's support to the Marxist rebels attempting to overthrow the Sultanate. The insurrection in Oman will not be described here in detail. In brief, the rebellion broke out in 1965 in Dhofar province, which borders South Yemen, in reaction to the harsh rule of Sultan Sa'id bin Taymur. Under the influence of the new government in Aden, the rebels became radicalized in 1968 and formed the Popular Front for the Liberation of the Occupied Arab Gulf (PFLOAG). This organization had the announced intention of overthrowing British-backed governments in Bahrain, Qatar, the Trucial States (as they were called before becoming the UAE), and Oman. In June 1970 Sultan Sa'id was overthrown not by PFLOAG, but by his son Qabus with British support. Sultan Qabus launched a modernizing effort to develop Oman. South Yemen continued to support PFLOAG, but after much fighting, Omani forces with British, Iranian, and Jordanian assistance finally defeated the rebels at the end of 1975.

Since South Yemen gave political and military support to the Omani rebels, it was not surprising that relations between Aden and Muscat became hostile and that there were direct clashes between the armed forces of the two countries. On May 6, 1972, the Omani government announced that the Sultan's air force had bombed PDRY positions from which guns had been firing on the Omani border post of Harbut. The PDRY quickly denounced this violation of their airspace and accused Oman of having violated it 119 times since June 1970. Later in the same month, Omani forces were withdrawn from Habrut and the post there was destroyed. Believing South Yemen to be responsible, Omani forces attacked a base near Hauf in PDRY territory.[48]

The Omani government charged that on November 18, 1973, a PDRY Il-28 bomber had attacked an Omani military base in Dhofar. It also accused the PDRY of sending its own soldiers to fight alongside the PFLOAG, of continuing to shell Omani positions from inside the PDRY, and of sending armored cars to attack Omani forces.[49] In October 1975, during the final offensive that would defeat the rebels by the end of the year, Omani aircraft attacked Hauf again in reprisal for continued shelling into Oman from the PDRY. Muscat claimed to have destroyed the rebels' headquarters and cut off their supply line from Hauf into Dhofar. The following month, though, the Omani government claimed that shelling of Omani territory from longer-range guns than before had begun from Jadib—about five and a quarter miles inside South Yemen.[50] The Omani government later claimed in December 1975 that some 300 to 400 regular PDRY soldiers retreated over the border along with the defeated rebels. Sultan Qabus declared that the ten-year war had come to an end on December 11, 1975.[51] A final cease-fire between Aden and Muscat came into effect March 11, 1976 (two days after the establishment of Saudi-PDRY diplomatic relations),[52] but on November 24 the PDRY shot down an Iranian aircraft that Aden said had violated its airspace. Muscat claimed the aircraft had never left Oman, but this was difficult to believe since the pilot was captured in the PDRY.[53]

As with South Yemen's clashes with Saudi Arabia, the Soviet Union strongly supported Aden's position when fighting took place between PDRY and Omani forces. Moscow quickly repeated PDRY charges that Omani forces had crossed the border.[54] There was, however, a limit to the extent to which the Soviets would publicly condone South Yemeni support to PFLOAG. At first Moscow seemed reluctant to help the Omani rebels, since they were perceived to be pro-Chinese. When the Shah of Iran began to send troops to fight in Dhofar beginning in 1972, Aden vigorously denounced his policy, but the Soviets were hesitant to do so. Despite Moscow's condemnation of the Shah after the Iranian revolution, while he was in power it tried hard to have friendly ties to Tehran. As part of this policy, the Soviets did not criticize the Shah's actions in the same manner as those of the Sultan or his British and Jordanian allies.[55] In November 1976, when South Yemen shot down the Iranian aircraft, Radio Moscow was careful to give both the PDRY's and the Iranian government's versions of what happened.[56]

Yet if Aden saw Moscow as annoyingly agreeable to seeing Iranian troops on the PDRY border, South Yemeni leaders were quite happy to learn that their conservative Arab neighbors were also displeased about the situation. Indeed, the presence of Iranian troops in Oman seems to have been an important impetus for the PDRY, on the one hand, and Saudi Arabia and the other Arab Gulf states, on the other, to reconcile their differences. The conservative states attempted to mediate between Oman and South Yemen both before and after the insurrection ended with the hope that normalized relations would lead to the withdrawal of Iranian forces from the Peninsula.[57] When the PDRY shot down the Iranian aircraft in November 1976, Saudi Arabia did not side with conservative Oman but instead mediated between Tehran and Aden as well as arranged for the Iranian pilot to return home.[58] Although Aden's ties to Muscat did not improve, its relations with Saudi Arabia did for a while, leading to speculation that with Saudi aid the PDRY might turn away from the Soviets.[59]

Whereas Aden regarded its support to PFLOAG as a foreign policy priority, the Soviets seemed to regard it as something of an embarrassment that hindered Moscow's ties with the other states of the region. The conservative states of the Peninsula, however, gave the Soviets no credit for the nuances in their public statements expressing less than full support for Aden. Had the Soviets emphasized the Iranian threat to both South Yemen and the conservative Arab states, they may have been more successful at earning their gratitude. This, however, would have alienated Iran and only pushed the Shah into an even closer alliance with the United States. The budding friendship between Aden and Riyadh, which Moscow was apprehensive about, ended soon anyway, and the last Iranian troops left Oman in February 1979, at the time of the fall of the Shah. The PDRY-Omani border clashes, then, are an example of less than full Soviet support to South Yemen, which resulted from Moscow's complex foreign policy objectives calling for good relations with many countries and from Aden's up to then single-minded purpose of promoting revolution in Oman no matter how this might affect its ties with its other neighbors.

Conflicts with North Yemen

The details of the 1972 and 1979 PDRY-YAR border wars as well as South Yemeni support for the NDF insurgency in 1979–82 were discussed in the previous chapter and so will not be repeated here. A common theme in all of them is that while the Soviets did not assist North Yemen, they did not give much aid to South Yemen either. Unlike the conflicts with Oman and Saudi Arabia when the Soviets publicly supported Aden, Moscow attempted to remain evenhanded and neutral in its commentary when fighting took place between the Yemens.

Hostilities between North and South in 1972 were preceded by the killing of a North Yemeni shaykh and sixty-five of his men on February 21. Sanaa claimed they were being paid by the PDRY but were lured to the South and murdered because they had not undertaken the disruptive acts in the North they had been hired for; Aden admitted to killing them but said it did so because the northerners were a YAR-sponsored invasion party. Although the Sanaa government did not want it, the tribes of North Yemen sought revenge, and in the spring sporadic fighting took place on the border. This soon halted, and an uneasy peace was maintained until September 26, when fighting broke out between the PDRY and regular YAR armed forces. The fighting stopped on October 19, and the leaders of both countries signed a peace accord and unification agreement on October 28.[60]

There were several press reports that the Soviets had given military assistance to Aden during both periods of fighting in 1972 and that the Sanaa government was angry about this. However, Soviet statements were careful to blame the fighting not on either Yemeni government, but on Saudi Arabia, Zionism, and imperialism instead.[61] Moscow called for both sides to stop fighting and negotiate during the conflict and then praised the success of the Arab League mediation effort in bringing the war to an end. In one statement, the Soviets did indicate that the North was responsible for the conflict, but even then they blamed the "reactionary" tribes and not the Sanaa government.[62] By contrast, Aden sought to portray the USSR as committed to the PDRY, not as neutral. During the October fighting, Prime Minister 'Ali Nasir Muhammad went so far as to proclaim, "the Soviet Union will not stand by with folded arms in the event of an invasion of South Yemen."[63] The PDRY evidently would have preferred a strong commitment to it during the fighting with Sanaa and not the evenhanded stance that the USSR in fact adopted.

Fighting broke out again between the two Yemens on February 24, 1979. Washington announced an emergency arms package for the YAR, to be paid for and shipped via Saudi Arabia. As before, the conflict did not last long; a cease-fire came into effect March 16, and the leaders of the two Yemens signed another unity agreement March 30.[64]

During the fighting, there were press reports of Soviet, Cuban, and

Ethiopian military aid to the PDRY.[65] Yet as in 1972, Soviet public statements deplored the conflict between two "progressive" states and called for the fighting to stop. Moscow blamed the United States and Saudi Arabia for attempting to exacerbate the war by aiding North Yemen but did not blame the YAR itself.[66] This contrasted with South Yemeni statements saying the North was guilty of aggression.[67] In the realm of action, the Soviets did in fact aid the PDRY by delivering fifteen MiG-23s, ten MiG-21s, ten Su-20s and other weapons during March 1979.[68] Nevertheless, the USSR once again attempted to remain neutral in a conflict between North and South Yemen in which Aden would have preferred that Moscow back it more openly. This experience may have contributed to Isma'il's decision to sign a treaty of friendship and cooperation with Moscow the following October in order to secure stronger Soviet support in the future.

The National Democratic Front, which had fought alongside PDRY troops in the 1979 war and had been active even before it, began an insurgency campaign later in 1979 against the YAR government that was not put down until mid-1982. The NDF was led by pro-PDRY Marxists but also included other groups disaffected by Colonel Salih's rule. The fighting, which was often interrupted by cease-fire accords, took place in the southern part of North Yemen (where the population is predominantly Shafei Sunni as in South Yemen, but not as in northern North Yemen, where Zaidi Shias form the majority and dominate the central government). In early 1982 YAR forces began a more vigorous effort to crush the NDF, which was finally defeated in May 1982.[69]

Although the North Yemenis complained on one occasion that South Yemen was giving the NDF Soviet weapons, the Soviets themselves barely even acknowledged that the NDF existed and never expressed support for it.[70] Aden, however, frequently broadcast news about the NDF, and PDRY leader Isma'il openly backed it. When 'Ali Nasir Muhammad came to power in April 1980, he attempted to play the role of mediator between Sanaa and the NDF even though PDRY aid to the NDF continued. Whether the PDRY should give full military support to the NDF became an issue in the power struggle between 'Ali Nasir and his powerful Defense Minister, 'Ali 'Antar. 'Antar favored military aid and was apparently able to provide some, but when the NDF was defeated he lost much of his influence. 'Ali Nasir, on the other hand, preferred to pursue friendly relations with the YAR government and not give military aid to the NDF, since the latter's prospects for success did not seem great. This view appears to have been shared by the Soviets, who did not want to see the insurgency lead the Sanaa government to turn away from Moscow and toward Washington. Moscow would have been pleased to see the NDF seize power but did not see its prospects for success as good. In this case both the Kremlin and 'Ali Nasir had an interest in downplaying the importance of the conflict.

From examining the South Yemeni revolution as well as Aden's clashes with Saudi Arabia, Oman, and North Yemen, it is clear that not only has the USSR never undertaken any major, highly visible actions to support the PDRY, but also that the Soviets have not fully backed Aden in most of them. There was greater Soviet military involvement in the non-Marxist North Yemeni revolution and civil war than in the South Yemeni revolution; in its public statements, Moscow often supported FLOSY, the group that lost. In the clashes between the two Yemens, the USSR was publicly neutral, and in the border clashes with Oman the Soviets did not join Aden in vigorously denouncing the intervention of the Shah of Iran on Muscat's behalf. Only in the case of Saudi-sponsored rebel incursions into South Yemen did the USSR appear to wholeheartedly support Aden.

Nevertheless, Soviet-PDRY ties do not seem to have suffered much from this lack of outspoken Soviet support for the PDRY's position during these conflicts. This lack of Soviet support may have contributed to Salim Rubayyi 'Ali's disenchantment with the USSR, but it obviously was not crucial to the pro-Soviet leaders who succeeded him. This was partly because in none of the conflicts after the revolution was the survival of the regime in such jeopardy as to require Soviet military intervention of some sort. However, even when the USSR was publicly the least supportive of Aden during its clashes with Sanaa, the PDRY was able to draw upon an ongoing Soviet military assistance program involving arms transfers and advisers.

THE MILITARY RELATIONSHIP

The extent to which the USSR gave military assistance to the NLF and FLOSY before independence, directly or indirectly via Egypt, is not clear. The first known Soviet arms transfer to independent South Yemen was a relatively small shipment of light weapons and military vehicles in the summer of 1968.[71] At that time the South Yemeni army still relied heavily on the arms Britain had supplied to the Federation's armed forces.

Over the years, the USSR has continued to supply Aden with arms. Unlike North Yemen, which also relies heavily on Soviet arms but has also received significant arms transfers from the United States, France, West Germany, Italy, and others, South Yemen has received major supplies of weapons only from the USSR.[72] As of July 1984, the PDRY's inventory of Soviet weapons included 30 Mig-17, 48 MiG-21, 25 Su-20/22 fighters and interceptors, 30 Mi-8 and 15 Mi-24 helicopters, an unspecified number of SA-2, SA-3, SA-6, SA-7 surface-to-air missiles, 450 T-54, T-55, and T-62 main battle tanks, and several naval vessels, including 10 fast attack craft.[73]

According to Hosmer and Wolfe, Soviet arms transfers to Aden were worth less than $20 million in 1965–69 (really only 1968–69), more than $150 million in 1970–74, and about $230 million in 1975–80.[74] ACDA has given somewhat higher figures: $32 million in 1964–73 (really 1968–73), $160 million in 1973–77, and $775 million in 1978–82.[75] These levels of Soviet arms transfers are close to what Moscow has provided North Yemen. Considering that the PDRY has only a quarter the population of the YAR but all three of its armed services are slightly larger and possess more sophisticated Soviet weapons, these military assistance figures really indicate that Moscow has armed the South much more intensively than the North.[76]

There have also been significant numbers of Soviet, Cuban, and East German military advisers in South Yemen over the years. About 50 Soviet military technicians and advisers first arrived in Aden during January 1969.[77] Since then, the combined number of Soviet, Cuban, and East German advisers has been estimated by some at extremely high levels such as 8,000 or even 15,000.[78] According to the International Institute for Strategic Studies (IISS), the CIA, and the State Department, though, these numbers have been much lower. These latter sources indicate that there were about 200 Soviet military advisers in the PDRY in 1973–74, 350 by 1977, 550 by 1978, 1,000 to 1,500 by 1979–80, and 1,500 up to the present. The number of Cuban advisers had reached 350 in 1977, grew to 1,000 in 1978–79, and then fell to about 300 by 1984. The East Germans have usually been estimated at 100, though the IISS put their number at 325 in 1982 and then 75 in 1983 and 1984.[79]

It is difficult to judge whether there have been serious problems in the Soviet–South Yemeni military relationship, since, unlike Sanaa, Aden has said little about them (Moscow has not revealed much either). At first the Soviets appeared hesitant about giving military assistance to Aden, for even though South Yemen expelled its few British military advisers in January 1968, the Soviets sent only a minor package of small arms by the following summer and waited until January 1969 before sending some MiGs and about fifty advisers. A technical and military accord was signed in August 1968, and when President ash-Shaabi visited Moscow in January 1969, more military aid was agreed to. In April 1969, over fifty South Yemenis went to Moscow for training as pilots, thus beginning a stream of South Yemeni personnel who would travel to the USSR for military training—a total of 1,115 for the years 1969-81.[80]

China was also active in sending military advisers to South Yemen, at first to aid the Omani rebels and beginning in 1971 to assist the People's Militia—a paramilitary organization directly responsible to the NLF and intended, if necessary, to counter the army (which, along with the air force, the Soviets initially concentrated on training). It has been reported that Salim Rubayyi 'Ali intended the People's Militia to counter Soviet influence as well.[81] With the defeat of the Omani rebels in 1975 and the increase of Cuban influence in the People's Militia, the role of Chinese military advisers declined, and by 1977 there were none left in the PDRY.[82]

The PDRY did not establish diplomatic relations with Cuba until 1972, but their military ties grew rapidly after that. Cuban advisers arrived in 1973 and have concentrated on training the People's Militia and air force pilots.[83] Ties with East Germany were established after ash-Shaabi's overthrow in 1969, and by 1970 East Germany had already begun assisting Aden with internal security.[84] They are believed to have exerted a strong influence on the PDRY intelligence service from that time up to the present.[85]

Several high-level military officers from Russia and the PDRY have exchanged visits.[86] Notable among these were the visits of Admiral Gorshkov, commander of the Soviet navy, to Aden in December 1974, May 1978, and March 1983. When the Soviet navy was expanding its operations around the globe in the early 1970s, Soviet naval planners must have seen Aden as an important base for resupplying the Soviet Indian Ocean fleet, which had to operate thousands of miles from the nearest Soviet ports in either the Black Sea or Vladivostok. After the navy lost its bases first in Egypt and then in Somalia, the importance of Aden became even greater (especially since the coastal region of Moscow's new ally, Ethiopia, was being contested by Eritrean guerrillas).[87] Aden served as a crucial transshipment point for Soviet military assistance to Ethiopia during the conflict with Somalia over the Ogaden, and it could play a similar role if the Soviets became militarily involved in the region again.

What military facilities the Soviets actually use in the PDRY is not exactly clear. Both Moscow and Aden have over the years vociferously denied that there is any Soviet base in South Yemen at all.[88] While this might be technically correct in the sense that the USSR does not have a sovereign military base, the Soviets do use military facilities officially (though perhaps only nominally) controlled by the South Yemenis. The Soviets certainly use both naval and air facilities at Aden (some PDRY aircraft are believed to be operated by Soviet and Cuban crews).[89] Reports that the USSR has built submarine pens and that it uses facilities elsewhere such as Mukalla are less certain.[90] There have been persistent reports, emanating mainly from Oman and South Yemeni exile groups, that the USSR has built large-scale military facilities on the PDRY-controlled island of Socotra, but these appear to be greatly exaggerated.[91]

On October 25, 1979, Leonid Brezhnev and 'Abd al-Fattah Isma'il signed a treaty of friendship and cooperation lasting for twenty years from ratification and renewable every five years thereafter.[92] Article 5 of the treaty calls for both countries "to continue to develop cooperation in the military sphere on the basis of the relevant agreements concluded between them in the interests of strengthening their defense capability." Both sides also called for the creation of an Asian security system (art. 10) and pledged not to enter military alliances or otherwise take actions directed against the other (art. 12). In case of war, the treaty says only the following: "In the event of situations arising which create a threat to peace, the parties will seek to make immediate contact with a view to coordinating their positions in the interests of eliminating the threat which has arisen or restoring peace" (art. 11). Unless there were stronger commitments made in an unpublished annex, this treaty does not enjoin the USSR to come to South Yemen's defense if the latter is attacked, but merely calls for mutual consultations. Whether the Soviets ever would or could invoke the treaty to overtly intervene in South Yemen to prevent it from abrogating the treaty remains to be seen. Both Aden and Moscow have insisted that the treaty is not directed against any third party and does not threaten any other nation.

The PDRY also signed treaties of friendship and cooperation with East Germany on November 17, 1979, Ethiopia on December 2, 1979, and Libya and Ethiopia on August 19, 1981 (a protocol for cooperation between the South Yemeni and Bulgarian defense ministries was also signed April 2, 1980).[93] The tripartite treaty signed by Libya, Ethiopia, and the PDRY stated that "an aggression against one should be considered an aggression directed against all" and pledged the other parties to assist the one attacked "in all necessary ways" (art. 16). Yet for all the publicity the trilateral treaty aroused, military cooperation between the PDRY and Ethiopia on the one hand and Libya on the other has not been great. Distance, declining oil revenues, and the absence of a purely Marxist-Leninist orientation have all served to limit Qadaffi's ability and willingness to assist his allies. Bilateral military cooperation between Aden and Addis Ababa, however, has been more substantial. In addition to serving as a way station for Soviet and Cuban aid to Ethiopia, the IISS stated, in 1980 there were 1,000 PDRY troops plus a PDRY MiG-17 squadron based in Ethiopia, and some PDRY troops may still be there.[94] There have also been reports that Ethiopian troops aided South Yemen in its 1979 war with the YAR, but the veracity of these is doubtful considering Addis Ababa has been unable to defeat its opponents at home in Eritrea, Tigre, and elsewhere ever since the Ethiopian revolution.[95]

Moscow and Aden have not said much about the details of their military relationship, but as a result of the presence of Soviet, Cuban, and East German military advisers, Soviet use of PDRY military facilities, and Aden's series of treaties of friendship and cooperation, it appears that South Yemen is as closely tied militarily to the Soviet bloc as any state can be without actually being a member of the Warsaw Pact.

THE ECONOMIC RELATIONSHIP

As was mentioned previously, Aden's economy suffered considerably as a result of Britain's withdrawal and the closing of the Suez Canal. In addition, a large-scale exodus of people seeking better economic opportunities as well as escape from political repression by the new government threatened to seriously erode the South Yemeni work force. It was halted in 1973 when the government put a stop to free emigration.[96] The new government's radical policies meant that little economic assistance was forthcoming from the West, especially after the poorly compensated nationalization of most foreign firms in 1969. Owing to both great economic need and their own ideological orientation, the South Yemeni leaders hoped to receive large-scale assistance from the socialist states. The

Soviets, however, have not been particularly generous, especially in the early years of the republic.

Between 1967 and 1981, the USSR has given only about $205 million in economic assistance to Aden. Of this amount, the Soviets gave only $15 million by 1974; the bulk of Soviet assistance has come since 1978 (after the pro-Soviet faction seized power). The Chinese, on the other hand, were more generous during the early years of the republic; they provided $79 million in aid all together, but they have given nothing at all since 1974. South Yemen has also received some $125 million from Eastern Europe and over $200 million from Arab sources.[97]

The USSR and Eastern Europe have also sent an increasing number of economic aid technicians to the PDRY; in 1976 they numbered 400, and by 1981 this had risen to 2,700. Chinese experts also served in South Yemen and continued to do so after China stopped giving Aden any loans or grants. Cuban economic experts reached a high of about 500 in 1978 but dropped to 150 by 1981.[98] In addition, the number of academic students from South Yemen studying in the USSR and Eastern Europe has been growing every year; from 30 in 1967 their numbers increased to 1,335 at the end of 1981.[99]

The Soviet Union and South Yemen have signed several economic and technical cooperation agreements since 1969. In addition, Soviet economists have assisted Aden in drawing up its economic plans ever since the first three-year plan of 1971–74. The PDRY also joined the Council for Mutual Economic Assistance (CMEA) as an observer. In 1980, the two governments established the Standing Committee on Economic and Technical Cooperation to coordinate all Soviet assistance to Aden's development efforts. So far it has met once each year, alternating between Moscow and Aden.[100]

Among the most important development projects that the USSR has undertaken in South Yemen are a fish canning plant at Mukalla that produces 1.5 million cans annually, fishing port facilities at Aden with refrigerator installations, a fish meal plant, other aid to the fishing industry, a network of dams in the interior, a series of artesian wells, water storage tanks, a three-hundred-bed hospital, tractor and agricultural machinery workshops, additional types of workshops, and several other small projects. In addition, the USSR is constructing a thermoelectrical station in Aden to operate a water desalinization system and a factory to produce 250,000 tons of cement annually.[101] From a total turnover of only 4.5 million rubles in 1970, Soviet-PDRY trade grew to a high of 98.9 million rubles in 1981 but fell to 73.0 million in 1982. This trade consists mainly of Soviet exports to Aden and few imports from there.[102]

Although South Yemeni leaders frequently praise the USSR for its "selfless" economic assistance, the low level of Soviet aid when the PDRY so desperately needs it must be disappointing. Even the staunchly pro-Soviet Isma'il once criticized Soviet aid to Aden as "inadequate" compared with what Moscow gave Cuba.[103] One problem with Soviet aid is that some projects take a very long time to complete. Another is that the Soviets have not given much aid for industrial development but have concentrated on projects that have helped Moscow. The Soviet effort to develop the PDRY fishing industry is a case in point, since the USSR then imports frozen fish and fish meal from Aden in exchange for Soviet goods.[104] Similarly, when the PDRY took over the unprofitable British Petroleum oil refinery in 1977, the USSR sent 400,000 barrels (about 1 million metric tons) there—apparently enough to service its naval and merchant ships in the Red Sea and Indian Ocean area, but less than its 8 million metric ton capacity or even 3.4 million metric tons per year needed for the refinery to break even. The Soviet ambassador to Kuwait stated that the USSR would not increase the quantity of oil it refines at Aden because "no profit is gained from this operation."[105]

South Yemeni leaders, particularly 'Ali Nasir Muhammad, have expressed the hope that oil would be found, but although Soviet exploration efforts began in the early 1970s, they did not find much.[106] Apparently exasperated with the lack of Soviet success, Aden asked Western oil companies to explore, and one of them (the Italian AGIP; Azienda Generale Italiana Petroli) found oil off the coast in the Gulf of Aden and in the Hadramaut (the Soviets seem to have found some as well, but statements about it have been vague).[107] It is not certain how much oil exists in South Yemen, but the fact that a Western firm obtained positive results so much more quickly than the Soviets is striking. The PDRY has also been awarding more contracts to Western firms lately and not relying as much on the USSR and its allies.[108]

Soviet aid may appear stingy and of low quality to the South Yemenis, but the Soviets were probably not happy that such a desperately poor country expected so much from them. The Soviets appeared less than enthusiastic when the radical leaders who came to power in 1969 nationalized foreign-controlled enterprises.[109] This only served to weaken the South Yemeni economy, and the USSR was unwilling to subsidize Aden as it did Havana. Even after 'Ali (who attempted to follow a Chinese model of development) was ousted, the Soviets were critical of the way the pro-Soviet leaders in Aden ran their economy. For example, a July 1979 *Pravda* article noted that PDRY workers were leaving jobs in industry, construction, agriculture, and fishing because they could get higher wages in the services sector. In addition, a poor state pricing policy was blamed because the fish catch was only 20 percent of what it should have been.[110] The Soviets see rational PDRY economic policies as an important factor in spurring economic development in South Yemen.

Despite its Marxist-Leninist government and close ties to Moscow, South Yemen has received less Soviet economic aid than has non-Marxist North Yemen. The YAR has a much larger population than the PDRY, which might justify greater Soviet aid on the basis of need, but of course for Moscow economic need is less important that political factors in making decisions about what level of aid to provide different countries. In comparing Soviet aid to both Yemens, it must be noted that the USSR gave more assistance to Sanaa during the period 1956–75 and much less thereafter, whereas it gave little to Aden from 1967 to 1977 but much more from 1978 to the present. Nevertheless, the reason the PDRY as a close Soviet ally has not received even more from the USSR is possibly that Moscow's political influence is so strong in Aden that it has not had to compete with others for influence there, especially since the West has given little aid to the PDRY. To have influence in Sanaa, though, the Soviets have had to compete with others, and indeed Moscow's total economic aid to the YAR has been about the same as Washington's. Yet if Soviet economic assistance as well as Soviet support during times of conflict have not been as great as Aden may have hoped for, the Soviets must derive their influence in some other way, which will become evident as we examine the Soviet role in Aden's internal politics.

SOVIET ROLE IN PDRY INTERNAL POLITICS

Unlike North Yemen, the Soviets did not have friendly relations with the prerevolutionary regime in South Yemen because it was under British control. As in North Yemen, in their public commentary about the successive rulers of independent South Yemen, the Soviets praised each one while he was in power but quickly embraced whoever ousted him.

Although they later repeated his successors' denunciations of him as "right wing" the Soviets were highly supportive of Qahtan ash-Shaabi while he was in power. Ash-Shaabi declared that South Yemen would pursue "scientific socialism" almost immediately after taking office. It was also ash-Shaabi who went to Moscow in January–February 1969 and signed the first Soviet–South Yemeni economic and technical agreement that provided for Soviet military assistance as well. The Soviets had much praise for him, and when his opponents succeeded in passing several radical measures at the Fourth Congress of the NLF held at Zinjibar in March 1968, the Soviets described some of their proposals as "petty bourgeois." Yet once ash-Shaabi had been ousted, Moscow quickly embraced the new leftist leadership.[111] There does not appear to be any evidence—or even a serious claim—that the Soviets engineered ash-Shaabi's overthrow.

The three leading figures of the leftist regime were Isma'il (Secretary-General of the NLF), 'Ali (Chairman of the Presidential Council and Assistant Secretary-General of the NLF), and 'Ali Nasir Muhammad (Defense Minister and later Prime Minister after the dismissal of Haitham). Between 1969 and 1978, Moscow frequently and floridly praised the pro-Soviet Isma'il, who made several visits to the USSR and often met with the highest Soviet leaders.[112] The Soviets also often praised 'Ali Nasir, and he too made a number of visits to the USSR.[113] With regard to 'Ali, statements made by the Soviets during this period were positive, but they mentioned him much less frequently than the other two. The Soviets particularly praised 'Ali when he visited Moscow in November 1972 and signed an economic and technical agreement there. 'Ali himself cited the value of Soviet economic aid, though he seemed at least as appreciative of Chinese and Saudi aid.[114]

The Soviets did not criticize 'Ali directly before his overthrow, but there were occasions when they criticized unnamed leaders for policies they did not approve of. For example, in 1969 and 1970 Moscow scored "impatient" leftists "who wish to nationalize everything and put everything on a cooperative basis" and who thus might "ruin the economy utterly and undermine the faith of the peoples in socialist principles."[115] Later, in 1976, Moscow denounced "rightists" for normalizing relations with Saudi Arabia "in the belief that establishment of political and business contacts between Aden and Riyadh might lead to the 'de-ideologization' of the progressive South Yemeni regime, the erosion of the revolution."[116] 'Ali was the most prominent figure associated with the attempt to promote "revolutionary" economic development and later détente with Riyadh; the latter Soviet statement shows just how threatening to its interest Moscow considered this policy. Immediately after 'Ali was overthrown, Moscow vociferously repeated all the various charges that Isma'il and 'Ali Nasir had made against him. Among other things, he was accused of having secret contacts with the United States and Saudi Arabia and wanting to transform the PDRY into a reactionary regime, being guilty of "leftist extremism" (no contradiction between this charge and the one of working for reaction was even acknowledged), and trying to "cast aspersions on the correctness" of relations with the USSR.[117] In addition, 'Ali was persistently accused of opposing the creation of a vanguard Marxist-Leninist party. After the unification of the NLF with the smaller communist and Ba'th parties in 1975 and the signing of a party cooperation protocol between the new UPONF and the Communist Party of the Soviet Union, the often-predicted formation of a "vanguard party" did not take place. This was apparently because 'Ali opposed it on the basis that the formation of an official Marxist-Leninist party would alienate the PDRY's conservative neighbors and force Aden to rely all the more on Moscow. The Yemeni Socialist Party came into being less than four months after 'Ali was executed.[118]

A question in dispute is to what extent the Soviets, Cubans, and East Germans were involved in the events of June 24–26, 1978, when YAR President al-Ghashmi was assassinated by a South Yemeni bomb in Sanaa and Salim Rubayyi 'Ali was ousted and then executed in Aden. That the Soviets disapproved of 'Ali because of his desire to distance Aden from Moscow seems obvious, but whether Moscow also called for his overthrow is not. Soviet involvement in the plot to kill al-Ghashmi seems doubtful, since it has been Soviet policy to maintain good relations with North Yemen and this incident worsened them. Isma'il, on the other hand, openly desired to see the Sanaa government overthrown. Once al-Ghashmi was dead and fighting broke out in Aden between forces supporting 'Ali and Isma'il, it is not clear what role the Soviets played. A report published at the time said that the Soviets shipped 500 Cubans from Ethiopia to Aden and that Soviet and Cuban forces actively assisted Isma'il.[119] The Soviets immediately denied this,[120] and its truth has never been confirmed. There is not enough evidence available to make a final judgment on the Soviets' role in 'Ali's overthrow.

One thing, however, is certain: whether or not they were involved, the Soviets definitely benefited from the coup, since a strongly pro-Soviet leader then took control. As soon as these events occurred, the process that 'Ali had begun of restoring ties to the United States was abruptly ended, as was the policy of friendship with Riyadh as an alternative source of aid and influence. The rise of Isma'il also meant that the PDRY was unlikely to expel the Soviets as Egypt and Somalia had done and as 'Ali appeared to want to do.

The Soviets had tremendous praise for Isma'il both before and after June 1978.[121] Moscow had good reason to praise him, because he was so very pro-Soviet. It was Isma'il who said that Soviet-PDRY ties "should reflect a basically principled and not a pragmatic nature"[122] meaning that South Yemen should be close to the USSR even if it meant losing aid from the conservative Arab states. Ties with Moscow grew closer in October 1978 through the creation of the Yemeni Socialist Party, with close ties to the Communist Party of the Soviet Union, and in October 1979 through the signing of the treaty of friendship and cooperation.

It appeared at first that Isma'il would share power with 'Ali Nasir Muhammad, who became Chairman of the Presidential Council after 'Ali, but in December 1978 the Presidential Council was abolished and a Supreme People's Council created with Isma'il as President of its Presidium.[123] 'Ali Nasir appeared to be the junior partner, with only the post of Prime Minister, but the Soviets often praised him too, and he met with Soviet leaders on several occasions.[124]

Whether this praise for 'Ali Nasir meant that the Soviets connived with him in overthrowing Isma'il on April 21, 1980, is not clear. A disagreement between the two leaders had apparently taken place over whether Aden should support revolutionary groups in neighboring countries as Isma'il wanted or whether it should cooperate with the established governments of even conservative states in order to receive economic aid from them as 'Ali Nasir advocated.[125] Fred Halliday saw Isma'il's overthrow as evidence that Soviet influence in Aden was not very strong, since a pro-Soviet leader was ousted.[126] It seems, however, that the Soviets were happy to see Isma'il leave because his hostility toward his neighbors was frustrating Soviet efforts to improve relations with them. The Soviets praised Isma'il right up until the time of the coup. Once it occurred, though, Brezhnev quickly congratulated 'Ali Nasir. Isma'il had officially "resigned for health reasons" (though he showed no signs of ill health during his visit to Libya the week before he resigned), and a few months later he was reported to be in Moscow "for medical treatment."[127] Once again, whether or not the Soviets engineered the coup, they did indeed benefit from it, since 'Ali Nasir's policy of improving ties to Saudi Arabia and other conservative Arab states has led to a renewal of economic assistance from them while at the same time the PDRY has remained firmly allied to the USSR.

Since 'Ali Nasir Muhammad's assumption of the three top leadership posts, Soviet praise for him has been fulsome, as was by now to be expected. 'Ali Nasir, in turn, continually lauded Soviet-PDRY ties, expressing particular devotion to the 1979 treaty of friendship and cooperation.[128] Moscow has also issued favorable commentary on two PDRY defense ministers who are political rivals of 'Ali Nasir. 'Ali 'Antar, to whom 'Ali Nasir had lost the post of defense minister in 1977, was widely reported to be seeking to increase his power via the army. 'Ali Nasir relieved him of his post in April 1981 but appointed him First Deputy Chairman of the Council of Ministers (first deputy prime minister) and Minister of Local Government the following month.[129] The Soviets have had little to say about 'Ali 'Antar since then but have praised his successor as defense minister, Salih Muslih Qasim (appointed in August 1981).[130] Both 'Antar and Qasim wanted to provide large-scale assistance to the National Democratic Front of North Yemen in order to topple the Sanaa government, whereas 'Ali Nasir opposed this.[131] The failure of the NDF in the spring of 1982 led to a diminution in influence of both 'Antar and Qasim, though they continued to hold their positions.

In August and September 1982 there were reports that 'Ali Nasir left the Arab Summit Conference at Fez early because of a coup plot being launched by Isma'il and some of his former associates, but these appear to have been exaggerated.[132] In May 1984 'Ali Nasir apparently lost a round in the ongoing power struggle when five new full members were added to the Politburo, including Qasim ('Antar was already a member). 'Ali Nasir Muhammad in February 1985 gave up the post of prime minister while remaining head of the party and chief of state. The new Prime Minister, Haydar Abu Bakr al-'Attas, had until then been Minister of Installations (construction). Had the prime ministership gone to 'Ali 'Antar or Salih Muslih Qasim, this would have signaled a serious weakening of 'Ali Nasir Muhammad's position. Al-'Attas, however, is believed to be a technocrat and an ally of 'Ali Nasir Muhammad, and so the former's elevation is not necessarily a threat to the latter. It should not be forgotten, though, that 'Ali Nasir Muhammad was able to seize full power in 1980 from the post of prime minister alone.[133] That rivals to 'Ali Nasir exist and that Isma'il is still somewhere indicates that should 'Ali Nasir ever start pursuing policies the Soviets disapprove of, as 'Ali did, there are others Moscow could support in overthrowing him, and who would pursue pro-Soviet policies. In addition to divisions among the PDRY leadership, close ties between the two countries' parties and armies as well as the presence of Soviet,

Cuban, and East German advisers in South Yemen greatly aids the exercise of Soviet influence in Aden.

FOREIGN POLICY ISSUES

The broad outlines of the evolution of South Yemen's foreign policy have already been discussed. What will be examined here are the differences between Moscow and Aden over foreign policy in the past, their virtual identity of views at the present, and the PDRY's foreign policy position toward various issues and countries.

Despite their later condemnation of him, the Soviets had few foreign policy differences with ash-Shaabi. It was he who pushed for close relations with Moscow and who signed the first major economic and technical cooperation agreement. Ash-Shaabi also had good relations with China and maintained ties with the West (including the United States at a time when other Arab countries had broken relations with Washington).[134] After ash-Shaabi was overthrown by the leftists, certain differences between Moscow and Aden emerged. When Bahrain, Qatar, and the UAE became independent in 1971, the USSR attempted to establish friendship and exchange ambassadors with them. The PDRY, however, refused to recognize them and tried unsuccessfully to exclude them as well as Oman from membership in the United Nations and the Arab League. At that time Aden hoped to see Marxist revolution spread beyond Oman to those countries as well. The South Yemenis also opposed the November 1967 United Nations resolution on Palestine—which the USSR had sponsored. Aden criticized such Soviet friends (at the time) as Egypt and Algeria for having "petty bourgeois" governments.[135] The South Yemenis complained that Moscow did not think they could fight "imperialism" using their own methods.[136] In addition, Aden's close friendship with Peking must have been a source of concern for Moscow. In short, South Yemeni revolutionary exuberance, which was not succeeding in exporting revolution, threatened not only to hinder Moscow's attempts at establishing ties with the conservative Arab governments, but even to interfere with its relations with other pro-Soviet Arab states. Yet despite these differences and South Yemeni disappointment over the USSR's seeming lack of revolutionary enthusiasm, Moscow was able to maintain friendship and avoid a rupture with Aden.

From this leftist extreme, PDRY foreign policy suddenly shifted to the right in 1975–77 when 'Ali established diplomatic relations with Bahrain, Qatar, and the UAE in 1975 and with Saudi Arabia in 1976. 'Ali also worked for better relations with Sanaa. After the defeat of the PFLO in 1975, mediation efforts with Muscat were begun, but these were not successful. Finally, an effort was undertaken to improve relations with the West, including the United States. The Soviets were critical of 'Ali's friendship with Riyadh and feared that Saudi economic assistance would diminish Soviet influence in Aden.[137] 'Ali also participated in the Taiz conference of March 1977 at which the PDRY, YAR, Somalia, and Sudan called for a Red Sea "zone of peace." Although the Soviets have also called for a Red Sea zone of peace, they condemned this conference as an attempt to turn the Red Sea into an "Arab lake" directed against the Marxist, non-Moslem Ethiopian government that was facing Moslem insurgency in Eritrea.[138]

Unlike the previous leftist thrust to Aden's foreign policy, which all the top PDRY leaders supported, the shift to the right was supported by 'Ali but not by Isma'il. The continued pursuit of this policy, then, was dependent on 'Ali's remaining in a strong position domestically. 'Ali appeared to be dominant in the summer of 1977, when another Saudi aid agreement was announced in June and when 'Ali visited Riyadh in July and ratified the agreement in August.[139] However, the growing conflict in the Horn of Africa led to a sharp division among the PDRY leadership over whether to support Ethiopia or Somalia in the Ogaden and later whether to back the Eritrean secessionists (many of whom were Marxists) as Aden had before or to support the Marxist government in Addis Ababa. In August 1977, after the visit of Interior Minister Qasim to Ethiopia, Al-Ahram reported that South Yemeni military experts were aiding the Ethiopians both in Eritrea and in the Ogaden.[140] What apparently happened was that 'Ali was unable to stop the Isma'il faction from helping the Ethiopians and from allowing the Soviets to use Aden to ship military supplies to Ethiopia (these shipments became especially heavy in December 1977 following Somalia's abrogation of its treaty of friendship and cooperation with the USSR the previous month).[141] 'Ali tried desperately to reverse the pro-Ethiopian tilt and even met with Somali leader Siad Barre in late November, but to no avail.[142] As a result of this, Saudi Arabia in November 1977 canceled all economic aid, lobbied with the other Gulf states to oppose Aden, and remobilized the South Yemeni exile forces on the border that had been inactive since the Saudi-PDRY rapprochement of March 1976.[143] 'Ali was politically weakened already, and these actions taken by Riyadh weakened him further. The Eritreans charged in April

1978 that South Yemeni pilots were flying missions against them for Ethiopia and produced a man whom they claimed was a captured PDRY pilot.[144]

After 'Ali was executed in June 1978, Isma'il put renewed emphasis on revolution. He encouraged opposition in the YAR both before and after the 1979 war and appeared to have renewed support to the PFLO, which became more active in 1979 than at any time since its defeat in 1975. Despite his claims of wanting to improve relations with both the United States and Saudi Arabia, the budding rapprochement with Washington abruptly came to an end, and relations with Riyadh deteriorated further (relations with China also deteriorated sharply).[145] Following the June 1978 coup, Saudi Arabia put its armed forces on alert, and Radio Free South Yemen began anticommunist broadcasts.[146] Finally, Aden's relations with pro-Soviet Iraq also deteriorated through a series of incidents in which an anti-Ba'th, Marxist Iraqi professor was murdered in Aden; the PDRY authorities blamed the Baghdad government and stormed the Iraqi embassy to capture the culprits, then put them on trial. By March 1980, relations between them were so bad that Iraq began sponsoring South Yemeni opposition groups.[147] Although the Soviets did not publicly complain about it, Isma'il's dogmatic foreign policy radicalism was hurting Soviet efforts to improve relations with the conservative Arab states. South Yemen's dispute with Iraq was also unwelcome, since disagreements between its allies only put demands on Moscow to choose between them that the Soviets do not want to face.

When 'Ali Nasir Muhammad came to power in April 1980, he immediately moved to improve Aden's ties with North Yemen, Saudi Arabia, and the smaller Gulf states. His visits to Sanaa, Riyadh, Kuwait, and Abu Dhabi in June and July of 1980 led some to believe that he was willing to reduce PDRY reliance on Moscow in exchange for aid from the Gulf states.[148] Aden also approached several Western governments, including West Germany, France, and Italy, concerning the creation of joint commercial ventures and improving relations generally. Although South Yemen and the United Kingdom had never broken diplomatic relations since the former's independence, in 1983 the two exchanged ambassadors for the first time since 1975.[149] Saudi-PDRY relations also improved, but problems still remain—an armed clash reportedly occurred along their border in December 1983. In February 1985, following the return of Isma'il to Aden, KUNA mistakenly reported that he had become the head of the Yemeni Socialist Party (instead, he received a post in the YSP sec-

retariat). The clandestine radio Voice of the Free Sons of the Yemeni
South (probably based in Saudi Arabia) then suddenly appeared and
severely criticized the Aden government for serving the interests of the
USSR.[150] Despite the activities of the NDF, both Yemens have worked to
improve their relations. South Yemen has also normalized its relations
with Oman; in October 1982 the two arrived at a normalization agreement
with the help of Kuwait and the UAE.[151] In October 1983 Muscat and
Aden agreed to establish diplomatic relations, and 'Ali Nasir Muhammad
and Sultan Qabus have even begun to send each other congratulatory messages on their respective national days. There are still some issues they
disagree on (an agreement on delimiting their common border has yet to
be achieved, and each country has called upon the other to remove foreign
forces from its territory), but the fact that the PDRY has been willing to
have ties with Oman at all as well as greatly reducing its aid to the PFLO
is an unusual development given Aden's previous hostility toward Muscat.[152]

From the early 1970s when the Shah of Iran sent troops to Oman,
Aden had poor relations with Tehran and criticized the Shah's policies to a
much greater extent than the Soviets. The PDRY welcomed the revolutionary government that came to power in Iran and was pleased that it
pulled the remaining Iranian troops out of Oman. Diplomatic relations
were established in April 1980, and since the outbreak of the Iran-Iraq war
in September 1980, South Yemen has supported Tehran and not Baghdad.
This, of course, has not improved the PDRY's already poor relations with
Iraq. Even after the Iraqi army was pushed out of Iran and the Ayatollah's
forces have been fighting in Iraq, Aden continued to favor Iran, though
now its position is more neutral. South Yemen, Syria, and Libya are the
only Arab nations that have supported Iran; the others all support Iraq. In
pursuing this policy, Aden appears to have differed somewhat from Moscow, which has tilted toward Iraq and issued hostile statements about Iran
after the tide of war changed.[153]

This, however, appears to be the only foreign policy difference that
exists between Aden and Moscow. On virtually all other issues their
views are identical. On the Middle East, South Yemen has retreated from
its earlier radical position critical of the Soviets for not helping the Arabs
enough, and both governments have frequently emphasized their similar
views.[154] Along with Syria, Libya, Algeria, and the PLO, South Yemen is
a member of the Rejectionist Front opposed to the U.S.-arranged Camp
David agreement between Israel and Egypt and any other partial settle-

ment agreement such as the abortive May 1983 Israeli-Lebanese accords. Like the USSR, the PDRY has called for an overall settlement of the Middle East problem, including the creation of a Palestinian state. In the 1973 Middle East war, South Yemen joined North Yemen and Egypt in blockading the Straits of Bab al-Mandab to prevent ships going to or from Israel via the Red Sea. If there is any difference between the positions of Moscow and Aden on the Arab-Israeli conflict, it is that the USSR has recognized Israel's right to exist whereas the PDRY has not. This difference, however, is one that both governments have chosen to ignore, since their policies on this issue are so similar in all other respects.

South Yemen has become particularly close to Syria, which in 1980 signed its own treaty of friendship and cooperation with Moscow. Aden sent some 700 troops to participate in the Syrian-dominated Arab League force in Lebanon but withdrew them in December 1977 (though apparently not because of any dispute with Damascus; a PDRY infantry battalion of 500 soldiers was reported to be in Syria in mid-1982).[155]

Aden has maintained good relations with the radical Palestinians such as George Habash, but despite its friendship with Syria it has also been friendly with Yasir Arafat. During 1983, when Syrian-supported Palestinian rebels drove Arafat's forces out of Lebanon, both Moscow and Aden signaled their displeasure by issuing statements supporting the PLO and calling for Palestinian unity. The PDRY also agreed to accept some of Arafat's fighters, as did several other Arab countries.[156] Nevertheless, it was clear that neither Moscow nor Aden intended to make an issue of the PLO in their relations with Syria.

Although the PDRY is clearly a radical Arab state, its views on the Arab-Israeli conflict put it more in the mainstream of Arab foreign policy than Egypt. Indeed, it was Aden's quick condemnation of the Camp David accords that helped it restore its relations with the Arab League soon after its expulsion for involvement in the death of YAR President al-Ghashmi in June 1978. However, on other issues, the PDRY is definitely outside the Arab mainstream. While most other Arab nations (except Libya and to some extent Syria) support the efforts of the Eritrean Moslems to gain their independence, South Yemen strongly supports the Ethiopian government and has close politico-military relations with it. On Eritrea, the PDRY has stated that it favors a peaceful settlement to the conflict but has emphasized that it has no differences with Addis Ababa on this issue.[157] Similarly regarding Afghanistan, Aden immediately recognized the Marxist government that came to power there in 1978.[158] When the Soviets invaded at the end of December 1979, Syria and South Yemen were the only two Arab countries that refused to attend the Islamic summit conference that condemned Moscow. Indeed, Aden has vocally defended Soviet policy in Afghanistan since then.[159] Finally, Aden has often repeated Soviet claims that Soviet Moslems are free to worship as they please and that they do not suffer from any form of discrimination.[160]

Although 'Ali Nasir Muhammad has improved relations with North Yemen, Saudi Arabia, and Oman, has sought a greater degree of Western and other nonsocialist involvement in the PDRY economy, and has generally presented a more moderate image to the world than Isma'il, he has shown no real sign of differing with the Soviets on foreign policy issues or of moving away from his close politico-military ties with the USSR as some had hoped he would. Indeed, Aden's new moderation is definitely in Soviet interests, since it has led to the renewal of economic aid from the GCC states and so alleviated Moscow's burden of being the PDRY's sole benefactor. Further, a moderate PDRY presents a less threatening image to the GCC states and might help Moscow eventually establish diplomatic ties with them. Whether the PDRY will revive its goals of spreading Marxist revolution to its neighbors cannot be foretold, but it is clear that different PDRY leaders (sometimes the same one) have followed different foreign policy paths, and this could happen again. For the present, though, it is likely that 'Ali Nasir will continue his moderate policy toward the PDRY's neighbors while remaining firmly tied to the USSR.

CONCLUSION

To what extent does the Soviet Union control the foreign and domestic policies of the PDRY? That Isma'il and 'Ali Nasir have pursued different policies ever since the pro-Soviet coup of 1978 shows that Soviet control of Aden is not complete. But because of the leadership struggles that are a chronic feature of South Yemeni politics, it is doubtful that any leader could remain in power without the support of the Soviets. Moscow could easily ally with his rivals to oust any leader it did not like.

Could the Soviets ever be expelled from South Yemen as they were from Egypt and Somalia? Despite the presence of Soviet, Cuban, and East German advisers, the Soviets could not move as easily to stop the PDRY from leaving the Soviet bloc as they can in Eastern Europe. It is thus conceivable that the South Yemenis could successfully implement a decision to expel the Russians and abrogate their treaty of friendship and cooperation. However, for this to occur, one crucial condition must first be met: the entire South Yemeni leadership must be united behind the decision to get rid of them. Although not impossible, it is highly unlikely that this condition will be met owing to the state of rivalry that exists among the PDRY leaders. This rivalry makes unity among them difficult, and the memory of what happened to 'Ali serves to discourage any leader from attempting to detach Aden from Moscow without the support of the rest of the PDRY leadership. As a result, it is doubtful that the South Yemenis could ever expel the Soviets.

Because Soviet influence has become so strong in South Yemen since the June 1978 coup, no PDRY leader would diverge too far from the Soviets in foreign policy if he wished to remain in power. Still, that Isma'il remained in power from June 1978 until April 1980 and that his foreign policy had a revolutionary bent whereas 'Ali Nasir, who has been in power since then, has pursued a more moderate line indicates that Moscow is willing to tolerate a certain amount of variation in Aden's foreign policy. Indeed, the Soviets may well be ambivalent about what role they want the PDRY to play.

The Soviets would, of course, welcome a successful attempt by Aden to spread Marxist revolution to other countries on the Peninsula. At present, however, the obstacles to this are much greater than the opportunities: the GCC states with their prosperous economies and strong governments do not seem likely candidates for Marxist revolution, and even the poor and weak North Yemeni government was able to put down a Marxist insurrection in 1982. Thus, even if his rivals ousted 'Ali Nasir Muhammad and began promoting revolution on the Peninsula, the Soviets could be expected not to support this policy wholeheartedly and to look for a more moderate leadership if the revolutionary policy failed. Moscow appears to recognize that South Yemen has extremely limited value in expanding Soviet influence in the area. Indeed, it can become a hindrance to Moscow if Aden firmly supports revolutionaries even when they cannot succeed and this policy only induces the PDRY's neighbors to rely more heavily on the West. Aden's present value to Moscow, then, is that it provides significant military facilities in a region where the Soviets want to maintain a strong presence and need a safe base from which they can help allies in future conflicts, as they did in Ethiopia. Although the Soviets are closely allied to the Marxist governments of Ethiopia, Mozambique, and Angola, only South Yemen does not face armed internal insurgents who have not yet been defeated, even after many years. The Soviets at present do not have to worry about a powerful opposition movement attacking their facilities or sabotaging their efforts to give military help to Marxist allies in a future conflict in the region. But if the prospects for revolution on the Peninsula ever do improve, South Yemen could well be instrumental in furthering the spread of Marxism-Leninism there.

Oman

3

The two Yemens are strategically important not only because they neighbor Saudi Arabia, but also because they border on the Straits of Bab al-Mandab, which guard the southern entrance of the Red Sea. Yet even if the Red Sea were blocked to sea traffic between the Mediterranean and the Indian Ocean, as it was from 1967 to 1975 when the Suez Canal was closed, shipping can still travel the long way around Africa. The same cannot be said about the Straits of Hormuz, through which all sea traffic to and from the Persian Gulf must pass. Western Europe, Japan, and to a lesser extent, the United States are dependent on the Gulf for much of their oil, and if the Straits of Hormuz were ever blocked the West would certainly face an oil shortage and a perhaps large increase in petroleum prices. The importance of the Straits of Hormuz could be reduced if a vastly greater pipeline network were built across Arabia to either the Indian Ocean, the Red Sea, or possibly the Mediterranean, but this network would take a long time to construct and would be vulnerable to attack. Alternative oil sources could also be discovered and developed, but the West cannot afford to rely upon this prospect to meet its immediate oil needs. If the Straits were blocked at present, the crisis this would cause could not be alleviated in the short run unless they were reopened, possibly by force.

The two nations that lie athwart the Straits of Hormuz are Iran and Oman. While the Shah of Iran was in power, the West's access to the Gulf was not in doubt. However, when the Islamic revolutionary government came to power, which has been generally hostile to the West and since 1983 has been threatening to blockade the Straits, the West has been dependent on Oman's remaining friendly to keep the Straits open.

What a pro-Soviet government in Muscat would do about the Straits is not clear. Neither the USSR nor Oman would necessarily want to halt the oil traffic in peacetime, but during a period of high tension or conflict between America and Russia the Soviets might want to close the Straits in order to harm the West militarily and economically. Nor would the United States be able to open them so easily if Soviet military forces were stationed in Oman. Further, a Marxist might be willing to see the Straits closed simply because, unlike the output of Iran and the other oil-exporting Gulf states, the comparatively modest amount of oil Oman produces does not have to be shipped through them.

Such a scenario, of course, is highly speculative. The possibility, however, demonstrates the importance of this one country's being friendly to the West, for if Oman were hostile the West could not depend on Khomeini's Iran as an ally to keep the Straits open. In examining the possibility that this scenario might occur, two questions that must be looked at are: (1) What are the prospects that the present government in Muscat will become allied to Moscow? and (2) What are the prospects that the present pro-Western government there will be overthrown by Soviet- and South Yemeni–backed revolutionaries?

As far as the first question is concerned, it may be quickly answered that there is very little likelihood that the Kremlin and the Sultan will become close allies. Sultan Qabus has frequently stated that he is unwilling even to establish diplomatic relations with the USSR. Similarly, in contrast to their periodic friendly overtures toward Saudi Arabia, the Soviets have never expressed friendliness toward the Sultan.

The possibility of Marxist insurgency in Oman is a more serious concern, since there was a rebellion in Oman's Dhofar province to the south from 1965 to 1975. The leadership of this rebellion became dominated by Marxist-Leninists in 1968 and received varying degrees of support from South Yemen, China and the USSR. The insurgents were ultimately defeated by the Sultan's forces, but this was done only with the help of British, Iranian, and Jordanian forces. The Shah of Iran maintained troops in Oman even after the war, but these were withdrawn in February 1979 at the time of his overthrow. The Popular Front for the Liberation of Oman is still in existence, and should insurgency break out again under its leadership or that of some other group, there is doubt whether the Sultan's forces alone could defeat the rebels or obtain effective foreign military assistance to do so. At present, the possibility of renewed insurgency appears remote owing to the strength of the Sultan's government, the relative economic prosperity Oman has enjoyed under his rule, and the extreme weakness of the former rebels.

HISTORICAL BACKGROUND

The Omani government officially puts the country's population at 1.5 million, but in reality the figure is somewhere in the range of 800,000 to 1 million. Though Moslem, the majority of the population are neither Sunni nor Shia but are adherents of a different rite called Ibadhism. An Ibadhi state was founded in Oman in the eighth century A.D., and although Oman was at times occupied by the empires of Arab Sunnis from the north or Persian Shias from across the Gulf, Ibadhism helped form the rallying point for the more than two hundred Omani tribes to reassert the country's independence. In addition to the Ibadhis, about one-quarter of the population are Sunnis. In Dhofar province, which is separated from the Omani heartland to the north by five hundred miles of desert, the population is ethnically distinct from the Omanis, speaks its own dialect known as Jibali, and is predominantly Sunni. There are also Shia communities in Oman, which number only about 2 percent of the total population, and non-Arab communities including Hindus, Baluchis, and Pakistanis. Some of these have been in Oman for generations; others are short-term migrant workers.[1]

In Omani history, the Ibadhi state was headed by an Imam whose main functions were religious but who gradually acquired secular authority as well. A unique feature of the Imamate was that the tribal and religious leaders selected a candidate for Imam who was then "elected" or acclaimed by the people. The Imamate was not always strong domestically, and it was replaced by a dynasty of kings for some 250 years until the fifteenth century. Even after their restoration, the Imams remained weak and were not able to prevent the Portuguese from capturing the port of Muscat in 1507. In the next century, the head of the Yaaribah tribe became Imam; he greatly strengthened the Imamate by driving the Portuguese completely out of Oman by 1650. Under the leadership of the Yaaribah, Oman went on to build a large navy and commercial fleet and to seize other Portuguese colonies in East Africa as well as to conquer Gwadar on what is now the coast of Pakistan. Contrary to the accepted norms of Ibadhism, however, the Yaaribah introduced the principle of hereditary rule. Increasing internal opposition weakened the Imamate, and in 1737 the last Yaaribah Imam asked the Persians to help him stay in power.[2]

The tribes who revolted against the Yaaribah also fought among themselves. During this struggle, the tribes coalesced into two broad confederations—the Hinawi and the Ghafiri—that still exist. Broadly, the

Hinawi tended to be ethnically South Arabian or Yemeni as well as completely Ibadhi, while the Ghafiri tended to be North Arabian and to include Sunni tribes as well as Ibadhi. There were many exceptions, however, and much switching back and forth between the two confederations occurred over the years. A sort of balance of power emerged between the two confederations, and it evolved that no one could become Imam without support from both and that an Imam would have great difficulty in carrying out military operations unless both confederations supported him.[3]

In 1744 Ahmad bin Sa'id led forces that defeated the Persians and drove them out of Oman. In 1749 he was elected Imam and thus became the founder of the Al Bu Sa'id dynasty, which continues to rule Oman to this day. Ahmad ruled from the interior until his death in 1783, when his son Sa'id became Imam. Sa'id, however, was a weak ruler, and the following year he yielded temporal authority to his son Hamad in Muscat while he retained the title of Imam and remained in the interior. Thus it came about that there was an imam in interior Oman and a "saiyid" (lord) and later sultan at Muscat.[4]

During the reign of Saiyid Sa'id bin Sultan from 1806 to 1856, coastal Oman was stronger and more prosperous than the interior. Under him, the Omani empire flourished in East Africa and Zanzibar, and the economy grew through commerce largely based on the export of East African slaves to Arabia. Sa'id became more interested in his overseas empire than in Oman itself and eventually moved his court permanently to Zanzibar. When he died in 1856 his eldest son became ruler in Muscat, but another son seized power in Zanzibar. This division of the Omani empire was made permanent through British arbitration in 1861. This, combined with the ending of the slave trade by the British, greatly weakened Muscat's authority. An Ibadhi revival movement toppled the Sultan in 1868, and a new Imam of all Oman was then elected who in 1869 drove Saudi forces out of Buraimi (over which the two countries would again clash in 1952–55). In 1871, however, the new Imam was killed. From then until 1913 the Hinawi and Ghafiri continued to oppose the Muscati sultans, but they also were in conflict with each other. The Al Bu Sa'id dynasty became progressively weaker through the remainder of the century, and the Omani economy suffered a prolonged depression owing to the loss of maritime commerce to European steamships. The interior tribes made several raids on Muscat, but their own internal divisions did not allow them to hold it for long. The greatly weakened sultans were able to remain in power only with the aid of the British.[5]

As with Aden, British involvement in Oman began as a response to Napoleon's invasion of Egypt and the fear that he would threaten the British position in India. The first Anglo-Omani agreements were signed in 1798 and 1800 and provided for British representation in Muscat. Further Anglo-Omani accords in 1822, 1839, August 1845, October 1845, and 1873 progressively limited and then finally abolished the slave trade and slavery in Oman. The Canning Award of 1861, which divided Zanzibar and Oman, also provided for the former to pay the latter a subsidy. Soon thereafter the Zanzibaris defaulted, but the British agreed to pay the subsidy, which they did up until 1970. Oman never became a formal British protectorate as did the Trucial States (later UAE), Qatar, Bahrain, and Kuwait, but this was due to an 1862 Anglo-French agreement that required French consent to any dilution of Omani independence by the British. Nevertheless, by the end of the 1890s, the Muscati sultans were unable to act independently from the British. In 1891 Sultan Faysal bin Turki (ruled 1888–1913) signed an agreement not to alienate any portion of his territory to any foreign power except Britain. After Muscat was overrun by tribes from the interior in 1895, the British agreed to defend the capital from attack. Although he needed the British to protect him from his subjects, Faysal attempted to counter Britain's growing influence over him by allowing the French a coaling station at Bandar Jissa. However, the British put a stop to this plan in 1899 when the Sultan was invited on board a British warship in Muscat and then forced to renounce the agreement with France under threat that the British would immediately bombard his capital. The next two Sultans, Taymur bin Faysal (1913–31) and Sa'id bin Taymur (1932–70), were forced to sign letters agreeing to seek British advice in important matters in order to obtain British recognition.[6] Though Oman was formally independent, the Sultan had become little more than a British vassal.

The interior tribes greatly resented the influence of the British, and when in 1912 the British and the Sultan attempted to reduce the flow of arms into the interior by setting up a central warehouse for all imported arms, the tribes were so incensed by this threat to their traditional livelihood that in 1913 the Hinawi and Ghafiri were able to unite. They elected a strong Imam, Salim al-Kharusi, who led several attacks on Muscat that had to be fended off by British Indian troops. A stalemate ensued, and after Imam Salim was assassinated in July 1920 the tribes were willing to settle their differences with the Sultan. In September 1920 a treaty was signed at the coastal town of Sib whereby the Sultan agreed to respect the autonomy of the interior and the tribes agreed not to hinder the Sultan's authority on the coast. Throughout the reign of Imam Muhammad bin 'Abdallah al-Khalili (1920–54), this agreement was observed.[7]

The search for oil would bring an end to interior Oman's isolation. In August 1952 Saudi forces occupied part of the Buraimi oasis. Sultan Sa'id bin Taymur raised a tribal force to drive them out, but he was stopped by the British, who did not want a conflict to erupt between Muscat and Riyadh in which the United States might support the latter (the Arabian-American Oil Company—ARAMCO—reportedly encouraged the Saudis to occupy Buraimi in order to obtain the oil believed to be there); this did little to increase the respect of the Omani tribes for the Sultan. Imam Muhammad, who had worked to keep interior Oman independent from Riyadh as well as Muscat, died in May 1954. The new Imam, Ghalib bin 'Ali, and his tribal sponsors then actively sought aid from the Saudis to fend off the Sultan, who had sent survey parties from Petroleum Development Oman into the interior. In October 1955 forces of the Sultan as well as the ruler of Abu Dhabi expelled the Saudis from Buraimi; in December the Sultan's forces occupied all of interior Oman, meeting little resistance.[8]

Imamate forces who had fled to Saudi Arabia returned to Oman in June 1957 and launched a revolt. With the help of several tribes, they pushed the Sultan's forces out of the main towns of the interior. The Sultan had to call for British military assistance, and Anglo-Omani forces were able to retake most of the interior by August 1957. The rebels retreated to Jebal Akhdar (Green Mountain), where they held out until another Anglo-Omani assault completely routed them in January 1959. The Imam and other rebel leaders, however, escaped to Saudi Arabia and later moved to Iraq. They mounted only minor terrorist activity until 1961, but Imamate forces did manage to have the "question of Oman" put before the United Nations General Assembly every year until 1971, when the Sultanate finally became a member.[9]

The 1957–59 rebellion was a traditional tribal revolt. The rebellion that began in Dhofar to the south in 1965 also began this way but was transformed into a Marxist insurrection.

THE DHOFAR REBELLION

The Dhofar region abuts the PDRY and has a population of about 60,000. It is unusual for Arabia in that it experiences an annual monsoon and during the rainy season is lush and green. Between the coastal plain and the desert behind it is a mountainous area ideally suited for guerrilla warfare. In modern times, Dhofar first came under Muscat's rule in 1829, but the Sultan's forces soon withdrew. In 1879 the Sultan's forces again took Dhofar, and Oman's rule has been more or less continuous there ever since.[10]

Sultan Sa'id bin Taymur frequently visited Dhofar between 1945 and 1955, and in 1958 he made Salalah (Dhofar's capital) his permanent home, never visiting Muscat again. Sa'id's rule was extremely harsh. To achieve a degree of autonomy from the British, he kept his government's expenditures low, rapidly eliminated all of Oman's previous debts, and never again borrowed money from the British or anyone else. As a consequence, he did not spend much for development. Oman remained in an extremely poor state until the end of his rule in 1970, even though it started exporting oil in 1967. In 1965 (the year the rebellion broke out) there were only five privately owned cars, three primary schools, and one twelve-bed hospital in all of Oman. Taxation was heavy and emigration forbidden, though some managed to leave illegally. Sa'id believed that contact with the wider world and development efforts would lead to rising expectations that could not be met, and then to revolution; through keeping Oman poor and ignorant, he thought this could be avoided. Conditions in Dhofar, where the Sultan lived, were particularly harsh; the population was subjected to a series of petty restrictions regarding personal appearance, dress, transportation, employment, and entertainment.[11] It was hardly surprising that a rebellion broke out.

Minor skirmishes between the Sultan's forces and some Dhofari tribal forces supported by Saudi Arabia took place in 1963 and 1964. These tribal elements joined with members of the Dhofar branch of the Arab Nationalist Movement, the Dhofar Charitable Association (organized by the ANM to raise money for revolution under the guise of charity), and the Dhofar Soldiers' Organization (a loose-knit group of Dhofari soldiers and policemen serving in Oman, Saudi Arabia, and elsewhere in the Gulf) in forming the Dhofar Liberation Front (DLF). Despite the arrest of some forty to sixty DLF members in April and May 1965, the DLF was able to hold its first congress June 1–9, 1965, at Wadi al-Kalim in central Dhofar. The congress elected an eighteen-member executive committee and issued a manifesto calling for the overthrow of the Sultan. A DLF ambush of a government patrol on June 9, 1965, became the event from which the Marxists would date the formal beginning of the revolution. At this time, however, tribal and nationalist forces were predominant in the DLF, and not the Marxists.[12]

In the next couple of years the DLF launched sporadic raids in Dhofar, including an attempted assassination of the Sultan in April 1966 that nearly succeeded. By 1967 it was suffering from the loss of Saudi and Egyptian aid as well as from a government offensive, but it received a tremendous boost at the end of the year when the radical National Liberation Front came to power in Aden. South Yemen would provide a sanctuary and supply base for the Dhofari rebels and would fundamentally influence the character of the rebellion. At the second congress of the DLF held at Hamrin in central Dhofar September 1–20, 1968, the Marxist-Leninists seized control of the movement. The congress ousted all but three of the previous eighteen-man executive committee, elected a new twenty-five-man committee, adopted "scientific socialism" and declared its aim not only to bring Marxist revolution to all Oman but also to the Trucial States, Qatar, and Bahrain (which were all still British protectorates). The congress also changed the name of the movement to the Popular Front for the Liberation of the Occupied Arab Gulf (PFLOAG). At this point some of the non-Marxist leaders, including Yusuf al-'Alawi, who later became Omani Minister of State for Foreign Affairs, broke away from the movement and continued to call themselves the DLF.[13]

From September 1968 until July 1970, PFLOAG launched successful military offensives that pushed the Sultan's Armed Forces (SAF) and its British advisers out of most of Dhofar. The guerrillas came to control the entire province except the area immediately surrounding Salalah and its airfield.[14] A second group called the National Democratic Front for the Liberation of Oman and the Arab Gulf (NDFLOAG, which, like PFLOAG, was founded by ANM members) attempted to launch a revolt in the interior of northern Oman where the Imamate rebellion had taken place, but this was quickly put down by the SAF.[15]

The fact that rebellion had also broken out in the north was quite alarming to the British, who feared that the Sultan's harsh policies would soon lead to a general revolt they could not control. On July 23, 1970, Sultan Sa'id was overthrown in a coup led by his son Qabus (whom the father had kept under virtual house arrest in Salalah after his return from Sandhurst and a term in the British army). The British never formally admitted directing the coup, but statements later made by British officials who were there at the time indicated that they had; indeed, it is highly doubtful that Qabus could have pulled off the coup without their help.[16]

The new Sultan quickly criticized the oppressive rule of his father, announced economic and social reforms, and proclaimed an amnesty for rebels who surrendered—which two hundred did in only a month.[17]

These new policies served to build public support for the new Sultan, as did a serious error on the part of PFLOAG shortly after the coup. Seeing that the populace reacted favorably to the new Sultan's reforms, a PFLOAG group in eastern Dhofar advocated that the rebels negotiate an agreement with him. The PFLOAG leadership in South Yemen not only refused to implement such a policy but insisted that its advocates be put on trial, which probably would have meant death for them. When the PFLOAG leadership sent units to eastern Dhofar to quell this revolt within its ranks, many in the east surrendered to the Sultan's forces. This had the effect of decreasing the number of rebels, opening up the eastern Dhofar to the SAF, and allowing the British and the Omanis to form units (called firqats) of Dhofar irregulars drawn largely from ex-rebels to fight against PFLOAG.[18]

According to John Akehurst, commander of the Dhofar Brigade during the last part of the campaign, PFLOAG's strength at its height in 1970–71 was 2,000 full-time guerrillas, 4,000 part-time militiamen, and an uncertain number of sympathizers among the Dhofari population. Defections from PFLOAG to the Sultan took place, but these numbers were not substantially reduced until 1974.[19] PFLOAG held its third congress at Rakyut in Western Dhofar on June 9, 1971, during which it formalized its administrative and economic policies. On December 22, 1971, a unification congress was held at Ihlish (also in Dhofar) at which PFLOAG and NDFLOAG joined forces. The new organization was named the Popular Front for the Liberation of Oman and the Arab Gulf (still PFLOAG—the term "occupied" was dropped to reflect the fact that Bahrain, Qatar, and the UAE had become independent). After an abortive attack by PFLOAG on the town of Mirbat in July 1972, government forces seized the offensive for the duration of the war.[20]

The Sultan's forces expanded from about 3,000 at the time of the coup to over 14,000 by 1974 (of which 6,000 were Baluchis). Some 300 British officers and men were also in Oman either as part of the Special Air Services (which trained the firqats) and other U.K. units or else on secondment or contract with the Sultan's forces. Most of the officers in the SAF, including all the top commanders, were British. In late 1973 the Shah of Iran sent a battle group of 1,200 soldiers to Dhofar; this was withdrawn in October 1974 but replaced two months later with an Iranian force that rose to 4,000–4,500 before the end of the war. In addition, a Jordanian army engineering squadron served temporarily in Dhofar, and the firqat force grew to about 1,000 by 1974.[21] Foreign military assistance to the Sultan's war effort was obviously significant.

After its defeat at Mirbat in July 1972 and the increase in SAF and allied forces, PFLOAG operations were severely hampered. At a general congress convened July 1, 1974, PFLOAG granted "organizational independence" to its non-Omani components (of which the only significant one was the Bahrain National Liberation Front), altered its goal from spreading revolution throughout the entire Gulf to influencing Oman alone, and changed its name to the Popular Front for the Liberation of Oman (PFLO).[22] These changes reflected not only the Front's diminished expectations, but also South Yemen's hope to obtain economic assistance from the oil-rich Gulf states and to reduce obstacles to improved relations with them.

In late 1974 government forces completed a defensive barrier known as the Hornbeam Line west of Salalah. It consisted of some thirty-five miles of barbed wire and mines, stretching from the coast into the interior, and was constantly patrolled by Omani forces. This and another such line called the Damavand Line completed farther to the west in 1975 were instrumental in cutting off arms and supplies sent from South Yemen to PFLO guerrillas in interior Dhofar. At the end of January 1975 the PFLO announced that the condition of its forces was "critical" and appealed for assistance. In a final offensive lasting from October to early December 1975, government forces were able to take control over all of Dhofar, pushing most PFLO forces that did not surrender, along with some 250 PDRY soldiers, across the border into South Yemen. On December 11, 1975, the Sultan declared victory over the insurgents. Sporadic incidents, mainly shelling from South Yemen, continued for a few months, but this largely ended March 11, 1976, when a Saudi-mediated cease-fire between Muscat and Aden came into effect. It was estimated that some 120 guerrillas were still in Dhofar in December 1975, but they were unable to obtain supplies, and their numbers rapidly dwindled to about 50 through surrenders over the next few months.[23] Akehurst said later that much of the Sultan's victory was due to rapid and continuous civil aid efforts made wherever government forces took control of a village, which gave the local population an incentive for seeing that the guerrillas did not return.[24] This helped end the cooperation between the population and the guerrillas that had made the latter so strong before.

These events did not go unnoticed in the Soviet Union. Indeed, even during the 1957–59 Imamate revolt, the Soviets as well as the Chinese expressed support for the rebels both while the fighting was going on and long afterward.[25] In October 1963 *Izvestiia* published a statement by the Imam of Oman expressing his confidence that the USSR would give aid to the Omani people if asked.[26] There appears to be no evidence, however, that the Soviets gave the Imamate cause anything beyond verbal support in the media and at the United Nations. In 1964 articles appeared criticizing the Imam for keeping interior Oman so isolated.[27] Despite their antipathy for the Muscat government and its British supporters, Moscow and the Imam (who relied mainly on conservative Saudi Arabia) had little in common.

The Soviet press paid little attention to the activities of the Dhofar Liberation Front in 1965–68. After the DLF transformed itself into the overtly Marxist-Leninist PFLOAG, the Soviets occasionally expressed sympathy for it but appeared reluctant to give greater support. This reluctance appears to have stemmed from two factors: (1)PFLOAG's goal of spreading revolution beyond Oman to the Arab states of the Gulf threatened to harm Moscow's efforts to improve its ties with the conservative states of the region, especially Iran; and (2) PFLOAG received support and training from China and generally appeared to be strongly pro-Peking. In September 1969 a PFLOAG statement noted that its arms came from China but complained about the Soviet Union, "We do not say that the Soviet Union has totally discarded us. We are still hopefully trying in this direction."[28]

Despite this appeal and PFLOAG's outward neutrality in the Sino-Soviet dispute, the Front patterned itself on the Chinese revolutionary model. The People's Republic of China (PRC) first granted a small amount of military aid to the DLF when the first DLF delegation visited Peking in June 1967. Chinese aid grew stronger through 1970. In 1971, however, the PRC appeared to become less interested in the Front. Shortly after Peking established diplomatic relations with Kuwait and Iran in 1972, Chinese aid to PFLOAG ceased altogether. According to Hashim Behbehani, who interviewed several PFLO officials after the war, in 1972 Peking called on PFLOAG to confine its aims to Oman. When PFLOAG did not comply, Chinese aid stopped. When PFLOAG finally did this in 1974 and changed its name to PFLO, Peking was no longer interested in helping it.[29] Thus, by 1972, PFLOAG switched from relying mainly on the Chinese for aid to relying mainly on the Soviets.

Even before Chinese aid to PFLOAG ceased, the Soviets began to indicate a degree of approval (if not support) for the group. In 1969, *New Times* praised the Front's espousal of "scientific socialism" and later in the year *Pravda* correspondent A. Vasil'ev actually visited guerrilla-held Dhofar and wrote several articles about it.[30] PFLOAG delegations also visited Moscow in both 1969 and 1970 at the invitation of the Soviet Afro-Asian Solidarity Committee, but no meetings with Soviet government or Party officials were announced.[31] In September 1971, after Chinese interest in PFLOAG had noticeably declined, another Front delegation visited the USSR and this time was received by Konstantin Katushev, a secretary of the CPSU (Communist Party of the Soviet Union) Central Committee. PFLOAG later told Aden News Agency that the Soviets offered to "double" their aid to the Front at this time.[32]

After these meetings, Soviet press coverage of the Dhofar rebellion greatly increased, especially during the years 1973 through 1975. On several occasions the Soviet media reported PFLOAG claims that the Front controlled "90 percent" or "almost all" of Dhofar's territory and population.[33] The Soviets repeatedly condemned Britain, Jordan, Saudi Arabia, and the United States for giving military assistance to the Sultan, but unlike PFLOAG they seldom criticized the Shah of Iran, with whom Moscow hoped to maintain good relations.[34] Moscow often repeated PFLOAG reports on the high level of casualties being inflicted on the "imperialists."[35] Once Radio Moscow angrily criticized the British press for printing stories on PFLOAG members defecting to the Sultan.[36]

Through the end of 1973 the Soviets seemed to believe that PFLOAG would be successful in its revolutionary efforts, at least in Dhofar and possibly in all of Oman as well. To them, the Sultanate of Oman was merely a larger version of the British-protected sultans in South Yemen that the National Liberation Front had overthrown. The first indication in the Soviet press that Moscow realized the contest was in doubt came in January 1974 during an Omani government offensive. In the Soviet view, the Sultanate would surely fall without British and other external support, and this alone was frustrating PFLOAG.[37] The "blatant" Iranian intervention also began to be criticized.[38] The change of name from PFLOAG to PFLO was noted with little comment.[39] By 1975, instead of predicting the success of the rebels in defeating the Sultan as they had done before, the Soviets were saying that the Sultan and his backers had failed to defeat the rebels up to then and would not succeed in the future.[40] In November 1975, when the PFLO was close to being defeated *Krasnaia Zvezda* admitted that "the question of the rebels is . . . complicated" but still predicted that the "forces of reaction" were "doomed to failure."[41]

Despite the PFLO's appeals for assistance and Soviet awareness of the Front's increasing military problems, the USSR did not offer much help politically. The Soviets would report statements by Front leaders expressing gratitude for Moscow's help, although what this entailed, especially in military terms, was not specified.[42] When the Soviet media described the aid the USSR was giving to the rebels, they would use phrases such as "Soviet citizens . . . are by the side of the patriots" or "the Oman people's just struggle meets with the understanding and support of the peoples of the socialist community."[43] While the "people" may have sided with it, the fact that neither their government nor the Party in Moscow would go on record as doing so indicated that the USSR did not intend to make a great effort to save the Front. The PFLO sent delegations to the USSR again in November 1972, September 1973, and March 1975, but these visits were all at the invitation of the Soviet Afro-Asian Solidarity Committee and no further meetings with government or Party officials were announced.[44] Despite their expressions of gratitude to the USSR, the Dhofari rebels must have been sorely disappointed.

Regarding actual Soviet military assistance to the rebels, Moscow supplied a modest quantity of weapons via South Yemen, including 122-mm Katyusha rockets, RPG-7 recoilless rifles, antitank rockets, antipersonnel mines, mortars, machine guns, rifles, and ammunition.[45] In August 1975 the PFLO began using Soviet SA-7 surface-to-air missiles (SAMs) including the more advanced SA-7B version.[46] The PFLO did not bring large, difficult-to-maneuver Soviet artillery pieces into Dhofar, but these were used to fire across the border into Oman from inside the PDRY.[47] In 1973 Cuban military advisers arrived in South Yemen, and these were believed to have helped train Omani rebels at several camps in the PDRY.[48] Omani guerrillas also went to China, North Korea, and the USSR at various stages of the conflict. By 1975, however, the situation of the PFLO was so desperate that it could not spare enough guerrillas to take up all the training slots that the Soviet military offered.[49] Soviet military advisers were never seen in Dhofar. With the exception of one Chinese killed in early 1968, the only non-Omanis that the Sultan's forces met in Dhofar were PDRY soldiers.[50]

While the Soviets did indeed give some military aid to the Omani guerrillas, what they gave was too little and came too late to even keep the insurrection alive, much less help it succeed. It is understandable that the

115

Soviets would not want to do too much for the Dhofaris as long as the latter appeared to be under strong Chinese influence. There was a period, however, after the decline of Chinese support in 1971 and before the buildup of the Sultan's forces as well as intervention of a large Iranian force in 1973, when greater Soviet aid to the guerrillas might have driven government forces out of Salalah or at least made the air base there unserviceable. This could have vastly complicated the Sultan's efforts to retake Dhofar. Soviet assistance to the rebels in mounting operations in northern Oman would also have distracted government forces from Dhofar and conceivably rallied the Sultan's opponents there. After the buildup of progovernment forces, the small size of both the rebel fighters and the Dhofari population from which they drew support, combined with the PFLO's inability to spread the revolution to northern Oman, ensured that the guerrillas could not overthrow the Sultan. Whether substantially greater Soviet military assistance to the PFLO in the later stages of the war could have extended the life of the insurrection is not clear. It should be noted, though, that the successful economic development program mounted by the Omani government eroded much of the popular base of support for the PFLO and even encouraged defections from the Front itself. Moscow did send sophisticated SAMs to the guerrillas at the very end of the war, but the USSR was unwilling to give significant military assistance to the PFLO in an attempt to prolong the insurgency. Indeed, despite claims in Oman and the West that the entire conflict was a communist-inspired attempt to seize all Oman and control the Straits of Hormuz, the Soviets appear not to have been involved in most of it and to have participated only desultorily during the final years.

INTERNAL POLITICS

In that Moscow supported both the Imamate and later the Dhofar rebels, it is not surprising that it was critical of Sultan Sa'id bin Taymur and of his son Sultan Qabus bin Sa'id. Sultan Sa'id drew heavy criticism from the Soviets; one writer described him as the "most gloomy, disgusting person in the wicked little world of feudal sovereigns in the Persian Gulf zone."[51] At no point during the 1950s or 1960s did Moscow ever appear willing to establish diplomatic ties with the Sultan's government. It was the Soviet view that even though Oman was not officially a British protectorate like the Trucial States, Britain in fact ruled it as one. Since Sultan Sa'id's government did not join either the United Nations or Arab

League and maintained diplomatic relations only with Britain and India, this Soviet view was understandable.

The Soviet reaction to the coup of July 23, 1970, was different from Soviet policy toward most changes of government in other Peninsula countries. Moscow has usually made overtures for improved bilateral relations when new governments came to power either by coups or by the traditional means, as when a ruler died in Saudi Arabia or (after their independence) the smaller Arab Gulf countries. When Qabus came to power, however, the Soviets immediately denounced him as a British puppet whose reforms were merely public relations ploys to make himself more popular than his father.[52] Nor was there any Soviet attempt to establish friendly relations with the new government as there was with Bahrain, Qatar, and the UAE when they became independent the following year. Since Oman was never formally a protectorate, there was no formal independence for the country, and it was the Soviet view that the new government remained under British control. Yet while the new Sultan has continued to seek the advice of British officials, he did not formally agree to accept British advice as did his father and grandfather. Moscow did not think it would happen, but the reign of Sultan Qabus did bring change to Oman in the form of economic development and broader participation in international relations, including membership in the United Nations and Arab League as well as diplomatic ties with many countries including (eventually) China, Yugoslavia, and Romania. Further, contrary to Soviet predictions, the Sultan was able to achieve popular support that he still enjoys.

The Soviet press continued to vilify Sultan Qabus both for the remainder of the war and later. After the isolation of Oman during Sa'id's regime, the Soviets appeared to be both surprised and annoyed at Qabus's success in receiving support and recognition from the Arab countries and Iran. Qabus made several statements accusing Moscow and Aden of being the main backers of the Omani rebels and saying the insurgents were directed by the "world communist movement"; this brought an immediate Soviet response to the effect that the insurgency arose out of local causes and that the Sultan was making "anti-Soviet" statements in order to obtain Western aid or even intervention.[53] Later the Soviets criticized him for allowing the United States to use military facilities on Masirah Island and for participating in U.S. Rapid Deployment Force plans and related military exercises.[54]

None of Moscow's commentary about Oman has ever been friendly or favorable, nor has Moscow publicly called for diplomatic ties with Muscat as it has with the other governments of the region with which it does not have relations. Nevertheless, since the normalization agreement between Oman and the PDRY was made in late 1982, there has been a noticeable difference in Soviet commentary about Oman. Instead of condemning Oman for allowing the United States to hold RDF exercises on Omani territory as Moscow did in 1981, from late 1982 the Soviets criticized the United States for holding these exercises in Oman (as well as Somalia, Sudan, and Egypt) but did not equate Oman with the United States. Indeed, the Soviets sometimes portrayed Oman as a victim of U.S. "militarism."[55] In addition, instead of denouncing the Sultan for actions or statements taken by the Omani government that displeased Moscow, the Soviets have blamed these on his assistants such as Yusuf al-'Alawi, the former rebel who became Minister of State for Foreign Affairs.[56] Still, whereas Soviet commentary on Saudi Arabia and the other GCC countries is sometimes friendly and sometimes not, the Soviets have yet to issue favorable commentary about Oman. All that can be said is that they appear to have become less critical.

Regarding the opposition, the Soviets continued to make statements supporting the PFLO. Although the fighting came to an end in December 1975, the Soviets on several occasions in 1976 reported that the struggle continued and that the rebels were not defeated.[57] In 1977 and 1978, reports of PFLO "victories" disappeared, but the Front was still portrayed as being determined to continue the fight. Other statements on Iranian and Chinese aid to the Sultan admitted that the rebels had in fact been defeated.[58] Genuine optimism about the Front's prospects revived in 1979 when all the remaining Iranian troops left Oman when the Shah's regime fell. By this time there were only about 300 Iranian troops left in Oman, but both the Soviets and the PFLO claimed that 3,000 Iranians had left and concluded that the Sultan was now more vulnerable.[59] A PFLO delegation visited Moscow April 24–29, 1979 (apparently the first one to do so since 1975), and received lots of media coverage while there. As usual, however, the delegation was invited to the USSR by the Soviet Afro-Asian Solidarity Committee, and no meetings with government or Party officials were reported.[60] The PFLO did manage to mount a few military operations inside Dhofar during 1978–80, but these were small-scale hit-and-run attacks, and even the PFLO later admitted that they "did not have the same momentum and level" as during the earlier insurgency.[61] A charge made by both the Soviets and the PFLO, which

Muscat hotly denied, was that the Iranian troops were replaced by 7,000 Egyptian soldiers.[62]

From 1980, Soviet reports of the Front's determination to fight on practically disappeared. Instead, PFLO statements were cited on several occasions denouncing Omani military cooperation with the United States.[63] A delegation from the Organization of Omani Youths (a PFLO affiliate) attended the nineteenth Komsomol (Soviet youth organization) congress in May 1982, and Moscow praised the PFLO's own congress of 1982.[64] Several South Yemeni statements of support to the PFLO were made during 1982 as well, but after the Oman-PDRY normalization agreement was signed in the autumn, Aden cut off the PFLO's radio broadcasts, and both the Soviet and South Yemeni media have practically ceased reporting its activities.[65] Ending hostile propaganda campaigns was one of the points agreed to in the Aden-Muscat accord, and the PDRY has so far honored its commitment and kept the PFLO inactive. The Front, however, does continue to exist.

Perhaps the USSR did not make any friendly overtures to the new Omani government in July 1970 because Moscow initially thought the guerrillas would succeed in overthrowing the Sultan. It is not clear whether Moscow's reduced criticism of Oman since the Muscat-Aden normalization has been accompanied by a Soviet diplomatic effort to improve relations. Whether it has or not, though, Soviet policy toward Oman so far must be described as a failure. By supporting the rebels during the war, Moscow ensured that the Sultan's government would be hostile toward it, yet not supporting them sufficiently was an important factor in the PFLO's defeat. By continuing to give verbal support to the rebels after the war when they had almost no chance of succeeding, the Soviets only further induced the Sultan to rely heavily on the West. Even now, when Oman-PDRY ties have improved, Muscat insists that it will not establish diplomatic relations with Moscow until the USSR ceases interfering in its internal affairs.[66] Pursuing a policy of outward hostility toward the government without effective support to its opponents, then, has meant that the Soviets have been unable to achieve any influence in Oman and are unlikely to in the future even though Soviet hostility toward Muscat has diminished.

FOREIGN POLICY ISSUES

Besides the now small risk of internal rebellion, the two most important security concerns for Oman have been threats from South Yemen and threats to the Straits of Hormuz. Both of these concerns have been heightened by actual or potential Soviet involvement in them. While the potential threat from South Yemen has diminished in recent years, the threat to the Straits has increased as a result of the Iran-Iraq war.

Oman has seen South Yemen as a security threat not only because of PDRY aid to the Dhofari rebels, but also because of the presence of Soviet, Cuban, and East German military personnel there who could assist a direct South Yemeni attack on Oman.[67] This Omani fear was heightened by the Soviet-PDRY treaty of friendship and cooperation signed in October 1979 and the tripartite treaty of August 1981 linking South Yemen, Ethiopia, and Libya. Nevertheless, the number of Soviet-bloc military advisers in South Yemen has not been very great, and Omani officers have indicated that the PDRY has not kept large numbers of troops near the Omani border and that its forces as a whole suffer from poor training, old equipment, low morale, and chronic absenteeism.[68] Part of the reason Muscat had up until late 1982 repeatedly stated that the Soviet presence in Aden was a threat to the entire Arabian Peninsula was to dissuade the other monarchies of the region from assisting Aden in response to South Yemen's friendly overtures to them while at the same time it remained hostile toward Oman. Similarly, Moscow and Aden have portrayed the presence of Iranian, British, and now American forces in Oman as a threat not only to South Yemen but to the entire Peninsula in an effort to isolate Muscat from the other monarchies.[69]

Efforts to mediate between Muscat and Aden were made by the Arab League while the insurrection was still in progress, but these failed.[70] Further efforts were made by Saudi Arabia at the time of its own rapprochement with South Yemen in March 1976. Secret meetings between high-level Omani and PDRY Foreign Ministry officials were reported to have taken place in both Muscat and Riyadh during 1977, but while Oman publicly supported the mediation effort, South Yemen denied it was even taking place, and these efforts failed as well.[71] Kuwait and the UAE resumed the attempt, and in May 1982 Muscat and Aden agreed to settle their differences. After an initial meeting in Kuwait in July 1982, delegations from the two sides met again there at the end of October and signed a normalization agreement that came into effect November 15, 1982.[72] Both sides agreed to establish normal relations and resolve all differences peacefully, negotiate a border agreement, not allow foreign troops to use their territory to attack or threaten the other country, stop all hostile propaganda campaigns, and, in principle, establish diplomatic relations.[73] The

Soviets welcomed the agreement wholeheartedly.[74] In late October 1983, further progress was made when Muscat and Aden did establish diplomatic relations, though neither has yet opened an embassy in the other country.[75] The border committee met again in January 1983, October 1983, and January 1985, but a final agreement has not yet been achieved on this issue, though the differences are believed to be minor.[76] While still wary of each other, the two countries have succeeded in reducing the level of tension and hostility between them.

Oman and many of its Western allies have long feared a Soviet threat to the Straits of Hormuz. It is not clear exactly what Moscow either intends or could accomplish there, but the fact that the Soviets could act to disrupt, control, or halt the flow of oil through the Straits has made the possibility a concern. This threat seemed remote in the past, but the Soviet invasion of Afghanistan in December 1979 increased Oman's fears that the Straits were vulnerable.[77] More than any other nation in the region, Oman has sought to protect itself and the Straits through military alliance with the West, especially the United States and the United Kingdom. Muscat has permitted the United States to use military facilities in Oman for the RDF and has proposed a formal military link between the GCC states and the West and even Omani membership in the North Atlantic Treaty Organization (NATO) as an observer.[78] The other GCC states have been unwilling to become as closely allied to the West as has Oman, and all five of them have asked Oman to reduce its military links with it.[79] Oman has also voiced its concern about the Soviet threat to the Straits more than any of the GCC states. Muscat vehemently criticized Brezhnev's 1980 Persian Gulf peace proposals to neutralize the region, calling them "interference" in the internal affairs of the Gulf states and saying that the Soviet invasion of Afghanistan demonstrates Moscow's hostile intentions toward the area.[80] Oman has also complained about the presence of Soviet naval vessels and aircraft in the vicinity of the Straits, though no clashes with them have been reported.[81] For their part, the Soviets have repeatedly denounced Oman for its "anti-Soviet" stand. Moscow portrays Oman as attempting to instill fear of the USSR as an excuse to introduce U.S. military forces into the region.[82] Moscow's description of Oman as acting on behalf of U.S. interests may have been designed to isolate Oman from the other GCC states. Despite their discomfort over Oman's overt military links with America and Britain, however, the other GCC states have maintained their close friendship with Muscat.

More than any other recent event, the Iran-Iraq war that began in September 1980 has underlined the vulnerability of the Straits of Hormuz. Unlike the USSR, which has repeatedly denied that it poses any threat to the Straits, revolutionary Iran has threatened to close them. Tehran has on several occasions stated that if Iraq manages to cut off Iranian oil exports, Iran would then close the Straits and thereby severely affect oil exports from all the Gulf countries. When Iraq acquired several French Super Entendard aircraft with Exocet missiles, which might well be able to destroy Iranian oil export facilities at Kharg Island, Iran renewed its threats. On October 15, 1983, Ayatollah Khomeini himself warned that Iran would close the Gulf to all shipping and destroy Western oil interests in the region in response to an Iraqi attack.[83] The sea lanes for the Straits lie entirely in Omani territorial waters, and the Sultan has pledged to keep them open. He has also stated that neither Oman nor the GCC could do this alone.[84] The United States government has responded to these Iranian threats by stating that it would not allow Iran to close the Straits and would act to keep them open.[85] Washington sent a task force of naval vessels including an aircraft carrier to the area, and on January 21, 1984, the U.S. Department of Defense issued a notice that ships and planes coming within five miles of the task force would risk being fired upon.[86]

The Soviet response to Iran's threats to close the Straits has been to urge both sides to end the war as soon as possible but to continue supplying arms to Iraq. Moscow has not indicated that it would make any response to a U.S. effort to keep the Straits open and has mainly confined itself to portraying the risk of American military intervention as yet another reason Iran and Iraq should end the war.[87] On March 8, 1984, however, a Soviet statement did say that the restrictions imposed on sea or air traffic in the Gulf are a violation of international law and that the USSR does not recognize them.[88] While the Soviets have apparently not yet actually challenged the U.S. five-mile limit, the statement serves to underline the fear that the Iran-Iraq war may lead to some form of Soviet involvement if Iran causes a crisis over the Straits.

Moscow and Muscat take opposing positions on several other foreign policy issues. Oman has condemned the Soviet invasion of Afghanistan and has been highly critical of the Soviet-Cuban role in Ethiopia and Angola.[89] Muscat has also expressed its disapproval of the Aden-Moscow treaty of friendship and cooperation and of the tripartite treaty linking the PDRY, Ethiopia, and Libya.[90] Moscow, in turn, has criticized Omani ties to the United States and Britain as well as Oman's efforts to link the GCC with the West.[91] The Soviets also denounced the establishment of diplomatic relations between Oman and the PRC in 1978 as part of the two countries' efforts to form a broader anti-Soviet alliance.[92] Even on the Arab-Israeli conflict, about which Moscow's views often correspond with even the most conservative Arab governments, Oman and the USSR disagree. The Soviets have vilified Oman for approving the Camp David peace accords signed by Egypt and Israel and for not breaking diplomatic relations with Cairo.[93] In August 1983 Yusuf al-'Alawi took the unusual step of calling upon Arab nations to recognize Israel, since Israel will remain in existence.[94] Unlike most other Arab states, Oman regards the USSR and not Israel as the main threat to the Arab world. Oman's main complaint against the United States is not that it supports Israel, but that it is not sufficiently anti-Soviet.[95] Owing to the Omani government's hostility toward all aspects of Soviet foreign policy, it does not seem likely that Moscow will ever be able to separate the Sultan from the United States or even establish diplomatic relations with Muscat so long as Qabus is in power. However, Moscow's diminished hostility toward Oman is probably less an indication of a strong Soviet effort to establish friendly ties with Muscat than it is an attempt to assuage the other GCC states' concerns about Soviet intentions toward the region and thereby induce them to improve their ties with Moscow as well as increase economic assistance to Aden.

CONCLUSION

The USSR does not appear likely to gain influence in Oman any time soon, either through luring the Sultan away from the West or though supporting internal opponents of his regime. Inside Oman, there is no longer any serious opposition to his rule. The one factor that appears to be most effective in ensuring domestic tranquility both in Dhofar and in the rest of the country is the tremendous economic growth that has taken place since 1970. It has been the Sultan's policy to see that the country's oil wealth is spread generally among the population via development projects, education, and government jobs.[96]

Economic prosperity and domestic tranquility in Oman present little opportunity for the Soviets to exploit discontent in order to weaken the Sultan, but how long will this situation last? In 1983, the Organization of Arab Petroleum Exporting Countries estimated that Oman's known oil reserves would only last twenty-three years at current rates of production;

Petroleum Development Oman estimated that they would last only thirty years.[97] At present, oil revenues contribute well over half of Oman's gross domestic product and almost all of the government's revenues.[98] While some progress has been made in developing agriculture, industry, and other revenue-producing sectors of the economy, unless substantially greater progress is made these alone will not suffice to support Oman's present standard of living without oil. As the country's oil reserves become depleted, Oman could well experience a serious economic decline, and this in turn could lead to domestic opposition to the Sultan.

In addition to potential economic problems, there are also potential political problems that could affect the stability of the Sultanate. Unlike Saudi Arabia, where there is a first and second crown prince or the other GCC states where the rulers have designated heirs, Sultan Qabus has no son, is not married, and has not named an heir. Should he die without one, political turmoil could erupt if the Sultan's uncles engage in a struggle over the succession. Even if the royal family were able to agree on a new sultan, there is no guarantee that the people would regard him as legitimate, especially if the British were seen to play a large role in bringing him to power as they did Qabus. But since Qabus is still relatively young (he was born in 1940), is currently in good health, and could still either marry and have a son or name an heir, the succession question is not a serious issue now, though it could become one.

Another threat to internal stability might arise from popular resentment against the strong British presence still in Oman, particularly in the military. All three services have a substantial number of British officers, even in very high positions.[99] The reason given for this is that Omanis are not yet capable of these tasks, but that they will replace the British as soon as they are ready. One British expatriate in Oman suggested that a more likely explanation is that the Sultan fears native Omanis in the highest positions would overthrow him, whereas he trusts the British more. If this is true, the Sultan could be expected to resist demands for more rapid Omanization in the armed forces, which might give rise to discontent. At this time, there is no strong evidence that the Omani public resents the British presence (or that of other foreigners including Americans). As the expectations of Omanis rise, resentment against the British presence not only in the military but in the government and the economy as well could build up if Omanization is not seen to be proceeding rapidly enough.

Finally, since coming to power in 1970 Sultan Qabus has exercised absolute political authority. Qabus originally appointed his uncle, Tariq bin Taymur, as Prime Minister, but he resigned in January 1972 because of his nephew's unwillingness to allow a parliamentary democracy in Oman.[100] In October 1981 the Sultan established a Consultative Council to advise him. Its membership, however, is not elected but is appointed by the Sultan. Further, the Council is allowed to make suggestions only in the realm of economic development; the Sultan has not yet permitted it any broader role in formulating foreign or domestic policy.[101] Should public pressure for an elected parliament arise, as it has in Kuwait and Bahrain, unwillingness on the part of the Sultan could lead to domestic opposition. As the case of neighboring Iran demonstrated, an absolute monarch who fosters economic development but suppresses the people's political aspirations is not necessarily secure on his throne.

If any of these potential problems ever become serious, the Soviets can be expected to exploit them by supporting the Sultan's opponents. The Soviets, however, cannot create these problems by their own actions. Since none of these potential threats to Oman's internal security are serious at present, there is little the Soviets can do to weaken the Sultan's government except wait for an opportunity to arise. Because of the importance of Oman in guarding the free flow of shipping through the Straits of Hormuz, Oman's future political evolution, whether peaceful or violent, will have crucial significance for the West.

Saudi Arabia

4

Saudi Arabia is clearly the most important state on the Arabian Peninsula. The Kingdom is the largest oil producer in the Organization of Petroleum Exporting Countries (OPEC) and is the second or third (depending on whether it chooses to produce more or less than the United States) largest oil producer in the world. Saudi Arabia also has immense oil reserves, unlike many of the other OPEC nations, which are expected to run out of oil by the turn of the century. Since Western Europe, Japan, and to a lesser extent the United States are dependent on imported oil, the continuation of Saudi oil exports is extremely important to them. As a result, the West is very sensitive about the prospect that the USSR might become influential in Saudi Arabia and act to control its oil exports.

Leaving aside here the unlikely scenario of a direct Soviet invasion or an attack by an ally of the Soviet Union such as South Yemen, the USSR could gain influence in Saudi Arabia through promoting either a revolution or a coup. Although there is at present no organized opposition capable of overthrowing or sustaining guerrilla warfare against the Saudi government, the number of absolute monarchies in the world has become smaller and smaller in modern history. This trend has certainly been in evidence in the Middle East, where monarchs have been overthrown in Egypt (1952), Iraq (1958), Yemen (1962), Libya (1969), Afghanistan (1973), and Iran (1979). Internal disturbances have taken place in Saudi Arabia, and the Soviets have on occasion indicated at least verbal support for Saudi opposition groups, including the Saudi Arabian Communist Party.

There is also the possibility that by diplomatic means the Soviets could induce the present Saudi government to become friendlier with Moscow and less friendly with Washington. This is what the Soviets have tried to do, frequently pointing out to Riyadh that the USSR supports the

126

Arab cause in the Arab-Israeli dispute whereas the United States opposes it by helping Israel. A change in Saudi Arabia's political orientation from West to East does not seem imminent, but the Saudis have sometimes issued statements that indicate a willingness to have better relations with the USSR. Yet while the Kremlin has been willing, Riyadh has not yet allowed Saudi-Soviet ties to develop even to the point of exchanging ambassadors. The extent to which the USSR both threatens America's alliance with the Kingdom through taking advantage of differences between the two countries and supports Saudi opposition movements will be examined here by analyzing the USSR's varying and often contradictory foreign policy toward Saudi Arabia.

HISTORICAL BACKGROUND

The modern history of Saudi Arabia began in the mid-eighteenth century when Muhammad bin Sa'ud, one of the many petty shaykhs of Nejd (central Arabia), joined forces with the religious reformer Muhammad bin 'Abd al-Wahab. Most of the Peninsula had come under the nominal authority of the Ottoman empire in the sixteenth century, but the Turks' control was weak. 'Abd al-Wahab saw that the Arabs of the region had reverted to superstitious and animistic practices, and he made his goal the restoration of Islam in its pure form. Through both conversion and force, Wahabism (as it became known in the West) and Saudi authority spread rapidly.[1] Ever since then, the power of the Al Sa'ud family has been inextricably linked with Wahabism; the Saudi royal family claims its right to rule largely on the basis of its commitment to the implementation and protection of Islamic principles. The ruler of Saudi Arabia is not only king, but also the Imam or religious leader of the nation.

By the early nineteenth century, the Al Sa'ud ruled not only Nejd, but also what is now the Eastern Province of Saudi Arabia abutting the Persian Gulf. In 1802–3, the Saudis captured most of the Hejaz (the western region bordering the Red Sea), including the holy cities of Mecca and Medina, and made raids as far north as Syria. The Ottoman Sultan decided to drive the Saudis out of the holy cities by having his viceroy of Egypt, Muhammad 'Ali, send an expeditionary force to the Peninsula in 1811. By 1813 the Egyptian-Turkish force had retaken Mecca and Medina, and after a long siege it captured and destroyed the Saudi capital of Daraiya in 1818. But the Egyptian-Turkish army did not remain in Nejd, and so the Saudis were able to resume their position there, establishing a new capital at Riyadh. The forces of Muhammad 'Ali defeated the Saudis again in 1837–38; this time the Egyptian viceroy was acting on his own to create an empire at the expense of the Ottoman Sultan, but his plan failed and he was forced to give up his conquests in 1841. The Turks took control of the Hejaz but did not extend their authority over Nejd. Thus Faysal bin Turki, the Saudi leader who had been captured by Muhammad 'Ali in 1838, was able to return to Nejd and restore his rule by 1843. His control also extended over the Eastern Province, but he chose not to encroach upon the Hejaz for fear the Turks might once again move into Nejd. Instead he tried to expand his realm over Bahrain, Qatar, the Trucial States, and Oman to the east and southeast, but he was frustrated in this by the British. Since formal boundaries were never agreed to, border tensions between Saudi Arabia and its smaller neighbors would reemerge in the mid-twentieth century.[2]

Faysal bin Turki died in 1865, and the power of the Saudis went into decline when his two sons, 'Abdallah and Sa'ud, quarreled over the succession. 'Abdallah asked the Turks to assist him, and they obliged by seizing the Eastern Province for themselves. Sa'ud died in 1875, leaving 'Abdallah in sole possession of a much truncated realm, but in 1885 Sa'ud's two sons overthrew him. The powerful Rashid family intervened and by 1891 were in complete control of what had belonged to the Al Sa'ud family, while the latter went into exile in Kuwait.[3] The Al Sa'ud concluded from this experience that rivalries within the royal family such as between 'Abdallah and Sa'ud could jeopardize both the country and the family's control over it and so must not be allowed to occur again.

The restoration of Saudi rule was brought about through the seizure of Riyadh from the Rashid by the future king 'Abd al-'Aziz (also known in the West as Ibn Saud), who led a small raiding party there from Kuwait in January 1902. 'Abd al-'Aziz was the son of 'Abdallah's and Sa'ud's younger brother 'Abd al-Rahman, who had himself been Imam of Riyadh for fifteen months before the Rashid expelled him in 1891. By 1905 'Abd al-'Aziz had driven the Rashid out of Nejd, and by 1913 he had retaken the Eastern Province from the Turks. To gain his support against the Ottomans, the British recognized 'Abd al-'Aziz as the independent Sultan of Nejd and its eastern dependencies.[4] With the collapse of the Ottoman empire at the end of the war, one of the Saudis oldest opponents had disappeared, but a new one arose in the form of the Hashemite Sharif Hussein of Mecca, who became King of the independent Hejaz.

'Abd al-'Aziz sought to spread his influence by organizing tribesmen into religiously motivated military camps known as *ikhwan* (brothers), which were sent progressively farther out in all directions from Nejd. With their help he seized Mecca from the Hashemites in 1924 and the following year took all of the Hejaz. The *ikhwan* also moved north, but here they ran into the British mandates of Transjordan and Iraq. To avoid war with the British, 'Abd al-'Aziz consented in the May 1927 Treaty of Jidda to respect-agreed upon frontiers. The *ikhwan,* however, wanted to be able to spread Wahabism as well as to continue raiding northward indefinitely. Seeing his agreement with the British as sacrilegious, part of the *ikhwan* revolted in 1928 and 1929 but were defeated. This was the most serious challenge to Saudi rule since its restoration in the twentieth century.[5] In 1934 'Abd al-'Aziz rounded out his conquests by capturing the Asir. The Idrisi family, who had been driven out of the Tihama region of Yemen by Imam Yahya, had ruled this area. When Imam Yahya attempted to take the Asir (which is ethnically Yemeni) for himself, Saudi forces moved as far south as Hodeida inside Yemen proper. They later withdrew from Yemen in exchange for Yahya's recognition of 'Abd al-'Aziz's rule in the Asir.[6] The Saudi-Yemeni border was only partially delimited, and so it has remained a source of tension between the two neighbors.

In January 1926, shortly after driving out the Hashemites, 'Abd al-'Aziz assumed the title of King of Hejaz, and in January 1927 he upgraded his title from Sultan to King of Nejd and its dependencies. It was not until September 1932, however, that he united his two kingdoms into a single Kingdom of Saudi Arabia, thus linking the royal family's name to the name of the country.[7] At first 'Abd al-'Aziz's treasury was chronically short of money; after the capture of the Hejaz, his main source of revenue was income derived from pilgrims visiting Mecca and Medina. In 1938, however, oil was discovered under a 1933 concession to Standard Oil Company of California, which would later form, with Texaco, Standard Oil of New Jersey, and Mobil, the Arabian-American Oil Company (ARAMCO).[8] While Saudi oil revenues were modest at first, they would grow progressively larger over the years. Thus began Saudi Arabia's close association with the United States, which developed even further during World War II when the Roosevelt administration began giving Lend-Lease aid to Riyadh in 1943, even through the latter was not technically eligible for it until the King declared war on Germany close to the end of the conflict in 1945 (by doing so, he made Saudi Arabia eligible to become a charter member of the United Nations). The United States also constructed and made use of an air base at Dhahran in the Eastern Province.[9]

'Abd al-'Aziz died in November 1953 and was succeeded by his son Sa'ud. In less than five years, King Sa'ud's mismanagement and extravagant spending brought the country to the verge of bankruptcy despite the growth in oil revenues. The royal family concluded that Sa'ud could not properly manage internal policy or deal effectively with external problems (which will be discussed later), and so in March 1958 it transferred executive authority to the Prime Minister, Crown Prince Faysal, while allowing Sa'ud to retain the title of King. Sa'ud managed to regain his authority in December 1960 but lost it again the following November as his health broke down. The struggle for power continued until November 1964 when the royal family, after receiving religious sanction from the *ulema* (the religious leaders and elders), deposed Sa'ud and proclaimed Faysal king.[10] This was the most serious leadership crisis Saudi Arabia has faced so far in the twentieth century; that they deposed Sa'ud showed that the royal family would not permit an incompetent monarch to continue ruling.

Faysal ruled as king from 1964 to 1975. He oversaw the development of the Kingdom's economy—first stabilization, followed by dramatic improvement in its finances. He also put an end to a plan for a constitution, a legislature, and elections that Sa'ud had halfheartedly supported but had later changed his mind about.[11] King Faysal was assassinated in March 1975 by a disgruntled nephew who was executed soon thereafter.[12] Faysal's younger brother Khalid succeeded him, but owing to his poor health he allowed his younger brother, Crown Prince Fahd, to exercise much authority. Khalid died on June 13, 1982, and Fahd has been king since then. He appointed his brother 'Abdallah crown prince and first deputy prime minister (since Faysal, the king has retained the title of prime minister) and another brother, Sultan, as second deputy prime minister.[13]

Since the death of Faysal, the crown prince and first deputy prime minister has always become king, and the second deputy prime minister has always become crown prince and first deputy prime minister. There is, however, no legal necessity for this. The royal family must approve the crown prince to become the new king upon the death of the old one, and the new king then chooses his crown prince. Succession to the throne usually but not necessarily passes to the next eldest son of King 'Abd al-'Aziz. When Faysal died, the next eldest surviving brother, Muhammad, was passed over in favor of Khalid. In each case of succession in

this century, the royal family has approved as king the man whom the previous king had designated crown prince. Because the succession is not
automatic, but open to a certain degree of choice, there is the possibility
that there will be disagreement within the royal family over who should sit
on the throne. Several observers have identified competing factions within
the royal family, but though these probably exist, the family has a much
greater interest in ensuring that the succession issue does not escalate into
an open struggle that could weaken the monarchy and lead to its collapse.[14]

SAUDI-SOVIET BILATERAL RELATIONS

It is not entirely proper to speak of Saudi-Soviet bilateral relations,
since the two countries have had extremely limited contact over the years,
and except for the period 1926–38 there have not even been diplomatic
relations between them. Nor has there been a protracted insurgency or
civil war inside Saudi Arabia that the Soviets could take advantage of, as
there was in the two Yemens and Oman. Instead, Saudi-Soviet bilateral
relations have been mainly limited to the realm of commentary by officials and the media, though a certain amount of trade has also taken
place.[15] Soviet commentary on Saudi Arabia has alternated between hostile statements about how the Saudi monarchy is the servant of American
imperialism and is increasingly opposed by the oppressed working
classes, and friendly statements noting that Saudi-Soviet cooperation
could do much to enhance the Arab cause in the Arab-Israeli dispute and
pleading for the establishment of diplomatic relations. Neither effective
internal opposition nor the exchange of embassies, however, has come
about. Saudi commentary on the Soviet Union has been generally negative, since the Saudis see the USSR and communism as the opponents of
Moslem principles and the conservative monarchy. Sometimes, though,
the Saudis say something favorable about the Soviets, thereby creating
fears in the West and hope in the USSR for a rapprochement between
Riyadh and Moscow.

In the 1920s, though, there appeared to be a much greater prospect
for Saudi-Soviet friendship. In August 1924 the Soviet Union succeeded
in establishing diplomatic relations with the Hashemite King Hussein of
the Hejaz, whose relations with the British were not good at that time.
When 'Abd al-'Aziz invaded the Hejaz and captured Mecca the following
October, the People's Commissar for Foreign Affairs, Chicherin, saw this
as a blow to Soviet foreign policy, since the first Arab state that Moscow

had established ties with was thus seriously weakened. The Comintern, however, welcomed 'Abd al-'Aziz's move, since they regarded him and Imam Yahya as truly independent Arab leaders opposed to British influence, whereas the Hashemite family, whom the British had installed as monarchs in Transjordan and Iraq, were dependent for their position on "imperialism." After 'Abd al-'Aziz completely took over the Hejaz in 1925 and assumed the title of King in January 1926, the USSR became the first country to acknowledge his rule over the Hejaz by according him diplomatic recognition on February 16, 1926. Happy to have his conquest recognized by one of the major European powers, the new King allowed the Soviet mission in Jidda to remain there (it was headed by Karim Khakimov, a Tatar Moslem who signed his letters "Agent and Consul General of the USSR").[16]

In 1926 'Abd al-'Aziz convened a Congress of Mecca to ratify his claim to the two holy cities. The USSR sent a delegation of Soviet Moslems, one of whom was elected vice-president of the Congress, and supported 'Abd al-'Aziz completely. Soon after this, the King became suspicious that the real aim of the Soviet mission in Jidda was to spread Marxist propaganda, and so he drew closer to the British. In 1927 the Soviets also recognized 'Abd al-'Aziz's elevation from Sultan to King of Nejd. Trade between the two countries had begun, with ships from Odessa bringing Soviet goods to Jidda. These goods, however, were dumped on the market at extremely low prices, so the Jidda merchants complained. In 1928 the King embargoed all Russian goods, and the Soviets were unable to persuade him to sign a trade agreement. As the King sought to limit his contacts with the USSR, Soviet interest in the Saudis soon waned, and commentary about them was sparse for the next few years. In May - June 1932, however, Prince Faysal (who later became king) visited the USSR, where he met President Kalinin, among others. The Soviets offered to forgive a debt of 30,000 pounds sterling that the Saudis had never paid, ironically, for the import of petroleum products. Moscow also offered a loan of 1 million pounds if the King would lift the trade embargo and sign both a commercial treaty and a treaty of friendship. The King later ended the trade embargo but did not sign any treaty or accept a loan.[17]

Saudi-Soviet relations then became fairly inactive. The Soviets saw that 'Abd al-'Aziz would not take active measures to challenge the British position in Arabia but was cooperating with London instead. Indeed, the Soviets themselves sought to cooperate with the British as the power of

Hitler's Germany grew stronger. Whether it was to improve relations with London or for some other reason, in 1938 the Soviets withdrew their diplomatic mission from Saudi Arabia as well as from Yemen, Turkey, Afghanistan, and Persia.[18] This was a move that the Soviets must deeply regret, for unlike Yemen, which agreed to resume diplomatic relations with Moscow in 1955, the Saudis did not do so.

Through the Second World War and until Stalin's death in 1953, there was very little Soviet writing about Saudi Arabia. The few references that were made in the late 1940s were generally hostile, accusing the Saudi monarch of having "sold out" to the oil companies and to the United States. The Soviets were especially bitter because the Saudis allowed the Americans to build and operate the air base at Dhahran.[19] This hostility reflected Stalin's generally pessimistic attitude regarding the Third World in the years before his death.

The new Soviet leadership, particularly Khrushchev, was much more optimistic about the prospects of Third World leaders' becoming allies or friends of the USSR. The Soviets were pleased by King Sa'ud's rejection of U.S. military aid in February 1954 and by his refusal in 1955 to join the Western-sponsored security pact that was to become the Central Treaty Organization (CENTO).[20] Following the momentous Czech-Egyptian arms deal—the first major arms agreement between the socialist bloc and a Third World state—the Soviets were hopeful that they could sell arms to the Saudis also. A situation arose that appeared to make such a deal possible. As was mentioned earlier, the boundaries between Saudi Arabia and the British-protected states to the south and east had not been firmly established. In 1952 Saudi forces occupied the Buraimi Oasis on the basis that it had been under Saudi rule in the nineteenth century. Both Riyadh and ARAMCO also hoped that oil would be found there. This oasis straddled the Oman–Abu Dhabi border, far inside what they regarded as their land, and it would have meant a substantial limitation of their respective territories if this move remained unchallenged. In October 1955 British, Omani, and Abu Dhabi forces retook the oasis and pushed the Saudis out. Both Prince Faysal and Soviet officials were cited in the Western press as claiming that Saudi Arabia was considering resuming diplomatic ties with Moscow and buying Soviet arms, but the Saudi government officially denied both stories. The Soviets did, however, express support for the Saudi position in the Buraimi Oasis dispute. The Soviets were also hopeful about the prospects for friendship with Riyadh, since King Sa'ud then seemed willing to follow Nasser's lead by signing a security pact with Egypt and Syria in October 1955 (which was joined by Yemen the following year) and allowing Egyptian military advisers into Saudi Arabia. Saudi Arabia, Yemen, and Egypt also worked to weaken the British position in Aden—a policy the Soviets supported too.[21]

King Sa'ud and Nasser did not remain on friendly terms for long, and in August 1956 the King expelled all Egyptian military advisers. After a brief period of renewed solidarity during the Anglo-French-Israeli invasion of Suez and Sinai in October 1956, they began to exchange increasingly hostile polemics. The Soviets wanted to prevent their relations with both states from worsening, but as Saudi Arabia turned closer to the United States (in 1957 the King renewed the U.S. lease on Dhahran air base), the Soviets became more critical. By 1958 Soviet writers came to the conclusion that Saudi Arabia had "joined the imperialist camp" and changed from praising Wahabism as a progressive, anti-British movement to condemning it as an instrument of the reactionary rulers to oppress the masses.[22]

Over the next few years the Soviets did sometimes feel optimistic about the Saudis. When Faysal took control of the government in 1958, they applauded his call for Saudi Arabia to pursue "positive neutrality" but later they grew impatient with a neutrality that allowed ties to the United States but not to the USSR. The Soviets were also encouraged when Saudi-Egyptian relations became less hostile at times. They were especially pleased when in 1961 the Saudis announced that America would not be allowed to renew the lease on Dhahran air base when it expired in 1962. By September 1962 the two governments seemed on the verge of restoring diplomatic relations. In that month the Mayor of Riyadh traveled to Soviet Central Asia and the Saudi Ambassador to the United Nations, Ahmad Shukairy (who later became the first head of the PLO), went to Moscow and was warmly received by Khrushchev. These were the first publicly acknowledged visits to the USSR by Saudi officials since Faysal went there in 1932. There was even a report that the Saudis asked the Russians to sell them arms, but because Sa'ud would not allow the presence of Soviet military advisers in the Kingdom, the Soviets would not agree.[23] But however warm their relations were about to become, they suddenly turned extremely cold with the outbreak of the North Yemeni revolution on September 26, 1962.

Soviet commentary was bitterly critical of Saudi support to the Yemeni royalists, while the Saudis were equally critical of Soviet support for the large Egyptian army presence in Yemen to support the republicans.

The Saudis saw Nasser's actions in Yemen as a threat to themselves, which Egypt's bombardment of Saudi territory several times did little to alleviate.[24] At one point there seemed to be a thaw in Saudi-Soviet relations. After Brezhnev and Kosygin ousted Khrushchev in October 1964 and Faysal deposed Sa'ud the following month, the Soviets sent Faysal their congratulations, and the King allowed a Soviet journalist to enter the country—the first to do so since the 1930s. Faysal told him that Saudi Arabia had no quarrel with the USSR or prejudice against Russians, and that there were "no obstacles" to improving bilateral relations.[25] The Soviets lauded the new King, as they did the improvement of Saudi-Egyptian relations that took place as the result of efforts to bring about a cease-fire and arrange a political settlement in Yemen. The Yemeni peace efforts failed, however, leading to renewed Saudi-Egyptian polemics, and since Moscow sided with Cairo, the USSR and Saudi Arabia once again became hostile toward each other.[26]

Egyptian involvement in the Yemeni civil war continued until the defeat of Israel in the June 1967 Arab-Israeli conflict induced Nasser to agree to withdraw his troops from the Peninsula in exchange for Saudi assistance and an end to Saudi aid to the Yemeni royalists. Nasser was no longer a threat to Saudi Arabia, but King Faysal was concerned over the increase in Soviet advisers and weapons that were sent to Egypt. Further, when the last Egyptians left Yemen and the republicans were besieged by the royalists in Sanaa, the USSR itself airlifted arms and supplies to the capital as well as provided some pilots for the YAR's aircraft in order to save the republic. The Saudis were infuriated by this move and threatened to continue aiding the royalists, but by early 1968 Moscow's interest in North Yemen waned as its attention shifted to competing with China for influence over the Marxist government that had come to power in South Yemen in November 1967.[27] The Saudis supported South Yemeni émigrés who attempted several times to overthrow the NLF government or make the Hadramaut in the east independent during 1968–73; in response, the Soviets gave military assistance to Aden in order to defeat these efforts. In addition, the USSR gave some support to the Marxist rebels in Oman whereas Saudi Arabia decided to help Sultan Qabus, who overthrew his oppressive father in 1970.[28] In the late 1960s and early 1970s, then, the Saudis and the Soviets were in a struggle for influence over these three countries that bordered directly on the Kingdom. It is little wonder, then, that the Saudis did not react favorably to Soviet overtures to establish friendly bilateral relations.

By mid-1970 the North Yemeni civil war had ended with the republicans victorious. These were moderate republicans, though (the radical ones had been defeated by them in 1968), who were willing to be reconciled with most of the royalists and with the Saudis. When Nasser died in September 1970, Sadat came to power in Cairo; in July 1972 he expelled most of the Soviet military advisers in Egypt.[29] In 1973 Iranian troops arrived in Oman to help suppress the Marxist insurgency; while the Saudis were happy to see the guerrillas contained, they also found that they had a common interest with Aden to see the Shah's forces removed, since both regarded him as a threat.[30] The October 1973 War saw Saudi Arabia join other Arab oil producers in an embargo on oil exports to the United States in protest over American support to Israel. King Faysal had in the past received congratulatory telegrams from the Soviet President on Saudi National Day (September 23) and had sent his thanks, but in 1973 Faysal for the first time sent congratulations to Podgorny on the anniversary of the October Revolution (November 7).[31] There was speculation again that Saudi-Soviet relations would be resumed and even that the King would travel to Moscow, but this did not occur.[32] Faysal had little faith in Soviet protestations of friendly intentions, and he insisted that the USSR was linked to Israel and that both opposed the Arabs.[33] He remained hostile toward the Soviets until his death in March 1975.

When Khalid assumed the throne, the security situation in the southern part of the Peninsula had greatly improved. The Omani rebels were on the defensive and would be defeated by the end of the year. South Yemeni President Salim Rubayyi 'Ali had begun making efforts to improve Aden's relations with the smaller Gulf emirates. Aden would establish diplomatic relations with Bahrain, Qatar, and the UAE in 1975 and with Saudi Arabia in March 1976.[34] Egypt's ties to the United States were growing, and Sadat would abrogate his treaty of friendship and cooperation with Moscow in 1976.[35] While Moscow and Riyadh did not cease to be critical of each other, there were some more friendly statements, as when Crown Prince Fahd said that Riyadh wanted good relations with both East and West and that Saudi Arabia might "settle" its relations with the USSR.[36] The Soviets welcomed all such statements but were annoyed by the Saudi desire to have friendship "without embassies."[37]

However, as Moscow and Riyadh continued to compete for influence in both South Yemen and the Horn of Africa, this mood of friendliness did not last. The Soviets hoped to remain on good terms with Somalia's leader, Siad Barre (with whom they had signed a treaty of friendship and cooperation in 1974), but they also hoped to gain an ally in much more populous Ethiopia, where there had been a revolution in 1974. The Somalis wanted to take the Ogaden region (which is ethnically Somali) from Ethiopia. Somalia tried to take the Ogaden by force, and when the Soviets gave military aid to Addis Ababa, Barre abrogated his treaty of friendship and cooperation with Moscow and expelled Soviet and Cuban military advisers, all with Saudi encouragement, at the end of 1977. But the Somali invasion failed, largely because the USSR and Cuba gave military support to Ethiopia while the United States did not support Somalia, since the Carter administration did not want to be seen aiding the violation of Organization of African Unity (OAU) strictures regarding the sanctity of borders established by the colonial powers—much to the disappointment of both the Somalis and the Saudis.[38]

These events also had a profound effect on South Yemen, since the pro-Saudi leader, 'Ali, was unable to stop his pro-Soviet rival, 'Abd al-Fattah Isma'il, from allowing the USSR to use South Yemen to transfer arms and advisers to Ethiopia. As 'Ali's position weakened, Riyadh's relations with Aden became increasingly strained until June 1978, when Isma'il overthrew 'Ali and Soviet influence became firmly established in Aden.[39] The Soviet and PDRY efforts to blame the killings of YAR leaders al-Hamdi (October 1977) and al-Ghashmi (two days before the Aden coup in June 1978) on Riyadh seemed intended to weaken Saudi influence in North Yemen and were one more cause of Saudi-Soviet tension.[40]

Saudi-American relations took a turn for the worse, however, after the U.S.–Egyptian–Israeli summit at Camp David in September 1978 produced a plan whereby Egypt would regain the Sinai Peninsula but only vague promises of "autonomy" for the Palestinians were offered. The Arab League summit held at Baghdad in November 1978 decided to condemn the agreement and expel Egypt from its membership; Saudi Arabia joined in this denunciation of U.S. policy, much to the surprise of American officials.[41] Seeing these strains in Saudi-American ties, Moscow launched a campaign to make friends with Riyadh. In a long article published in *Literaturnaia Gazeta* January 31, 1979, a Soviet expert on Arab affairs blamed Saudi Arabia's negative image of the USSR on the United States and Western Europe and said that this was sadly mistaken. Noting Saudi disappointment with U.S. policy toward the Middle East, he hoped Saudi-Soviet relations would improve.[42] The Saudi Foreign Minister, Prince Sa'ud al-Faysal, expressed his appreciation for Soviet support to the Arabs.[43] Several more friendly statements were issued from Moscow throughout 1979, and Crown Prince Fahd predicted that ambassadors would be exchanged at some point.[44]

Such friendly statements, however, soon gave way to hostile ones when the USSR invaded Afghanistan at the end of December 1979 and Riyadh became one of the chief organizers of the Islamic summit conference that met in January 1980 to condemn this action.[45] The Soviets soon began to criticize the Kingdom, though there were some signs of hope that the movement to improve relations could be revived. Moscow did, however, strongly object to Saudi aid to Pakistan and the Afghan rebels.[46] The Soviets also blamed the United States for stirring up Saudi fears about the "Soviet threat" and claimed the U.S. was the real threat to the Saudis.[47]

From 1981 to the present, the USSR and Saudi Arabia have issued generally negative commentary about each other. Occasionally, the Saudis have commented favorably on Soviet aid to the Arabs against Israel. The Soviets were extremely happy when 'Abdallah (now the Crown Prince) deplored American policy toward the Arab-Israeli conflict while praising the Soviet stance on this issue.[48] There was another flurry of Soviet optimism over the possibility of improving relations at the end of 1982 when it was announced that the Saudi Foreign Minister would go to Moscow as part of a seven-nation Arab League delegation led by Jordan's King Hussein that wanted to visit the capitals of all five United Nations Security Council permanent members to seek a Middle East settlement.[49] Prince Sa'ud al-Faysal and the other members of the delegation met with Andropov, Tikhonov, and Gromyko December 3, and later the Prince and Gromyko had another meeting.[50] But soon after this visit the Saudi Information Minister ruled out any possibility of ties with Moscow.[51] In the first half of 1983, Soviet commentary about Saudi Arabia became very hostile indeed, with TASS accusing Riyadh of using torture against its internal opponents. What really seemed to annoy Moscow, however, was that the Saudis were using Afghanistan as an "excuse" for not establishing diplomatic relations with the USSR.[52]

The Saudis, however, appear serious in regarding Afghanistan as an obstacle to friendly relations with Moscow. At times, various Saudi leaders have again indicated that friendship with the USSR was possible.[53] But Saudi officials have made it clear that the USSR must meet four conditions before Riyadh will improve relations with Moscow: (1) Soviet forces must be withdrawn from Afghanistan; (2) the USSR and its allies must reduce their military presence in both South Yemen and Ethiopia; (3) the USSR must end all hostile propaganda against the Kingdom; and (4)

Soviet Moslems must be allowed greater freedom to practice their religion. The Saudis do not realistically expect the Soviets to meet these conditions and as a result do not foresee Saudi-Soviet relations improving any time soon.[54]

These four Saudi conditions, as well as the history of Soviet efforts to establish ties to Riyadh, show that the primary obstacle to friendly relations between the two nations is Soviet foreign policy in the region surrounding Saudi Arabia. While it wants good relations with Riyadh, Moscow has never regarded this goal as important enough to warrant not supporting governments or radical groups in neighboring countries opposed to Saudi interests.

THE USSR AND THE OPPONENTS OF THE SAUDI GOVERNMENT

The USSR has also hoped to see some form of political change that would bring a more "progressive" government to power in Riyadh, one that would be more friendly to the Soviets. There have indeed been many instances of opposition activity inside Saudi Arabia, ranging from distributing subversive literature to strikes, bombings, and coup attempts. Among the government's opponents have been oil workers, disaffected princes, members of the armed forces, radical groups, foreigners, the minority Shia population, and religious zealots such as those who seized the Grand Mosque at Mecca. The Saudi government has so far been able to hamper opposition activity both by imposing measures that restrict political action and by spreading the benefits of the country's oil wealth throughout the populace. Nevertheless, the government has not been able to stop it altogether. The Soviets have given several opposition groups favorable media coverage but little practical support.

Strikes by ARAMCO workers occurred in 1945, 1953, and 1956. These actions were ostensibly taken to rectify economic grievances, but in the later two political demands were put forward as well. The government sent soldiers to end the 1956 strike, and when it was over King Sa'ud issued a decree banning all strikes and work stoppages (though strikes have occurred since then). One of the leaders of the 1956 strike, Nasser Said, fled Saudi Arabia and set up an opposition group called the Union of Peoples of the Arabian Peninsula, about which more will be said later.[55] E. Primakov, a Soviet Orientalist, wrote in 1956 that these events showed it was the proletariat that was the "vanguard and leader of the Arabian peoples."[56] Almost a quarter-century later, another Soviet scholar noted that in addition to the banning of strikes and unions, wages and the general welfare of workers also improved to the point that these proletarians had become a "worker aristocracy" and that they had "temporarily lost their political activeness."[57] In other words, the Soviets do not expect a revolution to be started by workers who earn so much.

In 1962 Prince Talal had broken with King Sa'ud over the latter's refusal to permit a constitution or elected parliament. Talal, two of his brothers, and their associates went to Cairo in August 1962, where Nasser encouraged them to form the "Arab Liberation Front." The ALF, reflecting Talal's ideas, was a fairly moderate group, but in December 1962 it joined forces with the Marxist Saudi Arabian National Liberation Front (SANLF). Moscow saw this move as the beginning of a united front consisting of the Saudi proletariat, petty bourgeoisie, and "liberal feudals." Growing dissatisfied with Nasser, however, the errant princes were encouraged by Faysal's reform program, and after asking forgiveness they were allowed to come home the following year. The ALF collapsed, thereby dashing any Soviet expectations that disgruntled members of the royal family might effectively cooperate with more radical groups.[58]

Since then, the Soviets have observed that the Saudi royal family places great emphasis on maintaining its unity and do not seriously expect the family to allow any internal divisions to threaten its hold on power. Like many in the West, however, Soviet authors have attempted to identify factions in the royal family. One author saw Fahd and his six full brothers (all born of the same mother, Hassa bint Ahmad as-Sudairi) as resented by the other princes, especially Prince 'Abdallah, whose mother came from the Shammar tribe. He also saw the numerous sons of the ousted King Sa'ud as being banned from positions of responsibility and thus forming a "malcontents' group."[59]

The Saudi armed forces have also proved a disappointment to the Soviets; no Nasser has emerged from their ranks. After the North Yemeni revolution broke out in September 1962, several Saudi air force pilots defected to Egypt, and the entire air force was grounded while the government asked the United States to send planes to patrol Saudi skies.[60] Serious coup attempts occurred in June and September 1969, though few details are available.[61] There were also rumors of coup attempts by elements of the armed forces in 1970, 1977, 1980, and 1983, but it is doubtful that these are true.[62]

Since the armed forces have toppled many other Arab monarchs, the royal family has undoubtedly worried about this possibility, but in addition to the regular army, navy, and air force, Saudi Arabia possesses a separate National Guard. The National Guard is the descendant of the loyal *ikhwan* who did not revolt against King 'Abd al-'Aziz in the late 1920s and is drawn mainly from the tribes. While the mission of the regular armed forces is to protect the country against external attack, the National Guard's primary mission appears to be countering any possible internal opponents, including the regular armed forces.[63] While not impossible, a coup by the military is made more difficult by the existence of the National Guard, and tight internal security makes cooperation among potential coup plotters in the armed forces more difficult still.

There have also been a number of Saudi opposition groups since the 1950s. Those active in the 1950s were mainly reformist, such as the Labor Committee (which advocated trade unionism) and the Liberal Party and Reform Party (both of which called for a constitutional monarchy and a neutral foreign policy). Soviet writers were favorable to these groups but became more interested in the National Reform Front, which was founded in 1956 and then changed its name to the Saudi Arabian National Liberation Front in 1958. This group began by advocating political reform but became progressively more radical in its pronouncements, and by 1962 it was calling for the overthrow of the monarchy. The SANLF also cooperated with Prince Talal and his Arab Liberation Front until the latter made his peace with Faysal. In 1964 the SANLF united with other radicals in a Federation of Democratic Forces of the Arabian Peninsula.

After the outbreak of the Yemeni revolution, Nasser Said brought his pro-Nasser Union of Peoples of the Arabian Peninsula (UPAP) to North Yemen. From November 1966 to February 1967, this group carried out a series of bombings inside Saudi Arabia, but it was stopped by the authorities; in March 1967 seventeen UPAP members were publicly beheaded for the bombings and hundreds of Yemenis were deported. When the Egyptians withdrew from Yemen and the new YAR leadership that came to power in November 1967 made efforts to establish friendship with the Saudis, the UPAP was unable to remain in Yemen, and its reduced organization moved to Beirut.

Both the UPAP and the Federation of Democratic Forces of the Arabian Peninsula, as well as the Popular Democratic Party (founded by former Ba'thists and Nasserists and calling for a guerrilla war to overthrow the regime) were said to be involved in the two coup attempts of 1969.[64] Yet another organization, the Sons of the Arabian Peninsula, was described by one Israeli scholar as Marxist but by a Soviet scholar as part of the UPAP. The Sons were said to be active in 1970 but were reduced by a wave of arrests in 1971. They supposedly succeeded in recruiting members of the armed forces and were planning a coup when another series of arrests in 1972 ended their activity.[65]

Since the early 1970s these radical groups have apparently not been active inside Saudi Arabia and are kept alive only by Saudi émigrés in various Arab countries. One development that did take place was the transformation of the SANLF into the Saudi Arabian Communist Party (SACP) in 1975 at the Party's first congress. The Party's second congress was held in the summer of 1984, though exactly where was not announced. The General Secretary of the SACP Central Committee is Mahdi Habib; 'Abd al-Rahim Salih is also one of its leaders. SACP headquarters are rumored to be in either Lebanon or Cyprus. The organization is believed to have very few members.[66]

The Soviets have taken note of the activities of various opposition groups but have been careful not to claim that these groups operate with Soviet support. Their lack of success is attributed to the highly repressive Saudi internal security service, which the Soviets say is aided by the CIA and even Israeli Intelligence.[67] The Soviets have issued commentary about the SACP—apparently the most pro-Soviet opposition group—but have been reluctant to promote it.[68] An SACP member did attend the 26th CPSU Congress held at Moscow in 1981, but if he gave a speech the Soviets did not publish it as they did speeches of other nonruling communist party delegations.[69] For the most part, Soviet commentary on the SACP has not been on the Party's revolutionary activities but has merely cited it in support of Soviet policies and initiatives, such as the Brezhnev Persian Gulf peace proposals, or repeated its statements on the harsh internal conditions inside the Kingdom.[70] This low level of Soviet support to the SACP may well be due to Moscow's fear that any more would create yet another obstacle to normalized relations with Riyadh, though the Saudis are unhappy that Moscow gives the SACP even this small amount of publicity.

Along with Western observers, the Soviets have seen that there are a large number of guest workers (2 to 3 million by one estimate) in the Kingdom. These include Palestinians and Yemenis who some in the West fear might become a source of political unrest, but whom the Soviets see as "politically passive" since they are mainly interested in earning money "and are under the brutal control of the police and security authorities."[71]

Another source of unrest is the 6 to 10 percent of the Saudi population belonging to the Shia sect, concentrated in the Eastern Province where the oil fields are situated. The Shias have not shared equally in the benefit of the country's economic prosperity or obtained as good jobs as the majority Sunnis. In November 1979 and February 1980 there were disturbances in the Eastern Province that Saudi forces put down quickly. Both Western and Soviet observers viewed the Saudi Shias as being favorable to the revolutionary Shia government in Iran. Since these disturbances, however, the Saudi government has moved quickly to improve the economic condition of the people of the area. The Eastern Province has remained relatively peaceful since then. Though doubtful that this minority group in the population could organize itself into an opposition that would threaten the regime, the Shias remain, partly because of their proximity to the oil fields, a source of concern to Riyadh. There is a Saudi opposition group based in Tehran called the Islamic Revolutionary Organization of the Arabian Peninsula, but it has apparently had no more success inside the Kingdom than any other opposition movement. Although many see the Saudi Shias as pro-Iranian, it is not clear that they would be any less loyal to Riyadh than the Iraqi Shias are to Baghdad even when fighting Iran.[72]

The most dramatic act of rebellion against the Saudi monarchy was the seizure of the Grand Mosque at Mecca in November 1979 by a group of religious zealots. The Soviets portrayed the rebels as "gunmen" and "religious fanatics" as well as generally supported the Saudi government's efforts to defeat them, even though Soviet commentary was sympathetic to the Shias demonstrating in the Eastern Province at the same time.[73] The Saudis also denied that the Soviets had played any role in the seizure.[74] An important reason the Soviets may have supported Riyadh on this matter was that Moscow did not want to provoke hostility in the Islamic world by saying anything favorable about the rebels. As shown by the attacks made on the U.S. embassy in Pakistan and diplomatic installations in other countries by people believing rumors that the United States was behind the incident, the seizure was strongly opposed by Moslems in general. Two years later, though, Radio Moscow broadcast an SACP appeal on the second anniversary of the Mecca and Eastern Province "uprisings" calling for a united front of all Saudi opposition forces.[75] This changed tone undoubtedly reflected the chill in Saudi-Soviet relations following the Soviet invasion of Afghanistan.

Even when Saudi-Soviet relations have been friendlier than usual, the Soviets have favorably mentioned various of the monarchy's opponents.

However, even when Saudi-Soviet relations are hostile, the Soviets have not put much emphasis on the activities of the opposition; they do not seem to think it has had much chance of actually overthrowing the government. That the Soviets comment favorably on the Saudi opposition at all has hurt Moscow's chances for establishing diplomatic relations with Riyadh, since even on the occasions when the two governments seem friendly toward each other, a strong argument for those Saudis who oppose relations has been that the USSR would use an embassy and any other facilities in the country to aid and encourage the regime's opponents.

FOREIGN POLICY ISSUES

As we have seen, improvement in Saudi-Soviet relations has often been frustrated by differences over foreign policy issues. There are certain important foreign policy issues, however, on which Soviet and Saudi points of view appear to be similar. One of these is the Iran-Iraq war; neither Moscow nor Riyadh wants to see Iran defeat Iraq. Another is the Arab-Israeli conflict, in which both governments oppose Israel and support the Arab side. The extent to which Saudi and Soviet views are really similar on these issues, whether the degree of similarity that does exist has led to cooperation between them, and current Saudi and Soviet views on other issues will be examined here.

Iran-Iraq

As the Saudis have feared Soviet influence in Egypt and the Yemens, so have they feared Soviet influence in Iraq. Before the July 1958 revolution that ousted the Hashemite monarchy, this was not a major concern. Baghdad and Moscow had established diplomatic relations in 1944, but in 1954 Iraq broke them off, and in 1955 it joined the Western-oriented Baghdad Pact (which later became the Central Treaty Organization— CENTO) with Turkey, Iran, Pakistan, and the United Kingdom. When General Qasim took power in July 1958, though, he reestablished relations with Moscow, withdrew from the Baghdad Pact, and in 1959 expelled all British troops. The Soviets began providing military assistance to Qasim at this time. The Iraqi Communist Party grew in strength, but whenever the government cracked down on it, Moscow seemed to side with the government. During February–November 1963, the Ba'th Party held power and Moscow-Baghdad ties soured to the point where Soviet military assistance came to an end, but ties improved again while

General 'Arif and then his brother ruled, from November 1963 to July 1968. A coup then brought the Ba'th back to power under General al-Bakr, but this time the Soviets managed to get along so well with the Ba'th that on April 9, 1972, a Soviet-Iraqi treaty of friendship and cooperation was signed by Kosygin and al-Bakr. The Soviets then had some 1,000 military advisers in Iraq.

This development was considered threatening by both Saudi Arabia and Iran. After the great rise in oil prices that followed the October 1973 war, Iraq's revenues increased greatly, and Baghdad began to import goods and seek investment more from the West than the East. There was a substantial cooling in Soviet-Iraqi relations during the mid-1970s as Baghdad objected to Soviet support of Ethiopia against both Somalia and the Eritreans and the Iraqis diversified their arms supplies by buying weapons from Western Europe. Soon after July 1979, when Saddam Hussein, who had for several years been the "strongman" of Iraq, formally took power, Soviet-Iraqi relations improved somewhat as both nations vehemently opposed the American-sponsored Camp David accords. The Iraqis, however, were disturbed by the Soviet invasion of Afghanistan at the end of 1979. Baghdad also undertook a severe crackdown on the Iraqi Communist Party. When Iraq invaded Iran in September 1980, then, Soviet-Iraqi relations were not particularly close.[76]

Iran had traditionally had poor relations with Russia even long before the 1917 revolution, since much of Russian expansion into Central Asia in the nineteenth century took place at Iran's expense. In 1907, Britain and Russia agreed to divide Iran into a Russian sphere in the north and a British one in the south, leaving only a weakened independent government in the center. The new Soviet government renounced this agreement, but it soon became interested in Iran itself. In 1921 a Soviet-Iranian treaty was signed giving the Russians the right to send troops into Iran if forces threatening the USSR entered Iran's territory. The USSR and Britain again divided Iran in 1941 in order oust the pro-German Shah and provide a secure land route for the supply of Western arms to the Soviets. At the end of the war, the Soviets did not want to leave Iran, but under American pressure they did so in 1946, and two "autonomous" Marxist republics in Azerbaizhan and Kurdistan collapsed. Soviet support to the Tudeh (the Iranian communist party) continued, but after the 1953 U.S.-backed coup against the liberal Prime Minister Dr. Mossadegh, Iran became pro-Western. Iran joined the Baghdad Pact in 1955 and signed a security agreement with the United States in 1959; the Soviets objected to both actions. But when the Kennedy administration cut back on military aid to Iran the Shah decided to improve relations with Moscow, and Soviet-Iranian ties were good until 1972 when the Soviet-Iraqi treaty of friendship and cooperation was signed.

The Saudis had become worried about Iran's intentions, since the Shah had renewed a claim to Bahrain (which he later renounced), seized three islands in the Gulf from the UAE in 1971, and in 1973 sent troops to Oman. Like Moscow, Riyadh was not happy with the strong U.S.-Iranian military relationship that lasted from 1972 until the fall of the Shah in 1979. Both countries, however, worked to maintain good relations with Iran. The Islamic revolution that brought Ayatollah Khomeini to power was initially welcomed by Moscow because it ended Iranian-American military cooperation. But by 1980 it was evident that the Tehran government was not pro-Soviet, since the ayatollahs had condemned the USSR as the other "great satan" and opposed the Soviet invasion of Afghanistan. Moscow, however, hoped that its relations with Iran might improve on the basis of a common anti-American foreign policy and that more pro-Soviet elements such as the Tudeh might come to power.[77]

Iraq invaded Iran on September 22, 1980, in order to regain complete control of the Shatt al-Arab waterway (which Iraq had agreed to share in 1975 in return for the Shah's ending support to Kurdish rebels), seize territory such as Khuzestan, which had an ethnic Arab majority, and overthrow the government of Ayatollah Khomeini. The official Soviet position on the war was then and continues to be one of neutrality, urging both sides to end the conflict peacefully. At the beginning of the war, though, Moscow took measures that helped Iran and not Iraq. By late 1980 or early 1981, the USSR had ceased direct arms shipments to Iraq and had reportedly begun limited military assistance to Iran. Moscow's October 1980 signing of a treaty of friendship and cooperation with Iraq's archrival Syria, which openly favored Iran in the war, was considered an unfriendly act by the Iraqis.[78] This contrasted with Saudi Arabia, which joined all the other Arab countries (Syria, Libya, and to a lesser extent South Yemen being exceptions) in supporting Iraq.

Iraqi forces did well initially, but they soon became bogged down in Iran, and by 1982 the Iranians had pushed the Iraqis out of Iran and crossed into Iraq themselves. While still officially neutral, Soviet policy shifted to supporting Iraq. The Soviets had by this time realized that revolutionary Iran was as anti-Soviet as it was anti-American and that there was little opportunity for Soviet-Iranian cooperation. The suppression of the Tudeh in early 1983 also showed Moscow that pro-Soviet forces are not likely to come to power in Tehran. Although Iraq was suing for peace, Khomeini insisted that the war would end only when Saddam Hussein was ousted, Iraq agreed to pay reparations, and Baghdad admitted its guilt in starting the war. Iraq has indicated a willingness to provide some form of reparations (which it hopes the GCC would help provide), and Baghdad has agreed to an international tribunal to judge the question of responsibility for the war, but Saddam Hussein is not willing to relinquish power.[79] Continued Iranian prosecution of the war has led to the fear that Khomeini intends to install an Islamic government like his own in Baghdad and that after defeating Iraq he intends to spread his brand of Shia Islamic revolution by force to the Arab countries of the Gulf as well.

It is this fear of what Khomeini might do after defeating Iraq that obviously motivates Saudi Arabia to support Baghdad even though the Saudis have in the past been wary of Iraqi intentions toward the Peninsula. Saudi Arabia, Kuwait, and the other GCC states all have much smaller armies than Iraq has; they would be even less able than Iraq to defend themselves against Iran, and so they have been giving generous financial support to Baghdad to prevent this from happening. The Soviets have no desire to see Iran either overcome Iraq or establish a pro-Khomeini government in Baghdad, since this means that Moscow would probably lose a friend. Indeed, since the Tehran government has become hostile to the USSR, it is reasonable to conclude that whatever countries come under Iran's influence will also become hostile toward the USSR. Moscow might also fear that once having defeated Iraq, Tehran might turn its attention to spreading Islamic revolution to Afghanistan. In addition, the Soviets might fear both the appeal of Islamic revolution to the Moslem population of the USSR and the possibility of Iran's assisting Moslem rebels in Soviet Central Asia. While it is extremely doubtful that a revolt by Soviet Moslems could threaten to destroy the regime or even detach a part of the USSR from Moscow's rule, putting down such an attempt or governing an increasingly hostile populace is not a prospect the Soviet leadership would want to face.

Both Moscow and Riyadh, then, have a common interest in seeing that Iran does not defeat Iraq. Some observers have claimed that this common interest has led to Saudi-Soviet cooperation in supplying arms to Iraq even before 1982 when Moscow appeared to be tilting toward Iran. According to William Quandt, "early in 1981 the Saudis allowed Iraq to take delivery of 100 East European tanks at Saudi Red Sea ports. This soon became a regular practice, with East European and Soviet ships calling at the small port of Qadima north of Jidda to unload shipments of arms for Iraq."[80] Aryeh Yodfat claimed that Soviet aircraft landed at Saudi airfields with arms for transshipment for Iraq.[81] Such claims were denied by Saudi government officials.[82] Given Saudi sensitivity over any kind of Soviet presence and the fact that Soviet arms were openly delivered to the Jordanian Red Sea port of Aqaba for transfer to Iraq, these accounts are remarkable.[83] Yet even if the Saudis did allow the Soviets to directly deliver weapons or if Arab suppliers acting as intermediaries brought Soviet weapons into the Kingdom for retransfer to Iraq, Saudi-Soviet cooperation to save Iraq would seem to have certain natural limits, since their interests regarding Iraq are not the same.

Saudi Arabia would like to see Iraq throw out the Iranians but would not like to see Iraq become strongly allied to the USSR or allow in a Soviet military presence in order to do it. Similarly, Moscow would not like to see Iraq become closely linked with either the West or the conservative Arab states at the expense of its ties to the USSR. In the extreme case, Saudi Arabia would regard its own security as seriously threatened if the Soviets intervened militarily to save Iraq, and the USSR would be extremely unhappy to see Western military intervention for the same purpose. Thus, while neither Moscow nor Riyadh wishes to see Iraq defeated by Iran, the Soviets would like to retain or preferably increase their influence in Baghdad whereas the Saudis would like Soviet influence there to decline or end. Saudi and Soviet interests with regard to Iraq are basically competitive, not cooperative.

The Middle East

The USSR and Saudi Arabia have supported Iraq in its war with Iran for a relatively short time, but they have been arrayed on the same side of the Arab-Israeli conflict for a relatively long time. Moscow and Riyadh both supported the Arab side and opposed the Israelis during the 1956, 1967, and 1973 Middle East wars and during the 1982 Israeli invasion of Lebanon. Both have called for Israel to withdraw from all Arab territory occupied since June 1967 and for the creation of a Palestinian state on the West Bank and Gaza Strip. Both have had good relations with the Palestine Liberation Organization led by Yasir Arafat, though the Soviets have also supported more radical Palestinian groups such as the Popular Front for the Liberation of Palestine (PFLP) and the Popular Democratic Front for the Liberation of Palestine (PDFLP). In addition, both countries have strongly criticized the United States for supporting Israel.[84] As was mentioned before, several top Saudi leaders have made statements expressing appreciation for Moscow's position on the Arab-Israeli conflict. The Soviets have also frequently noted the closeness of Soviet and Saudi views on the Middle East and their common differences with the United States; Moscow has tried to convince Riyadh that Saudi-Soviet cooperation would greatly enhance the Arab cause.

For the most part, however, the Saudis have viewed Soviet foreign policy toward the Middle East as designed not to bring about a solution favorable to the Arabs but to enhance the influence of the USSR over the Arabs instead. King Faysal was particularly critical of the USSR; in his view, although Moscow said it helped the Arabs, it was Soviet military assistance to the Jews that allowed Israel to survive in 1948. He also blamed the USSR for the Arab defeat in June 1967; he accused the Soviets of falsely informing Nasser that the Israelis would not attack. Faysal claimed that if the Arabs had consulted the Soviets before starting the October 1973 war, the Soviets would again have colluded with the Israelis. He saw communism and Zionism as being united in a conspiracy against the Arabs and viewed the USSR and Israel as close allies no matter what they said publicly.[85] The Saudis criticized U.S. arms sales to Israel but accused the Soviets of providing Israel with soldiers by allowing large-scale emigration of Soviet Jews in the 1970s.[86]

Since the death of Faysal, the Saudi leadership has put less emphasis on the "communist-Zionist conspiracy" (though this notion does continue to appear), but it emphasizes that Israeli and Soviet foreign policies have a similar goal to keep the Arab states weak.[87] Israel wants to do this so that the Arabs cannot challenge it, and the Soviets want to increase their influence in Arab countries. Saudi leaders have frequently warned that continued U.S. aid to Israel only enhances Soviet penetration of the Arab world.[88] They also blamed insufficient Soviet support to Syria for that country's poor military performance during the Israeli invasion of Lebanon in the summer of 1982.[89]

The Soviets, for their part, have bitterly criticized the Saudis for equating Zionism with communism. They point to their support for the Arab cause as justifying Arab, including Saudi, appreciation of Soviet efforts. They used to fear that King Faysal's extremely negative view of the USSR would spread to other Arab countries.[90] Moscow has also regularly pointed to Saudi-U.S. military cooperation and the lack of Saudi support for the more radical Arab position as evidence of Saudi collusion with Israel.[91]

The Saudis have, however, made an effort to gain Soviet support for the moderate Arab position on a Middle East peace settlement. When the Saudis proposed the "Fahd Plan" in the summer of 1981 (which indirectly recognized Israel's right to exist by confirming the right of the states of the region to live in peace), the Soviets adopted an ambivalent stand on it. They said the Fahd Plan was similar to Soviet Middle East peace proposals, but they soon complained that it did not include a means for all sides to participate or call for a broad international conference—in other words, it did not provide any role for the Soviet Union as cochairman with the United States of a Geneva conference to settle the Middle East question, as Soviet proposals had called for. Moscow instead supported a proposal by the Steadfastness Front (Syria, Libya, Algeria, South Yemen, and the PLO) that did not recognize Israel's right to exist but advocated a more militant approach.[92] The Saudis, however, called on Moscow's Arab friends to persuade the Soviets to be more favorable to the Fahd Plan, and the Soviets welcomed Riyadh's call for a United Nations conference on the Middle East in November 1981, to include the USSR.[93] Although Riyadh failed to get the Fahd proposal accepted by the Arab summit conference at Fez in November 1981, owing to the objections of the Steadfastness Front states, a modified version was accepted by all (except Libya) at Fez the following September. The modified proposal called for the United Nations Security Council to provide guarantees for peace between "all states of the region" including an independent Palestinian state. After Syria's poor performance against Israel during the summer of 1982, the militant approach seemed unworkable. The Soviets responded favorably to the modified Fahd proposal, since calling for UN Security Council guarantees would make approval by the USSR necessary.[94]

The Saudi view has been and continues to be that the United States is more important than the USSR in bringing peace to the Middle East, since the U.S. has influence with Israel while the USSR does not.[95] But the Saudis have also reached the conclusion that it is necessary to have some degree of Soviet support for any Middle East peace plan to work, since Moscow might be able to influence the radical Arab states to accept it as well.[96] The Soviets, naturally, welcome the efforts of a conservative Arab state closely allied to the United States to bring the USSR into the Middle

East peace process when American foreign policy has sought to exclude Moscow from it.

As with the Iran-Iraq war, however, a similarity in Soviet and Saudi positions toward the Arab-Israeli conflict does not change the fact that the two governments' policies in this area are basically competitive, not cooperative. The Soviets have attempted to use the Middle East issue to extend and maintain their influence in the region. They have not always been successful at this, as their expulsion from Egypt showed, but currently they are influential in Syria. The Saudis, by contrast, seek a solution to the Arab-Israeli conflict, or at a minimum want to reduce U.S. aid to Israel, in order to eliminate Soviet influence in the Middle East. Indeed, the Saudis believe that if the Arab-Israeli conflict were resolved, or perhaps even if the United States stopped supporting Israel, Arab states would have little reason to ally with the USSR. Thus the Saudis feel that the USSR does not necessarily want to see the Middle East conflict resolved peacefully but would prefer it to simmer indefinitely so that at least one of the "confrontation states" will seek military assistance from it.[97]

Other Issues

In addition to their both opposing Israel, the USSR and Saudi Arabia are not friends with the People's Republic of China either. Yet Riyadh's refusal to establish diplomatic ties with Peking is of little comfort to Moscow, since the Saudis have not established relations with any other communist state either.

Yet even if the USSR and Saudi Arabia are not likely to become friends, the Soviets would be happy if Riyadh moved away from its close ties to the United States. To this end, Soviet commentary has emphasized that Saudi-U.S. military cooperation has allowed the United States to take advantage of Riyadh and to help Tel Aviv. When Israel bombed the Iraqi nuclear reactor in June 1981, the Soviets claimed that the American-flown AWACS based in Saudi Arabia did nothing to stop the Israelis from flying over Saudi territory to get to and from Iraq.[98] Soviet commentators have even claimed that the United States would take advantage of the Iran-Iraq war to move its forces into the region and then invade Saudi Arabia.[99]

Soviet commentary about Saudi Arabia often appears inconsistent. When the United States announces an arms sale to Riyadh, this is viewed as proof that Saudi Arabia is serving the interests of "American imperialism." Yet if the arms sale is canceled owing to the pressure of pro-Israeli

151

sentiment in Congress, U.S. policy is portrayed as anti-Saudi, and the Soviets appear to be almost as incensed as the Saudis that Washington will not sell all the arms Riyadh wants.

At other times Moscow has seemed convinced that there is no possibility of detaching Riyadh from Washington, and so it has tried to isolate Saudi Arabia from other Arab countries, including its smaller GCC neighbors. Although the Soviets backed Riyadh in its border claims against the British-protected coastal states in the 1950s and 1960s, after they all became independent the Soviets changed to supporting the latter's claims (particularly those of the UAE) and emphasizing the Saudi threat to them.[100] In both these efforts, however, Moscow has failed: Saudi Arabia remains closely linked to the United States and has increased its cooperation with the conservative Arab Gulf states by peacefully settling border issues and through the formation of the GCC.

Other issues over which Soviet and Saudi foreign policies have clashed in the past continue to divide them. After the North Yemeni civil war ended, the victorious republicans whom Moscow had supported would become reconciled to Riyadh and have little to do with Moscow. In late 1979 the USSR was able to renew its influence in Sanaa by providing arms to North Yemen after Saudi Arabia stopped delivering American weapons it had purchased on the YAR's behalf when the brief inter-Yemeni border war came to an end. The Soviets have continued to provide North Yemen with a relatively greater amount of military assistance and a smaller amount of economic assistance, while the Saudis have provided much economic but little military aid. The Saudis recognize that the YAR is trying to obtain as much as it can from both Riyadh and Moscow, but they do not think that North Yemen will become Marxist, especially since the YAR government defeated the NDF guerrillas in mid-1982. With regard to South Yemen, the Saudis are happy that 'Ali Nasir Muhammad has worked to establish friendly relations with Riyadh, Sanaa, and Muscat instead of attacking them, but they do not expect him to break away from Moscow. Riyadh continues to be concerned about the Soviet military presence in Aden. The Saudis also oppose Soviet-backed Ethiopia's attempt to conquer the Moslem insurgents in Eritrea. In 1982 the Saudis hosted a meeting at Jidda of the three main Eritrean guerrilla organizations, at which they agreed to cooperate; Eritrean leaders continue to thank the Saudis for their support.[101] Riyadh has continued to express support for and give aid to the Afghan guerrillas the Soviets are trying to conquer. The Saudis also opposed Brezhnev's Persian Gulf peace proposals made in December 1980, which called for outside powers not to establish military bases in the area and not to use or threaten to use force against any country of the region; the Saudis would apparently like to retain the option of having an American presence in the area if necessary.[102] In short, the Saudis have not dropped their opposition to Soviet foreign policy in these areas in order to seek cooperation with Moscow in others such as the Arab-Israeli conflict and the Iran-Iraq war.

OIL

As with the Arab-Israeli issue, the Soviets have for long attempted to use the oil issue to either separate Saudi Arabia from the United States or, barring this, to separate Saudi Arabia from the rest of the Arab nations. In the mid-1950s Soviet writers described Saudi Arabia as being completely controlled by ARAMCO, but in the late 1950s they began to see that the interests of the government and the oil companies often diverged. Throughout the 1960s, the Soviets condemned ARAMCO for making huge profits at the expense of the Saudi people and government. King Faysal was viewed as afraid to attempt to nationalize ARAMCO for fear of how "imperialism" would react.[103] The Soviets applauded the Saudis when in the 1970s they began to take an increasing stake in ARAMCO.[104] Moscow appears to have anticipated that nationalizing the oil company would involve tension between Saudi Arabia and the West, as when Iraq and Iran nationalized the oil companies in their countries; much to its regret, the oil companies involved have for the most part cooperated in ARAMCO's takeover and thus retained much of their role in Saudi Arabia.

The Soviets have frequently urged the Saudis to use the "oil weapon" against the United States because of Washington's support for Israel. Before the October 1973 war, Moscow saw Riyadh's failure to do so as proof that the Saudis were in league with "imperialism and Zionism."[105] When the Kingdom did join the Arab oil embargo against the United States and Holland during the war, the Soviets were very pleased. They urged the Saudis in particular to continue the embargo and to intensify it by withdrawing all their funds from Western banks.[106] Moscow has continued since then to urge Riyadh to "wield the oil weapon" and condemned it for not doing so.[107]

Since the 1973 oil price rise the Soviets have also heavily criticized the Saudis for working to keep petroleum prices lower than some (and on certain occasions all) of the other OPEC nations have wanted. For example, the Soviets complained bitterly when the Saudis wanted to lower the price of oil by forty cents a barrel in November 1974, to not raise it at all and later raise it by only 5 percent when most others wanted to raise it 15 percent in 1976–77, and to lower the price from $38 to $32 per barrel in 1981 when the others wanted to lower it only to $35.[108] In denouncing Riyadh over trying to keep the price of oil low, Moscow not only was attempting to drive a wedge between the Saudis and the other OPEC countries, but was also defending its own economic interests. The price of oil that the USSR exports to the West has closely followed OPEC prices.[109] Obviously, Moscow prefers to sell its oil for more rather than less.

Perhaps to a greater extent than with the Arab-Israeli issue, Moscow has failed in its efforts to divide the Saudis from the Americans or to isolate Riyadh from the other Arab countries through the oil issue. As is shown by Saudi Arabia's efforts to keep the price of oil lower than other OPEC states, the Saudis see it as in their interest to not endanger the economies of the United States and the West, since this would harm Saudi investments abroad as well as reduce the capacity of the West to purchase Saudi oil. In addition, the other OPEC states have no interest in seeing their relations with Saudi Arabia deteriorate, since the Saudi capacity to increase production and lower prices unilaterally could hurt them, while Saudi ability to also keep production low is of great importance to them if oil prices are to be kept relatively high.

CONCLUSION

Soviet foreign policy toward Saudi Arabia so far can only be judged a failure. Moscow's attempts to be friendly with Riyadh have not even resulted in diplomatic relations since Stalin withdrew his mission to Jidda in 1938. Nor have the Soviets been able to bring about a shift in Saudi foreign policy from close relations with the United States to neutrality between the superpowers; Moscow has been unable to exploit potential differences between Washington and Riyadh over foreign policy issues such as the Middle East and oil. Nor have the Soviets succeeded in promoting revolution or a coup that would bring to power a government more friendly to the USSR, since Saudi opposition groups have proved extremely weak. The Soviets can only hope that somehow either the government's view of the USSR or the prospects for the regime's opponents will change and thus provide them with an opportunity to gain some measure of influence in the country.

How might this occur? One change that would benefit the Soviets would be a new king, with different foreign policy views than his predecessors, who would want to have ties with Moscow. That the Soviets have warmly greeted every new Saudi king and promoted an improvement in Saudi-Soviet relations indicates that they have hoped for this. Though disappointed in the past, they could succeed in the future. Crown Prince 'Abdallah's positive statements about the USSR may be a sign that as king he would permit better Saudi-Soviet relations. However, Fahd made similar statements as crown prince (and even as king), but relations have not improved. In addition, a new king and probably the senior members of the royal family would have to be willing to overlook all the many foreign policy differences that have hitherto divided Moscow and Riyadh, including Afghanistan, South Yemen, and the Horn of Africa.

Another change that the Soviets hope for is a coup or revolution overthrowing the monarchy. Moscow can be expected to immediately recognize and offer support to any new Saudi government, just as it did with the Yemeni republicans even though the USSR enjoyed good relations with the Imamate. The Soviets would prefer a Marxist government to come to power but would welcome any government, particularly if it were anti-American and willing to become friends with the USSR. The Soviets could also be expected to give the rebels political and propaganda support if an insurrection broke out. Moscow would probably not attempt to become militarily involved itself or even offer direct military assistance until the insurgents actually came to power, though some military aid might go to the guerrillas before this via South Yemen, Ethiopia, and Cuba.

The weakness of the opposition and the strength of the central government in Saudi Arabia, however, make either a coup or a revolution seem unlikely in the near future. As long as revenues from oil exports allow the government to provide the populace with a high standard of living, discontent over economic issues is not likely to spark opposition to the government. Since known Saudi oil reserves are estimated to last until 2050 at current rates of production, economic decline and the political disruption this might cause do not seem imminent.[110] If there ever were a serious dispute within the royal family, such as a struggle over the succession, that gravely weakened the central government, others including the armed forces might be in a better position to seize power (perhaps with the

155

aid of the quarreling factions within the royal family). Yet despite rumors of disagreements among its members, the royal family appears determined to preserve its unity in order to preserve its rule; it knows that an outright succession struggle could lead to the loss of the throne.

Yet even without economic decline or a dispute within the royal family, some have tried and will undoubtedly try again to change the Saudi government by force. Political power and decision making involve only a relatively small group of senior princes. Despite occasional announcements that a written constitution and other steps toward political democratization are being studied, not even a consultative assembly with only advisory powers, as in Oman, has been established. Many Saudis, especially the Western-educated, nonroyal ones, would like to see some sort of political reform or change that would allow wider participation in political decision making.[111] Whether the present or future Saudi leadership would ever be responsive to such demands is difficult to say. What does seem clear, however, is that so long as economic prosperity, unity within the royal family, and tight internal security continue, the government will be in a strong position to stop any attempt to overthrow it.

What this means for the USSR is that while it would like to either improve relations with the present Saudi government or promote revolution in the Kingdom, it must wait for some kind of change to take place within Saudi Arabia for either of these two policies to succeed. If the past is a guide to the future, however, such a change will not arise soon.

Kuwait, the United Arab Emirates, Bahrain, and Qatar

Kuwait

The Soviet-Kuwaiti relationship is unique in that Kuwait is the only monarchical government on the Peninsula to have diplomatic ties with the USSR. The Soviet-Kuwaiti relationship, moreover, has gone beyond the exchange of ambassadors in its warmth and friendliness. Kuwait has purchased Soviet weapons for its armed forces, Soviet and Kuwaiti officials frequently travel to each other's countries and make joint statements in which both criticize the United States on many foreign policy issues, and the Kuwaitis have endorsed Soviet peace proposals for the Arab-Israeli conflict and the Persian Gulf. Moscow and Kuwait do not agree on everything, particularly on the Soviet invasion of Afghanistan, but unlike the other GCC countries that have cited Soviet foreign policy actions as a reason not to cooperate with the Kremlin, the Kuwaitis have downplayed their differences with the Soviets in the interests of continued good relations.

The Soviets value their ties with Kuwait because they can point to them as a successful example of peaceful coexistence between states with different social systems and attempt to persuade the other GCC states, especially Saudi Arabia, that Soviet relations with them would be equally cooperative. In addition, as shown by the Soviet media's rebroadcast of Kuwaiti government and newspaper statements, the Soviets are extremely pleased that an Arab monarchy criticizes the United States and praises the USSR. The Soviets undoubtedly feel that pro-Soviet statements emanating from Kuwait have greater propaganda value than similar ones from Moscow's Marxist allies in the Third World, since Kuwait is under no obligation to make them at all.

The Kuwaitis have worked for good relations with the USSR in the hope that the Soviets would not support opposition groups inside Kuwait as Moscow has done elsewhere in the Peninsula. In addition, the Kuwaitis have calculated that good Soviet-Kuwaiti relations would lead Moscow to discourage its friend Iraq from again acting on its claims to Kuwaiti territory. In other words, by being such a good friend to the USSR, the Kuwaiti government has sought to provide Moscow with an incentive for not assisting its external or internal opponents. And indeed, of the security threats that Kuwait now faces, none of the serious ones come from Marxists or are supported by the USSR.

At present Soviet-Kuwaiti relations appear to be quite harmonious. They were not always this good, however. For example, shortly after Kuwait's independence, the USSR vetoed Kuwait's application for membership in the United Nations. In addition, there was a period from the mid-1960s to the mid-1970s when the USSR and Kuwait had diplomatic ties but were not nearly as close as they became later. Here we will explore the reasons the Soviet-Kuwaiti relationship developed to its current friendly condition, unlike Soviet relations with the other GCC states, as well as the limits to the friendship.

HISTORICAL BACKGROUND

The history of modern Kuwait began in the early eighteenth century when tribesmen from inner Arabia migrated to the Gulf coast. The Al Sabah dynasty was founded in 1756 and has continued to rule up to the present. The town of Kuwait thrived on fishing, trading, and pearling. Throughout the eighteenth and nineteenth centuries, however, Kuwait's security was chronically in jeopardy from the Turks, the Persians, and the Saudis, all of whom wanted to control the area. Though the Kuwaiti shaykhs nominally recognized Ottoman suzerainty, they turned to the British to protect them from their neighbors. The British East India Company established a presence in Kuwait in the late eighteenth century, and in 1899 the British signed a treaty with Shaykh Mubarak whereby the British agreed to protect Kuwait in return for the Shaykh's promise not to cede territory to any power except the United Kingdom and not to have relations with any foreign government without British consent. This provided the Shaykh with an ally against any new Turkish assault and allowed the British to stop Germany and Russia from gaining Kuwait as an end point for planned railroad lines to the Persian Gulf. The Turks did not recognize the agreement at first, but in 1913 they signed an accord with the United Kingdom acknowledging Kuwait's autonomy, though this was never ratified owing to the outbreak of World War I. But Anglo-Kuwaiti relations were not always good. When Shaykh Salim supported the Turks in the war, the British imposed a blockade on Kuwait.[1]

In 1934 the Anglo-Persian Oil Company and the Gulf Oil Company were granted an oil concession and formed the Kuwait Oil Company. Production did not begin in earnest until after World War II, but since then it has been Kuwait's main source of income and has allowed the government to establish an extremely generous social welfare system for Kuwaiti citizens.[2]

In June 1961 the United Kingdom and Kuwait abrogated the 1899 agreement, Kuwait became formally independent, and the ruling shaykh assumed the title of Amir (prince). A new Anglo-Kuwaiti agreement was signed at this time whereby Britain would assist Kuwait if asked. Kuwait almost immediately invoked this new treaty when the Iraqi leader General Qasim seized the occasion of Britain's departure to claim all Kuwait as belonging to Iraq on the basis that it was administered by the Turks from Basra and the Ottomans never ratified the 1913 agreement acknowledging Kuwaiti autonomy (even though Iraq had recognized its border with Kuwait in 1932).[3] Citing alleged Iraqi troop movements toward the border, Kuwait requested a force of British soldiers, which began arriving in July and grew to 6,000. The Arab League, despite Iraqi objections, admitted Kuwait into its ranks and decided to support it against Baghdad. An Arab League force consisting of units from the UAR, Saudi Arabia, Jordan, and Sudan arrived in September to replace the British, who completely withdrew the following month. No fighting occurred, but the Arab League force (except for the UAR units, which left in December 1961) remained until February 1963 when Qasim was finally overthrown. In October 1963 the Iraqi government recognized Kuwait's independence.[4]

In May 1968, shortly after Britain announced that it would withdraw its forces from east of Suez by the end of 1971, Britain and Kuwait stated that their 1961 agreement would come to an end in three years (the 1961 agreement called for three years' advance notice for the termination of the treaty). At this point the new Ba'th government in Baghdad became increasingly threatening regarding the border issue. The approaches to the Iraqi port of Umm Qasr lay within Kuwaiti waters, and so Iraq claimed the Kuwaiti islands of Warbah and Bubiyan in order to rectify this as well as expand its extremely narrow coastline on the Persian Gulf. On March 20, 1973, after Kuwait rejected a draft treaty from Iraq by which Kuwait would have had to grant Baghdad the use of its territory, Iraqi forces attacked a Kuwaiti border post and reportedly landed on the two islands in question. Saudi Arabia moved troops to the Kuwaiti border as a gesture of support, but the Arab League merely called on both sides to resolve their dispute peacefully and did not act forcefully to protect Kuwait as it had in 1961. Iraqi forces withdrew from Kuwait in the first week of April, after Kuwait reportedly paid Baghdad a large sum of money. A formal border agreement was announced in June 1975, but its details were not released.[5] Some sources claim that the Iraqis did indeed obtain the use of Warbah and Bubiyan islands, though not ownership of them, but information on this point is sketchy.[6]

Other border incidents have occurred, but Kuwait's relations with Iraq have improved since the mid-1970s, especially after the outbreak of the Iran-Iraq war when Iraq came to rely heavily on Kuwait for financial support as well as for allowing goods to transit Kuwait overland to Iraq after the Iranians blocked Iraq's ports. Kuwaiti assistance to Baghdad has angered Tehran. The Iranian air attacks on targets in Kuwait in November 1980, June 1981, and October 1981 may have been intended as a warning not to aid Baghdad too much.[7] Kuwait also suffered a drop in oil exports following the stepped-up attacks on oil tankers by both Iran and Iraq in the spring of 1984, but it was still able to export most of its oil.[8]

Kuwait has had close relations with Saudi Arabia since independence, and their common border has not been a major problem, though some disagreements have been reported. In July 1975 they agreed to divide the administration of the Neutral Zone between them while continuing to share its oil revenues.[9] Kuwait is also a member of the GCC. Saudi Arabia revealed in November 1980 that a defense agreement exists between the two countries.[10] Kuwait, however, has refused to sign a bilateral internal security agreement with Riyadh (as all the other GCC states did following the attempted coup in Bahrain in 1981) or an overall GCC internal security accord, citing the incompatibility of such an agreement with Kuwait's laws.[11] Despite its small size, Kuwait has endeavored to assert its independence from its three powerful neighbors as well as the major powers.

In December 1961, for the first time Kuwaitis elected a twenty-member Constituent Assembly that drafted a constitution. Elections for a fifty-member National Assembly were held in January of 1963, 1967, 1971, and 1975. Kuwait, however, did not become a parliamentary democracy in the Western sense, since the Amir and not the Assembly has always chosen the prime minister (so far, this has always been the crown prince, though the man might not assume both offices at the same time). In addition, though elections were permitted, political parties were not. Nevertheless, a leftist opposition did exist that elected several members to the Assembly. They were led by Dr. Ahmad al-Khatib, who was also the head of the Arab Nationalist Movement branch in Kuwait. It was mainly this group's criticism and actions, which delayed legislation, that led the Amir on August 29, 1976, to dissolve the Assembly, suspend parts of the constitution, and limit the freedom of the press (Kuwait, like Lebanon, has been one of the few Arab countries to have a relatively independent press).[12] Elections were held for a new National Assembly in February 1981. No leftists won seats this time—partly owing to a redrawing of electoral boundaries—but five Sunni Moslem fundamentalists did, along with four members of the Shia community (down from ten in the previous Assembly). In the February 1985 elections, the fundamentalists were reduced to two seats while the left gained five seats (including one for Dr. Ahmad al-Khatib). Supporters of the government, though, still form the majority.[13] Despite the fact that the Assembly has come back into existence, the ability of the Amir to dismiss it and postpone elections as long as he pleases as well as to appoint a prime minister and cabinet without reference to the Assembly indicates that the Kuwaiti legislature is a relatively weak force compared with the Amir.

As in Saudi Arabia, succession to the throne is not automatic but is determined by the decision of the ruling family. A pattern has developed in Kuwait in which succession has alternated between two branches of the family, the al-Jabir and the al-Salim. Shaykh Mubarak, who ruled from 1896 until 1915, was succeeded first by his eldest son, Jabir (1915–17), and then by Mubarak's next son, Salim (1917–21). Jabir's son Ahmad then succeeded (1921–50) followed by Salim's son 'Abdallah (1950–65). The pattern was broken at this point when the throne passed not to an al-Jabir but to a younger son of Salim, Sabah (1965–77). When Sabah died on December 31, 1977, he was succeeded by one of Jabir's grandsons, Jabir al-Ahmad al-Jabir Al Sabah, who is the current Amir. Amir Jabir, in turn, appointed one of Salim's grandsons, Saad al-'Abdallah al-Salim Al Sabah, as crown prince and prime minister. Since independence, the ruling family has always chosen the designated crown prince to become the new amir when the old one died, and the new amir has moved quickly to consult with the family and appoint a new crown prince.[14]

161

SOVIET-KUWAITI RELATIONS

The USSR was not friendly toward Kuwait at first; before independence, Soviet writers portrayed the shaykh as being completely dependent
on the oil companies and the British, though one writer did note with
favor his refusal to join in a British-sponsored Persian Gulf federation. At
the time of Kuwait's independence, no Soviet congratulations were forthcoming, and the Soviets portrayed the country as still under British control.[15] When the USSR's ally General Qasim of Iraq laid claim to Kuwait,
Moscow remained neutral. This was not out of any love for Kuwait but
because another Moscow ally, Nasser of Egypt, vigorously opposed Iraq's
claim. When U.K. forces arrived, however, the Soviets strongly
denounced "British imperialism" and generally criticized Kuwait. In
November 1961 the USSR vetoed Kuwait's application for membership in
the United Nations because, even though British troops had completely
departed the previous month, the Soviets contended that the June 1961
Anglo-Kuwaiti accord meant that "Kuwait essentially remains a British
colony."[16]

Over the next year, the Soviet attitude toward Kuwait softened somewhat. When General Qasim was overthrown by the Ba'th Party in February 1963, the Soviets immediately repudiated his claim to Kuwait. The
Amir took advantage of the USSR's rapidly deteriorating relations with
the Ba'th government to propose the establishment of diplomatic relations, to which Moscow quickly agreed; ambassadors were exchanged in
June. In May 1963, Kuwait finally gained admission to the United
Nations with the enthusiastic support of the Soviet Union.[17]

The Soviet attitude toward Kuwait once again grew cool when in
November 1963 the Ba'th was ousted and a new, pro-Soviet government
came to power in Baghdad. In May 1964, during his visit to Cairo,
Khrushchev gratuitously denounced Kuwait in a speech disparaging the
notion of Arab unity: "There is such a state as Kuwait . . . There is some
little ruler sitting there, an Arab of course, a Moslem. He is given bribes.
He lives the life of the rich, but he is trading in the riches of his people.
He never had any conscience and he won't ever have any. Will you come
to terms with him on unification? It is easier to eat three puds of salt than
to reach agreement with him, although you are both Arabs and Moslems."[18] The Kuwaiti government was highly offended by this and threatened to break off diplomatic relations, though it did not.[19]

After Khrushchev's ouster in October 1964, the new Soviet leadership adopted a more cordial attitude toward Kuwait. The Kuwaiti Deputy Prime Minister and Finance Minister (now the Amir) visited Moscow in November 1964, and a Soviet economic delegation went to Kuwait the following February to sign a technical assistance agreement. A cultural exchange agreement was signed in March 1967, and the Kuwaitis bought a number of cargo ships from the USSR. The Soviets were especially pleased by the May 1968 announcement that the 1961 Anglo-Kuwaiti accord would be terminated.[20]

By the early 1970s Soviet-Kuwaiti relations had become outwardly friendly, but like Saudi Arabia and Iran, Kuwait grew to fear the growing ties between Moscow and Baghdad, especially after the signing of the Soviet-Iraqi treaty of friendship and cooperation in April 1972. Despite the fulsome Soviet praise for Kuwait on the tenth anniversary of diplomatic relations between the two countries in March 1973,[21] the Kuwaitis were dismayed at the USSR's support for Iraq in the Iraq-Kuwait border clash that broke out later the same month. Iraq seized Kuwait's Al-Samitah border post on March 20, and the next day TASS cited a Radio Baghdad broadcast blaming Kuwait for the conflict.[22] In addition, Admiral Sergei Gorshkov, commander of the Soviet navy, and a contingent of Soviet naval vessels arrived in Iraq on April 3 (two days before Iraqi forces withdrew from Kuwaiti territory) and remained until April 11.[23] One Kuwaiti newspaper reported that Soviet military advisers were present in Umm Qasr and other areas in Iraq near the Kuwaiti border, and it accused the USSR of siding with Iraq.[24]

The Soviets, however, attempted to play down their support to Iraq; aside from the March 21 TASS broadcast, Moscow did not blame Kuwait for the conflict and hardly ever referred to it publicly. As the conflict drew to a close in early April, *New Times* blamed its outbreak on Britain for not drawing a good border between the two neighbors and urged Baghdad and Kuwait to resolve their differences peacefully.[25] Soviet-Kuwaiti relations soon resumed their outward friendliness, with a delegation from the Kuwaiti National Assembly visiting the USSR in July and the Amir sending his congratulations to Podgorny on the anniversary of the October Revolution.[26]

As a result of this experience, the Kuwaitis determined to have a closer relationship with the USSR so that Moscow would not support Baghdad in any future Kuwait-Iraq crisis. Kuwait sought to accomplish this by purchasing arms from the USSR, and in January 1974 a Kuwaiti military delegation went to Moscow for the first time.[27] The Soviets,

though, reportedly refused to sell arms to Kuwait out of concern that this
might harm their relations with Iraq.[28] But Kuwait persisted, and another
military delegation visited the USSR in September–October 1975. The
Soviets finally relented and sent a military delegation to Kuwait with an
arms offer in March 1976, shortly after the United States had denied a
Kuwaiti arms request. At this point, however, the Kuwaitis became
ambivalent about the deal; they did not want to purchase Soviet arms if it
meant Soviet military instructors would arrive with them or if Kuwaiti soldiers had to go to the USSR. The Kuwaitis feared this might lead to Marxist subversion within the ranks of their armed forces, and so they insisted
on having Egyptian and Syrian military instructors as well as buying only
those Soviet weapons that these Arab trainers were familiar with.[29] The
Soviets agreed to this condition, and in December 1976 an agreement
worth $400 million was reported to be in the offing, but by March 1977,
when the agreement was actually signed, the Kuwaitis had cut this back to
$50 million. At this time they purchased a number of SA-7 SAMs and
Soviet artillery pieces.[30]

Although this arms agreement took over three years to arrange, it did
lead Moscow to put a greater value on Kuwait's friendship. When tension
arose along the Kuwait-Iraq border again in mid-1977, the Soviets
remained strictly neutral and applauded the mutual troop withdrawal of
one kilometer from the border.[31] In February 1980 the Soviets sold
Kuwait an additional arms package worth over $200 million, which
included one hundred SA-6 and one hundred SA-7 SAMs as well as a
number of FROG-7 ("Luna") SSMs.[32] Up to 1984, Kuwait kept its military relationship with the USSR strictly limited.[33] It did not send any students to the Soviet Union or other communist countries for military
training and did not allow Soviet military advisers in Kuwait.[34] Kuwait
has also purchased much more in arms from the United States, United
Kingdom, and France and has even allowed military instructors from the
West into the country.[35] Indeed, the Kuwaiti armed forces are primarily
equipped with Western weapons. U.S.-Kuwaiti security cooperation has
increased in recent years, especially since the December 1983 bombings
by pro-Iranian terrorists and the spring 1984 escalation in attacks against
oil tankers in the Gulf by Iran and Iraq.[36]

In the summer of 1984, though, Soviet-Kuwaiti military cooperation
increased as well. The Kuwaiti Defense Minister visited Washington in
April 1984 and obtained a certain (undisclosed) amount of American
security assistance, but he was denied permission to purchase Stinger

shoulder-fired SAMs. The United States had recently denied these weapons to both Jordan and Saudi Arabia because of fears in Congress that the weapons could fall into the hands of terrorists and be used against Israel. When attacks on tankers heated up in the spring, though, the Reagan administration rushed four hundred Stingers to Saudi Arabia, invoking emergency provisions to bypass the necessity for congressional approval. Kuwait also requested Stingers but was denied, even though it promised they would not be used against Israel. When the Kuwaiti Defense Minister visited Moscow in July 1984 (a visit that had already been planned), the Soviets reportedly agreed to sell Kuwait everything it wanted in a deal worth over $300 million (though, as in 1974–77, the deal may actually be worth considerably less). According to the Kuwaiti press, Soviet military advisers would be sent to Kuwait, and by January 1985 some Kuwaiti military personnel had already been sent to the USSR for military training.[37]

The Kuwaitis desire a military relationship with the USSR not only to obtain weapons to enhance their security, but also to induce the Soviets to be friendly toward Kuwait and not support groups or nations hostile to it. For the Soviets, selling arms to Kuwait is one way to convince Saudi Arabia and the other conservative monarchies that they too can benefit from a military relationship with the USSR.

In other aspects of Soviet-Kuwaiti bilateral relations, trade between the two countries had grown from 700,000 rubles in 1960 to a high of 36.6 million rubles in 1978, but it fell to only 6.1 million rubles in 1982.[38] In the 1960s Moscow provided limited technical assistance to Kuwait, primarily sending a small number of technicians to train fishermen in the use of fishing boats sold to Kuwait by the USSR.[39] Since the mid-1970s, though, the Soviets have not provided economic or technical advisers to Kuwait. In addition, the USSR has not made any grants or loans to Kuwait for economic development, since Kuwait is so wealthy that it has had no need for them.[40] Indeed, a Soviet scholar recently suggested that Kuwait should finance projects in the USSR.[41] The original Soviet-Kuwaiti cultural and scientific cooperation agreement was signed in March 1967, and several two-year exchange program accords have been agreed to since then.[42] But the level of these exchanges has been limited: ten students attended university in the USSR at the end of the 1960s, and since then the number has apparently remained quite low even though the two-year exchange program agreed to in September 1978 specifically called for Kuwaiti students to study in the USSR.[43] The two countries have also signed an airline agreement whereby Aeroflot has been allowed to fly to

Kuwait, a television and radio cooperation protocol to exchange programs, and an accord between TASS and KUNA (the Kuwaiti News Agency) for exchanging news.[44] Yet despite the degree of interaction that all these agreements imply, there has really been little contact between the two societies except for high-level visits.[45]

The Soviet view of Kuwait's internal politics has changed from completely negative during the Khrushchev era to mainly positive mixed with some criticism. In the early 1960s the Soviets saw the Amir as being in league with the oil companies and the "imperialists" and did not seem to note the formation of a state oil company—a policy that the Soviets praised others for implementing.[46] Beginning with the Brezhnev era, the Amir and his government have been portrayed in an increasingly favorable light. Soviet commentators applauded Kuwait's moves to take larger and larger shares and finally complete control of the foreign oil companies operating on its territory.[47] They also noted with favor the development of Kuwait's social services and trade unions and were particularly pleased when Kuwait's unions affiliated with the Soviet-sponsored World Federation of Trade Unions in 1972.[48] They have occasionally scolded Kuwait for investing so much of its oil revenues in the West and not using the money to develop industry and agriculture at home, but they praised Kuwait for its role in the 1973 oil embargo and, unlike Saudi Arabia, for usually being willing to raise the price of oil.[49] Moscow was critical, though not greatly so, of the dissolution of the National Assembly in 1976 and lauded its revival in 1981.[50] The one aspect of Kuwait's internal situation that Moscow has continued to criticize most often is the harsh economic conditions and lack of civil rights that the non-Kuwaitis, who form the majority of the population, experience as compared with the relative opulence enjoyed by Kuwaiti citizens.[51]

Soviet writers have recognized that there has been opposition activity in Kuwait, beginning with the reformist Young Kuwaiti movement of the 1930s and including various workers' strikes over the years.[52] Since Kuwait's independence, though, the Soviets have been careful not to express support for any Kuwaiti opposition movements. Although there may be communists in the country, there does not appear to be a pro-Soviet Kuwaiti communist party.[53] The Soviets noted that the goal of PFLOAG (Popular Front for the Liberation of the Occupied Arab Gulf) was to spread revolution to Oman, Bahrain, Qatar, and the Trucial States (now UAE). While some members of PFLOAG may have hoped to bring revolution to Kuwait as well, Soviet commentators did not include Kuwait in their descriptions of PFLOAG's revolutionary goals.

The one occasion when Moscow appeared to overtly support a Kuwaiti opposition leader was in December 1972, when Dr. Ahmad al-Khatib, head of the Arab Nationalist Movement branch in Kuwait, visited the USSR as the guest of the Soviet Afro-Asian Solidarity Committee (the supposedly unofficial Soviet organization that supports national liberation fronts in Asia and Africa). Soviet commentary at the time, however, described him not as an ANM leader, but as a member of the Kuwaiti National Assembly and emphasized how good Soviet-Kuwaiti relations were.[54] Moscow has not expressed approval for opposition activity by pro-Iranian Islamic fundamentalist groups in Kuwait or for the Islamic Jihad organization's bombing of the American and French embassies and several government buildings in December 1983.[55]

Far from supporting or even expressing sympathy for antigovernment groups, the Soviets have gone to great lengths to convince the Kuwaiti government that the USSR "cannot possibly interfere in the internal affairs of any other state."[56] But as a 1975 crackdown on leftists in Kuwait demonstrated, Kuwait is sensitive about this issue.[57] The government wants to avoid (and has successfully done so) friendly government-to-government relations with the USSR leading to Soviet support of Marxist or other opposition groups. There is a large Soviet embassy in Kuwait as well as embassies from many other communist countries, but one former Soviet diplomat complained that Kuwait's tight internal security makes Soviet contact with Kuwaiti society, let alone dissidents, very difficult.[58] Soviet commentary on Saudi Arabia, Oman, and Bahrain has frequently supported the actions or statements of Marxist opposition groups. The absence of similar Soviet commentary about Marxists in Kuwait seems designed not only to maintain good relations with the Kuwaiti government, but perhaps also to signal the other GCC states that establishing diplomatic relations with the USSR will end Moscow's public support of opposition groups in them too.

It is in the realm of foreign policy that the Soviets have come to particularly value friendship with Kuwait, for even though Kuwait is ruled by an amir instead of a "vanguard party" the two governments have similar foreign policy views on many issues. Foremost among these is the Arab-Israeli dispute. The Kuwaiti government and media have frequently endorsed the Soviet call for an overall Middle East peace conference to solve the Arab-Israeli dispute and create a Palestinian state. Kuwait has also vilified the United States for supporting Israel, criticized Egypt and the United States for the Camp David accords, and praised Soviet support to the Arabs. Kuwaiti and Soviet officials have often stated that their views on this issue are "identical."[59] This, however, is not completely true. In the 1970s some Kuwaiti newspapers criticized Moscow for allowing Jews to emigrate from the USSR to Israel and allegedly add to the latter's armed forces (one paper went as far as to state that Moscow's permitting Jewish emigration was "proof" that the USSR actually aided Israel, since the USSR did not allow Soviet Moslems to emigrate to fight for the Palestinians).[60] On other occasions Kuwaiti papers have complained that the USSR gave the Arabs only defensive weapons and not offensive ones (as the United States gave to Israel) and thus prevented the Arabs from defeating Israel.[61] The Kuwaiti media also expressed disappointment over Soviet "passivity" during the Israeli invasion of Lebanon in 1982.[62] In recent years, however, the Kuwaiti press has been less critical of Soviet policy toward the Middle East, since Jewish emigration from the USSR has all but stopped and the Soviets have been more generous than in the past in supplying arms to Syria (whose hard-line stance against Israel Kuwait vocally supports).

The Kuwaiti government has also expressed its general approval of Soviet foreign policy toward the Persian Gulf. Kuwait was the only GCC member to welcome Brezhnev's Persian Gulf peace proposals of December 1980, which called for banning all outside forces and military bases from the area.[63] It is a deeply held tenet of Kuwaiti foreign policy that the military presence of one superpower in the Gulf will lead to the presence of the other as well, possibly bringing a confrontation between them that will hurt all the states of the Gulf. Although Soviet naval forces have indeed been present in the Gulf, the United States has had a larger military presence in the form of a small naval force permanently stationed there and facilities in Oman and sometimes Bahrain. More worrying to the Kuwaitis are U.S. Rapid Deployment Force plans; they fear that if the United States greatly increases its military presence in the region, the USSR will follow suit. But if the U.S. does not build up its forces in the Gulf, the Kuwaitis feel certain the USSR will not do so either. American claims that the United States must have a Rapid Deployment Force ready because of the Soviet threat to the Gulf are simply dismissed by many Kuwaitis, who believe that the Soviet threat does not exist and that the

U.S. cites it only as a pretext to move forces into the Gulf and dominate the region itself.[64] The Soviets, not surprisingly, agree with these views.

The Soviet military presence in South Yemen is of concern to Kuwait, as it is to Oman and the other GCC states. Oman seeks to counter the Soviet presence in the PDRY and any future PDRY-backed rebel activity in Dhofar by having a British and American military presence in the Sultanate. The Kuwaitis have sought to deal with the problem in a completely different way: Kuwait has hoped that if the hostility between Oman and South Yemen could only be brought to an end, neither country would have any reason for allowing a foreign military presence. With Oman and South Yemen free of foreign troops, the entire Persian Gulf/Arabian Peninsula area would be less likely to become the scene of a superpower competition or confrontation, hence enhancing the security of all the states of the area.[65]

Thus Kuwait worked hard to bring about the normalization of relations between Muscat and Aden that finally took place in October 1982. So far, however, neither Oman nor South Yemen has moved to dismiss the foreign military presence. Ever since South Yemen became independent under a radical government, the Kuwaitis have argued that unless it receives aid from the West or the rich Arab states, the country's poverty will force it to turn toward the USSR and encourage Aden to be hostile toward its neighbors. Since 'Ali Nasir Muhammad came to power in 1980, South Yemen's relations with all its neighbors have been at their most cordial, but Aden has still not given up its close ties to Moscow.

Kuwait has repeatedly urged the five other GCC states to establish diplomatic relations with the USSR, but so far it has failed. The most vocal opponent of such a move is Oman, which sees the USSR as a threat and has proposed that the GCC act as a military alliance in conjunction with the West to counter it. This is precisely what the Kuwaitis want to avoid; they want the GCC to remain neutral. One Kuwaiti official revealed that Moscow's greatest objection to the GCC was that Oman was a member while at the same time being linked militarily to the West.[66] The Kuwaitis believe that if the GCC is not hostile toward the USSR, the USSR will not be hostile toward the GCC. Kuwait's officials were disturbed at the announcement of the tripartite treaty signed by South Yemen, Ethiopia, and Libya, but in reaction to it the Amir called for better GCC–East bloc ties.[67]

Kuwait has objected to certain Soviet foreign policy actions, including the invasion of Czechoslovakia in 1968, aid to India in the Indo-Pakistani war of 1971, aid to Ethiopia in fighting the Moslem rebels of Eritrea, and the invasion of Afghanistan.[68] The Kuwaitis, however, have not regarded any of these events as important enough to justify interrupting their friendly relations with Moscow. For example, Kuwait quickly announced that it "rejects" the Soviet intervention in Afghanistan at the end of 1979, and a Kuwaiti delegation attending the Islamic Conference of January 1980 endorsed its call for the USSR to withdraw, but it did not break diplomatic relations with the USSR or join in the boycott of the 1980 Moscow Olympics.[69] In February 1980 Radio Moscow in Arabic applauded the Kuwaiti Foreign Minister's statement that Soviet actions in Afghanistan did not threaten Kuwait or the other nations of the Gulf.[70]

Another issue that some GCC states including Saudi Arabia see as a bar to relations with the Soviets is Moscow's treatment of Soviet Moslems. By contrast, Kuwaiti officials have praised what they see as the freedom of belief that Soviet Moslems enjoy and hence do not see freedom for Islam in the USSR as a problem.[71]

Kuwait has become rhetorically, if not always actually, pro-Soviet in its foreign policy, but it has a conservative, anticommunist regime. The Soviets have come to value the friendship of the present government, but they would probably welcome immediately any force that overthrew the Amir and established a "progressive" regime. What is the likelihood of the present Kuwaiti government being overthrown?

Kuwait has the enviable advantage of having over two hundred years of proven oil reserves at current rates of production.[72] Social unrest as a result of oil reserves being exhausted, then, is not a concern. A potential cause for discontent is the lack of political freedom. Only about 3 percent of Kuwait's population votes in the elections; suffrage is limited to adult male Kuwaiti citizens. Further, the National Assembly has only limited functions. The press, while freer than most in the Arab world, is still subject to government interference, as the frequent suspension of newspapers for making statements the government does not like testifies. There has been opposition to the amir-dominated government in the past, and there continues to be some at present. The influence of the leftist opposition has declined in recent years while the strength of the Moslem fundamentalists has grown. Nevertheless, through sharing the oil wealth, the Kuwaiti government has managed to keep its citizens content.

More worrisome are the large number of non-Kuwaitis, mainly from other Arab nations, living and working in the country. The proportion of non-Kuwaitis has grown from 45 percent in 1957 to 58.5 percent in 1980.[73] In addition, about a quarter of the total population of Kuwait is Shia; it is feared that many Shias in Kuwait are sympathetic to Iran's Ayatollah Khomeini, unlike Kuwait's Sunni government, which supports Iraq.[74] There is concern that the non-Kuwaitis' poorer economic condition may provide the motive and their large numbers the opportunity for taking over the country. Soviet statements of sympathy for the plight of the non-Kuwaitis indicate that Moscow would welcome such a move. Kuwait's tight internal security and the lack of freedom for non-Kuwaitis to organize themselves in any way, however, would make such a move difficult.

Although the Soviets would welcome a revolution in Kuwait, as long as the opposition there remains weak the Soviets will do nothing to promote political change, since this would probably result in the Kuwaiti government ending its friendship with the USSR. Of course the primary threat to Kuwait now is not an internal one, but the external one from Iran. Kuwait, however, is not likely to ask its Soviet allies for protection against Iran, since it fears any large Soviet presence could result in the weakening and overthrow of the regime.

What has Kuwait gained from friendship with the USSR? Most of all, Kuwait's close ties to Moscow have ended Soviet hostility to Kuwait and have provided the Soviets with an incentive not to support their allies (such as Iraq, South Yemen, or national liberation groups) in plans hostile to Kuwait. However, should the Amir's government ever become seriously weakened for any reason, it could not then count on the USSR's friendship.

The United Arab Emirates, Bahrain, and Qatar

Of all the countries of the Arabian Peninsula, the Soviets have paid the least attention to the United Arab Emirates, Bahrain, and Qatar. Moscow has made attempts to establish diplomatic relations with all three since their independence in 1971, but so far it has failed. Moscow has also halfheartedly tried to drive a wedge between these three on the one hand and Saudi Arabia and the United States on the other and has indicated some support for revolutionary groups in them, also without success. More recently, Moscow has focused its efforts just on trying to create normal ties with each of the three, for although it has failed to do so up to the present, if it succeeds even with one, this could lead to relations with the other two and perhaps with Saudi Arabia as well.

HISTORICAL BACKGROUND

UAE

The UAE is a federation of seven separate emirates (Abu Dhabi, Dubai, Sharjah, Ras al-Khaimah, Umm al-Qaiwain, Ajman, and Fujairah), each with its own ruler. In times past this area was variously known as the Pirate Coast, Coastal Oman, the Trucial Coast, and the Trucial States. The Portuguese, Dutch, Saudis, Omanis, and British all vied for influence over this region in the seventeenth and eighteenth centuries, but by the early nineteenth century the British came to predominate. In 1806, 1809, and 1818 the British sent military expeditions against the states of the region in response to their attacks on British vessels. In 1820 the British signed a peace treaty with these states as well as Bahrain to suppress piracy and the slave trade, and in 1835 the shaykhs signed a maritime truce in which they promised to end hostilities by sea against one another during the pearl diving season. This truce was renewed every year until 1853, when a perpetual truce was signed whereby Britain agreed to protect them from outside attack as well as enforce the peace among them. Fearing the growth of French, Russian, and German influence at the end of the nineteenth century, in 1892 Britain signed a further round of treaties in which they all agreed not to cede their territory to anyone except the United Kingdom or have relations with any foreign government without British permission.[75]

Britain's announcement in January 1968 that it would withdraw from the region by 1971 provided the inducement for these states (some of which are very small), along with Bahrain and Qatar, to form a federation. Several problems, including disputes over border issues and the degree of influence each state would have, prevented rapid agreement on federation, and both Bahrain and Qatar decided against joining in order to become independent instead. On December 2, 1971, the UAE came into being as an independent state (Ras al-Khaimah refused to join at first, but it did so in February 1972), and a new treaty of friendship was signed with the United Kingdom replacing all previous treaties between the emirates and London. The UAE also became a member of the United Nations and the Arab League in December 1971.[76]

The oil boom came relatively late to the emirates compared with Saudi Arabia, Bahrain, and Kuwait. Abu Dhabi began to produce oil only in 1962, Dubai in 1969, Sharjah in 1974, and Ras al-Khaimah in 1984. At present, Abu Dhabi produces 80 percent of the UAE's total production and Dubai produces 18 percent. Abu Dhabi's current oil reserves will also last over a century at current rates of production, but Dubai's will last only twelve years unless more is discovered. In addition to its greater oil wealth, Abu Dhabi also has a larger population and more territory than all the others combined.[77] As a result it has been the most powerful of the UAE states, and its ruler, Shaykh Zayid bin Sultan Al Nuhayan, has been UAE President ever since independence.

This has led some of the other rulers, especially those of Dubai and Ras al-Khaimah, to resist the growth of federal authority, since they fear this will lead to dominance by Abu Dhabi and diminution of their power within their own realms (each emirate is an absolute monarchy). One of the main items of dispute is the integration of the armed forces; Dubai has kept its army separate from the federal forces. Other issues not agreed upon are the questions of abolishing borders between emirates, transforming the present provisional constitution into a permanent one, and holding popular elections instead of having the seven rulers appoint representatives to the forty-member Federal National Council (an advisory body with no legislative functions). Yet despite these differences, there has been cooperation among the seven on a considerable number of issues. Dubai's support for the union has also been gained because its ruler, Shaykh Rashid bin Sa'id Al Maktum, not only has been Vice-President of the UAE since independence, but also has been Prime Minister since 1979.[78]

The most important governing body in the UAE is the Supreme Council of Rulers, consisting of the seven amirs (Abu Dhabi and Dubai each have the right to veto decisions of the majority).[79] This body elects the President and Vice-President. Shaykh Zayid has been elected President and Shaykh Rashid Vice-President at the elections in 1971, 1976, and 1981; their current terms expire in December 1986. The presidency of the UAE, then, is not a hereditary office. Each of the seven amirs, however, is a hereditary ruler. As with the other GCC countries, succession is not predetermined; new rulers are chosen by the respective ruling families. The emirates have not been free from dynastic power struggles. In August 1966, Shaykh Zayid came to power in Abu Dhabi when the ruling family, with British approval, ousted Shaykh Shakbut, who had ruled since 1928 and refused to spend much money on economic development (much like Sultan Sa'id of Oman, who was deposed in 1970). Shaykh Zayid, like Sultan Qabus later, immediately reversed this policy. In Sharjah, the British and the ruling family ousted the pro-Nasser Shaykh Saqr and replaced him with his cousin Khalid in June 1965. After the British left, Saqr attempted to return to power in January 1972, but although he seized the palace and killed Khalid, he and his supporters were captured by Khalid's brother Sultan, who then became Amir.[80] Other successions, though, have been more peaceful, as in 1981 when the ruling families of Ajman and Umm al-Qaiwain chose the designated heirs apparent when the old amirs died.[81]

The population of the UAE has risen from 179,000 in 1968 to over 1,040,000 in 1980. Most of this increase has been due to the influx of foreign workers, mainly to Abu Dhabi and Dubai. The UAE government estimated in 1982 that 90 percent of the work force consisted of foreigners. It appears that UAE citizens form only a quarter or less of the country's population.[82] There is also a strong Shia and Iranian influence in Dubai (the ruling families are all Sunnis). Strikes and disturbances by foreign workers over both economic and political issues have occurred (a Palestinian group attempted to assassinate the Syrian Foreign Minister visiting Abu Dhabi in October 1977 but ended up killing the UAE Minister of State for Foreign Affairs instead),[83] but increasingly forceful measures have been taken to control them. One potentially serious problem is that a large proportion of the armed forces consists of foreigners (mainly Arabs) whose willingness to fight for the UAE and lack of susceptibility to foreign influence are not completely certain.

In foreign affairs, the UAE has been primarily concerned with its stronger neighbors. At the end of November 1971, just before independence, Iran seized three small islands in the Gulf that had been administered by Sharjah and Ras al-Khaimah.[84] The UAE and Iran established normal diplomatic relations in October 1972, but neither the Shah nor the Ayatollah has moved to give the islands back. The UAE has not attempted forceful action against its much stronger neighbor to the north to retake the islands, though it has reiterated its claim to them.[85] Saudi Arabia had claimed large tracts of land from Abu Dhabi, but in 1974 and 1977 it was agreed that the UAE would keep most of it, including the Buraimi Oasis.[86] Ras al-Khaimah has also had a minor border dispute with Oman over which agreement has been reached in principle, though an actual settlement remains elusive.[87]

Bahrain

Bahrain was dominated by the Portuguese in the sixteenth century and the Persians in the seventeenth and eighteenth centuries until the Al Khalifa family, from the Peninsula, ousted them in 1783 and established the present dynasty. Over the next several decades, the Bahraini shaykhs faced threats from the Turks, Persians, Saudis, and Omanis (who captured the island briefly). In 1861 the British signed a treaty with the Bahraini shaykh whereby he agreed to observe the perpetual maritime truce and cease trading in slaves in exchange for British recognition and protection. Further treaties were signed in 1880 and 1892 binding Bahrain neither to cede territory to any power except Britain nor to have relations with foreign governments without British permission. On August 15, 1971, Bahrain became independent. Bahrain also signed a treaty of friendship with the United Kingdom, replacing all previous treaties, and was quickly accepted as a member of both the United Nations and the Arab League. Shaykh Isa bin Salman Al Khalifa, who succeeded his father on the throne in November 1961, took the title of Amir upon independence and has ruled Bahrain up to the present. The Amir's son Hamad is heir apparent and Minister of Defense, and the Amir's brother is Prime Minister.[88]

Oil was discovered in Bahrain in 1932. Its production has declined from 76,000 barrels per day in 1970 to 45,000 b/d in 1981. In 1983 OAPEC estimated that Bahrain's known oil reserves would last only twelve years at current rates of production. Bahrain, however, shares equally with Saudi Arabia an offshore oil field that now provides over half of Bahrain's oil revenues. Bahrain also earns money from its oil refinery (capacity 250,000 b/d, most of which is pumped from Saudi Arabia), banking, and trade.[89]

In December 1972 elections were held for a Constituent Assembly to draft a constitution. The Assembly (composed of twenty elected members and twenty-two others appointed by the Amir) was dominated by conservatives. A constitution was promulgated the following June declaring Bahrain to be an Islamic state and the *sharia* to be the source of legislation. At the first (and only) elections held December 3, 1973, for the newly created National Assembly, ten of the thirty members elected were leftists, calling themselves the "Popular Bloc of the Left" (political parties, though, were forbidden). As in Kuwait, the prime minister and cabinet were responsible not to the Assembly, but to the Amir. The proceedings of the National Assembly were highly acrimonious; not a single piece of legislation was passed. On August 26, 1975, the

Amir dissolved the Assembly, and no elections have been held since then.[90]

Bahrain's population has traditionally been more politicized than those of the other conservative Gulf states. From the mid-1950s to the mid-1970s, the leftists were the most prominent opponents of the government. Since the Iranian revolution, though, the influence of the left has been reduced while that of the Islamic fundamentalists has grown. This is particularly disturbing because while the ruling family and most of the elite are Sunnis, about 55 percent of Bahrain's population are Shias—many of whom support Ayatollah Khomeini. Bahrain's population growth in recent years has been much less dramatic than that of the UAE; from 216,000 in 1971 to 359,000 in 1981. Of these, two-thirds are Bahrainis.[91]

Beginning in 1927, Iran claimed Bahrain as one of its provinces on the basis of previous Persian rule. Although this claim was ignored as long as the British were present, the Shah renewed it after London's 1968 announcement that Britain would withdraw from the Gulf. But after United Nations mediation, the Shah renounced his claim in May 1970. Shortly after the Iranian revolution, however, an ayatollah renewed Iran's claim to Bahrain, but the new Tehran government denied that this was an official act and sent a resident ambassador to Bahrain in July 1979. Relations between the two countries have become strained, though, because of the Bahraini government's fear that Tehran is supporting the Shia opposition, especially the Islamic Front for the Liberation of Bahrain, and because of Iran's complaints over the Manama government's treatment of Shias. On December 13, 1981, Bahraini authorities thwarted an attempted coup by the Islamic Front and accused Iran of backing it. Despite Iranian denials, Bahrain quickly moved to sign an internal security accord with Saudi Arabia.[92]

Since independence, Bahrain's relations with its neighbors and the West have been generally good. The British had allowed the United States to use a naval base in Bahrain for a small flotilla since the late 1940s; in December 1971 the United States and Bahrain signed an agreement allowing America to continue using it. At the time of the October 1973 Middle East war, Bahrain announced that it would terminate the agreement, but it later reversed its decision. At the end of June 1977 the agreement finally was ended, but Bahrain has continued to allow the United States to use its facilities. Saudi Arabia reportedly has been allowed to maintain air defense facilities on Bahrain. A causeway between the two countries is nearing completion.[93]

Qatar

The Al Khalifa held sway over Qatar before they took Bahrain from the Persians in 1783. They continued to dominate the peninsula until the 1870s when the Al Thani shyakhs of Doha (now Qatar's capital) accepted Turkish suzerainty and drove the Al Khalifa out. The Turks remained in Qatar until World War I, and it was only in 1916 that the Al Thani signed an agreement not to cede territory to any power except Britain or to have relations with foreign governments without British consent. Qatar became independent on September 1, 1971, a new treaty of friendship with the United Kingdom was signed replacing all previous agreements, and Qatar soon joined the United Nations and the Arab League. Of Qatar's current population of about 250,000, only about 50,000 are Qataris, while the rest are immigrant workers. Oil was discovered in Qatar in the 1930s but was not produced until 1949. In 1983 Qatar pumped 310,000 barrels of oil per day (down from 570,000 b/d in 1973), and at this rate of production its current reserves are expected to last for twenty-nine years.[94]

Upon the abdication of his father, Shaykh Ahmad bin 'Ali Al Thani became ruler of Qatar in 1960. Ahmad, however, was not particularly interested in ruling and spent much of his time outside the country—he stayed in Switzerland when Qatar became independent in September 1971. Earlier, in April 1970, the ruling family and the British had compelled him to transfer day-to-day authority to his younger cousin, Shaykh Khalifa bin Hamad Al Thani. On February 22, 1972, while Ahmad was hunting in Iran, Khalifa seized power for himself and has been Amir ever since (Ahmad died in 1977). A struggle then took place within the ruling family over whether the Amir's younger brother or younger son would become heir apparent; a compromise was finally reached in 1977 when the Amir appointed his elder son Hamad heir apparent and Minister of Defense. Qatar has had a provisional constitution since 1970, but it has not been put fully into effect and power remains in the hands of the Amir. There is a consultative assembly with at first twenty, and since 1975, thirty members elected under a limited suffrage, but this body has only advisory powers.[95]

In foreign relations, there was a territorial dispute between Qatar and Saudi Arabia over the base of the Qatar peninsula, but this was resolved in

Qatar's favor in 1965. Members of Qatar's ruling family are Wahabis, as are the Saudis, and relations between Doha and Riyadh are very close. There is still a dispute outstanding over Hawar Island, less than a mile off Qatar's west coast, which Bahrain claims and where both hope there may be oil deposits. Though still not settled, the dispute has not involved conflict between the two countries and is currently under mediation.[96]

SOVIET VIEWS AND ACTIONS

In the late 1960s the Soviets bitterly opposed British-sponsored plans for a federation of the Trucial States along with Bahrain and Qatar even though the radical Arab governments of the UAR, Algeria, and Iraq all welcomed the idea. They saw the proposed federation as a British plan to pretend to grant independence to the emirates but really retain control over them. Moscow warned that this federation would fail, just as the British-sponsored Federation of South Arabia did in South Yemen.[97] Before their independence, Soviet writers were vehemently hostile toward the Gulf rulers and sided with Saudi Arabia in its territorial claims against Abu Dhabi, including the Buraimi Oasis.[98]

As independence for the UAE drew near, the Soviets relented and stated that a federation just might help these small states break away from "imperialism."[99] Unlike South Yemen, which opposed the UAE's admission to the United Nations and the Arab League and supported PFLOAG's goal of bringing revolution to the former Trucial States, Moscow immediately recognized the independence of the UAE in December 1971. An exchange of cables took place between Soviet President Podgorny and UAE President Shaykh Zayid in which both expressed the desire to establish diplomatic relations.[100] A Soviet delegation arrived in Abu Dhabi at the end of January for talks on this subject, and on February 15, 1972, the UAE government announced that the two countries had agreed to have diplomatic ties and exchange embassies.[101] But two months later a Beirut paper announced that the UAE had abandoned these plans; the UAE President stated the following year that Saudi Arabia had opposed the Soviet-UAE rapprochement and that the UAE could not afford to ignore Saudi desires.[102]

The Soviets appear to have accepted this setback stoically and continued to issue generally favorable commentary about the UAE. Moscow changed its view of the Saudi-UAE border dispute and began supporting the UAE instead.[103] On the Iranian seizure of the three islands in the Gulf in 1971, the Soviets indicated their support for the UAE by citing criticism of Tehran's action by other Arab states, but they did not directly criticize the Shah (with whom Moscow wanted to have good relations).[104]

Moscow has occasionally criticized the UAE government, as in early 1977 when the UAE was the only OPEC member that joined Saudi Arabia in its opposition to a 15 percent oil price rise and in 1978 when the UAE, along with Egypt, Saudi Arabia, and Qatar, formed the Arab Military Industrial Organization (this was seen as serving "imperialism"). Moscow has also been critical of the dichotomy between Abu Dhabi and Dubai as the rich emirates and the others as poor ones as well as the UAE's reliance on Western technicians.[105] *Krasnaia Zvezda* once denounced the UAE for buying so much Western military equipment.[106]

In their limited commentary on UAE internal politics, the Soviets have supported Shaykh Zayid and increased authority for the federal government, including plans to integrate the UAE's armed forces.[107] In reporting a 1979 student demonstration in the UAE, *New Times* did not portray this as a protest against "reactionary rule" as it easily could have done, but presented it as a basically progovernment demand for further unity and centralization within the UAE.[108] Since independence, the Soviets have had very little to say about opposition movements in the UAE. Although they supported PFLOAG's actions in Oman, the fact that Moscow immediately moved to establish relations with the UAE after it became independent showed that the USSR did not strongly support the PFLOAG/Aden call for revolution in the emirates.

In November 1978 the UAE Defense Minister revealed that his country would not buy Soviet SAMs but would purchase similar Western weapons instead. What was surprising about this announcement was not that the UAE had turned down a Soviet arms offer, but that it had considered buying Soviet arms at all. The Defense Minister further revealed that the UAE does buy light Eastern bloc weapons for which it can bring in Arab military instructors familiar with them to train UAE forces.[109] It is not clear whether the UAE buys these weapons directly from the Eastern bloc or from other Arab countries with large stockpiles of them.

In recent years, contacts between the USSR and the UAE have increased. In March 1982 the UAE Interior Minister went to Moscow, ostensibly for medical treatment, but brought an "official delegation" with him; this was the first visit by UAE officials to the Soviet Union.[110] Since the fall of 1982, Aeroflot has been flying in and out of Abu Dhabi and Dubai. The Soviets and several Eastern European countries have taken part in trade exhibitions in the UAE, though Soviet exports to the UAE remain low.[111] In June 1984 Intourist and a local travel agency sponsored a series of charter flights for UAE tourists to visit the USSR.[112] All this activity has fueled speculation that the Soviet Union and the UAE will soon establish diplomatic relations, as has the establishment of diplomatic relations between Abu Dhabi and Peking in November 1984 (the UAE's first with a communist country).[113] Such speculation has occurred before, though, and nothing has come of it.

Before Bahrain's independence, Soviet writers were hostile not only to the British presence there, but also to the rule of the Al Khalifa. The introduction of relatively advanced social and labor legislation by Shaykh Isa in the 1960s was not credited to him at all but was attributed to the increasing strength of the national liberation movement that forced him to adopt these measures. The Soviets were also encouraged that the Bahrain National Liberation Front (BNLF—a Marxist group founded in 1955) was active in the country and that antigovernment strikes occurred in 1938, 1954–56, 1963, and 1965.[114] With regard to Iran's claim to Bahrain, the Soviets did not support it, though they did not strongly oppose it either.[115]

When Bahrain became independent in August 1971, the Soviet attitude toward it grew markedly more friendly even though the PDRY and PFLOAG (which the BNLF had joined) denounced Bahrain's independence as "false." The Soviets decried the treaty of friendship with the United Kingdom and the agreement to permit American use of the naval base, but their commentary saw the United States and the United Kingdom as attempting to keep control and portrayed Bahrain as a victim of "imperialism" rather than a collaborator. The Soviets also repeatedly asked permission to establish an embassy in Bahrain, but the latter "shelved" the request owing to pressure from "some neighbors."[116]

The Soviet attitude toward Bahrain became much less friendly after the Amir dissolved the National Assembly in August 1975 and suppressed the leftists who had been active in 1974–75. Their critical attitude has persisted: even when Bahrain abrogated the base agreement with the United States, it was classified by Soviet writers as being as reactionary as Oman, and both were said to use U.S. arms to suppress the leftists.[117] In 1978 Radio Moscow described Bahrain as not being fully independent because of the presence of Western banks and oil firms, the continued visits by U.S. Navy vessels, and Saudi influence.[118]

The Soviets also increased their coverage of the BNLF after 1975, even though it has been less active since then. Soviet media have publicized BNLF statements denouncing the dissolution of the National Assembly and repression against leftists. The BNLF has also praised Soviet foreign policy actions, such as the intervention in Afghanistan and the Brezhnev Persian Gulf peace proposals, that the Bahraini government opposes. The Soviets have given more coverage to the BNLF than to the Saudi Arabian Communist Party, citing by name several leaders of the former including 'Ali Sulayman, Yusuf al-Hassan, 'Abdallah 'Ali, and Muhammad Ahmad Salim.[119] Moscow also hailed the agreement on unity of action between the BNLF and the Popular Front of Bahrain (another Marxist group) in March 1981.[120] The Soviets do not appear to support the much stronger Islamic Front, though after its coup attempt of December 1981, Radio Peace and Progress broadcast a BNLF statement saying that neither Iran nor the USSR was to be blamed for internal opposition to the Bahrain government.[121] Moscow would undoubtedly like to see the BNLF come to power in Bahrain, but it does not realistically expect this.

Although the Soviet attitude toward Bahrain has been relatively negative in recent years, top Soviet leaders still send the Amir (as well as the leaders of all other GCC states except Oman) greetings on his country's independence day and exchange telegrams on certain other occasions. Thus the Soviets keep hoping to establish normal ties with the Amir. Because of Bahrain's experience of having an active leftist opposition that was verbally supported by the USSR, the Bahrain government is much less likely than the UAE to permit the establishment of diplomatic relations with Moscow; it will probably maintain close ties with both Saudi Arabia and the United States instead.

The Soviets have said the least of all about Qatar. In the late 1950s and early 1960s, they saw evidence of a "growing" working-class struggle. They denounced the suppression of a spring 1963 strike demanding political rights and a share in the country's increasing wealth. Moscow saw the struggle being continued by the "National Liberation Front of Qatar" and the "Organization for the National Struggle of Qatar."[122] These groups, however, have not been active since then and probably have ceased to exist (if they ever really did). Just as with the UAE and Bahrain, Moscow hailed Qatar's independence. The Soviets also welcomed the February 1972 coup in which Shaykh Khalifa (then Prime Minister) overthrew Ahmad to become Amir. The first Soviet citizen (a journalist) ever to visit Qatar had only a short time before the coup interviewed Khalifa, who at that time expressed interest in better relations with the USSR. Since then, however, the Amir has made no move to establish diplomatic ties to Moscow.[123] The Soviets have criticized Qatar for its close contacts with the West and for participating in the Arab Military Industrial Organization and have praised it for opposing America's Middle East policy.[124] Because of its particularly close ties to Riyadh, Qatar is not likely to establish diplomatic relations with the USSR.

The UAE, Bahrain, and Qatar, along with Saudi Arabia, Oman, and Kuwait, are members of the Gulf Cooperation Council that was founded in May 1981. Just before its creation and during the first year of its existence, Soviet commentary about the GCC was hostile. Moscow feared the organization would invite a greater U.S. military presence into the region.[125] In 1982 and 1983 the Soviets appeared to be less worried about this possibility and issued mainly factual accounts of its meetings and activities.[126] By 1984 the Soviets seemed to develop a more favorable view of the GCC and praised its calls for no foreign interference in the region.[127]

The views of the UAE, Bahrain, and Qatar on foreign policy issues regarding the Soviets tend to be similar. In the 1973 Middle East war and the 1982 Israeli invasion of Lebanon, they all supported the Arab side and condemned both Israel and its American supporters. They all denounced the Camp David peace accords as well. In general, their views on the Arab-Israeli conflict agree with Soviet policy and disagree with American policy—as the Soviets have often pointed out—though sometimes the newspapers of these countries complain that the Soviets are not doing enough to help the Arab cause. All three countries oppose Soviet assistance to Ethiopia in suppressing the Moslem Eritrean rebels and the Soviet invasion of Afghanistan (Bahrain and Qatar did not attend the 1980 Moscow Olympics because of Afghanistan, but the UAE did).[128] The governments and especially the media of these three countries have expressed opposition to U.S. Rapid Deployment Force plans and what they see as American exaggeration of the Soviet threat to the Gulf. Nevertheless, none of them were willing to accept the Brezhnev Persian Gulf peace proposals, which would have banned all outside forces from the region.

One important reason the rulers of the Trucial States, Bahrain, and Qatar accepted British protection in the nineteenth and early twentieth centuries was that they feared encroachment by other powers, among them the Saudis. When the British withdrew from the area in 1971, though, the Soviets were unable to transform their continuing concern over dominance by Saudi Arabia into friendship with the USSR. Part of the reason Moscow did not succeed was that Saudi Arabia adopted a conciliatory posture toward its smaller neighbors and that there were strong bonds of religion, culture, and, most important, type of government that the leaders of these three countries shared with Riyadh and not with Moscow. Further, although the British deposed several rulers in these states while exercising their "protectorate" they did not dismantle the principle of shaykhly rule. These weak governments feared that the Soviets might try to subvert this principle even with a much smaller presence than the British ever had. Soviet support for PFLOAG's activities in Oman only confirmed these fears. Yet leftist forces were extremely weak in Qatar and the UAE, and while stronger in Bahrain, they could not avoid being crushed by the government in 1975.

Although these three countries all maintain tight internal security, their governments may become vulnerable to attempts to overthrow them by Shias, foreign workers, leftists, or other forces. Their small size and their proximity to Saudi Arabia, however, make the suppression of any such attempt by Saudi forces relatively easy, as demonstrated by Saudi assistance to Bahrain in crushing pro-Iranian forces in Bahrain in December 1981.[129] In Bahrain, Qatar, and the UAE, then, revolution appears to have little chance to succeed unless it occurs first in Saudi Arabia or unless Riyadh somehow becomes too weak to intervene—both highly unlikely. Thus, Soviet efforts to befriend these three countries have failed because both they and Saudi Arabia have feared the Soviets would attempt to promote revolution in them, while the halfhearted Soviet efforts to encourage revolution have failed because the left in them was so weak.

Conclusion

The USSR has up to now failed completely in its efforts to either promote revolution or ally with the established governments in Saudi Arabia, Oman, the UAE, Bahrain, and Qatar. Moscow has good relations with Kuwait, to which it sells arms, but this relationship is limited since Kuwait is basically a conservative emirate. If the Soviets gave even media support to Kuwaiti opposition groups, the Kuwaiti government could be expected to quickly suppress its opponents and become much less friendly with the Soviets. In North Yemen the situation is more complicated. The YAR government has good relations and a treaty of friendship and cooperation with the Soviets, and Sanaa wishes to continue receiving military and economic assistance from them as well as from the West and the Saudis. However, the North Yemenis are unwilling to become closely aligned with any country politically or militarily. The North Yemeni government fought border wars with South Yemen in 1972 and 1979 and defeated PDRY-backed rebels in 1982. Should another border war break out or Marxist insurgents grow strong again, Sanaa might ask for help from the West but would probably not break relations with Moscow for fear the Soviets would then support Aden and North Yemen's internal opponents all the more strongly. At present, though, the YAR government is relatively strong, and it might become even stronger if its 1984 oil discovery leads to more oil finds from which Sanaa can draw revenue. Moscow's one true success on the Peninsula has been South Yemen, but instead of strongly backing this country's previous efforts to export revolution, the Soviets have preferred that Aden have friendly, or at least calm, relations with its neighbors and so not harm Moscow's efforts to establish friendly relations with them.

Up to the present, then, Soviet efforts to gain influence in the Peninsula have met with only limited success. If it has indeed been the Kremlin's aim to control the Peninsula's oil, these efforts have been extremely unsuccessful. Nor do the Soviets appear likely to accomplish any more in the near future. The GCC states' booming economies and tight internal security eliminate much of the incentive as well as the opportunity for revolution or other political change. Moscow's less than wholehearted support for left-wing opposition groups in these countries indicates that since the failure of the Omani revolution the Soviets have concluded that there is little profit in assisting rebels who are not likely to come to power. Since the mid-1970s the USSR has tried hardest to establish good relations with the GCC countries, but except for Kuwait the latter have remained suspicious of Moscow owing to Soviet support for rebels in the past, continuing favorable media coverage of these groups, and foreign policy actions such as intervention in Ethiopia and Afghanistan, which the GCC states consider a direct threat to themselves. Thus, except for Kuwait, Moscow has not even been able to establish diplomatic ties with the GCC countries, nor does it seem likely to do so in the near future.

If the present state of stability continues in their internal politics and in their close relations with the West, the Soviets cannot expect to gain any more influence in the GCC countries by attempting either to promote revolution or to befriend the conservative governments in power. But how long will this stability last? Since the GCC states are among the few remaining absolute monarchies left in the world, it seems only reasonable to anticipate that some form of political change will occur in them. Although the Soviets can probably do little to instigate it, political change occurring in the GCC could provide Moscow with the opportunity to weaken Western influence, strengthen Soviet influence, and ultimately gain control of the region's oil.

What are some of the possible, though not necessarily probable, forms that political change in the GCC could take? What would be the likely Soviet reaction to them, and what opportunities would they offer the Soviets to expand their influence? One change that could occur is that the Soviet Union might succeed in establishing diplomatic relations with some or all of the five GCC states it does not yet have such ties with. The Soviets would obviously be happy about this, but if no other political change took place, this would probably not lead to an expansion of Soviet influence. As with Kuwait, the Soviets would probably be so concerned about maintaining diplomatic relations that they might cease giving political or propaganda support to opposition groups in the GCC. Having embassies in the GCC countries would allow the Soviets more contact with people there, but the embassy personnel would undoubtedly be monitored so closely that they would have little opportunity to aid Marxist subversion. Western officials and media tend to predict the rise of Soviet influence in the area when officials of GCC states, especially Saudi Arabia, even hint at the possibility of exchanging ambassadors, but this is not a change that would necessarily harm Western interests or greatly benefit Soviet ones. Indeed, it is unusual that a country as important as Saudi Arabia does not have relations with the USSR.

Another change that could take place is the seizure of power in any one of these states by a member of the ruling family who otherwise might have to wait a long time or not come to power at all. The likely Soviet response would be to recognize the new ruler immediately with the hope that he would then seek friendly relations with the USSR, as Kuwait has. The Soviets are unlikely to express hostility to a member of the royal family who seized power, as they did when Sultan Qabus of Oman overthrew his father in 1970; the Soviets saw Qabus as a British puppet and seemed to anticipate that the Marxist rebels would soon overthrow him anyway. Yet even when Moscow does recognize ruling family members who seize power, as it did the new Qatari Amir who ousted his cousin in 1972, this will not necessarily result in greater influence for the Soviets.

A more serious political change in these countries would be a coup d'état by the military. Once again, the Soviets could be expected to recognize the new government immediately. If the new military government was leftist or even less conservative than the monarchy it replaced (not a very difficult feat), the new leadership would probably recognize the USSR and eventually receive military assistance from the USSR as even moderate Arab states such as Jordan and Kuwait have done. A leftist, anti-Western military government, though, would not want to be dominated by the Soviets.

A Marxist insurgency in one of the GCC countries would undoubtedly receive Soviet political support and low-level military assistance (perhaps via South Yemen). Based on its past actions, the USSR would probably not give large-scale military support or intervene on behalf of the insurgents for fear that this might lead to Western intervention and a possible clash between the superpowers. Indeed, the Soviets would rather see a long-lasting insurgency sap the government's strength and the West's will to support it effectively. Should a Marxist government succeed in coming to power, the Soviets would recognize it and might act quickly to sign a treaty of friendship and cooperation as well as gain military facilities on its territory. This would be the best of all possible political changes that the Soviets could hope for in the Peninsula.

Instead of Marxist or leftist forces, a strong Islamic fundamentalist movement could rise up in the GCC countries. If the Soviets followed the same course of action they did in Iran, they would do or say little to support the Islamic fundamentalists until the monarchy was on the verge of collapse, when they would suddenly embrace the rebels. They would recognize Islamic fundamentalist governments immediately, but as in Iran, might gain very little influence with them even though the fundamentalists could be strongly anti-Western. Indeed, the rise of Islamic fundamentalism on the Peninsula might be unwelcome to the Soviets, for it could threaten not only the pro-Western monarchies but also the pro-Soviet Marxist government of South Yemen.[1]

Another type of political change could occur if the central governments of the GCC states somehow lost much of the internal strength they have now but were too strong to be overthrown. This could result from greatly diminished oil revenues owing to an (unlikely) oil price decline of dramatic proportions. These countries might then see a host of tribal and other forces become influential and vie for power, as is occurring now in North Yemen. The Soviets would seize the opportunity to gain influence by supporting some of these groups, but as in North Yemen, other foreign powers would support different groups, making complete control of the country by pro-Soviet forces difficult.

It is also possible that the GCC states could evolve into constitutional monarchies with popularly elected parliaments. Kuwait has advanced furthest along this path, though it still has a long way to go. The Soviets would also welcome this change and would hope that elected parliaments might influence their governments to have friendly relations with the USSR and to support Soviet foreign policy positions on various issues, just as Kuwait does. The Soviets fear, however, that should "bourgeois democracy" become entrenched in these countries, the governments would not want to come under Soviet domination, nor would the people necessarily support revolutionary forces if they could change their leaders through elections.

Finally, there is also the possibility that there will be little or no significant internal political change in the GCC countries owing to the difficulty in bringing about any of the changes mentioned above. No matter what kind of internal change threatened to occur in the UAE, Bahrain, or Qatar, the relatively small size of these countries as well as their close proximity to Saudi Arabia would allow the Saudis to intervene militarily to put a stop to any change they considered undesirable. The Saudis would also be able to intervene in Kuwait if the forces seeking political change were not strongly supported by either Iraq (not likely at present) or Iran (difficult unless it defeats Iraq). In Oman, the Sultan's highly professional armed forces could probably defeat any internal threat, but if help was needed the British would probably provide it as they did during the Dhofar insurgency. It is also doubtful that a leftist military coup could take place in Oman as long as almost all the top military posts are held by British officers.

With the possible exception of Oman, then, the internal security of the GCC states relies primarily on the internal stability and strength of Saudi Arabia. Each of these possible changes seems particularly unlikely in the Kingdom. There may be differences within the royal family, but it understands from past experience in the nineteenth century that lack of family unity can mean the loss of the throne. A military coup would also be difficult because security within the armed services hinders cooperation among potential plotters, and even if they could combine they would have to confront the loyalist National Guard. A Marxist or other revolt simply does not seem feasible at present since the government is so strong and other forces, including foreign workers, are so tightly controlled. Nor does a drastic fall in the price of oil seem likely, which could weaken the central government and allow other forces to become more powerful. The transformation of the Kingdom into a constitutional monarchy also seems doubtful, since the royal family does not seem willing to move along this path at all. The rise of Islamic fundamentalism is possible, but it is not likely that Khomeini's Iranian Shia variety will take root in this predominantly Sunni Arab country. Finally, if no other political changes take place, the Saudis are not likely to change their views about establishing relations with the Soviets. No political change in Saudi Arabia and the GCC, then, means no gain in influence for Moscow.

There are, of course, also several potential external threats to the GCC states. The most ominous one at present stems from the Iran-Iraq war. Should Iran manage to defeat Iraq, Tehran might decide to turn against the militarily much weaker GCC states. Moscow might be pleased to see these pro-Western governments under attack or even overthrown, but it would not necessarily gain from this owing to Iranian hostility toward the USSR. If Iran either defeats Iraq or manages to replace Saddam Hussein with a pro-Iranian government in Baghdad, the Soviets would lose an important friend. If the Iranians then turn against Kuwait, Moscow will also lose a friend. Should Iranian influence then spread to the rest of the GCC, these countries would not become friendly with the USSR either. In addition, if the Iranians succeeded in controlling the GCC, they could also threaten to bring Islamic revolution to Marxist South Yemen as well, which would be a serious blow to the Soviets. Finally, Iranian control of the Arabian Peninsula would not help the Soviets in gaining control of the region's oil, though it would reduce Western influence there.

Yet to do all this (and it is not clear that Tehran intends to), Iran must first defeat Iraq, which is proving to be an extremely difficult task. The USSR as well as several Western states (particularly France) are sending modern weapons to Baghdad, and the GCC states are giving Iraq economic and financial assistance. One way in which the Soviets could expand their influence with the GCC countries is if the latter feel increasingly threatened by Iran but cannot obtain the arms they want from the United States or the West. They may then conclude that to defend themselves they have no choice but to have ties with Moscow and buy Soviet arms. The Kuwaiti news media, if not Kuwaiti government officials, compared the American refusal to sell the emirate Stinger antiaircraft missiles in the spring of 1984 with the USSR's willingness to meet all Kuwait's requests and concluded that the USSR was more reliable than the United States in helping Kuwait enhance its security.

Although many Americans would not think so, the GCC countries seriously regard Israel as a threat to their security. The Israeli attack on a country as far away as Iraq in the summer of 1981 heightened this fear. If the Israelis ever bombed or launched any form of attack on any of the GCC countries, the Soviets would stand to gain considerably, especially if the United States did little or nothing to stop the attack or continued giving military aid to Israel afterward. The Soviets could also benefit if the United States helped the Israelis attack another Arab state with equipment or facilities based in the GCC, as when the U.S.-flown AWACS in Saudi Arabia were widely accused by Arabs of deliberately ignoring Israeli warplanes or even helping them cross Saudi airspace on the bombing mission to Iraq. There would be strong pressure on the GCC governments by other Arab states as well as their own people and even officials to move away from the United States. The USSR would then renew its efforts to build friendly ties with these states and perhaps offer military assistance to help defend them against Israel. In these circumstances, their offers might be accepted. Even without an Israeli attack on the GCC, the Soviets will continue to try to take advantage of the GCC states' unhappiness over American support to Israel.

Marxist insurgency in North Yemen could also threaten Saudi Arabia especially if the revolutionaries succeeded in coming to power, subduing all of North Yemen, allowing a Soviet military presence in the country, and perhaps uniting with the South. With the two Yemens united, or at least cooperating with each other and the Soviets, they could focus their attention on attempting to spread revolution either in Oman or in Saudi Arabia. They might incite the ethnically Yemeni population of Saudi Arabia's Asir Province (just to the north of North Yemen) and attempt to reclaim it. At any rate, a Marxist North Yemen with its very large population, either alone or combined with the South, would pose a much greater security threat to the Saudis than South Yemen alone. But this does not seem likely to happen. Colonel Salih may be overthrown by the army at some point, but a future military government in Sanaa would probably be no more willing to be dominated by the Soviets (or anyone else) than the present or past ones. At this time the government of Colonel Salih is relatively strong, whereas his Marxist opponents are weak. Even if a Marxist government came to power in Sanaa, it would find subduing the conservative tribes extremely difficult, especially since the latter would receive Saudi aid. North Yemeni politics are relatively unstable, but this instability cannot easily be taken advantage of to promote Marxism. Yet even if the Soviets gained influence in North Yemen via a successful Marxist revolution or closer relations with the non-Marxist government, the Saudis would be extremely frightened and would probably seek increased U.S. military assistance.

Finally, South Yemen could attempt to invade or promote revolution in any of its three neighbors, but unless this was strongly supported by the USSR (and so far none of the PDRY's conflicts with its neighbors have been), it would probably not succeed. Their main result would most likely be to induce South Yemen's neighbors to seek greater military assistance, and perhaps even intervention, from the West. A large-scale Soviet, Cuban, or East German military buildup in the PDRY, whether intended to support an invasion or not, would also lead the GCC countries to turn to the West for military assistance. Thus, even if the hard-liners in the present power struggle in Aden succeed, the Soviets would probably not want them to attempt to either promote revolution in any of its neighbors or mount an invasion against them, both to avoid failure and to keep the GCC states from allying more closely than ever with the West.

Yet if none of these several possible internal or external political changes seem particularly likely to occur, it does not seem reasonable to expect that there will be no political changes in the Arabian Peninsula that could harm the interests of the West and enhance those of the USSR. The USSR is either unable or unwilling to promote such changes itself, but it will strive to reduce Western influence and increase its own should any of them occur. The West as a whole, and the United States in particular, must give some thought to how it should act to best preserve its interests if and when political change does come to the Peninsula.

Of all the Third World countries that have been declared "vital" to Western interests, those of the Arabian Peninsula really are so because the West depends so heavily on their oil—a dependence that is likely to grow in time, since this region has the world's largest concentration of oil reserves. Some have argued, though, that the West should not be particularly concerned about who controls this region, since they will have just as much interest in selling oil to the West for hard currency as the West has in buying it from them. They point out that after the downfall of the Shah brought an extremely anti-Western government to power in Tehran, the Iranians continued to sell oil to the West. Similarly, the Iraqi government is friendly toward the USSR and rhetorically anti-Western, but it also has sold as much oil as it could to the West. Radical, pro-Soviet governments in the Arabian Peninsula would want to do the same, they argue.

This argument seems excessively optimistic. If the Soviets came to have as much influence in Saudi Arabia and the GCC countries as they now have in South Yemen, the USSR and its new allies could for political reasons independent of the economic self-interest of the Peninsula countries decide to reduce or deny the West's access to the region's oil. The West cannot rely on pro-Soviet Marxist leaders not to do this even though it could mean a precipitous loss of income for them, especially if there were Soviet and Cuban forces in the country and a divided leadership that Moscow could manipulate, as in Aden. Pro-Soviet governments on the Peninsula might well, with Moscow's approval, continue to sell oil to the West, but the fact that they could threaten to deny oil unless the West (especially Western Europe and Japan) made political concession is reason enough for the West to vigorously oppose Soviet efforts to gain influence that could lead to control over the Arabian Peninsula.

But does this mean that the West, particularly the United States, will have to act forcefully to prevent any political change in the Arabian Peninsula for fear it might lead to Soviet control over the area? This seems neither possible nor desirable. There are certain kinds of changes, such as insurrections, where Western intervention could prove extremely costly in terms of lives and money. And as with America's intervention in Vietnam, a substantial proportion of Western electorates might object. There is, after all, a strong likelihood that forces other than the most pro-Soviet ones would indeed want to continue selling oil to the West and would not have any interest in seeing the USSR come to control the region. Attempting to suppress these forces might backfire and induce them to invite the Soviets in to assist and protect them, which they might not do if they did not have to face Western opposition.

Because the Arabian Peninsula is so extremely important to the West, the United States cannot afford to merely express its opposition against the forces of change that might rise in these countries while not making sufficient effort to stop them as it has so often done elsewhere. By expressing hostility toward these forces of change, the United States would surely risk inducing them to become pro-Soviet (if they were not to begin with) and ask for Soviet assistance. At the same time, by taking little or no action to stop them from coming to power, the United States would risk that these forces might succeed, either with or without Soviet help, and might then invite the USSR to help protect them against America, which has indicated hostility toward them.

Political change in the GCC states, then, will pose a serious dilemma for the United States, forcing it to choose between two relatively stark options: America must either act decisively—perhaps forcefully—to defend the current pro-Western regimes, or it must immediately establish good relations with the forces of change. If the United States gives insufficient support to the present regimes and indicates hostility to the forces of change without doing much to stop them, this could be disastrous for Western interests. For if the present monarchies are overthrown, the Soviets can be expected to immediately offer aid and support to the new governments. To avoid this, the United States either must stop such forces from coming to power, or it must ally with them or, at the minimum, influence them to remain neutral and not invite the Soviets in should they succeed in gaining power.

There are certain kinds of political change where the course of action the West should take seems fairly clear. If the five GCC countries that have not done so already decide to follow Kuwait's lead in establishing diplomatic relations with the USSR and even buying weapons from it, the United States should accept this. Having relations like these with the USSR, as Kuwait demonstrates, does not mean that these states have become pro-Soviet. If a change of government occurs because one member of a ruling family overthrows another, the United States would be ill advised to become involved in an intrafamily power struggle, but instead should be willing to have good relations with any monarch. Obviously the West would not object if these absolute monarchies became Western-style constitutional monarchies. At the other extreme, the United States should respond forcefully to defend the present GCC governments in the event they are attacked or threatened by external forces and *if the GCC governments request U.S. assistance.*

It would be more difficult for the West to judge how to react to violent internal change, particularly in Saudi Arabia. If a military coup took place, there might be little the West could do but accept it for fear the new leaders otherwise might turn to the Soviets. In case of a rebellion or insurrection led by Marxists, Arab nationalists, Islamic fundamentalists, or whomever, the West would naturally want to support the friendly governments in power, and with Western military assistance the insurgency might well be ended, as in Oman. But if the monarchies no longer commanded general popular support, Western intervention might be a futile effort and lead the rebels to turn more toward the Soviets than they would otherwise have been inclined to do.

What the United States should or should not do in the event of political change harmful to Western interests, such as domestic upheaval, insurgency, or invasion, cannot be decided here. Much will depend on the specific circumstances at the time. There are some things, however, that the United States can do to prevent change harmful to Western interests and thus perhaps avoid the difficult choice between military intervention and attempting to befriend new forces that may be hostile. One action the United States has taken to preserve its interests in the region is to form a Rapid Deployment Force. The RDF, though, is designed mainly to deter and oppose a Soviet invasion of the area, but as I have argued here, that is probably the least likely contingency. Some measures should be taken to guard against a Soviet invasion, since the absence of such measures could only encourage the Soviets by reducing the risks of such an operation. However, since other kinds of change are more likely, something should be done to prepare for them as well. The RDF, of course, could be used to intervene against insurgency in the Arabian Peninsula, and this might prove successful, as did British aid to Oman in ending the rebellion there. Yet should the insurgents prove to be strong, the central governments weak, and the conflict long, the American public would be unlikely to support American involvement in "another Vietnam." Obviously it would be best to prevent the conditions that could give rise to an insurrection to begin with. Other policies are required to prevent the loss of Western influence in the Peninsula either through rebellion or through successful Soviet diplomacy.

This is a task for which guidelines are difficult to set, especially since the prospect of internal rebellion or of Soviet diplomatic gains in the GCC states seems extremely remote at this time. One thing it is necessary to keep in mind is that while the West may value the Arabian Peninsula mainly because of its oil, the countries there do not consist of oil fields alone but also include people and governments with aspirations and fears of their own. To preserve its interests, the West should avoid taking actions that alienate both the people and the governments of the region or that would separate the people from their governments.

One area in which the United States should exercise caution is its plans to defend the Peninsula. Many in the region have concluded, as I have, that a Soviet attack on the Gulf or the Peninsula is not likely. U.S. government claims that the Soviets do pose a strong threat to the region, and American efforts to gain military facilities in the GCC countries in order to guard against it, are looked upon with skepticism. Many newspapers in the region repeat the Soviet argument that the USSR does not represent a threat to the region at all, and they see American claims that Moscow does as only an excuse for the United States to move armed forces in and take control of the Gulf itself. When the United States repeatedly and publicly asks the GCC states for military facilities (even though they have already indicated they do not want to grant them) but then Washington refuses to sell them certain weapons they request for their defense needs, these doubts are increased. Indeed, if the Arab world and the GCC countries' own media generally perceive America as attempting to dominate the region, the GCC governments may fear that they will appear to be American puppets and risk becoming weak domestically if they give the United States the military facilities it wants. Instead of publicly advising the GCC states on what they should do to enhance their security, the United States should give such advice only privately and should be responsive to meeting their security needs as they define them when they ask for such assistance.

Another point of contention between the Peninsula states and the United States is the Arab-Israeli conflict. As this study has shown, every Peninsula government (except perhaps Oman) objects strongly to U.S. military and other support for Israel when Israel is occupying Arab territory. The GCC governments in particular fear that, because they cooperate closely with Washington, radical Arab governments as well as internal opponents will seek to overthrow these conservative governments since they are close to the United States and, by implication, to Israel. Yet if these governments were seriously threatened by internal or external forces that objected mainly to their continuing links to the United States while it continues to support Israel, the GCC governments could be expected to try to save themselves by loosening or even severing their ties with the United States and perhaps developing relations with the USSR. If this occurred and the GCC governments still remained threatened by internal and external opponents, it would be very difficult for the United States to intervene and save them, since all involved in the struggle would be anti-American.

The possibility that this will occur is not insignificant, and because the region is so important the United States should take steps to see that it does not. This would mean adopting a more balanced policy toward the Arab-Israeli conflict in which the United States would be less pro-Israeli and more evenhanded and neutral regarding their quarrel. It may be the emotional inclination of many Americans to support Israel, but the military and economic needs of the West make it essential that the United States maintain close, friendly relations with the GCC countries as well. It is very much in America's strategic interests to see that Israel does not undertake actions that undermine U.S.-GCC relations and not to support Israel if it does. The United States cannot afford to allow its support for Israel to alienate the GCC countries so much that they feel forced to reduce their ties to America and perhaps increase them with the USSR.

An Iranian victory in the Iran-Iraq war could lead to an Iranian invasion of the GCC countries or Iranian support for Islamic fundamentalists there. It is in America's interest, then, to see that Iraq is not defeated. This does not mean that the United States should intervene against the Iranians especially since the Tehran government's extreme anti-Sovietism coincides with U.S. interests. The West would not benefit if the present Iranian government or a future one invited Soviet influence into Iran because it was so afraid of the United States. Indeed, Washington and Tehran have several interests in common, whether or not either of them now recognizes it. But since Iranian troops are in Iraq (and despite the fact that Iraq started the war), America should take steps to see that the Baghdad government is not defeated. For without Iraq's army, half a million strong, standing in the way, the task of preventing Iran from overthrowing the GCC governments would be much more difficult for the United States. Above all, the United States should avoid giving the GCC states the impression that it would not help them fend off Iranian threats and thus perhaps lead them to seek Soviet military assistance in protecting themselves.

Because of North Yemen's large population and potential for presenting a more serious threat to Saudi Arabia than South Yemen alone if a pro-Soviet government came to power in Sanaa, the United States should more actively assist the YAR in order to prevent the USSR from gaining influence there. It is in neither America's nor Saudi Arabia's interest that North Yemen should have to turn to the USSR for arms to defeat PDRY-backed Marxist insurgents, as happened in 1979–82. Should a stronger insurgency ever break out, the USSR cannot be relied upon to save the non-Marxist government in Sanaa. If Saudi Arabia is unwilling, for whatever reason, to buy U.S. arms for retransfer to the YAR, then the United States should provide direct military assistance to Sanaa based on long-term loans. Nevertheless, the United States should not become too closely identified with the present military regime in the YAR, if only because North Yemen's experience indicates that at some point it will eventually give way to a new government. The United States should also provide economic assistance designed to benefit the people, work toward eliminating the economic causes of revolt, and give any new regime an incentive to maintain good relations with the U.S. Types of economic assistance that might be provided include further work in building and maintaining roads, construction of schools, hospitals, clinics, and training centers for teaching technical skills and the English language, and help for greater numbers of Yemeni students to pursue their education in the United States.

Finally, the United States should be receptive to overtures by the present South Yemeni government or a future one for normal bilateral relations. Others have argued that the United States should not allow the restoration of diplomatic ties with Aden because the PDRY would only request military and economic aid that Washington would not want to provide and because the hard-line faction might seize upon renewed ties to Washington as an excuse to purge the moderates.[2] These arguments, however, do not seem convincing. A government so closely allied to the USSR militarily is not likely to ask for or even want U.S. military assistance. While Aden might wish to receive American economic assistance, it would not expect to gain any unless it modified its external policies in a direction less hostile to the West. But the United States really cannot expect such a reorientation unless the South Yemeni leaders realize that friendly cooperation with the United States is possible. We will never know whether a quick and favorable American response to Salim Rubayyi 'Ali's overtures for friendship with the United States in 1977 and 1978 would have prevented his overthrow in June 1978 and kept the Soviets from gaining predominant influence in the country. The lesson that other South Yemeni leaders probably drew from this experience is that America cannot be relied upon to help those who want to decrease the PDRY's dependence on the USSR and increase its ties to the West. Like improved relations between South Yemen and its three neighbors, normal relations between Washington and Aden might give even the hard-liners an incentive not to take actions that would harm the relationship. A U.S. initiative to reestablish diplomatic ties with the PDRY, however, would be inadvisable now while there is a serious power struggle going on. Nevertheless, it would be in America's interest to respond favorably to any South Yemeni initiative for improved relations.

The Soviets have had only limited success in gaining influence in the Arabian Peninsula countries and none in obtaining control over their oil. The USSR, however, will undoubtedly persist in its efforts to gain influence there either through attempting to ally with the present governments of the region or through supporting revolution against them whenever the opportunity arises. It is very much in the interests of America and the West to see that the Soviets do not succeed. This can best be accomplished not only by taking steps to guard against a Soviet invasion, which does not seem very likely to occur anyway, but also by adopting the other measures recommended here to prevent the spread of Soviet influence to this vital region through less dramatic but more likely means.

Notes

INTRODUCTION

1. *BP Statistical Review of World Oil* (London: British Petroleum, June 1985), pp. 8, 16.

2. Ibid., p. 2.

3. A Russian warship first visited the Gulf in 1893, and abortive attempts were made in 1895 and 1897 to gain Bandar 'Abbas on the Persian side of the Gulf for a possible railroad terminus and coaling station. Russian flotillas came to the Gulf again in 1901 and 1902, and in 1903 they were accompanied by French vessels. The Russians subsidized a steamship line that began sailing from Odessa to Muscat and Kuwait in 1901, but this was unprofitable and did not last long. The Russians also had a plan to build a railroad from Tripoli in what is now Lebanon to Kuwait in order to have a transit route bypassing the British-controlled Suez Canal, but as with German plans to build a railroad from Berlin to Baghdad with a terminus at Kuwait, the British prevented this.

After 'Abd al-'Aziz ibn Sa'ud conquered Riyadh in 1902, Holden and Johns claim that he met the Russian consul to Bushire (then a principal Persian port) in Kuwait in early 1903. According to the Soviet historian A. M. Vasil'ev, however, the Russian consul met with 'Abd al-'Aziz's father and not the conqueror himself. After the Russian defeat in the Russo-Japanese War in 1905 and the Anglo-Russian entente of 1907, the Russian threat to British interests in the Gulf faded.

According to William R. Crawford, a Deputy Assistant Secretary of State during the Carter administration, "The Russian objective was clearly stated more than 100 years ago at the Constantinople Convention, that the Red Sea and the southern entrance thereto were a legitimate area of Russian military hegemony."

See Abdullah Muhammad Morsy, *The United Arab Emirates: A Modern History* (London: Croom Helm; New York: Barnes and Noble, 1978), pp. 28-30; Robert Geran Landen, *Oman since 1856: Disruptive Modernization in a Traditional Society* (Princeton: Princeton University Press, 1967), pp. 100, 251, 261; David Holden and Richard Johns, *The House of Saud: The Rise and Rule of the Most Powerful Dynasty in the Arab World* (New York: Holt, Rinehart and Winston, 1981), pp. 26-30; A. M. Vasil'ev, *Istoriia Saudovskoi Aravii (1745–1973)* (Moscow: Nauka, 1982), p. 236; and U.S. Congress, House Committee on Foreign Affairs, Subcommittee on Europe and the Middle East, *Proposed Arms Transfers to the Yemen Arab Republic,* 96th Congress, 1st session (Washington, D.C.: U.S. GPO, 1979), pp. 3-4.

4. See John Baldry, "Soviet Relations with Saudi Arabia and the Yemen, 1917–1938," *Middle Eastern Studies* 20, 1 (January 1984): 53-80. These events will be discussed in further detail in the chapters on North Yemen and Saudi Arabia.

5. A. Yodfat and M. Abir, *In the Direction of the Persian Gulf: The Soviet Union and the Persian Gulf* (London: Frank Cass, 1977), pp. 31-32.

6. Central Intelligence Agency, *Prospects for Soviet Oil Production,* ER 77-10270 (Washington, D.C.: CIA, April 1977). See also CIA, *The International Energy Situation: Outlook to 1985,* ER 77-10240U (Washington, D.C.: CIA, April 1977), and CIA, *Prospects for Soviet Oil Production: A Supplemental Analysis,* ER 77-10425 (Washington, D.C.: CIA, July 1977).

7. U.S. Congress, Joint Economic Committee, Subcommittee on International Trade, Finance, and Security Economics, *Allocation of Resources in the Soviet Union and China—1981,* 97th Congress, 1st session (Washington, D.C.: U.S. GPO, 1982), p. 85.

8. David Wilson, *Soviet Oil and Gas to 1990* (Cambridge, Mass.: Abt Books 1982), pp. 2-4, 172.

9. *BP Statistical Review of World Oil* (London: British Petroleum, June 1984), pp. 2, 5, 8, 20, and Central Intelligence Agency, *Handbook of Economic Statistics, 1984,* CPAS 84-10002 (Washington, D.C.: CIA, September 1984), pp. 130-132.

10. Wilson, *Soviet Oil and Gas,* ch. 5.

11. Mark Wood, "Soviets Cite Problems in Siberian Oil Output," *The Washington Post,* May 28, 1984, pp. E2-E3, and Gary Lee, "Soviet Oil Output Shows a Decline," *The Washington Post,* April 13, 1985, pp. A1, A14.

12. Jonathan Steele, *Soviet Power: The Kremlin's Foreign Policy—Brezhnev to Andropov* (New York: Simon and Schuster, 1983), p. 204. See also Ed A. Hewett, *Energy Economics and Foreign Policy in the Soviet Union* (Washington, D.C.: Brookings Institution, 1984), p. 163.

13. "Calling Iran's Bluff—for a While," *The Economist,* February 25, 1984, p. 64.

CHAPTER 1: NORTH YEMEN

1. On the pre-Islamic history of Yemen, see Robert W. Stookey, *Yemen: The Politics of the Yemen Arab Republic* (Boulder, Colo.: Westview Press, 1978), ch. 1.

2. For more on the religious divisions of North Yemen, see Manfred W. Wenner, *Modern Yemen: 1918–1966* (Baltimore: Johns Hopkins Press, 1967), pp. 30-36.

3. Stookey, *Yemen,* p. 133.

4. Ibid., p. 146.

5. Wenner, *Modern Yemen,* pp. 42-45.

6. This was the treaty of Da'an, which was signed in October 1911 but ratified by the Turks only in September 1913; ibid., pp. 47-48.

7. Ibid., pp. 71-78.

8. Ibid., pp. 142-147.

9. Ibid., pp. 147-164.

10. Ibid., pp. 152-156; Eric Macro, *Yemen and the Western World since 1571* (New York: Frederick A. Praeger, 1968), pp. 111-113; and Stephen Page, *The USSR and Arabia: The Development of Soviet Policies and Attitudes towards the Countries of the Arabian Peninsula, 1955–1970* (London: Central Asian Research Centre, 1971), pp. 17-18.

11. Wenner, *Modern Yemen*, pp. 169-171.

12. Stookey, *Yemen*, pp. 213-223.

13. Wenner, *Modern Yemen*, pp. 182-183.

14. Macro, *Yemen and the Western World*, p. 114.

15. Page, *USSR and Arabia*, pp. 37-38.

16. Wenner, *Modern Yemen*, pp. 184-185, 188-189.

17. Stookey, *Yemen*, pp. 223-225.

18. Wenner, *Modern Yemen*, pp. 124-128.

19. Ibid., pp. 128-130.

20. *Keesing's Contemporary Archives*, September 29–October 6, 1962, pp. 18997-98.

21. For narratives of the Yemeni civil war, see Dana Adams Schmidt, *Yemen: The Unknown War* (New York: Holt, Rinehart and Winston, 1968), and Edgar O'Ballance, *The War in the Yemen* (London: Faber and Faber, 1971). For an analysis of Egyptian policies in Yemen, see A. I. Dawisha, "Intervention in the Yemen: An Analysis of Egyptian Perceptions and Policies," *The Middle East Journal* 29, 1 (Winter 1975): pp. 47-63.

22. O'Ballance, *War in the Yemen*, chs. 10–11.

23. Stookey, *Yemen*, pp. 266-272.

24. Robin Bidwell, *The Two Yemens* (Singapore: Longman/Westview, 1983), pp. 271-274.

25. J. E. Peterson, *Yemen: The Search for a Modern State* (Baltimore: Johns Hopkins University Press, 1982), pp. 192, 196, and *Keesing's Contemporary Archives*, December 9, 1977, p. 28716.

26. Peterson, *Yemen*, p. 121, and *Keesing's Contemporary Archives*, December 9, 1977, pp. 28715-16.

27. *Keesing's Contemporary Archives*, November 3, 1978, p. 29292, and *Middle East Contemporary Survey*, vol. 2, 1977–78 (New York: Holmes and Meier, 1979), pp. 794-800.

28. *Keesing's Contemporary Archives*, November 3, 1978, pp. 29291-92.

29. Ibid.

30. Ibid., and *Keesing's Contemporary Archives*, March 16, 1979, p. 29505.

31. J. E. Peterson, *Conflict in the Yemens and Superpower Involvement*, Occasional Papers Series (Washington, D.C.: Georgetown University Center for Contemporary Arab Studies, December 1981), and Nigel Harvey, "New Stability Emerges—but for How Long?" *Middle East Economic Digest*, November 5, 1982, pp. 24, 27.

32. "For the Record," *The Washington Post*, May 23, 1983, p. A22.

33. *Keesing's Contemporary Archives*, March 16–23, 1963, and O'Ballance, *War in the Yemen*, p. 73.

34. O'Ballance, *War in the Yemen*, p. 155.

35. Page, *USSR and Arabia*, p. 75.

36. Ibid., pp. 74-75.

37. Ibid., p. 75. In the autumn of 1962, the royalists captured three Soviets who landed a helicopter near Marib in what they mistakenly thought was republican-controlled territory. The royalists charged that they were Soviet military advisers participating in combat operations. The three Soviets, however, turned out to be civilian air pilots who had been in Yemen since the days of Imam Ahmad; see Schmidt, *Yemen*, p. 65, and *Keesing's Contemporary Archives*, March 16–23, 1963, p. 19299.

38. O'Ballance, *War in the Yemen*, p. 108.

39. *Keesing's Contemporary Archives*, February 8–15, 1964, p. 19891, and O'Ballance, *War in the Yemen*, ch. 5. The Soviet Union objected to the United Nations Yemen Observation Mission (UNYOM) because it had been arranged by the UN Secretary-General and not the Security Council. When the Security Council voted to approve UNYOM, the USSR abstained. UNYOM entered Yemen in June 1963 under a limited mandate by which it was not allowed to make contact with the royalists. The mission received little cooperation from any party and was finally withdrawn in September 1964.

40. *Keesing's Contemporary Archives*, April 11–18, 1964, p. 20006, and O'Ballance, *War in the Yemen*, pp. 123-124. As-Sallal also visited China June 1–11, 1964, and signed a ten-year treaty of friendship as well as economic and technical agreements in Peking; see *Keesing's Contemporary Archives*, January 16–23, 1965, p. 20530.

41. Richard E. Bissell, "Soviet Use of Proxies in the Third World: The Case of Yemen," *Soviet Studies* 30, 1 (January 1978): 93.

42. O'Ballance, *War in the Yemen*, ch. 9, and *Keesing's Contemporary Archives*, October 9–16, 1965, p. 21003.

43. Page, *USSR and Arabia*, p. 88.

44. Ibid.

45. O'Ballance, *War in the Yemen*, p. 158, and *Keesing's Contemporary Archives*, February 25–March 4, 1967, p. 21891.

46. Bidwell, *Two Yemens*, pp. 214-215.

47. Page, *USSR and Arabia*, p. 89.

48. Ibid., and O'Ballance, *War in the Yemen*, pp. 175-176.

49. Cited in Raymond L. Garthoff, *Soviet Military Policy: A Historical Analysis* (New York: Frederick A. Praeger, 1966), p. 213.

50. Georgi Mirsky, "The Proletariat and National Liberation," *New Times*, no. 18 (May 1964): 6.

51. Cited in Garthoff, *Soviet Military Policy*, p. 214.

52. Page, *USSR and Arabia*, pp. 88-89.

53. Ibid., p. 89.

54. Vladimir Sakharov, a Soviet diplomat who was based in Hodeida at the

time and later defected to the United States, described a violent attack made by the citizens of Hodeida against the Soviet consulate there because of the Arab defeat. Sakharov blamed the Chinese for having incited the mob. See Vladimir Sakharov, *High Treason* (New York: Ballantine Books, 1980) pp. 161-163.

55. Page, *USSR and Arabia*, p. 108, and O'Ballance, *War in the Yemen*, p. 184.

56. Bissell, "Soviet Use of Proxies," p. 96.

57. Ibid., pp. 97-98, and Page, *USSR and Arabia*, pp. 108-109.

58. Bissell, "Soviet Use of Proxies," pp. 98-99.

59. Ibid., p. 97, and *Keesing's Contemporary Archives*, February 24–March 2, 1968, p. 22548.

60. *Keesing's Contemporary Archives*, February 24–March 2, 1968, p. 22548.

61. Bidwell, *Two Yemens*, pp. 216-217.

62. Schmidt, *Yemen*, p. 296, and Page, *USSR and Arabia*, p. 108.

63. Bidwell, *Two Yemens*, pp. 216-217.

64. O'Ballance, *War in the Yemen*, p. 197.

65. Schmidt, *Yemen*, p. 297.

66. Bissell, "Soviet Use of Proxies," p. 101.

67. Ibid., and L. N. Kotlov, *Iemenskaia arabskaia respublika* (Mosocw: Nauka, 1971), pp. 214-215.
The PRF-government conflict was also based partly on Shafei-Zaidi rivalry, with the PRF having many Shafeis and the government dominated by Zaidis. Another such clash took place in Sanaa in August 1968 as a result of differences between Zaidi and Shafei army officers; the Zaidis again emerged more powerful; see *Keesing's Contemporary Archives*, February 15–22, 1969, p. 23200.

68. Charles B. McLane, *Soviet-Third World Relations*, vol. 1, *Soviet-Middle East Relations* (London: Central Asian Research Centre, 1973), p. 116, and Aryeh Y. Yodfat, *The Soviet Union and the Arabian Peninsula* (London: Croom Helm; New York: St. Martin's Press, 1983), p. 4.

69. Bidwell, *Two Yemens*, pp. 239-240.

70. Cited in ibid., p. 102.

71. Page, *USSR and Arabia*, p. 110.

72. Ibid., pp. 109-110, and *Keesing's Contemporary Archives*, June 27–July 4, 1970, p. 24053, and August 1–8, 1970, p. 24114.

73. *Keesing's Contemporary Archives*, October 9–16, 1971, p. 24876, and January 1–7, 1973, p. 25654.

74. Stookey, *Yemen*, p. 268, and *At-Tali'ah* (Kuwait), November 6, 1971, pp. 12-13, in Joint Publications Research Service (JPRS) 55005, *Translations on the Near East*, no. 704 (January 21, 1972): 37-41.

75. Damascus MENA in Arabic, March 28, 1972, in *Foreign Broadcast Information Service: Middle East and North Africa Daily Report* (hereafter referred to as FBIS ME), March 29, 1972, pp. B1-B2.

76. Aden ANA in Arabic, March 13, 1972, in *FBIS ME,* March 14, 1972, pp. B2-B3.

77. Baghdad INA in Arabic, March 11, 1972, in *FBIS ME,* March 13, 1972, p. B1.

78. Damascus MENA in Arabic, March 28, 1972, in *FBIS ME,* March 29, 1972, pp. B1-B2.

79. Moscow in Arabic, March 17, 1972, in *Foreign Broadcast Information Service: Soviet Union Daily Report* (hereafter referred to as FBIS SU), March 21, 1972, B3-B4.

80. See Moscow in Arabic, April 4, 1972, in *FBIS SU,* April 5, 1972, pp. B4-B5, and Moscow in Arabic, April 11, 1972, in *FBIS SU,* April 13, 1972, pp. B4-B5.

81. Moscow in Arabic, March 21, 1972, in *FBIS SU,* March 22, 1972, pp. B1-B2.

82. Norman Kirkham, "Yemen to Get MIGs," *The Sunday Telegraph,* March 5, 1972, p. 2.

83. *Keesing's Contemporary Archives,* July 15-22, 1972, p. 25368.

84. Ibid., January 1-7, 1973, p. 25654.

85. Baghdad INA in Arabic, July 18, 1972, in *FBIS ME,* July 19, 1972, p. B1.

86. That this story circulated, though, is an indication that Soviet-YAR relations were not good; Cairo MENA in Arabic, August 4, 1972, in *FBIS ME,* August 7, 1972, p. B1.

87. Kamaran Island lies just off the coast of North Yemen in the Red Sea north of the YAR port of Hodeida and is relatively far from the PDRY. The British seized the island from the Turks in 1915 and ruled it from Aden. South Yemen inherited it from the British upon independence in 1967. After the YAR occupied it in October 1972, the subject of the island's disposition arose. Once the unity agreement of November 1972 was signed, Sanaa argued that it should not return Kamaran to Aden, since after unity the island would belong to all Yemen; *Rose al-Yusuf* (Cairo), December 11, 1972, pp. 20-22, in JPRS 58191, *Translations on the Near East,* no. 897 (February 8, 1973): 1-6.

Although it has been ruled by North Yemen since 1972, many maps published since then still mark it as belonging to South Yemen. This error is probably the result of the general lack of knowledge in the West about Yemeni affairs.

88. *Keesing's Contemporary Archives,* January 1-7, 1973, p. 25655.

89. "Milestone in Yemeni History," *New Times,* no. 40 (October 1972): 16-17; Moscow TASS International Service in English, October 1, 1972, in *FBIS SU,* October 2, 1972, p. B9; Moscow in Arabic, October 6, 1972, in *FBIS SU,* October 10, 1972, p. B8; Moscow in Arabic, October 14, 1972, in *FBIS SU,* October 16, 1972, pp. B10-B11; Moscow TASS International Service in English, October 15, 1972, in *FBIS SU,* October 16, 1972, p. B11; Moscow in Arabic, October 17, 1972, in *FBIS SU,* October 19, 1972, pp. B7-B8; Moscow in Arabic, October 24, 1972, in *FBIS SU,* October 25, 1972, pp. B1-B2; and Moscow in Arabic, October 31, 1972 in *FBIS SU,* November 1, 1972, pp. B6-B7.

90. Yodfat, *Soviet Union,* pp. 4-5, and Bidwell, *Two Yemens,* p. 240. Bidwell also wrote that "around the same time a Russian contingency plan for the invasion of the YAR in conjunction with the PDRY came by chance or design into the hands of

the Sanaa authorities." Bidwell gives no source for this report, but even if such a plan was found, it might well have been a fabrication.

91. Damascus MENA in Arabic, October 3, 1972, *FBIS ME,* October 3, 1972, p. B3. See also *Al-Muharrin,* October 7, 1972, in *FBIS ME,* October 10, 1972, p. B1.

92. Cairo MENA in Arabic, October 4, 1972, in *FBIS ME,* October 5, 1972, p. B3.

93. Cairo MENA in Arabic, October 23, 1972, in *FBIS ME,* October 24, 1972, p. B1.

94. Paul Martin, "N. Yemen Premier Threatens to Resign If No Political Solution Is Found to Conflict with the South," *The Times,* October 23, 1972, p. 5.

95. Cairo MENA in Arabic, October 23, 1972, in *FBIS ME,* October 24, 1972, p. B1.

96. *Ath-Thawrah,* October 5, 1972, p. 2, in *FBIS ME,* October 17, 1972, pp. B3-B4.

97. *Keesing's Contemporary Archives,* March 16, 1979, p. 29505.

98. Peterson, *Yemen,* pp. 124-125.

99. *Keesing's Contemporary Archives,* April 18, 1980, p. 30197.

100. Ibid., p. 30198, and Cairo MENA in Arabic, March 7, 1979, in *FBIS ME,* March 8, 1979, pp. C8-C9.

101. Kuwait KUNA in Arabic, March 8, 1979, in *FBIS ME,* March 9, 1979, pp. C3-C4.

102. U.S. Congress, House Committee on Foreign Affairs, Subcommittee on Europe and the Middle East, *U.S. Interests in, and Policies toward, the Persian Gulf,* 96th Congress, 2d session (Washington, D.C.: U.S. GPO, 1980), pp. 418-419.

103. Ibid. U.S. Secretary of State Cyrus Vance sent a note to Soviet Ambassador Anatoly Dobrynin protesting the presence of Soviet and Cuban military advisers in the PDRY on March 6, 1980; *Keesing's Contemporary Archives,* April 18, 1980, p. 30198.

104. Ruszkiewicz testimony in U.S. Congress, *U.S. Interests in, and Policies toward, the Persian Gulf,* pp. 100-120, 422-427.

105. *Keesing's Contemporary Archives,* April 18, 1980, p. 30198.

106. Ibid.

107. Moscow TASS in English, February 27, 1979, in *FBIS SU,* February 28, 1979, pp. F3-F4.

108. Moscow in Arabic, February 28, 1979, in *FBIS SU,* March 1, 1979, p. F8.

109. O. Anichkin, "Vmeshatel'stvo pentagona," *Izvestiia,* March 18, 1979, p. 5, and V. Vinogradov, "Nagnetaiut napriazhennost'," *Krasnaia Zvezda,* April 18, 1979, p. 3.

110. Moscow World Service in English, March 7, 1979, in *FBIS SU,* March 8, 1979, p. F5.

111. Moscow TASS International Service in Russian, March 13, 1979, in *FBIS SU,* March 14, 1979, p. F5.

112. Moscow Domestic Service in Russian, March 21, 1979, in *FBIS SU,* March 22, 1979, H11.

113. Kuwait KUNA in Arabic, March 8, 1979, in *FBIS ME,* March 9, 1979, pp. C3-C4, and *Keesing's Contemporary Archives,* April 18, 1980, p. 30198.

114. International Institute for Strategic Studies, *The Military Balance 1979–80* (London: IISS, 1979), p. 105. Soviet arms deliveries to the PDRY were also said to be made during the summer of 1978 and in February 1979 just before the fighting began; U.S. Congress, House Committee on Foreign Affairs, Subcommittee on Europe and the Middle East, *Proposed Arms Transfers to the Yemen Arab Republic,* 96th Congress, 1st session (Washington, D.C.: U.S. GPO, 1979), pp. 27-28.

115. U.S. Congress, *Proposed Arms Transfers to the Yemen Arab Republic,* pp. 27-28.

116. *Middle East Contemporary Survey, 1978–79* (New York: Holmes and Meier, 1980), pp. 64-65.

117. Cited in U.S. Congress, *Proposed Arms Transfers to the Yemen Arab Republic,* p. 60. When asked about the statements by U.S. Energy Secretary James Schlesinger on the U.S. intervention in the area to protect the oil fields, Salih replied, "we will not be a tool in U.S. hands nor in those of the Soviet Union." His statement was mistakenly interpreted in the West to be North Yemeni criticism of U.S. aid to the YAR as constituting intervention; Dan Morgan, "U.S. Expedites N. Yemen Arms; Saudis Cautious," *The Washington Post,* March 10, 1979, pp. A1, A11.

118. Kuwait KUNA in Arabic, March 1, 1979, in *FBIS ME,* March 2, 1979, p. C2.

119. Peterson, *Conflict in the Yemens,* pp. 24-25.

120. *Keesing's Contemporary Archives,* April 18, 1980, p. 30199, and *Middle East Contemporary Survey, 1978–79,* pp. 64-66.

121. Ibid.

122. According to one source, there were six leftist groups: the Yemeni Revolution Democratic Party, the Democratic People's Union, the Vanguard Popular Party, the Yemeni Labor Party, the Revolutionary Resistance Party, and the pro-Iraqi Ba'th Party; *Middle East Contemporary Survey, 1976–77* (New York: Holmes and Meier, 1978), p. 653.

According to Yemeni sources, this list is correct except for the pro-Iraqi Ba'th Party. Relations between Sanaa and Baghdad have been good, especially in recent years, and so the Iraqi Ba'thists have not encouraged opposition to the YAR government. The Syrian Ba'thists, however, have often been at odds with Sanaa, partly because Sanaa has good relations with Damascus's rival, Baghdad. The Ba'thist elements in the NDF, then, have been pro-Syrian.

123. *Middle East Contemporary Survey, 1977–78,* p. 794.

124. Ibid., pp. 797, 797.

125. Baghdad INA in English, August 20, 1978, in *FBIS ME,* August 22, 1978, p. C6.

126. Aden Domestic Service in Arabic, January 5, 1979, in *FBIS ME,* January 9, 1979, pp. C2-C3. The name "13 June Front" refers to the date in 1974 when al-Hamdi seized power. These officers supported al-Hamdi but objected to al-Ghashmi and Salih.

127. *Middle East Contemporary Survey, 1978–79,* pp. 895-896, and *Middle East Contemporary Survey, 1979–80* (New York: Holmes and Meier, 1981), p. 827.

128. Kuwait KUNA in English, March 4, 1980, in *FBIS ME,* March 7, 1980, pp. C12-C13, and *Keesing's Contemporary Archives,* April 18, 1980, p. 30199, and March 6, 1981, p. 30743.

129. *Keesing's Contemporary Archives,* March 6, 1981, p. 30743. It was also reported that the NDF infiltrated certain of the northern tribes, especially the Bakil, who were opposed to Salih and Saudi influence. According to Bakil shaykhs I interviewed, however, the Bakil leaders did not cooperate with the NDF but were opposed to it instead. One of the primary aims of the NDF is to rid the YAR of the influence of the shaykhs, as they did in the southern YAR villages they took control of. Wishing to preserve tribal influence, the Bakil as well as the Hashid do not want to see the NDF gain strength.

130. *Middle East Contemporary Survey, 1979–80,* pp. 828-829.

131. Clandestine DNF [NDF] Radio in Arabic, August 11, 1980, in *FBIS ME,* August 20, 1980, pp. C5-C6. See also Clandestine DNF Radio in Arabic, August 16, 1980, in *FBIS ME,* August 19, 1980, p. C7.

132. "YAR," *FBIS ME,* September 4, 1980, p. ii.

133. "Yemen," *FBIS ME,* November 12, 1980, p. iii; "YAR," *FBIS ME,* December 22, 1980, p. iii; and *Keesing's Contemporary Archives,* March 6, 1981, p. 30744.

134. Kuwait KUNA in Arabic, January 26, 1981, in *FBIS ME,* January 29, 1981, p. C2.

135. *Middle East Contemporary Survey, 1980–81* (New York: Holmes and Meier, 1982), p. 869.

When asked in an interview whether the YAR government decision to "liquidate" the NDF had been matched by an NDF decision to "topple the regime" an NDF official replied that "the front's decision so far has been to seek to thwart the DNF's liquidation and, consequently, the slogan to topple the regime has not been raised"; *As-Siyassah,* September 7, 1981, p. 15, in *FBIS ME,* September 9, 1981, pp. C7-C9.

136. "YAR, PDRY," *FBIS ME,* November 2, 1981, p. iii.

137. "PDRY-YAR," *FBIS ME,* November 27, 1981, p. iii, and *Keesing's Contemporary Archives,* March 12, 1982, p. 31379. Under the terms of the agreement, the border area was to be demilitarized and the cease-fire overseen by a tripartite committee made up of YAR, NDF, and PDRY representatives.

According to *Le Monde,* the cease-fire agreement was prepared by the Amir of Kuwait and was signed by Salih and NDF leader Sultan 'Umar "in the presence of" 'Ali Nasir Muhammad; Jean Gueyras, "L'Unité entre les deux Yemens n'est pas une entreprise utopique nous declare M. Salem Saleh Mohamed," *Le Monde,* May 7, 1982, p. 6. See also Jean Gueyras, "La 'guerre civile oubliée'," *Le Monde,* November 18, 1981, p. 7.

138. *Keesing's Contemporary Archives,* March 12, 1982, p. 31379. The agreement was publicized now only because 'Ali Nasir Muhammad had not consented to its publication earlier. His rival, 'Ali Antar, had apparently objected to it. See Laurie Mylroie, "Politics and the Soviet Presence in the People's Democratic Republic of Yemen: Internal Vulnerabilities and Regional Challenges," N-2052-AF (Santa Monica, Calif.: Rand Corporation, December 1983), p. 57.

139. London *Ash-Sharq al-Awsat,* March 31, 1982, p. 1, in *FBIS ME,* April 1,

1982, pp. C8-C9. According to *Al-Majallah,* "Certain sources say that President 'Ali Nasir Muhammad could be sincere in his desire to curb the sabotage operations the NDF is carrying out against the north, but . . . it is difficult to make the NDF comply with this desire at a time it is protected by the Russian umbrella, whose designs and objectives are difficult for any [PDRY] president to disregard unless he is willing to expose his life to danger"; *Al-Majallah,* January 29–February 5, 1982, p. 1, in *FBIS ME,* February 3, 1982, p. C7.

140. Ibid.

141. David B. Ottaway, "North Yemen's War: Sanaa Turns to Soviets for Military Aid," *The Washington Post,* April 21, 1982, pp. A1, A19. Accounts differ on exactly what types of aircraft were shot down. NDF General Secretary 'Umar told Agence France Presse that "two government planes were shot down last week around al-Bayda' "; Paris AFP in English, March 15, 1982, in *FBIS ME,* March 15, 1982, p. C8. *Ash-Sharq al-Awsat* reported that the NDF had shot down one U.S. F-5, one Sukhoi, and one helicopter; *Ash-Sharq al-Awsat,* March 31, 1982 p. 1, in *FBIS ME,* April 1, 1982, p. C9. In April, the NDF told Agence France Presse that it had "shot down two fighter planes and a helicopter" again without specifying what type they were; Paris AFP in English, April 15, 1982, in *FBIS ME,* April 15, 1982, p. C9. However, 'Umar did admit to Damascus's *Al-Ba'th* that the NDF had shot down two U.S. fighter planes "and one Sukhoi aircraft in Al-Bayda' province"; *Al-Ba'th,* March 22, 1982, p. 10, in *FBIS ME,* April 16, 1982, p. C7. Finally, YAR Prime Minister al-Iryani told *Le Monde,* "In March SAM-2 missiles handled by the NDF guerrillas shot down two Sanaa Army [*sic*] Sukhoi-22 aircraft—both missiles and aircraft being Soviet-made"; Eric Rouleau, "Le Chef du gouvernement de Sanaa accuse le régime d'Aden de fomenter la guerre civile à l'intérieur du pays," *Le Monde,* May 7, 1982, p. 6. Although the YAR government was not happy that Soviet weapons supplied to it were being destroyed by other Soviet weapons operated by the NDF, the NDF could not have been pleased that a Marxist liberation organization such as itself had to confront Soviet weapons in the hands of its "reactionary" opponents.

142. The NDF also called for Sanaa to cut its ties with Saudi Arabia and return to Riyadh $400 million in Saudi aid. Paris AFP in English, March 15, 1982, in *FBIS ME* March 15, 1982, p. C8.

143. *Keesing's Contemporary Archives,* March 1983, p. 32049.

144. Some of these NDF "proposals" however, were somewhat unrealistic for a force that was being defeated. Citing an NDF statement issued in Aden, Radio Monte Carlo reported that the NDF had proposed "a truce to the Sanaa Government during which the Front will stop all military operations provided government forces return to their barracks and stop arresting individuals and all military preparations"; Radio Monte Carlo in Arabic, April 18, 1982, in *FBIS ME,* April 19, 1982, p. C6.

145. *Keesing's Contemporary Archives,* March 1983, p. 32049.

146. Beirut *As-Safir,* March 28, 1982, p. 12, in *FBIS ME,* April 20, 1982, pp. C14-C15. 'Umar also mentioned an "agreement for coordination" reached in July 1981 between the NDF and the 13 June Front; this indicates that the latter did not become fully integrated into the NDF in January 1979. 'Umar also charged that YAR forces were being aided by tribal forces, Moslem Brothers, Iraqis, Jordanians, and British experts who had served in Oman.

147. Harvey, "New Stability Emerges," pp. 24, 27.

148. Moscow TASS in English, February 27, 1979, in *FBIS SU,* February 28, 1979, pp. F3-F4.

149. Rouleau, "Chef du gouvernement," p. 6. According to al-Iryani, the three YPUP leaders who were also members of the YSP Politburo were Yahya ash-Shami, Muhammad Qasim ath-Thawr, and 'Umar; this does not appear to be true. The YPUP is the political wing of the NDF. Rouleau said it was founded in February 1982, but in a letter to me Fred Halliday said it was founded in March 1979; Halliday to Katz, May 21, 1984.

150. Paris AFP in English, May 9, 1982, in *FBIS ME,* May 10, 1982, p. C9, and *The Wall Street Journal,* May 10, 1982, p. 1.

151. Baghdad INA in Arabic, May 10, 1982, in *FBIS ME,* May 11, 1982, p. C8.

152. Rouleau, "Chef du gouvernement," p. 6. Al-Iryani also said that "Moscow could probably advise it [the PDRY] not to equip the rebels on our territory but I do not think it can give it orders to that effect."

153. Kuwait *Al-Watan,* May 25, 1982, pp. 11, 15, in *FBIS ME,* June 1, 1982, C9, and Kuwait *Ar-Ra 'y al- 'Amm,* June 7, 1982, pp. 19, 22, in *FBIS ME,* June 9, 1982, C8-C10.

154. Macro, *Yemen and the Western World,* pp. 117-118.

155. International Institute for Strategic Studies, *The Military Balance 1984–85* (London: IISS, 1984), pp. 72-73.

156. Stephen T. Hosmer and Thomas W. Wolfe, *Soviet Policy and Practice toward Third World Conflicts* (Lexington, Mass.: Lexington/D. C. Heath, 1983), pp. 17, 23, 32, 43, 74. Hosmer and Wolfe do not actually give a figure for the years 1975-80. The figure of $420 million was derived by subtracting the totals they gave for the years 1955-74 from their overall figure for the years 1955-80 of more than $500 million. Since the figures Hosmer and Wolfe gave were not precise, my derived figure of $420 million for 1975-80 must not be regarded as precise either.

157. U.S. Arms Control and Disarmament Agency, *World Military Expenditures and Arms Transfers, 1964-1973* (Washington, D.C.: U.S. GPO, 1975), p. 70; U.S. Arms Control and Disarmament Agency, *World Military Expenditures and Arms Transfers, 1968-1977,* (Washington, D.C.: U.S. GPO, 1979), p. 156; and U.S. Arms Control and Disarmament Agency, *World Military Expenditures and Arms Transfers, 1972-1982* (Washington, D.C.: U.S. GPO, 1984), p. 97. These ACDA figures are estimates of the value of arms actually delivered. Thus there is a large discrepancy between the value of the arms package that the Carter administration said it would transfer to the YAR through Saudi Arabia in 1979 ($490 million) and the value of U.S. weapons that the YAR received ($230 million in 1978-82).

In the ACDA estimates, figures of total arms imports per country from all sources together are given on an annual basis, but imports per country from specific sources are given only for five-year periods (ten years in the earlier editions). The annual arms imports per country from specific sources apparently remain classified.

158. Page, *USSR and Arabia,* p. 37.

159. As with arms transfers, different sources give different figures for the number of Soviet advisers in the YAR. They agree, however, on the general trend of a

decline to a low level by the mid-1970s lasting until 1979, after which the number grew in the 1980s.

See International Institute for Strategic Studies, *Military Balance, 1973–74*, p. 7; ibid., *1975–76*, p. 9; ibid., *1981–82*, p. 14; ibid., *1982–83*, p. 17; ibid., *1983–84*, p. 18; ibid., *1984–85*, p. 22; Central Intelligence Agency, *Communist Aid to Less Developed Countries of the Free World, 1977*, ER 78-10478U (Washington, D.C.: CIA, November 1978), p. 3; CIA, *Communist Aid Activities in Non-Communist Less Developed Countries, 1978*, ER 79-10412U (Washington, D.C.: CIA, September 1979), p. 4; CIA, *Communist Aid Activities in Non-Communist Less Developed Countries, 1979 and 1954–79*, ER 80-10318U (Washington, D.C.: CIA, October 1980), p. 15; U.S. Department of State, Bureau of Intelligence and Research, *Soviet and East European Aid to the Third World, 1981*, DOS Pub. 9345 (Washington, D.C.: U.S. GPO, February 1983), p. 14; and Bidwell, *Two Yemens*, pp. 286-287, 328.

160. U.S. Department of State, *Soviet Aid*, p. 15.

161. Sanaa *Ath-Thawrah*, January 10, 1971, pp. 1, 4, in *FBIS ME*, January 18, 1971, pp. B1-B2; Sanaa *Ath-Thawrah*, March 17, 1971, p. 2, in *FBIS ME*, March 30, 1971, pp. B1-B2; Sanaa *Ath-Thawrah*, September 3, 1971, p. 1, in *FBIS ME*, September 15, 1971, p. B1; Baghdad INA in Arabic, December 12, 1971, in *FBIS ME*, December 13, 1971, p. B1; and Sanaa Domestic Service in Arabic, December 21, 1971, in *FBIS ME*, December 22, 1971, pp. B1-B2.

162. Bidwell, *Two Yemens*, pp. 239-240.

163. Cairo DPA in English, January 18, 1973, in *FBIS ME*, January 19, 1973, p. B2.

164. Damascus MENA in Arabic, October 3, 1972, in *FBIS ME*, October 3, 1972, B3.

165. Baghdad INA in Arabic, May 3, 1973, in *FBIS ME*, May 7, 1973, p. B3.

166. Sanaa *Ath-Thawrah*, July 31, 1973, p. 8, in *FBIS ME*, August 15, 1973, p. B1.

167. Sanaa *Ath-Thawrah*, February 12, 1974, in *FBIS ME*, March 1, 1974, p. B2.

168. Kuwait *As-Siyassah*, February 13, 1975, pp. 1, 13, in *FBIS ME*, February 24, 1975, p. C3, and Moscow Radio Peace and Progress in Arabic, April 11, 1975, in *FBIS SU*, April 14, 1975, pp. F2-F3.

169. Cairo *Akhbar al-Yawm*, July 19, 1975, p. 5, in *FBIS ME*, July 24, 1975, p. C1.

170. *Keesing's Contemporary Archives*, April 16, 1976, p. 27682.

171. Doha QNA in Arabic, June 16, 1976, in *FBIS ME*, June 17, 1976, p. C2.

172. Moscow TASS in English, November 14, 1975, in *FBIS SU*, November 18, 1975, p. F6, and Sanaa Domestic Service in Arabic, October 6, 1976, in *FBIS ME*, October 7, 1976, p. C1. The YAR did, however, expel the TASS correspondent from Sanaa. The Soviets saw this as an "unfriendly" act, expressed "regret" over it, and blamed it on "forces which would like to damage Yemen-Soviet relations"; Moscow TASS in English, August 5, 1977, in *FBIS SU*, August 8, 1977, p. F1.

173. "Pribytie delegatsii," *Krasnaia Zvezda*, April 8, 1978, p. 1, and Sanaa Domestic Service in Arabic, June 10, 1978, in *FBIS ME*, June 13, 1978, p. C4.

174. Moscow in Arabic, July 27, 1978, in *FBIS SU*, July 28, 1978, p. F4; Iurii Zhukov, "Otvlekaiushchii manevr," *Pravda*, July 31, 1978, p. 5; and Moscow in Arabic, February 13, 1979, in *FBIS SU*, February 16, 1979, p. F9.

175. Sanaa Domestic Service in Arabic, January 26, 1979, in *FBIS ME*, January 29, 1979, p. C3.

176. Doha QNA in Arabic, January 30, 1979, in *FBIS ME*, January 30, 1979, p. C5.

177. International Institute for Strategic Studies, *Military Balance, 1979-80*, p. 105.

178. London *Al-Hawadith*, March 28, 1980, pp. 21-23, in *FBIS ME*, April 3, 1980, p. C6.

179. Paris *An-Nahar al-'Arabi wa ad-Duwali*, December 6-12, 1981, p. 17, in *FBIS ME*, December 15, 1981, p. C6, and *Keesing's Contemporary Archives*, March 12, 1982, p. 31379. It was also reported at the same time that Salih immediately asked the Saudis for a grant of $1 billion so that the YAR could purchase additional Soviet weapons.

180. Kuwait *Ar-Ra'y al-'Amm*, June 7, 1982, pp. 19, 22, in *FBIS ME*, June 9, 1982, p. C10.

181. Kuwait *As-Siyassah*, May 17, 1983, in *FBIS ME*, May 20, 1983, p. C6; "Treaty of Friendship and Cooperation between the USSR and YAR," *Pravda*, October 11, 1984, p. 2, in *FBIS SU*, October 11, 1984, pp. H3-H5; and "Correction to USSR-YAR Friendship Treaty," in *FBIS SU*, October 17, 1984, p. H7.

The 1984 treaty is valid for twenty years initially and will automatically be renewed every five years thereafter unless either side abrogates it. According to Dusko Doder, "The Soviets had established modest treaty arrangements with North Yemen in 1964 . . . but these treaty arrangements expired long ago." This is not true; the 1964 treaty was valid for five years initially and called for automatic renewal for additional five-year periods unless either party abrogated it. See Dusko Doder, "Soviets, N. Yemen Sign Treaty," *The Washington Post*, October 10, 1984, pp. A19, and *Keesing's Contemporary Archives*, April 11-18, 1964, p. 20006.

182. Indeed, the Soviets rarely refer to Soviet military advisers in the YAR. In an interview with *As-Siyassah*, though, the Soviet Ambassador to the YAR, Dr. Oleg Peresypkin, admitted there were Soviet military advisers in North Yemen "at the request of the Yemeni Government" but he did not specify their numbers or mission; Kuwait *As-Siyassah*, January 9, 1981, p. 19, in *FBIS SU*, January 15, 1981, p. H4.

183. International Institute for Strategic Studies, *Military Balance, 1984-85*, pp. 22, 26, 73, 120.

184. Page, *USSR and Arabia*, p. 89; Central Intelligence Agency, *Communist Aid to the Less Developed Countries of the Free World, 1976*, ER 77-10296 (Washington, D.C.: CIA, August 1977), p. 13; CIA, *Communist Aid, 1977*, p. 6; CIA, *Communist Aid, 1978*, p. 10; CIA, *Communist Aid, 1979*, p. 20; U.S. Department of State, *Soviet Aid*, p. 19; and U.S. Department of Commerce, Bureau of the Census, *Statistical Abstract of the United States, 1982-83*, (Washington, D.C.: U.S. GPO, 1982), pp. 829, 832.

185. *Keesing's Contemporary Archives*, March 6, 1981, p. 30743.

186. *Vneshniaia torgovlia SSSR, 1922–1981 gg.* (Moscow: "Financy i Statistika" 1982), pp. 16-17, and *Vneshniaia torgovlia SSSR v 1982 g.* (Moscow: "Financy i Statistika" 1983), p. 11.

187. "North Yemen: The Answer Lies in the Soil," *The Economist,* May 15, 1982, pp. 87-88. For a detailed study of the YAR economy, see *Yemen Arab Republic: Development of a Traditional Economy* (Washington, D.C.: World Bank, 1979). At the time of this report the YAR enjoyed a current account surplus because even though it imported much and exported little, the rapid growth in remittances of Yemeni workers in the oil-rich Arab states more than compensated (ibid., p. 227). More recently, however, remittances have leveled off and exports have remained low, but imports have grown, thus creating larger current account deficits for the YAR; "North Yemen: The Answer Lies in the Soil," pp. 87-88, and Warren Richey, "North Yemen: Land of Donkeys and Camels Learns to Cope with Toyotas, Radios . . . and Canned Peas," *The Christian Science Monitor,* January 14, 1983, pp. 12-13.

188. Page, *USSR and Arabia,* pp. 89, 110; Central Intelligence Agency, *Communist Aid, 1976,* p. 10; CIA, *Communist Aid, 1977,* p. 11; CIA, *Communist Aid, 1978,* p. 18; CIA, *Communist Aid, 1979,* p. 22; and U.S. Department of State, *Soviet Aid,* p. 23.

189. Page, *USSR and Arabia,* p. 89; CIA, *Communist Aid, 1976,* p. 9; CIA, *Communist Aid, 1977,* p. 9; CIA, *Communist Aid, 1978,* p. 15; CIA, *Communist Aid, 1979,* p. 21; and U.S. Department of State, *Soviet Aid,* p. 21.

190. Manama Gulf News Agency in Arabic, April 20, 1978, in *FBIS ME,* April 21, 1978, p. C2.

191. Beirut *An-Nahar,* September 16, 1972, p. 9, and September 23, 1972, p. 9, in JPRS 57393, *Translations on the Near East,* no. 847 (November 1, 1972): 68-81.

192. Sanaa *Ath-Thawrah,* April 24, 1972, p. 1, in *FBIS ME,* May 2, 1972, pp. B2-B3.

193. Page, *USSR and Arabia,* pp. 33, 48, 65, 74, 76, 77.

194. Ibid., p. 108.

195. Pyotr Perminov, "Problems and Policies," *New Times,* no. 44 (October 1981): pp. 24-25.

196. Moscow TASS in English, June 25, 1978, in *FBIS SU,* June 26, 1978, p. F3; Moscow Domestic Service in Russian, June 26, 1978, in *FBIS SU,* June 27, 1978, p. F1; Moscow TASS in English, June 26, 1978, in *FBIS SU,* June 27, 1978, p. F1; Moscow TASS in English, June 27, 1978, in *FBIS SU,* June 28, 1978, p. F2; Moscow TASS in English, June 28, 1978, in *FBIS SU,* June 29, 1978, p. F2; Moscow TASS in English, July 3, 1978, in *FBIS SU,* July 5, 1978, pp. F4-F5; Moscow in Arabic, July 6, 1978, in *FBIS SU,* July 7, 1978, pp. F6-F7; Moscow TASS in English, July 12, 1978, in *FBIS SU,* July 18, 1978, p. F1; Moscow TASS in English, July 15, 1978, in *FBIS SU,* July 17, 1978, p. F2; Moscow Domestic Service in Russian, July 24, 1978, in *FBIS SU,* July 26, 1978, p. F8; and A. Usvatov, "Provocation," *New Times,* no. 28 (July 1978): 16-17.

197. P. Perminov, "Gorizonty respubliki," *Izvestiia,* October 29, 1982, p. 5.

198. P. Perminov, "Problems and Policies," pp. 24-25.

199. V. Peresada, "Sbrasyvaia gruz proshlogo," *Pravda,* October 26, 1981, p. 6.

200. Moscow in Arabic, October 26, 1977; *FBIS SU,* October 27, 1977 p. F2; and "Zaiavlenie natsional'nogo fronta severnogo Iemena," *Krasnaia Zvezda,* October 27, 1977, p. 3

201. "North Yemen," *New Times,* no. 2 (January 1979): 7.

202. A. Stepanov, "The Sana Assassination," *New Times,* no. 43 (October 1977): 14-15.

203. For an analysis of Yemeni unity, see Ursula Braun, "Prospects for Yemeni Unity," conference paper presented at the Symposium on Contemporary Yemen, Centre for Arab Gulf Studies, University of Exeter, July 15–18, 1983.

204. See, for example, *Al-Mustaqbal,* March 8, 1980, p. 13, in *FBIS ME,* March 13, 1980, p. C6.

205. The USSR-PDRY treaty was condemned by Shaykh 'Abdallah al-Ahmar; Doha QNA in Arabic, March 22, 1980, in *FBIS ME,* March 26, 1980, pp. C6-C7.

206. Muscat *'Uman,* October 6, 1982, p. 3, in *FBIS ME,* October 8, 1982, p. C2. See also Kuwait KUNA in Arabic, November 24, 1981, in *FBIS ME,* November 24, 1981, p. C1.

207. The YAR, however, has not criticized the bilateral PDRY-Ethiopia treaty friendship and cooperation signed December 2, 1979. Ethiopia also signed a treaty of friendship and cooperation with the USSR on November 20, 1978; *Keesing's Contemporary Archives,* April 18, 1980, p. 30199.

208. Cairo DPA in Arabic, May 13, 1979, in *FBIS ME,* May 17, 1979, p. C2, and Kuwait *As-Siyassah,* November 4, 1981, pp. 10-11, in *FBIS ME,* November 5, 1981, p. C7.

209. There were rumors that a Saudi-YAR border clash took place as recently as early 1984; Kuwait As-Siyassah, April 22, 1984, p. 16; in *FBIS ME,* April 24, 1984, pp. C6-C7.

210. Moscow TASS in English, March 13, 1973, in *FBIS SU,* March 14, 1973, p. B5.

211. Herbert H. Denton, "PLO Evacuees in North Yemen Miss Delights of City," *The Washington Post,* January 10, 1984.

212. V. Kudriavtsev, "Teni nad krasnym morem," *Izvestiia,* April 16, 1977, p. 4.

213. Baghdad INA in Arabic, May 26, 1977, in *FBIS ME,* May 27, 1977, p. C1.

214. Sanaa Domestic Service in Arabic, February 13, 1980, in *FBIS ME,* February 14, 1980, pp. C8-C10.

215. London Reuter in English, February 8, 1980, in *FBIS ME,* February 11, 1980, p. C4.

216. Kuwait *As-Siyassah,* January 9, 1981, p. 19, in *FBIS SU,* January 15, 1981, p. H4.

217. Kuwait *Ar-Ra'y al-'Amm,* May 4, 1981, p. 19, in *FBIS ME,* May 6, 1981, p. C4.

218. Sharjah *Al-Khalij,* May 13, 1981, p. 9, in *FBIS ME,* May 15, 1981, pp. C1-C2.

219. "Oil Found in North Yemen," *Financial Times,* July 12, 1984, p. 3, and Kenneth Cline, "North Yemen Oil Find May Enliven Politics," *The Christian Science Monitor,* October 4, 1984, p. 11.

CHAPTER 2: SOUTH YEMEN

1. On the history of South Yemen before the arrival of the British, see Robert W. Stookey, *South Yemen: A Marxist Republic in Arabia* (Boulder, Colo.: Westview Press; London: Croom Helm, 1982), ch. 2.

2. Robin Bidwell, *The Two Yemens* (Singapore: Longman/Westview, 1983), pp. 16-17, 28-29.

3. Ibid., pp. 32-34. At the time, the British also feared that the French were collaborating with the Egyptian potentate Muhammad 'Ali to threaten the British position in India. In the 1830s Muhammad 'Ali came to rule much of the Arabian Peninsula, including the east coast of the Red Sea from Aqaba to Bab al-Mandab. The British were afraid that if they did not take Aden, Muhammad 'Ali would do so and thus deny them its use. In 1840 Muhammad 'Ali's power crumbled, and he had to submit to the authority of the Ottoman Sultan against whom he had rebelled earlier.

4. Ibid., pp. 43-44. A French attempt to buy a coastal town from a local shaykh in 1870 also came to nothing owing to British and Turkish efforts.

5. Ibid., pp. 46-49, and Stookey, *South Yemen*, pp. 39-41.

6. Stookey, *South Yemen*, p. 41, and Manfred W. Wenner, *Modern Yemen 1918–1966* (Baltimore: Johns Hopkins Press, 1967), pp. 44-45.

7. Bidwell, *Two Yemens*, pp. 59-65. The British seized Kamaran Island off the North Yemeni coast from the Turks in 1915 and did not give it back when North Yemen became independent in 1918. The YAR seized it from South Yemen during the 1972 border war.

8. Wenner, *Modern Yemen*, pp. 158-164.

9. There are several good accounts of the last years of British rule in Aden. These include Charles Johnston, *The View from Steamer Point* (London: Cox and Wyman, 1964); Tom Little, *South Arabia: Arena of Conflict* (New York: Praeger, 1968); Julian Paget, *Last Post: Aden, 1964–1967* (London: Faber and Faber, 1969); Kennedy Trevaskis, *Shades of Amber* (London: Hutchinson, 1968); and R. J. Gavin, *Aden under British Rule, 1839–1967* (New York: Barnes and Noble, 1975). For a more recent and scathing account of British policy, see J. B. Kelly, *Arabia, the Gulf and the West* (New York: Basic Books, 1980), ch. 1.

10. Kelly, *Arabia*, pp. 9-12, and Bidwell, *Two Yemens*, pp. 98-99.

11. Bidwell, *Two Yemens*, pp. 137-138.

12. Kelly, *Arabia*, p. 12.

13. Fred Halliday, *Arabia without Sultans* (Harmondsworth, Middlesex: Penguin Books, 1974), pp. 195-197.

14. Kelly, *Arabia*, pp. 19-27.

15. Ibid., pp. 5, 11-12, 21, and David A. Russell, "South Yemen: From Colonialism to Communism" (unpublished manuscript, August 1, 1981), pp. 21, 185.

16. Kelly, *Arabia*, pp. 12-27, and Russell, "South Yemen" pp. 185-187, 190.

17. Halliday, *Arabia without Sultans*, pp. 189-195, Kelly, *Arabia*, pp. 24-25, and Joseph Kostiner, "Arab Radical Politics: Al-Qawmiyyun al-Arab and the Marxists in the Turmoil of South Yemen, 1963–1967," *Middle East Studies* 17, 4 (October 1981): 454-476.

18. Halliday, *Arabia without Sultans*, pp. 207-213, and Kostiner, "Arab Radical Politics."

19. Kelly, *Arabia*, pp. 39-40.

20. *Keesing's Contemporary Archives*, December 16-23, 1967, pp. 22411-18.

21. Ibid., p. 22417.

22. Halliday, *Arabia without Sultans*, pp. 227-240, *Keesing's Contemporary Archives*, July 12-19, 1969, pp. 23451-52, and August 21-28, 1971, p. 24788.

23. Bidwell, *Two Yemens*, pp. 245-246, and Halliday, *Arabia without Sultans*, pp. 249-250.

24. *Keesing's Contemporary Archives*, November 3, 1978, p. 29290.

25. Ibid., pp. 29289-90.

26. *Keesing's Contemporary Archives*, March 16, 1979, pp. 29507-8, and April 18, 1980, p. 30199.

27. Stephen Page, *The USSR and Arabia: The Development of Soviet Policies and Attitudes towards the Countries of the Arabian Peninsula, 1955-1970* (London: Central Asian Research Centre, 1971), pp. 17, 31, 37-38.

28. Ibid., pp. 49-50.

29. Ibid., p. 64. See also an extremely valuable collection of Soviet articles about South Yemen from 1964 until early 1968 published as *The Soviet Attitude toward the N.L.F. and FLOSY* (Background Brief no. 83, 1968), pp. iii, 1-14. There is no indication who published this collection, but it appears to be the work of the U.S. Foreign Broadcast Information Service.

30. *Soviet Attitude toward the N.L.F. and FLOSY*, p. iii. Makkawi was dismissed because he had called for the British to negotiate with the NLF soon after they had banned it in June 1965. As the leader of FLOSY, Makkawi must have subsequently come to regret that the British did not take even more repressive measures against the NLF.

31. Ibid., pp. iv-v, 23, 66.

32. Ibid., pp. v, 29.

33. Ibid., pp. v-vi, 33-35, 45-46, 53.

34. The many British accounts of the war make no mention of direct large-scale Soviet assistance to the NLF; indeed, the British themselves appear to have done more to help it than the Russians, since as the former withdrew they gave control of territory to the Federation's South Arabian Army, which then gave control to the NLF.

35. *Keesing's Contemporary Archives*, July 12-19, 1969, p. 23452, Bidwell, *Two Yemens*, pp. 16-17, and Halliday, *Arabia without Sultans*, p. 256.

36. *Keesing's Contemporary Archives*, January 1-7, 1973, p. 25654.

37. Riyadh Domestic Service in Arabic, March 22, 1973, in *FBIS ME*, March 23, 1973, p. B1. Aden denied this charge and claimed that the Saudis were allied to Israel; Aden Domestic Service in Arabic, March 24, 1973, in *FBIS ME*, March 26, 1973, pp. B1-B2.

38. Baghdad INA in Arabic, April 9, 1971, in *FBIS ME*, April 9, 1971, p. B1 (the Aden paper cited was *Ash-Shararah*, April 8, 1971).

39. *Keesing's Contemporary Archives*, July 1-7, 1973, p. 25654.

40. Kuwait *Ar-Ra'y al-'Amm*, October 17, 1972, p. 9, in JPRS 57576, *Translations on the Near East*, no. 860 (November 21, 1972): 1-5.

41. Aden *14 October,* September 12, 1972, p. 2, in JPRS 57379, *Translations on the Near East,* no. 845 (October 25, 1972): 32-34; and *Middle East Contemporary Survey, 1976–77* (New York: Holmes and Meier, 1978), p. 554.

42. According to the account of Soviet defector Vladimir Sakharov, who was a Soviet diplomat in North Yemen during 1967, FLOSY leader Makkawi had close ties to the Soviets then and maintained them after the NLF came to power. If this is true, the Soviets appear to have stopped supporting Makkawi by 1972. He then joined the Saudi-sponsored exiles in the United National Front. See Vladimir Sakharov, *High Treason* (New York: Ballantine Books, 1980), pp. 159, 280, 288.

It was also in September 1972 that Makkawi condemned the USSR; Tripoli *Al-Balayh,* September 1972, p. 3, in JPRS 57742, *Translations on the Near East,* no. 870 (December 12, 1972): 1-4.

43. Page, *USSR and Arabia,* p. 113; Moscow TASS International Service in English, March 16, 1971, in *FBIS SU,* March 17, 1971, p. B6; Moscow Radio Peace and Progress in English, April 4, 1972, in *FBIS SU,* April 5, 1972, pp. B3-B4; A. Mikhailov, "Intrigi vokrug demokraticheskogo Iemena," *Pravda,* August 1, 1972, p. 5; Moscow Radio Peace and Progress in English, August 1, 1972, in *FBIS SU,* August 2, 1972, p. B9; Moscow in Arabic, September 3, 1972, in *FBIS SU,* September 5, 1972, pp. B9-B10; Moscow in Arabic, September 24, 1972, in *FBIS SU,* September 26, 1972, p. B11; and Moscow in Arabic, December 15, 1972, in *FBIS SU,* December 18, 1972, p. B6.

44. Yuri Gvoydev, "Democratic Yemen: Problems and Aims," *New Times,* no. 48 (November 1972): 14-15.

45. Page, *USSR and Arabia,* p. 113.

46. Aden *Ath-Thawri,* June 9, 1970, pp. 4, 5, 7, in JPRS 51194, *Translations on the Near East,* no. 505 (August 18, 1970): 35.

47. Baghdad INA in Arabic, August 28, 1972, in *FBIS ME,* August 28, 1972, p. B1. In addition, the Defense Minister 'Ali Nasir Muhammad stated in May 1971 that he had recently told Soviet Defense Minister Grechko in Moscow of "the dangers facing the Yemeni revolution" and that Soviet officials expressed "full readiness" to give additional military aid; Aden ANA in Arabic, May 18, 1971, in *FBIS ME,* May 19, 1971, p. B1.

48. *Keesing's Contemporary Archives,* January 1-7, 1973, pp. 25654-55.

49. Muscat *'Uman,* March 30, 1974, p. 5, in JPRS 62244, *Translations on the Near East,* no. 1179 (June 14, 1974): 1-2.

50. *Keesing's Contemporary Archives,* December 8–14, 1975, p. 27483. In August 1974, PFLOAG changed its name to Popular Front for the Liberation of Oman (PFLO).

51. *Keesing's Contemporary Archives,* May 7, 1976, p. 27716.

52. Ibid.

53. *Keesing's Contemporary Archives,* May 20, 1977, p. 28353. The aircraft was shot down just before the opening of a conference of Gulf foreign ministers in Muscat on November 25 that was attended by Bahrain, Iran, Iraq, Kuwait, Qatar, Saudi Arabia, Oman, and the UAE.

54. See, for example, "Aggression in South Arabia," *New Times,* no. 21 (May

1972): 11, 13; Moscow TASS International Service in English, May 12, 1972, in *FBIS SU,* May 15, 1972, p. B2; Moscow in Arabic, May 13, 1972, in *FBIS SU,* May 15, 1972, pp. B2-B4; and Mikhailov, "Intrigi," p. 5.

55. In January 1973 Radio Moscow called the United States, United Kingdom, Saudi Arabia, Oman, and Jordan Aden's enemies but did not mention Iran even though its troops were in Dhofar; Moscow in Arabic, January 23, 1973, in *FBIS SU,* January 24, 1973, pp. B7-B9.

Sometimes Moscow would cite PDRY statements about Iran but would not offer its own criticism; see Moscow TASS in English December 6, 1973, in *FBIS SU,* December 7, 1973, p. F1. See also A. Vasil'ev and V. Peresada, "Opasnye zamysly," *Pravda,* November 4, 1975, p. 5.

56. Moscow in Persian, November 26, 1976, in *FBIS SU,* December 2, 1976, pp. F5-F6.

57. Kuwait *Ar-Ra'y al-'Amm,* July 15, 1973, p. 3, in *FBIS ME,* July 31, 1973, pp. B2-B3; Amman *Ar-Ra'y,* March 27, 1977, p. 11, in *FBIS ME,* March 28, 1977, p. C1; Doha QNA in Arabic, June 6, 1977, in *FBIS ME,* June 7, 1977, p. C1; Doha QNA in Arabic, June 26, 1977, in *FBIS ME,* June 28, 1977, p. C1. The PDRY, though, publicly denied that a mediation effort was going on; Aden Domestic Service in Arabic, April 5, 1977, in *FBIS ME,* April 7, 1977, p. C11.

58. Aden Domestic Service in Arabic, December 20, 1976, in *FBIS ME,* December 21, 1976, p. C8; and Riyadh Domestic Service in Arabic, December 28, 1976, in *FBIS ME,* December 29, 1976, p. C1.

59. Vincent Ryder, "Move to Reduce Russian Influence," *The Daily Telegraph,* December 1, 1975, p. 4.

60. *Keesing's Contemporary Archives,* January 1–7, 1973, pp. 25654-55.

61. See notes 91, 92, and 101 in chapter 1.

62. See note 93 in chapter 1.

63. Juan de Onis, "Southern Yemen Cites Soviet Support," *The New York Times,* October 7, 1972, p. 12.

64. *Keesing's Contemporary Archives,* April 18, 1980, pp. 30197-201.

65. See notes 111–113 in chapter 1.

66. See notes 119–124 in chapter 1.

67. See, for example, Aden Domestic Service in Arabic, March 9, 1979, in *FBIS ME,* March 13, 1979, p. C8.

68. International Institute for Strategic Studies, *The Military Balance, 1979–80* (London: IISS, 1979), p. 105.

69. See chapter 1, pp. 39-43.

70. For the YAR's complaints, see Eric Rouleau, "Le Chef du gouvernement de Sanaa accuse le régime d'Aden de fomenter la guerre civile à l'intérieur du pays," *Le Monde,* May 7, 1982, p. 6.

71. Page, *USSR and Arabia,* p. 112.

72. See U.S. Arms Control and Disarmament Agency, *World Military Expenditures and Arms Transfers, 1964–1973* (Washington, D.C.: U.S. GPO, 1975), p. 70; U.S. Arms Control and Disarmament Agency, *World Military Expenditures and Arms Transfers, 1968–1977* (Washington, D.C.: U.S. GPO, 1979), p. 156; and U.S. Arms

Control and Disarmament Agency, *World Military Expenditures and Arms Transfers 1972-1982* (Washington, D.C.: U.S. GPO, 1984), p. 97.

73. International Institute for Strategic Studies, *Military Balance, 1984-85,* p. 73.

74. Stephen T. Hosmer and Thomas W. Wolfe, *Soviet Policy and Practice toward Third World Conflicts* (Lexington, Mass.: Lexington/D. C. Heath, 1983), pp. 32, 43, and 74. The authors did not give a figure for the years 1975-80. The figure of $230 million given here was derived by subtracting the totals they gave for the years 1965-74 from the overall figure of more than $400 million they gave for the years 1955-80 (the USSR, of course, gave nothing to Aden during the years Britain ruled it). Since the figures Hosmer and Wolfe gave were not precise, my derived figure for 1975-80 cannot be regarded as precise either.

75. See note 72.

76. International Institute for Strategic Studies, *Military Balance, 1983-84,* pp. 64-65.

77. Page, *USSR and Arabia,* p. 113.

78. The wilder estimates of Soviet bloc military advisers in the PDRY include one made by the Cairo weekly *Akhir Sa'ah* that Soviet and Cuban troop strength in South Yemen rose to 8,000 after the 1979 YAR-PDRY war and that Polish and Czech ships [*sic*] had brought large quantities of weapons to Aden; Cairo MENA in Arabic, May 9, 1979, in *FBIS ME,* May 10, 1979, p. C4. Kuwait's *As-Siyassah* put the Soviet and Cuban presence at 9,000 at the time the USSR-PDRY treaty of friendship and cooperation was signed in October 1979 and predicted the total would rise to 15,000 by the end of the year; Doha QNA in Arabic, October 27, 1979, in *FBIS ME,* October 29, 1979, pp. C4-C5. In September 1979 Radio Moscow cited a U.S. State Department denial of a *Die Welt* story that the Soviets, Cubans, and East Germans were training a 40,000-man force in the PDRY made up of Yemenis, Palestinians, and Ethiopians to seize the region's oil fields; Moscow in German, September 9, 1979, in *FBIS SU,* September 11, 1979, p. H2.

It has also been reported that the number of Soviet bloc advisers in South Yemen rose from 1,000 to 4,000 shortly after Somalia denounced its treaty of friendship and cooperation with Moscow and expelled the Soviets and Cubans in November 1977 (Bidwell, *Two Yemens,* pp. 291-292), that their number reached about 6,600 by the time of the June 1978 coup (Aryeh T. Yodfat, *The Soviet Union and the Arabian Peninsula* [London: Croom Helm; New York: St. Martin's Press, 1983], p. 52), and that 2,700 Cuban troops and 150 Soviet advisers were transferred from Ethiopia to South Yemen during the 1979 war between the two Yemens (Kuwait KUNA in Arabic, March 8, 1979, in *FBIS ME,* March 9, 1979, pp. C3-C4). Sudanese sources stated in March 1982 that in addition to 1,500 Soviet troops in South Yemen, there were also 4,000 Cubans and 1,000 East Germans; Khartoum SUNA in Arabic, March 23, 1982, in *FBIS ME,* March 25, 1982, p. C4.

79. International Institute for Strategic Studies, *Military Balance, 1973-74,* p. 7; ibid., *1974-75,* p. 9; ibid., *1975-76,* p. 9; ibid., *1980-1981,* p. 12; ibid., *1981-82,* pp. 14, 19, 96; ibid., *1982-83,* pp. 17, 22, 103; ibid., *1983-84,* pp. 18, 22, 109; ibid., *1984-85,* pp. 22, 26, 120; Central Intelligence Agency, *Communist*

Developed Countries of the Free World, 1977, ER 78-10478U (Washington, D.C.: CIA, November 1978), p. 3; CIA, *Communist Aid Activities in Non-Communist Less Developed Countries, 1978,* ER 79-10412U (Washington, D.C.: CIA, September 1979), p. 4; CIA, *Communist Aid Activities in Non-Communist Less Developed Countries, 1979 and 1954-79,* ER 80-10318U (Washington, D.C.: CIA, October 1980), p. 15; and U.S. Department of State, Bureau of Intelligence and Research, *Soviet and East European Aid to the Third World, 1981,* DOS Pub. 9345 (Washington, D.C.: U.S. GPO, February 1983), p. 14.

80. Page, *USSR and Arabia,* p. 114, and U.S. Department of State, *Soviet Aid,* p. 15.

81. Richard F. Nyrop et al., *Area Handbook for the Yemens* (Washington, D.C.: U.S. GPO, 1977), pp. 149-150.

82. Ibid., pp. 150-151, and CIA, *Communist Aid, 1977,* p. 3.

83. Bidwell, *Two Yemens,* pp. 288-289.

84. For an early South Yemeni acknowledgment of East German assistance in internal security, see Aden *14 October,* June 21, 1970, p. 7, in JPRS 51211, *Translations on the Near East,* no. 507 (August 20, 1970): 43. On the establishment of Aden-East Berlin diplomatic relations, see *Keesing's Contemporary Archives,* November 1-8, 1969, p. 23645.

85. Stookey, *South Yemen,* pp. 104-105.

86. It was even reported that the purpose of Admiral Gorshkov's May 1978 visit to Aden was to secure expanded Soviet rights to naval facilities in South Yemen. When Salim Rubayyi 'Ali refused to grant them, the Soviets contrived his downfall the following month; Yodfat, *Soviet Union,* p. 48. This story, however, cannot be verified.

87. On the reported offer to give arms to the PDRY in exchange for a naval and air base, see Cairo MENA in Arabic, June 21, 1978, in *FBIS ME,* June 22, 1978, p. C2.

88. There have been a multitude of such statements emanating from both Moscow and Aden. See, for example, Damascus MENA in Arabic, January 31, 1978, in *FBIS ME,* February 1, 1978, p. B1; Aden Domestic Service in Arabic, September 4, 1974, in *FBIS ME,* September 6, 1974, p. C4; Moscow in English, September 5 1974, in *FBIS SU,* September 9, 1974, p. F6; Moscow TASS in English, September 11, 1974, in *FBIS SU,* September 13, 1974, p. F3; Manama Gulf News Agency in Arabic, July 13, 1978, in *FBIS ME,* July 13, 1978, p. C3; Moscow TASS in English, July 20, 1978, in *FBIS SU,* July 21, 1978, p. F3; Amman *Ar-Ra'y,* September 26, 1978, p. 8, in *FBIS ME,* September 27, 1978, pp. C3-C5; Moscow TASS in English, December 4, 1978, in *FBIS SU,* December 5, 1978, pp. F1-F2; Moscow TASS in English, December 12, 1978, in *FBIS SU,* December 14, 1978, p. F15; Kuwait *As-Siyassah,* February 7, 1979, p. 16, in *FBIS ME,* February 13, 1979, pp. C4-C7; Moscow Domestic Service in Russian, February 6, 1980, in *FBIS SU,* February 7, 1980, p. H1; Moscow TASS in English, February 28, 1980, in *FBIS SU,* February 29, 1980, p. H2; Moscow in Arabic, April 14, 1980, in *FBIS SU,* April 15, 1980, p. H4; Moscow in Arabic, March 22, 1981, in *FBIS SU,* March 24, 1981, pp. H1-H2; Aden Domestic Service in Arabic, November 19, 1981, in *FBIS ME,* November 20,

1981, pp. C4-C5; Doha QNA in Arabic, December 23, 1981, in *FBIS ME,* December 24, 1981, p. C5; and Aden Domestic Service in Arabic, March 13, 1982, in *FBIS ME,* March 15, 1982, pp. C6-C7.

89. International Institute for Strategic Studies, *Military Balance, 1983–84,* p. 65. According to former Prime Minister Muhammad 'Ali Haitham, the Soviets use a naval and air base in the PDRY; Cairo DPA in Arabic, August 12, 1976, in *FBIS ME,* August 13, 1976, p. C2. Bidwell wrote that Salim Rubayyi 'Ali told visiting U.S. Congressman Paul Findlay that the USSR "'does not and will not have a military base in Aden' but did have 'facilities'"; Bidwell, *Two Yemens,* p. 292.

90. See, for example, Cairo MENA in Arabic, August 31, 1978, in *FBIS ME,* September 5, 1978, p. C2; Kuwait KUNA in Arabic, December 23, 1978, in *FBIS ME,* December 28, 1978, p. C7; London *Al-Hawadith,* November 23, 1979, pp. 12, 13, in *FBIS ME,* November 27, 1979, p. C6; London *Al-Majallah,* November 29–December 5, 1980, pp. 12-16, in *FBIS ME,* December 3, 1980, pp. C3-C7; Paris AFP in English, January 20, 1980, in *FBIS ME,* January 21, 1980, p. C5; and London *Al-Hawadith,* December 11, 1981, p. 11, in *FBIS ME,* December 11, 1981, p. C9. See also Kelly, *Arabia,* pp. 471-472.

91. Page, *USSR and Arabia,* p. 115; Paris AFP in English, June 18, 1978, in *FBIS ME,* June 20, 1978, pp. C7-C8; Cairo MENA in Arabic, May 17, 1979, in *FBIS ME,* May 17, 1979, p. C6; Muscat Domestic Service in Arabic, March 17, 1981, in *FBIS ME,* March 19, 1981, p. C3; Muscat Domestic Service in Arabic, April 9, 1981, in *FBIS ME,* April 10, 1981, pp. C6-C7; Yodfat, *Soviet Union,* pp. 6, 46-47, 111-112; and Kelly, *Arabia,* pp. 471-472.

92. For details of the treaty, see *Keesing's Contemporary Archives,* April 18, 1980, p. 30199.

93. See ibid., and *Keesing's Contemporary Archives,* November 28, 1980, p. 30593, March 6, 1981, p. 30746, and January 15, 1982, p. 31280.

94. International Institute for Strategic Studies, *Military Balance, 1981–82,* p. 59, and ibid., *1983–84,* p. 68. Bidwell stated that 2,000 PDRY soldiers aided the Ethiopians against the Somalis in early 1978 but that they did not participate in the Eritrean campaign; Bidwell, *Two Yemens,* p. 292. According to the IISS, 500 PDRY soldiers (one infantry battalion) were stationed in Syria in 1982.

95. On Ethiopian troops in the PDRY, see *Die Welt,* September 7, 1979, pp. 1-5, in *FBIS ME,* September 11, 1979, pp. C6-C8. On the military strength of the Ethiopian opposition movements, see International Institute for Strategic Studies, *Military Balance, 1983–84,* p. 69.

96. Stookey, *South Yemen,* p. 89.

97. Central Intelligence Agency, *Communist Aid to the Less Developed Countries of the Free World, 1976,* ER 77-10296 (Washington, D.C.: CIA, August 1977), p. 13; CIA, *Communist Aid, 1977,* p. 6; CIA, *Communist Aid, 1978,* p. 10; CIA, *Communist Aid, 1979,* p. 20; U.S. Department of State, *Soviet Aid,* p. 19; and World Bank, *People's Democratic Republic of Yemen: A Review of Economic and Social Development* (Washington, D.C.: The World Bank, 1979), p. 98.

98. CIA, *Communist Aid, 1976,* p. 9; CIA, *Communist Aid, 1977,* p. 9; CIA, *Communist Aid, 1978,* p. 15; CIA, *Communist Aid, 1979,* p. 21; and U.S. Department of State, *Soviet Aid,* p. 21.

99. Page, *USSR and Arabia*, p. 114, and U.S. Department of State, *Soviet Aid*, p. 23.

100. For a chronology listing Soviet-South Yemeni economic agreements, see Russell, "South Yemen," pp. 21, 85. See also *The Middle East and North Africa, 1982–83* (London: Europa Publications, 1982), pp. 901-902; Moscow TASS in English, May 28, 1980, in *FBIS SU*, May 29, 1980, p. H2; Moscow TASS in English, March 19, 1981, in *FBIS SU*, March 20, 1981, p. H3; Moscow TASS in English, March 31, 1982, in *FBIS SU*, April 2, 1982, p. H3; and Aden Domestic Service in Arabic, February 17, 1983, in *FBIS ME*, February 18, 1983, p. C1.

101. Moscow TASS International Service in English, February 8, 1972, in *FBIS SU*, February 9, 1972, pp. B7-B8; Moscow TASS in English, March 31, 1982, in *FBIS SU*, April 2, 1982, p. H3; and Moscow in Arabic, October 25, 1983, in *FBIS SU*, October 27, 1983, pp. H2-H3.

102. Ministerstvo Vneshnei Torgovli, *Vneshniaia torgovlia SSSR, 1922–1981* (Moscow: "Financy i Statistika" 1982), pp. 18-19, and idem, *Vneshniaia torgovlia SSSR v 1982 g.* (Moscow: "Financy i Statistika" 1983), p. 11.

103. Hamburg DPA in English, November 14, 1972, in *FBIS ME*, November 15, 1972, p. B1. Isma'il made this statement shortly after returning from a visit to Cuba.

104. "Podpisan protokol," *Pravda*, December 11, 1982, p. 4. For details of a Moscow-Aden fish agreement, see Moscow Maritime Service in Russian, November 9, 1979, in *FBIS SU*, November 16, 1979, p. H7.

105. Doha QNA in Arabic, October 29, 1977, in *FBIS ME*, October 31, 1977, pp. C6-C7. See also Doha QNA in Arabic, June 25, 1977, in *FBIS ME*, June 28, 1977, p. C2, and Stookey, *South Yemen*, p. 85.

106. Soviet attempts to find oil in South Yemen began as early as 1971; see Cairo MENA in Arabic, December 31, 1971, in *FBIS ME*, January 4, 1972, p. B1.

107. Aden Domestic Service in Arabic, April 2, 1982, in *FBIS ME*, April 6, 1982, p. C7; Kuwait KUNA in English, October 30, 1983, in *FBIS ME*, October 31, 1983, p. C4; and Doha QNA in Arabic, November 12, 1983, in *FBIS ME*, November 15, 1983, pp. C1-C2. See also *Middle East and North Africa, 1982–83*, p. 903.

108. The Economist Intelligence Unit, *Quarterly Economic Review of Bahrain, Qatar, Oman, The Yemens*, no. 4 (1983): 21-22.

109. Page, *USSR and Arabia*, pp. 114-115.

110. Rakhim Esemov, "Preobrazhennyi krai," *Pravda*, July 8, 1979, p. 4. *Pravda* later cited 'Ali Nasir Muhammad on the PDRY's economic problems as being due to "growing pains"; see "K namechennoi tseli," *Pravda*, October 14, 1980, p. 4.

111. Page, *USSR and Arabia*, pp. 113-114. On events leading up to the 1969 coup, see Halliday, *Arabia without Sultans*, pp. 232-239.

112. Isma'il demonstrated his devotion to the USSR by attending many events in Moscow such as the Lenin centenary in April 1970, the 24th CPSU Congress in March 1971, the 25th CPSU Congress in February–March 1976, and the 60th anniversary of the October Revolution (November 1977). Isma'il also visited the USSR in June–August 1973 (during which he received "treatment" but also met with Brezhnev), July 1974 (when he met Podgorny and signed an economic and technical cooperation accord), June–July 1976 (only three months after attending the 25th

CPSU Congress), and October 1979 (when he signed the treaty of friendship and cooperation with Brezhnev). Isma'il made his last voyage to the USSR in the summer following his April 1980 "resignation" and remained there until early 1985. See Russell, "South Yemen," appendix C; Moscow TASS International Service in English, March 25, 1971, in *FBIS SU,* March 26, 1971, p. B5; Aden ANA in Arabic, April 14, 1971, in *FBIS ME,* April 15, 1971, p. B1; Aden ANA in Arabic, June 25, 1973, in *FBIS ME,* June 25, 1973, p. B4; Aden Domestic Service in Arabic, August 11, 1973, in *FBIS ME,* August 13, 1973, pp. B1-B2; Aden Domestic Service in Arabic, July 17, 1974, in *FBIS ME,* July 19, 1974, p. C1; Moscow TASS in English, July 18, 1974, in *FBIS SU,* July 18, 1974, p. F2; Aden Domestic Service in Arabic, March 7, 1976, in *FBIS ME,* March 8, 1976, p. C2; Aden Domestic Service in Arabic, June 25, 1976, in *FBIS ME,* June 28, 1976, p. C3; Moscow TASS in English, July 30, 1976, in *FBIS SU,* August 2, 1976, pp. F1-F2; "Vstrecha v TsK KPSS," *Pravda,* November 12, 1977, p. 2; Moscow TASS International Service in Russian, October 25, 1979, in *FBIS SU,* October 25, 1979, pp. H8-H9; and Kuwait KUNA in Arabic, July 7, 1980, in *FBIS ME,* July 8, 1980, pp. C8-C9.

113. 'Ali Nasir visited the USSR in September 1970, March–May 1971 (when he attended the 24th CPSU Congress and stayed on for talks with Grechko and Gorshkov), September–October 1971 (just after his appointment as Prime Minister), December 1972–January 1973 (when he met Kosygin), March 1973 (when he talked with Brezhnev and Grechko), September–October 1974 (when he met Kosygin and Grechko and then stayed for almost six weeks of "rest"), July 1977 (when he met Ustinov even though 'Ali Nasir was no longer Defense Minister), January–February 1978 (when he met Kosygin and signed another economic and technical cooperation accord), October 1978, July 1979 (for the Council for Mutual Economic Assistance session), May 1980 (shortly after Isma'il's "resignation"), March 1981 (when he met with Brezhnev and attended the 26th CPSU Congress), September 1982 (when he met with Brezhnev, Gromyko, and Chernenko), November 1982 (for Brezhnev's funeral), December 1982 (for the 60th anniversary of the USSR), September 1983 (when he met with Andropov), February 1984 (for Andropov's funeral), September 1984 (when he met Chernenko), and March 1985 (for Chernenko's funeral and to meet Gorbachev).

See Russell, "South Yemen," appendix C, Charles B. McLane, *Soviet–Third World Relations,* vol. 1, *Soviet–Middle East Relations* (London: Central Asian Research Centre, 1973), p. 89; Moscow TASS International Service in English, April 13, 1971, in *FBIS SU,* April 14, 1971, p. B4; Aden ANA in Arabic, May 1, 1971, in *FBIS ME,* May 4, 1971, p. B5; Moscow TASS International Service in English, September 30, 1971, in *FBIS SU,* September 30, 1971, p. B7; Moscow TASS in English, December 29, 1972, in *FBIS SU,* December 29, 1972, p. B6; Moscow TASS in English, March 8, 1973, in *FBIS SU,* March 8, 1973, pp. B13-B14; Moscow TASS in English September 15, 1974, in *FBIS SU,* September 16, 1974, p. F3; Moscow in Arabic, October 26, 1974, in *FBIS SU,* October 31, 1974, p. F1; Moscow TASS in English, July 28, 1977, in *FBIS SU,* July 29, 1977, p. F3; Moscow Domestic Service in Russian, July 29, 1977, in *FBIS SU,* August 1, 1977, pp. F1-F2; Moscow TASS in English, February 1, 1978, in *FBIS SU,* February 2, 1978, p. F8; Moscow Domestic

Service in Russian, February 2, 1978, in *FBIS SU,* February 3, 1978, pp. F2-F3; Moscow TASS International Service in Russian, July 2, 1979, in *FBIS SU,* July 3, 1979, p. H3; Moscow Domestic Service in Russian, May 28, 1980, in *FBIS SU,* May 29, 1980, pp. H1-H2; Moscow Domestic Service in Russian, March 3, 1981, in *FBIS SU,* March 4, 1981, pp. P32-P33; Moscow Domestic Service in Russian, March 7, 1981, in *FBIS SU,* March 9, 1981 p. H3; Moscow Domestic Service in Russian, September 14, 1982, in *FBIS SU,* September 15, 1982, p. H3; Moscow TASS in English, September 15, 1982, in *FBIS SU,* September 15, 1982, pp. H1-H5; Aden Domestic Service in Arabic, November 17, 1982, in *FBIS ME,* November 18, 1982, p. C11; Aden Domestic Service in Arabic, December 22, 1982, in *FBIS SU,* December 23, 1982, pp. P17-P19; "S rabochim vizitom," *Pravda,* September 28, 1983, p. 1; "Druzheskaia vstrecha," *Pravda,* September 30, 1983, p. 1; Aden Domestic Service in Arabic, February 15, 1984, in *FBIS ME,* February 15, 1984, p. C2, Moscow Domestic Service in Russian, October 3, 1984, in *FBIS SU,* October 4, 1984, p. H1; and Aden Domestic Service in Arabic, March 14, 1985, in *FBIS ME,* March 15, 1985, p. C1.

114. On 'Ali's one visit to Moscow, see Moscow TASS International Service in English, November 21, 1972, in *FBIS SU,* November 22, 1972, pp. B1-B2, and Moscow TASS International Service in English, November 24, 1972, in *FBIS SU,* November 27, 1972, p. B1.

In September 1976 and September 1977 there were reports that he would go to Moscow again, but he did not; see Baghdad INA in English, September 17, 1976, in *FBIS ME,* September 21, 1976, p. C3, and Baghdad INA in Arabic, September 10, 1977, in *FBIS ME,* September 14, 1977, p. C2.

115. A. Vasilyev, "Visiting South Yemen," *New Times,* no. 30 (July 1970): 26-29.

116. V. Alexandrov, "Dynamic Progress," *New Times,* no. 42 (October 1976): 15.

117. Moscow TASS in English, June 26, 1978, in *FBIS SU,* June 27, 1978, pp. F1-F2; and Moscow TASS in English, June 27, 1978, in *FBIS SU,* June 28, 1978, pp. F1-F2.

118. Moscow TASS in English June 29, 1978, in *FBIS SU,* June 30, 1978, pp. F4-F5.

Although the Soviets repeated Isma'il's charge that 'Ali opposed the creation of a vanguard party, TASS a few months earlier had cited 'Ali as being in favor of it. This is not easy to explain. Either the Soviets were trying then to signal 'Ali that support for the creation of a vanguard party in Aden was necessary in order for him to remain friends with Moscow or else they genuinely believed 'Ali did support the project. If the latter is true, this would indicate that the Soviets were not particularly displeased with 'Ali (especially in his politically weakened condition) and that the impetus for the dramatic events of June came from Aden, not Moscow. See Moscow TASS in English, January 31, 1978, in *FBIS SU,* February 7, 1978, p. F4.

According to Kuwait's *As-Siyassah,* the Isma'il-'Ali quarrel over the formation of the vanguard party had become quite bitter in early 1978 and Isma'il had arrested 150 officers loyal to 'Ali because of their opposition to it. 'Ali was described as opposing the creation of a party because it "would upset the political balance in the PDRY and would disrupt the PDRY's relations with the Arab world"; Doha QNA in Arabic, May 25, 1978, in *FBIS ME,* May 26, 1978, p. C2.

For more on the coup and the birth of the Yemeni Socialist Party (YSP), see *Middle East Contemporary Survey, 1977–78* (New York: Holmes and Meier, 1979), pp. 656-661, *Middle East Contemporary Survey, 1978–79* (New York: Holmes and Meier, 1980), pp. 715-717, and *Keesing's Contemporary Archives,* November 3, 1978, pp. 29289-90.

119. *Middle East Contemporary Survey, 1977–78,* p. 659.

120. Moscow TASS in English, June 28, 1978, in *FBIS SU,* June 29, 1978, p. F2.

121. See note 112.

122. Moscow in Arabic, October 19, 1978, in *FBIS SU,* October 20, 1978 pp. F5-F6.

123. Aden Domestic Service in Arabic, December 27, 1978, in *FBIS ME,* December 29, 1978, pp. C6-C8.

124. See note 113.

125. Cairo MENA in Arabic, August 11, 1979, in *FBIS ME,* August 13, 1979, pp. C4-C5.

126. Fred Halliday, *Soviet Policy in the Arc of Crisis* (Washington, D.C.: Institute for Policy Studies, 1981), pp. 93-94.

127. L. Brezhnev, "Tovarishchu Ali Naseru Mukhammedu," *Pravda,* April 23, 1980, p. 1, and L. Brezhnev, "Tovarishchu Ali Naseru Mukhammedu," *Pravda,* May 1, 1980, p. 1.

Neither Aden nor Moscow issued any vituperative commentary about Isma'il. Indeed, after his "resignation" he was named to the honorary post of Chairman of the YSP and awarded the Order of the 14th October. It was reported, however, that Isma'il was either detained or under house arrest for several months until he went into exile in the USSR. See *Middle East Contemporary Survey, 1979–80* (New York: Holmes and Meier, 1981), p. 827.

128. Moscow in Arabic, April 23, 1980, in *FBIS SU,* April 25, 1980, pp. H2-H3; Moscow TASS in English, April 27, 1980, in *FBIS SU,* April 29, 1980, pp. H3-H4; and Aden Domestic Service in Arabic, July 10, 1980, in *FBIS ME,* July 11, 1980, p. C3.

129. "Soviet Grip on South Yemen Tightened," *The Daily Telegraph,* April 30, 1981, p. 4. According to this article, 'Antar had been trained in Moscow and was a dedicated communist, but he "offended the Soviet Union and his South Yemeni colleagues by insisting on running the Defence Ministry himself, and refusing to take orders from Russian 'advisers.'"

See also *Keesing's Contemporary Archives,* July 24, 1981, p. 30996, and *Middle East Contemporary Survey, 1980–81* (New York: Holmes and Meier, 1982), pp. 717-720. This last source speaks of a failed coup attempt by 'Antar in February 1981 as well as 'Ali Nasir Muhammad's defeat of two other rivals. He dismissed Deputy Prime Minister 'Ali Salim al-Bayd and reportedly had executed former Foreign Minister Muhammad Salih Muti (who had been accused of links to Saudi Arabia). It is uncertain, however, how reliable these reports are.

That 'Ali Nasir Muhammad did not dismiss 'Ali Antar or take stronger action against him indicates that the PDRY leader may have feared him in the position of Defense Minister but valued his services otherwise. Not only did 'Ali Nasir appoint him Deputy Prime Minister and Minister of Local Government in May 1981, he also appointed him Vice Chairman of the Presidium of the Supreme People's Council in September 1982. However, it is also possible that 'Ali Antar was too strong for 'Ali Nasir to dismiss completely and that the appointment as Vice Chairman was intended by 'Ali Nasir to foster rivalry between 'Ali Antar and Salih Muslih Qasim. See also *Keesing's Contemporary Archives*, March 1983, p. 32050.

130. Moscow TASS in English, September 26, 1982, in *FBIS SU*, September 27, 1982, p. H7.

131. London *Ash-Sharq al-Awsat*, March 31, 1982, p. 1, in *FBIS ME*, April 1, 1982, pp. C8-C10.

132. On August 15, 1982, Kuwait's *As-Siyassah* reported that Muhsin ash-Shurbaji (PDRY director of intelligence and then Minister of State for National Security under Isma'il, who was sent into exile by 'Ali Nasir Muhammad as PDRY ambassador to Bulgaria) had unilaterally abrogated a PDRY-Bulgarian agreement whereby Bulgaria would establish a telephone network in Aden. Because of this act, 'Ali Nasir Muhammad called him home and then had him arrested at the airport. According to *Ash-Sharq al-Awsat*, however ash-Shurbaji's offense was more serious (this paper described him as PDRY ambassador to Yugoslavia). This account said Isma'il had flown to Yugoslavia to organize a coup plot with him against 'Ali Nasir Muhammad, but when 'Ali Nasir Muhammad learned of this, he recalled ash-Shurbaji for "consultations" then had him arrested and executed. It was reported that 'Ali Nasir left the Arab summit conference in Fez early "following press reports of an attempted coup d'état in his country."

As it turned out, however, 'Ali Nasir left Fez and went to Prague, where he reportedly met the leaders of Libya and Ethiopia, then went to Moscow where he met Brezhnev, and finally visited Bulgaria before returning home; his early departure from Fez appeared to be the result of disagreement with other Arab leaders more than anything else. In addition, *As-Siyassah* later reported that ash-Shurbaji had not been executed after all; this story, at least, was accurate, since in the spring of 1984 the same ash-Shurbaji was appointed Minister of Housing.

See Kuwait *As-Siyassah*, August 15, 1982, p. 1, in *FBIS ME*, August 16, 1982, pp. C3-C4; London *Ash-Sharq al-Awsat*, September 7, 1982, p. 1, in *FBIS ME*, September 8, 1982, p. C6; Kuwait KUNA in English, September 8, 1982, in *FBIS ME*, September 9, 1982, p. A3; Ad-Dammam *Al-Yawm*, September 12, 1982, p. 1, in *FBIS ME*, September 14, 1982, p. A5; Kuwait *As-Siyassah*, September 23, 1982, p. 1, in *FBIS ME*, September 24, 1982, p. C1; and Aden Domestic Service in Arabic, September 24, 1982, in *FBIS ME*, September 27, 1982, p. C10.

133. Aden Domestic Service in Arabic, May 21, 1984, in *FBIS ME*, May 23, 1984, pp. C8-C10; and Aden Domestic Service in Arabic, June 21, 1984, in *FBIS ME*, June 22, 1984, pp. C4-C6. 'Ali Nasir denied that there were differences among party leaders.

Al-'Attas was also elected to the YSP Politburo (along with one other individual) during the YSP Central Committee session just before be became Prime Minister. The YSP Central Committee also announced that "Comrade 'Abd al-Fattah Isma'il was appointed secretary of the general directorate of the YSP Central Committee Secretariat." KUNA then incorrectly reported that Isma'il had been appointed General Secretary of the YSP Central Committee (head of the party); 'Ali Nasir Muhammad still holds this post. Isma'il, though, is back in Aden and has an important position. This could mean that 'Ali Nasir has one more serious rival to contend with in Aden, but officials I spoke to think Isma'il is in poor health and does not pose a threat to 'Ali Nasir. I tend to credit this latter interpretation, since it is hardly conceivable that 'Ali Nasir Muhammad would have voluntarily given a high position to the man he ousted if Isma'il were strong and active. It is also possible, though, that Moscow engineered Isma'il's return to Aden as a warning to 'Ali Nasir not to become too friendly with the GCC countries. Then again, both 'Ali Nasir and Moscow may have wanted Isma'il back in Aden to encourage the GCC to give greater economic assistance to the PDRY so that Aden will not end its present moderate policy toward its neighbors and adopt a hostile one. The visit of the Saudi Foreign Minister to Aden in April 1985 indicates that the Kingdom might have just this concern.

Aden Domestic Service in Arabic, February 11, 1985, in *FBIS ME,* February 12, 1985, p. C4; Kuwait KUNA in Arabic, February 12, 1985, in *FBIS ME,* February 13, 1985, p. C3; Aden Domestic Service in Arabic, February 14, 1985, in *FBIS ME,* February 15, 1985, pp. C3-C4; Riyadh Domestic Service in Arabic, April 6, 1985, in *FBIS ME,* April 8, 1985, p. C4; Aden Domestic Service in Arabic, April 7, 1985, in *FBIS ME,* April 8, 1985, p. C5; and conversations with several U.S. government officials.

134. Page, *USSR and Arabia,* pp. 113-114.

135. Halliday, *Arabia without Sultans,* p. 254.

136. *Revolution Africaine,* October 20-26, 1972, pp. 19-33, in JPRS 57627, *Translations on the Near East,* no. 864 (November 29, 1972): 13-14.

137. Cairo MENA in English, March 27, 1976, in *FBIS ME,* March 30, 1976, p. C4.

138. *Keesing's Contemporary Archives,* May 13, 1977, p. 28348, and *Middle East Contemporary Survey, 1976-77,* pp. 556-560.

139. Riyadh Domestic Service in Arabic, June 15, 1977, in *FBIS ME,* June 16, 1977, p. C1; Riyadh Domestic Service in Arabic, July 31, 1977, in *FBIS ME,* August 1, 1977, p. C2; and Aden Domestic Service in Arabic, August 12, 1977, in *FBIS ME,* August 15, 1977, p. C2.

140. Cairo *Al-Ahram,* August 20, 1977, p. 1, in *FBIS ME,* August 23, 1977, p. C2.

141. *Middle East Contemporary Survey, 1977-78,* p. 665.

142. Aden Domestic Service in Arabic, November 27, 1977, in *FBIS ME,* November 29, 1977, p. C2.

143. *Middle East Contemporary Survey, 1977-78,* pp. 661-662.

144. Ibid., pp. 666-667.

145. *Middle East Contemporary Survey, 1978-79,* pp. 721-723, and Lt. Cmdr. Charles T. Creekman, Jr., "Sino-Soviet Competition in the Yemens," *U.S. Naval War College Review* 32, 4 (July-August 1979): 73-82.

146. South Yemen Freedom Radio [Clandestine] in Arabic, July 3, 1978, in *FBIS ME*, July 5, 1978, pp. C12-C13; and South Yemen Freedom Radio [Clandestine] in Arabic, July 4, 1978, in *FBIS ME*, July 5, 1978, pp. C13-C14.

147. *Middle East Contemporary Survey, 1978–79*, pp. 724-726, and *Middle East Contemporary Survey, 1979–80*, p. 667.

148. For an example of this view, see Kuwait KUNA in Arabic, July 10, 1980 in *FBIS ME*, July 10, 1980, pp. C5-C6. See also *Keesing's Contemporary Archives*, March 6, 1981, p. 30746.

149. *Keesing's Contemporary Archives*, March 6, 1981, p. 30745, and Nigel Harvey, "Aden Looks West," *Middle East Economic Digest*, October 21, 1983, p. 63.

150. Paris AFP in English, January 17, 1984, in *FBIS ME*, January 17, 1984, p. C3; Kuwait KUNA in Arabic, February 12, 1985, in *FBIS ME*, February 13, 1985, p. C3; and [Clandestine] Voice of Free Sons of Yemeni South in Arabic, February 18, 1985, in *FBIS ME*, February 19, 1985, p. C10.

151. *Keesing's Contemporary Archives*, March 1983, pp. 32048-49, and Manama *Gulf Daily News*, July 24, 1983, p. 1, in *FBIS ME*, July 26, 1983, p. C3.

152. Aden Domestic Service in Arabic, October 27, 1983, in *FBIS ME*, October 28, 1983, p. C1; Kuwait KUNA in English, October 30, 1983, in *FBIS ME*, October 31, 1983, pp. C1-C2; Aden Domestic Service in Arabic, November 19, 1983, in *FBIS ME*, November 21, 1983, p. C2; and Muscat Domestic Service in Arabic, November 29, 1983, in *FBIS ME*, November 30, 1983, p. C2.

153. The Soviets themselves seemed to note this very point; see Moscow in Persian, April 13, 1982, in *FBIS SU*, April 15, 1982, pp. H4-H5. See also *Keesing's Contemporary Archives*, March 6, 1981, p. 30747, and March 1983, p. 32049.

In April 1982, Aden and Tehran signed a "political and economic cooperation agreement" and in July 1982 they signed an agreement by which Iran would send crude oil to Aden to be refined as well as sell some of its crude to the South Yemenis. On the evolution of Soviet policy toward revolutionary Iran, see Zalmay Khalizad, "Islamic Iran: Soviet Dilemma," *Problems of Communism*, January–February 1984, pp. 1-20.

154. See, for example, Moscow Domestic Service in Russian, February 2, 1978, in *FBIS SU*, February 3, 1978, pp. F2-F3; "Sovmestnoe kommiunike o vizite v NDRI predsedatelia soveta ministrov SSSR A. N. Kosygina," *Izvestiya*, September 19, 1979, pp. 1, 4; "Sovmestnoe kommiunike," *Pravda*, May 31, 1980, pp. 1, 4; and Moscow TASS in English, September 15, 1982, in *FBIS SU*, September 16, 1982, pp. H6-H7.

155. *Middle East Contemporary Survey, 1977–78*, p. 665, and International Institute for Strategic Studies, *Military Balance, 1982–83*, p. 64.

156. Aden Domestic Service in Arabic, September 29, 1983, in *FBIS SU*, October 3, 1983, pp. H3-H5; and "Druzheskaia vstrecha," *Pravda*, September 30, 1983, p. 1. While both expressed support for the PLO, Moscow and Aden also praised Syria and did not openly criticize its treatment of the PLO.

'Ali Antar announced "the PDRY's readiness to become an arena of national dialogue for the Palestinian forces on the level of the PLO political program"; Aden

Domestic Service in Arabic, December 28, 1983, in *FBIS ME*, December 29, 1983, p. C1.

See also *Middle East Contemporary Survey, 1976–77*, pp. 558-559.

157. Doha QNA in Arabic, July 10, 1978, in *FBIS ME*, July 10, 1978, p. C5; *Der Spiegel*, December 4, 1978, pp. 188-93, in *FBIS ME*, December 5, 1978, p. C5; and Bidwell, *Two Yemens*, p. 292.

The PDRY insists that it does not have any of its own troops in Eritrea; Aden Domestic Service in Arabic, March 9, 1982, in *FBIS ME*, March 10, 1982, pp. C21-C22.

158. Moscow TASS in English, May 6, 1978, in *FBIS SU*, May 8, 1978, p. F5.

159. Aden Domestic Service in Arabic, January 8, 1980, in *FBIS ME*, January 9, 1980, p. C3; Moscow TASS in English, January 23, 1980, in *FBIS SU*, January 24, 1980, p. H3; Moscow TASS International Service in Russian, May 27, 1980, in *FBIS SU*, May 28, 1980, pp. H4-H7; and Kuwait KUNA in Arabic, July 8, 1980, in *FBIS ME*, July 8, 1980, pp. C6-C8.

160. See, for example, Moscow in Arabic, May 15, 1979, in *FBIS SU*, May 17, 1979, p. H7.

CHAPTER 3: OMAN

1. J. E. Peterson, *Oman in the Twentieth Century: Political Foundations of an Emerging State* (London: Croom Helm; New York: Barnes and Noble, 1978), pp. 19-23, and The Economist Intelligence Unit, *Quarterly Economic Review of Bahrain, Qatar, Oman, the Yemens,* annual supplement 1983, p. 34.

2. J. B. Kelly, *Arabia, the Gulf and the West* (New York: Basic Books, 1980), pp. 106-107, and Fred Halliday, *Arabia without Sultans* (Harmondsworth, Middlesex: Penguin Books, 1974), p. 268.

3. Peterson, *Oman*, pp. 112-114.

4. Ibid., pp. 26-27.

5. Kelly, *Arabia*, pp. 109-110, and Robert Geran Landen, *Oman since 1856: Disruptive Modernization in a Traditional Arab Society* (Princeton: Princeton University Press, 1967), pp. 365-387.

6. Peterson, *Oman*, pp. 139-143. For the letter signed by Sa'id bin Taymur in 1932 in which he agreed to seek British advice, see ibid., p. 224.

7. Kelly, *Arabia*, pp. 110-113.

8. Ibid., pp. 114-115, and *Keesing's Contemporary Archives*, March 31–April 7, 1956, p. 14782.

9. *Keesing's Contemporary Archives*, August 17–24, 1957, pp. 15709-12, and Peterson, *Oman*, pp. 180-187. In 1958 Sultan Sa'id sold the enclave of Gwadar, the last remnant of Oman's overseas empire, to Pakistan.

10. For a summary of Dhofari history through the nineteenth century, see Halliday, *Arabia without Sultans*, pp. 309-312.

11. Ibid., pp. 313-314, Peterson, *Oman*, pp. 187-188, and Kelly, *Arabia*, 119-120.

12. Halliday, *Arabia without Sultans*, pp. 314-318, and David Lynn Price,

Oman: Insurgency and Development, Conflict Studies, no. 53 (London: Institute for the Study of Conflict, January 1975), pp. 3-4.

13. Price, *Oman,* pp. 4-5, Halliday, *Arabia without Sultans,* pp. 366-370, and Hashim S. H. Behbehani, *China's Foreign Policy in the Arab World, 1955-75: Three Case Studies* (London: Kegan Paul International, 1981), pp. 143-146.

14. Halliday, *Arabia without Sultans,* pp. 323-325.

15. A third group, the Arab Labour Party of Oman (ALPO) also made its appearance at this time but was not militarily active. On both NDFLOAG and ALPO, see Behbehani, *China's Foreign Policy,* p. 153.

16. Ranulph Fiennes, *Where Soldiers Fear to Tread* (London: Hodder and Stoughton, 1975), p. 152, and John Townsend, *Oman: The Making of a Modern State* (New York: St. Martin's Press, 1977), p. 173.

17. John Akehurst, *We Won a War: The Campaign in Oman 1965-1975* (London: Michael Russell, 1982), p. 19, and *Keesing's Contemporary Archives,* September 5-12, 1970, p. 24175.

18. These events, known as the 12 September uprising, are best described in Behbehani, *China's Foreign Policy,* pp. 154-155.

19. Akehurst, *We Won a War,* p. 30.

20. Behbehani, *China's Foreign Policy,* pp. 156-158.

21. Ernest Oney, "The Iranian Intervention in Oman, 1973-1979," external research paper published by the U.S. Department of State, Bureau of Intelligence and Research, Office of Long Range Assessments and Research, September 1981, p. 3; Akehurst, *We Won a War,* pp. 36-38, 42; and *Keesing's Contemporary Archives,* June 17-23, 1974, pp. 26579-80, and February 24-March 2, 1975, p. 26988.

22. Behbehani, *China's Foreign Policy,* p. 159.

23. Major General K. Perkins, "Oman 1975: The Year of Decision," *RUSI Journal* 124, 1 (March 1979): 38-45, Akehurst, *We Won a War,* chs. 14-16, and *Keesing's Contemporary Archives,* May 7, 1976, p. 27716.

According to Akehurst, the PFLO guerrillas were extremely good fighters, but the PDRY troops who came to aid them in the fall of 1975 were fairly poor (p. 156).

24. Akehurst, *We Won a War,* pp. 183-184.

25. Stephen Page, *The USSR and Arabia: The Development of Soviet Policies and Attitudes towards the Countries of the Arabian Peninsula, 1955-1970* (London: Central Asian Research Centre, 1971), pp. 36-37, 51, 63.

26. "Narod Omana oderzhit pobedu," *Izvestiia,* October 10, 1963, p. 2.

27. See Page, *USSR and Arabia,* p. 82.

28. *Al-Hurriyah,* September 22, 1969, cited in ibid., p. 116.

29. Behbehani, *China's Foreign Policy,* p. 187. For a detailed analysis of China's relations with the Omani rebels, see ibid., ch. 7.

30. A. Vasil'ev, "Buntuiushchie gory Dofara," *Pravda,* September 29, 1969, p. 4; idem, "Partizanskimi tropami Dofara," *Pravda,* October 4, 1969, p. 4; and idem, "'My—ne raby,'" *Pravda,* October 12, 1969, p. 4.

31. Page, *USSR and Arabia,* p. 116, and Moscow in Arabic, September 21, 1971, in *FBIS SU,* September 24, 1971, p. B1. The Soviet Afro-Asian Solidarity Committee is the Soviet branch of the Afro-Asian People's Solidarity Organization (AAPSO), the nominally unofficial organization providing links between the socialist

states and national liberation groups. That the PFLOAG delegations' invitations were issued by this committee and not by the Soviet government or Communist Party is indicative of Soviet unwillingness to give strong support to PFLOAG.

32. Moscow TASS International Service in English, September 13, 1971, in *FBIS SU,* September 14, 1971, p. B3; Aden Domestic Service in Arabic, September 29, 1971, in *FBIS ME,* September 30, 1971, p. B2. PFLOAG claimed that its delegation met with not only Katushev, but also other unspecified members of the Politburo; it is difficult to ascertain where the truth lies. PFLOAG wanted to receive as much Soviet aid and support as it could. Yet even though the PFLOAG delegation met at least Katushev on this occasion, its invitation to the USSR was again issued by the Soviet Afro-Asian Solidarity Committee. See also Aden Domestic Service in Arabic, September 15, 1971, in *FBIS ME,* September 17, 1971, p. B1.

33. Moscow Radio Peace and Progress in English, March 23, 1972, in *FBIS SU,* March 24, 1972, pp. B6-B10; Moscow TASS in English, January 9, 1973, in *FBIS SU,* January 10, 1973, p. B10; and A. Leont'ev and V. Vinogradov, "Reshimost' naroda," *Krasnaia Zvezda,* January 13, 1974, p. 3. The Soviets also put Dhofar's population at 250,000—over four times its actual level.

34. See, for example, Moscow in Arabic, July 8, 1972, in *FBIS SU,* July 11, 1972, pp. B7-B8; Moscow Radio Peace and Progress, January 5, 1973, in *FBIS SU,* January 10, 1973, pp. B8-B9; K. Kapitonov, "Nepokorennyi Dofar," *Izvestiia,* January 10, 1973, p. 2; Moscow in Persian, February 12, 1974, in *FBIS SU,* February 14, 1974, pp. F6-F8; and Moscow in Persian, December 11, 1974, in *FBIS SU,* December 12, 1974, pp. F5-F6.

35. Moscow Radio Peace and Progress in English, January 19, 1972, in *FBIS SU,* January 20, 1972, pp. B7-B8; Moscow TASS in English, January 29, 1973, in *FBIS SU,* January 30, 1973, p. B5; Moscow TASS in English, March 12, 1973, in *FBIS SU,* March 13, 1973, p. B10; and Moscow TASS in English, May 21, 1973, in *FBIS SU,* May 23, 1973, p. B9.

36. Moscow in Arabic, March 13, 1973, in *FBIS SU,* March 15, 1973, pp. B14-B15.

37. Leont'ev and Vinogradov, "Reshimost' naroda," p. 3, and Moscow TASS in English, January 13, 1974, in *FBIS SU,* January 15, 1974, p. F8.

38. Moscow in Arabic, April 16, 1974, in *FBIS SU,* April 19, 1974, p. F5. See also Moscow TASS in English, October 20, 1975, in *FBIS SU,* October 23, 1975, pp. F6-F7, and Moscow in Persian, October 21, 1975, in *FBIS SU,* October 23, 1975, p. F7.

39. Moscow TASS in English, August 9, 1974, in *FBIS SU,* August 16, 1974, pp. F4-F5.

40. Moscow TASS in English, June 11, 1975, in *FBIS SU,* June 17, 1975, p. F6, and Moscow in Arabic, October 20, 1975, in *FBIS SU,* October 22, 1975, pp. F6-F7.

41. Iu. Gavrilov and V. Vinogradov, "Dofar: Bitva za svobodu," *Krasnaia Zvezda,* November 2, 1975, p. 3.

42. See, for example, Moscow Radio Peace and Progress in English, May 13, 1974, in *FBIS SU,* May 17, 1974, p. F14, and Moscow in Arabic, March 11, 1975, in *FBIS SU,* March 12, 1975, p. F10.

43. Moscow Radio Peace and Progress in Arabic, June 10, 1975, in *FBIS SU,* June 11, 1975, pp. F5-F6, and A. Sergeev, "V bor'be za svobodu," *Krasnaia Zvezda,* April 10, 1975, p. 3. See also Moscow in Arabic, October 8, 1974, in *FBIS SU,* October 9, 1974, p. F1.

Organizations such as the Soviet Afro-Asian Solidarity Committee and the World Peace Council also proclaimed their support for the Omani rebels. Yet while these organizations are controlled by the Soviets, they do not officially represent the Soviet Communist Party or the government. Instead, they represent "public opinion." See Moscow in Arabic, January 17, 1974, in *FBIS SU,* January 18, 1974, p. F7, and Moscow Radio Peace and Progress in Arabic, March 15, 1974, in *FBIS SU,* March 19, 1974, p. F6.

44. Aden Domestic Service in Arabic, November 5, 1972, in *FBIS ME,* November 7, 1972, p. B2; Moscow in Arabic, September 19, 1973, in *FBIS SU,* September 20, 1973, pp. F5-F6; and Moscow in Arabic, March 11, 1975, in *FBIS SU,* March 12, 1975, p. F10.

45. Bard E. O'Neill, "Revolutionary War in Oman," in Bard E. O'Neill, William R. Heaton, and Donald J. Alberts, eds., *Insurgency in the Modern World* (Boulder, Colo.: Westview Press, 1980), p. 224. In the summer of 1973, the Soviet Navy may also have sealifted about 200 guerrillas and their equipment from Aden to the eastern PDRY near the Oman border; Bradford Dismukes and James M. McConnell, eds., *Soviet Naval Diplomacy* (New York: Pergamon Press, 1979), p. 137.

46. Akehurst, *We Won a War,* pp. 142-143. On November 2, 1975, *Krasnaia Zvezda* noted that, according to the London *Times,* the "rebels have been using the latest equipment for the first time . . . including highly efficient anti-aircraft missiles." No mention was made of the fact that these weapons came from the USSR. Gavrilov and Vinogradov, "Dofar: Bitva za svobudu," p. 3.

47. Akehurst, *We Won a War,* p. 28.

48. David Lynn Price, "Moscow and the Persian Gulf," *Problems of Communism* 28, 2 (March–April 1979): 9. Price claimed that while visiting Dhofar in late 1974, he "could see PDRY/PFLO artillery positions across the border in South Yemen manned and directed by Cubans" (p. 9). He did not explain how he was able so positively to identify the Cubans or how he could tell they were actually directing PDRY artillery.

49. Behbehani, *China's Foreign Policy,* pp. 161-162.

50. Akehurst, *We Won a War,* pp. 26, 29.

51. G. G. Drambiants, *Persidskii zaliv bez romantiki* (Moscow: Mezhdunarodnye Otnosheniia, 1968), p. 48.

52. Dmitry Volsky, "The Fall of Sultan Said," *New Times,* no. 32 (August 1970): 26-27, and A. Vasil'ev, "Araviiskii tupik Londona," *Pravda,* August 7, 1970, p. 5.

53. Moscow in Arabic, March 24, 1973, in *FBIS SU,* March 27, 1973, pp. B16-B17; Moscow in Arabic, February 12, 1974, in *FBIS SU,* February 14, 1974, pp. F5-F6; Moscow in Persian, March 5, 1974, in *FBIS SU,* March 6, 1974, pp. F12-F13; Moscow TASS in English, March 28, 1974, in *FBIS SU,* March 29, 1974, p. F4; Moscow in Persian, April 4, 1974, in *FBIS SU,* April 5, 1974, p. F8; Moscow Radio Peace and Progress in Arabic, May 30, 1974, in *FBIS SU,* June 5, 1974, p.

F11; and Moscow in Arabic, January 14, 1975, in *FBIS SU,* January 15, 1975, pp. F6-F7.

54. L. Mironov, "Pentagon na Masire," *Krasnaia Zvezda,* January 6, 1977, p. 3; Moscow TASS in English, January 25, 1977, in *FBIS SU,* January 26, 1977, p. F6; Iu. Glukhov, "Opasnaia sdelka," *Pravda,* February 12, 1977, p. 5; V. Vinogradov, "Platsdarmy dlia interventsii," *Krasnaia Zvezda,* February 12, 1981, p. 3; Moscow TASS in English, February 12, 1981, in *FBIS SU,* February 13, 1981, pp. H1-H2; Moscow in Arabic, February 14, 1981, in *FBIS SU,* February 17, 1981, p. H1; and V. Peresada, "Nagnetaiut napriazhennost'," *Pravda,* February 17, 1981, p. 5.

55. Moscow Domestic Service in Russian, December 4, 1982, in *FBIS SU,* December 6, 1982, pp. H4-H5; Moscow in Arabic, December 6, 1982, in *FBIS SU,* December 7, 1982, pp. H2-H3; Moscow TASS International Service in Russian April 12, 1983, in *FBIS SU,* April 13, 1983, p. H1; Moscow TASS International Service in Russian, April 14, 1983, in *FBIS SU,* April 15, 1983, p. H1; Moscow Domestic Service in Russian, July 6, 1983, in *FBIS SU,* July 7, 1983, p. H3; and V. Murav'ev, "S dal'nim pritselom," *Krasnaia Zvezda,* July 9, 1983, p. 5.

Of course, merely because the Soviets have stopped criticizing Oman in some of their commentary since late 1982 does not mean they have ceased to do so in all of it. For some highly critical statements on the Sultan and his government, see Dmitry Zgersky, "Oman's 'Open Door,' " *New Times,* no. 44 (October 1982): 14-15; Moscow in Arabic, December 16, 1982, in *FBIS SU,* December 17, 1982, pp. H1-H2; and V. Mikhin, "Pod dudku Vashingtona," *Sel'skaia Zhizn',* April 26, 1983, p. 3.

56. V. Mikhin, "Omanskie 'Pravdoiskateli'," *Sovetskaia Rossia,* July 8, 1983, p. 5.

57. "Tainaia voina," *Pravda,* January 5, 1976, p. 4; Moscow in Arabic, March 9, 1976, in *FBIS SU,* March 11, 1976, pp. F2-F3; A. Filippov, "Patrioty nanosiat udary," *Pravda,* April 6, 1976, p. 5; and Moscow in Arabic, July 18, 1976, in *FBIS SU,* July 20, 1976, pp. F6-F7.

58. Moscow in Persian, January 28, 1977, in *FBIS SU,* February 2, 1977, pp. F7-F8; Moscow in Persian, December 6, 1977, in *FBIS SU,* December 7, 1977, p. F12; Moscow TASS in English, June 12, 1978, in *FBIS SU,* June 13, 1978, pp. F1-F2; and V. Fedorov, "V soiuze s reaktsiei," *Krasnaia Zvezda,* January 26, 1979, p. 3.

59. A. Kudryavtsev, "Looking for a New Prop," *New Times,* no. 11 (March 1979): 12; Moscow Domestic Service in Russian, April 9, 1979, in *FBIS SU,* April 10, 1979, pp. H2-H3; and Oney, "Iranian Intervention," p. 3.

60. Moscow in Arabic, April 27, 1979, in *FBIS SU,* May 2, 1979, p. H2; Moscow TASS in English, April 29, 1979, in *FBIS SU,* April 30, 1979, p. H4; "Vizit delegatsii," *Izvestiia,* May 1, 1979, p. 5; and Moscow in Arabic, May 6, 1979, in *FBIS SU,* May 8, 1979, pp. H1-H2.

61. Aden Voice of PFLO in Arabic, February 14, 1981, in *FBIS ME,* February 20, 1981, pp. C3-C4, and *Keesing's Contemporary Archives,* August 31, 1979, p. 29804. The PFLO also claimed another small attack inside Oman in early 1982; Aden Voice of PFLO in Arabic, March 9, 1982, in *FBIS ME,* March 11, 1982, p. C12.

In 1979 the PFLO launched a "new" strategy of waiting for Omani oil reserves to run out and bring economic chaos, thereby weakening the Sultan and providing an opportunity to renew its activities; see Fred Halliday, "Economic Decline in Oman: PFLO's New Political Strategy," *MERIP Reports,* no. 68 (May 1978): 18-21. So long as Oman's prosperity continues as it has, though, this strategy does not promise to be very effective.

62. For Soviet and PFLO claims, see Moscow TASS in English, January 16, 1979, in *FBIS SU,* January 17, 1979, p. F12; Moscow TASS in English, March 13, 1979, in *FBIS SU,* March 14, 1979, p. F8; Iu. Tyssovskii, "Sluga trekh gospod," *Izvestiia,* May 30, 1979, p. 5 (here 7,000 to 12,000 Egyptian troops were said to be in Oman).

For Omani denials of the presence of any Egyptian troops, see Manama Gulf News Agency in Arabic, February 25, 1979, in *FBIS ME,* February 26, 1979, p. C1; Rabat MAP in Arabic, March 1, 1979, in *FBIS ME,* March 2, 1979, pp. C2-C3; and Manama Gulf News Agency in Arabic, March 17, 1979, in *FBIS ME,* March 20, 1979, pp. C4-C5.

According to Bard O'Neill, "A high-ranking Egyptian officer acknowledged the presence of advisory personnel in Oman" in October 1979; O'Neill, "Revolutionary War in Oman," p. 233. The IISS also states that Egyptian armed forces are stationed in Oman but does not give numerical estimates; International Institute for Strategic Studies, *Military Balance, 1983–84,* (London: IISS, 1983), p. 54.

It appears, then, that there are some Egyptian troops in Oman, but probably not as many as the Soviets and PFLO claimed.

63. Moscow TASS in English, March 23, 1980, in *FBIS SU,* March 25, 1980, p. H3; Moscow in Arabic, June 6, 1980, in *FBIS SU,* June 9, 1980, p. H1; Moscow in Arabic, June 9, 1980, in *FBIS SU,* June 10, 1980, pp. H1-H2; Moscow TASS in English, November 6, 1980, in *FBIS SU,* November 7, 1980, p. H3; and Moscow in Persian, February 21, 1981, in *FBIS SU,* February 23, 1981, p. H6.

64. Aden Voice of PFLO in Arabic, May 26, 1982, in *FBIS ME,* May 28, 1982, pp. C2-C3; and Moscow TASS in English, June 18, 1982, in *FBIS SU,* June 21, 1982.

According to a study by Bettie and Oles Smolansky published in 1982, "The last [Soviet] reference to the activities of PFLO was published in *Pravda,* April 6, 1976. Nothing else has been said on that subject (before or after) until . . . January 1979." As the present study has shown, this statement is inaccurate. See Bettie M. Smolansky and Oles M. Smolansky, "The Sino-Soviet Interaction in the Middle East," in *The Sino-Soviet Conflict: A Global Perspective,* ed. Herbert J. Ellison (Seattle and London: University of Washington Press, 1982), p. 263.

65. With Oman-PDRY negotiations taking place in 1982 aimed at normalizing their relations, the PFLO appeared to sense that its freedom to broadcast would soon come to an end, and so in the summer of 1982 it embarked on an intense burst of activity. A "general conference" was held at Aden in June followed by a "general national congress" that lasted through August. The Voice of the PFLO devoted several broadcasts to reading a massive "draft constitution" for a proposed United Omani National Front meant to unite the PFLO with all other opponents of Sultan Qabus's rule. Much time was also devoted to the PFLO's history, a call to Omani soldiers to

revolt, and statements praising Soviet and South Yemeni support. The PFLO itself seemed to cast doubt on this last point the day before the Aden-Muscat accord was signed, when the Front vilified the Omani ruler's military cooperation with the United States and lamented that "Regrettably, there are those who listen to and believe these rulers." The PFLO made its final broadcast November 5, 1982 (ten days before the Oman-PDRY normalization agreement was ratified). Yet though it no longer has access to radio and is virtually ignored by both the Soviet and South Yemeni media, the PFLO does continue to exist.

In July 1984, Moscow International Service in Arabic reported a PFLO appeal to world public opinion for solidarity against Sultan Qabus. This PFLO statement was released not from Aden, but from Damascus.

See Aden ANA in Arabic, March 8, 1982, in *FBIS ME,* March 11, 1982, p. C12; Aden ANA in Arabic, May 18, 1982, in *FBIS ME,* May 21, 1982, p. C13; Aden Domestic Service in Arabic, June 9, 1982, in *FBIS ME,* June 10, 1982, p. C8; Aden ANA in Arabic, June 21, 1982, in *FBIS ME,* June 23, 1982, p. C6; Aden Voice of the PFLO in Arabic, July 28, 1982, in *FBIS ME,* July 30, 1982, pp. C3-C4 (first part of draft constitution—four more parts followed on succeeding days); Aden Voice of the PFLO in Arabic, August 27, 1982, in *FBIS ME,* September 1, 1982, pp. C5-C6; Aden Voice of the PFLO in Arabic, September 27, 1982, in *FBIS ME,* September 30, 1982, pp. C1-C2; Aden Voice of the PFLO in Arabic, October 26, 1982, in *FBIS ME,* October 27, 1982, pp. C5-C6; "PDRY," in *FBIS ME,* November 9, 1982, p. ii; Salalah Domestic Service in Arabic, November 15, 1982, in *FBIS ME,* November 16, 1982, pp. C2-C4; and Moscow International Service in Arabic, July 3, 1984, in *JPRS USSR Report: Political and Sociological Affairs,* August 9, 1984, p. 24.

66. Doha QNA in Arabic, April 3, 1983, in *FBIS ME,* April 4, 1983, pp. C4-C5; Muscat *'Uman,* May 29, 1983, p. 5, in *FBIS ME,* May 31, 1983, p. C3; Kuwait *Arab Times,* November 2, 1983, p. 6, in *FBIS ME,* November 4, 1983, pp. C3-C4; and Kuwait *Al-Anba,* January 29, 1984, p. 18, in *FBIS ME,* January 31, 1984, p. C3.

67. Muscat Domestic Service in Arabic, August 30, 1980, in *FBIS ME,* September 2, 1980, p. C1; Muscat Domestic Service in Arabic, March 17, 1981, in *FBIS ME,* March 19, 1981, p. C3; and Muscat Domestic Service in Arabic, June 8, 1981, in *FBIS ME,* June 9, 1981, pp. C2-C3.

68. Mark N. Katz, "Oman Security Gets a Boost in Soviet Urged Moderation," *The Christian Science Monitor,* January 18, 1983, p. 6. According to the IISS, there were 1,500 Soviet, 300 Cuban, and 75 East German military advisers in the PDRY in 1984; International Institute for Strategic Studies, *Military Balance, 1984–85,* pp. 22, 26, 120.

69. For examples of their charges against each other, see Moscow Radio Peace and Progress in Arabic, March 4, 1976, in *FBIS SU,* March 5, 1976, p. F1; Muscat Domestic Service in Arabic, March 10, 1976, in *FBIS ME,* March 11, 1976, p. C1; Glukhov, "Opasnaia sdelka," p. 5; Kuwait KUNA in Arabic, November 26, 1979, in *FBIS ME,* November 28, 1979, p. C2; and Muscat Domestic Service in Arabic, February 17, 1982, in *FBIS ME,* February 19, 1982, pp. C3-C4.

70. *Keesing's Contemporary Archives,* June 17–23, 1974, p. 26579.

71. Doha QNA in Arabic, March 31, 1977, in *FBIS ME,* April 1, 1977, p. C1; Aden Domestic Service in Arabic, April 5, 1977, in *FBIS ME,* April 7, 1977 p. C1; Doha QNA in Arabic, June 6, 1977, in *FBIS ME,* June 7, 1977, p. C1; and Doha QNA in Arabic, June 26, 1977, in *FBIS ME,* June 28, 1977, p. C1.

72. "PDRY-Omani Relations," in *FBIS ME,* May 7, 1982, p. ii; Kuwait KUNA in Arabic, July 7, 1982, in *FBIS ME,* July 8, 1982, p. C2; and Kuwait Domestic Service in Arabic, October 27, 1982, in *FBIS ME,* October 28, 1982, p. C1.

73. Salalah Domestic Service in Arabic, November 15, 1982, in *FBIS ME,* November 16, 1982, pp. C2-C4.

74. "Otnosheniia normalizuiutsia," *Pravda,* November 20, 1982, p. 4.

75. Aden Domestic Service in Arabic, October 27, 1983, in *FBIS ME,* October 28, 1983, p. C1.

76. Abu Dhabi Domestic Service in Arabic, January 27, 1983, in *FBIS ME,* January 28, 1983, p. C1; Kuwait KUNA in English, October 30, 1983, in *FBIS ME,* October 31, 1983, pp. C1-C2; and Muscat Domestic Service in Arabic, January 20, 1985, *FBIS ME,* January 22, 1985, p. C1.

77. Manama Gulf News Agency in Arabic, December 31, 1979, in *FBIS ME,* January 2, 1980, p. C2; and Kuwait KUNA in Arabic, July 7, 1980, in *FBIS ME,* July 7, 1970, p. C3.

78. *Keesing's Contemporary Archives,* July 25, 1980, p. 30379, and July 24, 1981, p. 30983, and "Oman," in *FBIS ME,* May 5, 1981, p. ii.

79. Paris AFP in English, December 4, 1981, in *FBIS ME,* December 7, 1971, p. C1.

80. Muscat Domestic Service in Arabic, December 17, 1980, in *FBIS ME,* December 18, 1980, p. C1; Manama Gulf News Agency in Arabic, January 27, 1981, in *FBIS ME,* January 27, 1981, p. C1; and Muscat Domestic Service in Arabic, January 27, 1981, in *FBIS ME,* January 28, 1981, p. C1.

Not surprisingly, the PFLO lauded the Soviet proposals; Aden Domestic Service in Arabic, December 14, 1980, in *FBIS ME,* December 16, 1980, p. C4.

81. Kuwait KUNA in English, April 8, 1980, in *FBIS ME,* April 9, 1980, p. C2; Muscat Domestic Service in Arabic, December 22, 1981, in *FBIS ME,* December 29, 1981, pp. C1-C3; and Muscat *'Uman,* September 7, 1983, p. 1, in *FBIS ME,* September 9, 1983, p. C2.

82. V. Peresada, "Vovse ne beskorystno," *Pravda,* January 20, 1980, p. 5, and Moscow Domestic Service in Russian, May 11, 1980, in *FBIS SU,* May 13, 1980, p. H2.

The Soviets apparently have some doubts as to how effective closing the Straits would be in denying Western access to the Gulf. According to TASS, the United States and Oman might build a "canal between the Persian Gulf and the Gulf of Oman to be used by battleships and other vessels in the event of the closure of the Straits of Hormuz" (Moscow TASS in English, July 3, 1981, in *FBIS SU,* July 7, 1981, p. H5.

83. *Keesing's Contemporary Archives,* December 1983, p. 32595.

84. Roger Matthews, "Strong Protection for the Oil Lanes," *Financial Times,* January 13, 1983, p. viii (of insert). The Straits are about twenty-four miles wide, and

the shipping lanes through them lie completely within the twelve-mile limit claimed by Oman. It is not certain if Iran recognizes Oman's claim to these waters, though Tehran has not seriously challenged it. See also Kuwait *Arab Times,* November 2, 1983, p. 6, in *FBIS ME,* November 4, 1983, pp. C3-C4.

85. Bernard Gwertzman, "Shultz Says Iran Won't Be Allowed to Blackmail U.S.," *The New York Times,* October 18, 1983, pp. A1, A12, and "President's News Conference on Foreign and Domestic Issues," *The New York Times,* February 23, 1984, p. A12. See also *Keesing's Contemporary Archives,* August 7, 1981, p. 31011, and December 1983, p. 32595.

86. John F. Burns, "TASS Says U.S. Acts in Persian Gulf Imperil Peace," *The New York Times,* March 8, 1984, p. A4.

87. The Soviets have warned that they "cannot be indifferent" to U.S. actions in the Gulf; see Konstantin Geivandov, "Eskalatsiia 'diplomatii kanonerok,'" *Izvestiia,* November 18, 1983, p. 5.

Although many statements warn of an impending crisis over the Straits, the Soviets have not said what they would do if one occurred. See, for example, Moscow Domestic TV Service in Russian, October 11, 1983, in *FBIS SU,* October 14, 1983, pp. H1-H2; Moscow TASS in English, October 12, 1983, in *FBIS SU,* October 14, 1983, p. H2; A. Gol'ts, "Greiut ruki," *Krasnaia Zvezda,* October 21, 1983, p. 3; Moscow Domestic Service in Russian, November 17, 1983, in *FBIS SU,* November 22, 1983, p. H8: and Moscow TASS International Service in Russian, February 21, 1984, in *FBIS SU,* February 23, 1984, pp. H9-H10.

88. "Zaiavlenie TASS," *Krasnaia Zvezda,* March 8, 1984, p. 3.

89. Muscat Domestic Service in Arabic, May 3, 1981, in *FBIS ME,* May 5, 1981, pp. C1-C2; Muscat *'Uman,* May 29, 1983, p. 5, in *FBIS ME,* May 31, 1983, p. C3; and Beirut *Monday Morning,* November 7-13, 1983, pp. 99-103, in *FBIS ME,* November 10, 1983, p. C4.

90. Muscat Domestic Service in Arabic, May 3, 1981, in *FBIS ME,* May 5, 1981, pp. C1-C2; and Muscat Domestic Service in Arabic, August 23, 1981, in *FBIS ME,* August 24, 1981, pp. C2-C4.

91. Moscow Radio Peace and Progress in Arabic, February 10, 1982, in *FBIS SU,* February 11, 1982, pp. H1-H2.

92. Moscow TASS in English, June 20, 1978, in *FBIS SU,* June 21, 1978, p. F5; and Moscow TASS in English, June 25, 1978, in *FBIS SU,* June 27, 1978, p. F3.

93. Moscow in Arabic, May 6, 1979, in *FBIS SU,* May 8, 1979, pp. H1-H2; and Moscow TASS in English, November 16, 1980, in *FBIS SU,* November 17, 1980, p. H9.

94. Kuwait KUNA in Arabic, August 2, 1983, in *FBIS ME,* August 3, 1983, p. C1.

95. Manama Gulf News Agency in Arabic, August 2, 1979, in *FBIS ME,* August 3, 1979, p. C4.

96. On Oman's economy, see The Economist Intelligence Unit, *Quarterly Economic Review of Bahrain, Qatar, Oman, the Yemens.*

97. "Report on Oil Reserves" *The New York Times,* June 3, 1983, p. D9, and Mark N. Katz, "War-Torn Dhofar . . . Only 39 Rebels Remain," *The Christian Science Monitor,* January 18, 1983, p. 6.

98. The Economist Intelligence Unit, *Quarterly Economic Review of Bahrain, Qatar, Oman, the Yemens,* annual supplement 1983, pp. 35, 44-45.

99. Until very recently, all three Omani armed services were commanded by British officers. In late 1984, an Omani (Major General Nasib bin Hamad al-Ruwaihi) was for the first time appointed commander of the army. But as of 1985, a British officer (Lt. Gen. John Watts) was still the overall commander of the armed forces and British officers were still in charge of the navy (Rear Adm. John Pierce Gunning) and the air force (Air Vice Mar. Erik Bennet). There are about one thousand Britons serving on contract with or seconded to the Omani forces, but only twelve U.S. military advisers in the Sultanate.

"People: Latest Appointments," *Jane's Defence Weekly,* November 17, 1984, p. 912; "A Wary North Eye," *The Economist,* September 15, 1984, pp. 32, 34; Judith Miller, "U.S. Is Said to Develop Oman as Its Major Ally in the Gulf," *The New York Times,* March 25, 1985, pp. A1, A8; and my conversations with several past and present U.S. and Omani officials.

100. Tariq also criticized the role played by the British in Oman; *Keesing's Contemporary Archives,* April 1-8, 1972, p. 25180.

101. For a detailed study of the formation and operation of the Consultative Council, see Dale F. Eickelman, "Kings and People: Oman's State Consultative Council," *The Middle East Journal* 38, 1 (Winter 1984): 51-71.

CHAPTER 4: SAUDI ARABIA

1. David Holden and Richard Johns, *The House of Saud: The Rise and Rule of the Most Powerful Dynasty in the Arab World* (New York: Holt, Rinehart and Winston, 1981), pp. 20-21.

2. Ibid., p. 23; J. B. Kelly, *Arabia, the Gulf and the West* (New York: Basic Books, 1980), pp. 226-227; and R. Bayly Winder, *Saudi Arabia in the Nineteenth Century* (London: Macmillan; New York: St. Martin's Press, 1965), chs. 1-7.

3. Winder, *Saudi Arabia,* chs. 8-9, and Kelly, *Arabia,* pp. 227-228.

4. Kelly, *Arabia,* pp. 228-229.

5. Ibid., pp. 230-238.

6. Manfred W. Wenner, *Modern Yemen, 1918-1966* (Baltimore: Johns Hopkins Press, 1967), pp. 142-147. According to some Yemenis, it is not just the border that is in dispute, but the entire question of which nation should rule the Asir.

7. Kelly, *Arabia,* pp. 235-236, and Holden and Johns, *House of Saud,* p. 96.

8. Kelly, *Arabia,* pp. 252-253.

9. Holden and Johns, *House of Saud,* p. 128, and George Lenczowski, *The Middle East in World Affairs,* 4th ed. (Ithaca and London: Cornell University Press, 1980), pp. 580-583.

10. Holden and Johns, *House of Saud,* chs. 13-14, and *Keesing's Contemporary Archives,* December 5-12, 1964, p. 20453.

11. Holden and Johns, *House of Saud,* pp. 213-216.

12. Ibid., pp. 379-383.

13. *Keesing's Contemporary Archives,* July 9, 1982, p. 31585.

14. See Holden and Johns, *House of Saud,* pp. 552-557, for a genealogy of King 'Abd al-'Aziz's male descendants.
15. Soviet exports to Saudi Arabia rose from only 0.2 million rubles in 1950 to 0.4 million rubles in 1960 but then expanded to 5.4 million in 1970 and 30.8 million in 1980. Soviet exports then declined to 25.5 million in 1981, 14.3 million in 1982, and 12.9 in 1983. Soviet trade figures state that the USSR bought nothing from Saudi Arabia in all these years except in 1983, when Moscow bought 156.5 million rubles worth of goods from Riyadh. See Ministerstvo Vneshnei Torgovli, *Vneshniaia torgovlia SSSR, 1922–1981* (Moscow: "Financy i Statistika," 1982), pp. 18-19, and Ministerstvo Vneshnei Torgovli, *Vneshniaia torgovlia SSSR v 1983 g.* (Moscow: "Financy i Statistika," 1984), p. 12.
16. John Baldry, "Soviet Relations with Saudi Arabia and the Yemen 1917–1938" *Middle Eastern Studies* 20, 1 (January 1984): 58-60; Ibrahim al-Rashid, ed., *Documents of the History of Saudi Arabia* (Salisbury, N.C.: Documentary Publications, 1976), pp. 214-215; and Holden and Johns, *House of Saud,* pp. 96-97.
17. Baldry, "Soviet Relations," pp. 60-64, Holden and Johns, *House of Saud,* pp. 107-108, and al-Rashid, *Documents,* pp. 220-224.
18. Baldry, "Soviet Relations," pp. 73-75, and Holden and Johns, *House of Saud,* p. 108.
19. Stephen Page, *The USSR and Arabia: The Development of Soviet Policies and Attitudes towards the Countries of the Arabian Peninsula, 1955–1970* (London: Central Asian Research Centre, 1971), p. 20.
20. Ibid., pp. 21, 25, 29.
21. Ibid., pp. 24, 25, 29-31. On Buraimi and Saudi Arabia's eastern frontiers, see Kelly, *Arabia,* ch. 2.
22. Page, *USSR and Arabia,* pp. 33, 35-36, 39. More recently, one Soviet author dated the transformation of Saudi Arabia into a reactionary state from 1956; A. Feoktistov, "Saudi Arabia and the Arab World," *International Affairs,* no. 7 (July 1977): 101.
23. Page, *USSR and Arabia,* pp. 50-51, 63-64.
24. Ibid., p. 78.
25. Ibid., p. 90.
26. Ibid., pp. 87-88, 92. Nasser and Faysal had agreed at a meeting in Jidda in August 1965 that Saudi Arabia would stop aiding the Yemeni royalists and Egypt would withdraw all its forces by October 1966. A conference of Yemenis from opposing sides was to meet and arrange for a transitional government and then a plebiscite. The two Yemeni sides did meet at Harad beginning in November 1965 but were unable to come to an agreement. Nasser, for his part, was both angered by Faysal's call with the Shah of Iran for an Islamic summit conference (which he saw as directed against him) and encouraged by the announcement of February 1966 that the British would leave Aden by 1968. Hoping to eventually spread his influence to South Yemen, Nasser increased the level of Egyptian forces in North Yemen (which in fact had been reduced), and so the war continued.
27. See chapter 1, on North Yemen, pp. 30-32.
28. See chapter 2, on South Yemen, pp. 76-80.

29. See Robert O. Freedman, *Soviet Policy toward the Middle East since 1970,* 3d ed. (New York: Praeger, 1982), pp. 75-91.

30. See chapter 2, on South Yemen, p. 80.

31. Riyadh Domestic Service in Arabic, November 7, 1973, in *FBIS ME,* November 8, 1973, p. B1.

32. Baghdad INA in Arabic, November 19, 1973, in *FBIS ME,* November 20, 1973, p. B5; Paris AFP in English, December 1, 1973, in *FBIS ME,* December 3, 1973, p. B4; and Beirut *An-Nahar,* December 2, 1973, in *FBIS ME,* December 6, 1973, p. B2.

33. See, for example, Tunis Domestic Service in Arabic, April 12, 1974, in *FBIS ME,* April 12, 1974, p. C1.

34. See chapter 2, on South Yemen, pp. 95-96.

35. Freedman, *Soviet Policy,* p. 236.

36. Riyadh Domestic Service in Arabic, July 3, 1975, in *FBIS ME,* July 9, 1975, p. C4.

37. Moscow in Arabic, July 8, 1975, in *FBIS SU,* July 10, 1975, pp. F3-F4; and Moscow in Arabic, July 17, 1976, in *FBIS SU,* July 19, 1976, pp. F7-F8.

38. For Saudi unhappiness on the lack of strong Western support for Somalia's operation in the Ogaden, see Jidda *'Ukaz,* January 27, 1978, p. 1, in *FBIS ME,* February 1, 1978, pp. C3-C4; and Riyadh Domestic Service in Arabic, March 6, 1978, in *FBIS ME,* March 10, 1978, pp. C3-C4.

39. See chapter 2, on South Yemen, pp. 96-97.

40. Moscow TASS in English, October 20, 1977, in *FBIS SU,* October 21, 1977, p. F1; Moscow TASS in English, July 13, 1978, in *FBIS SU,* July 14, 1978, pp. F6-F7; and V. Vinogradov and V. Chursanov, "Arabskii vostok v planakh imperializma," *Krasnaia Zvezda,* July 30, 1978, p. 3.

The Saudi News Agency criticized both Moscow and Aden for carrying stories that Riyadh was behind al-Hamdi's death. When al-Ghashmi was killed, the Saudis blamed the Soviets. While it was not clear to what extent the Soviets were involved in the June 1978 Yemeni events, most of the Arab League countries and Western observers generally saw the pro-Soviet South Yemeni leader 'Abd al-Fattah Isma'il as responsible for al-Ghashmi's death. See Riyadh SNA in Arabic, October 28, 1977, in *FBIS ME,* October 31, 1977, pp. C2-C3; and Riyadh SNA in Arabic, June 27, 1978, in *FBIS ME,* June 27, 1978, p. C1.

41. William B. Quandt, *Saudi Arabia in the 1980s: Foreign Policy, Security, and Oil* (Washington, D.C.: Brookings Institution, 1981), p. 114.

42. Igor' Beliaev, "Saudovskaia Aravia: Chto zhe dal'she?" *Literaturnaia Gazeta,* January 31, 1979, p. 14.

43. Manama Gulf News Agency in Arabic, March 3, 1979, in *FBIS ME,* March 5, 1979, pp. C1-C2; and London *Al-Hawadith,* March 2, 1979, pp. 20, 21, in *FBIS ME,* March 6, 1979, pp. C6-C10.

44. Fahd's statement appeared in Beirut's *As-Safir* on January 9, 1980—after the Soviet invasion of Afghanistan. The Saudis later insisted the interview was given before the invasion; see Quandt, *Saudi Arabia in the 1980s,* pp. 69-70.

For friendly Soviet statements about Saudi Arabia, see Moscow in Arabic, February 22, 1979, in *FBIS SU,* February 26, 1979, p. F9; Moscow in Arabic, March 5, 1979, in *FBIS SU,* March 6, 1979, pp. F4-F5; Moscow TASS in English, May 15, 1979, in *FBIS SU,* May 16, 1979, pp. H2-H3; Moscow in Arabic, September 23, 1979, in *FBIS SU,* September 24, 1979, pp. H4-H5; Moscow TASS in English, January 10, 1980, in *FBIS SU,* January 11, 1980, p. H3. This last broadcast was a summary of Prince Fahd's favorable comments on the USSR; undoubtedly the Soviets hoped they reflected his views even after the invasion of Afghanistan.

45. Riyadh SNA in Arabic, December 29, 1979, in *FBIS ME,* December 31, 1979, pp. C5-C6, and *Middle East Contemporary Survey, 1979–80* (New York: Holmes and Meier, 1981), pp. 706-707.

46. Moscow TASS in English, January 25, 1980, in *FBIS SU,* January 29, 1980, p. H7; Moscow TASS in English, February 13, 1980, in *FBIS SU,* February 20, 1980, p. H5; Moscow in Arabic, February 17, 1980, in *FBIS SU,* February 20, 1980, pp. H5-H7; and Moscow TASS in English, April 5, 1980, in *FBIS SU,* April 7, 1980, p. H4.

47. Moscow in Arabic, February 4, 1980, in *FBIS SU,* February 5, 1980, p. H4; Moscow TASS International Service in Russian, March 5, 1980, in *FBIS SU,* March 6, 1980, pp. H3-H4; V. Kudriavtsev, "Politika dezorientatsii," *Izvestiia,* April 6, 1980, p. 5; and Igor' Beliaev, "Kto zhe ugrozhaet Saudovskoi Aravii?" *Literaturnaia Gazeta,* July 9, 1980, p. 14.

48. Moscow in Arabic, November 6, 1981, in *FBIS SU,* November 9, 1981, pp. H4-H5. See also Moscow in Arabic, November 5, 1981, in *FBIS SU,* November 6, 1981, p. H1.

49. The delegation visited only Moscow, Peking, and Paris, since neither the United States nor the United Kingdom would receive it if PLO members were included and the delegation refused to visit Washington and London without them.

50. Moscow TASS in English, December 3, 1982, in *FBIS SU,* December 3, 1982, pp. H3-H4; and Kuwait KUNA in Arabic, December 3, 1982, in *FBIS SU,* December 6, 1982, pp. H3-H4.

51. Jidda Domestic Service in Arabic, December 11, 1982, in *FBIS ME,* December 13, 1982, p. C2.

52. "In Confrontation with Reaction," *World Marxist Review,* 26, 4 (April 1983): 37-38. See also Moscow Radio Peace and Progress in Arabic, January 5, 1983, in *FBIS SU,* January 6, 1983, pp. H3-H4; and Moscow TASS in English, February 23, 1983, in *FBIS SU,* February 24, 1983, pp. H3-H4.

53. As when Crown Prince 'Abdallah said in March 1983 that he favored establishing diplomatic ties to Moscow "at the right time," and when Saudi Ambassador to the U.S. Prince Bandar bin Sultan invited Soviet Ambassador Dobrynin to dinner as well as later telling the press that the Arabs would turn to "Moscow, Paris, and London" for weapons if they could not buy them from Washington. Riyadh SPA in Arabic, March 22, 1983, in *FBIS ME,* March 23, 1983, p. C1; Riyadh *Ar-Riyad,* April 12, 1984, p. 20, in *FBIS ME,* April 19, 1984, p. C8; and "Saudi Envoy Hosts Dinner for Dobrynin," Kuwait *Arab Times,* April 15, 1984, p. 1.

Prince 'Abdallah later said that Riyadh had no intention of establishing relations with the USSR or socialist bloc, and the Saudi Press Agency said Prince Bandar was "misquoted." Kuwait KUNA in English, November 21, 1983, in *FBIS ME,* November 22, 1983, p. C3; and Riyadh SPA in Arabic, April 17, 1984, in *FBIS ME,* April 18, 1984, pp. C1-C2.

54. Mark N. Katz, "Saudis Deny Rumors They Plan to Establish Ties with USSR," *The Christian Science Monitor,* May 9, 1984, p. 14.

55. Holden and Johns, *House of Saud,* p. 188, and Page, *USSR and Arabia,* p. 33.

56. E. Primakov, *Strany Aravii i kolonializm* (Moscow: Politizdat, 1956), p. 83.

57. A. Vasil'ev, "Saudovskaia Araviia mezhdu arkhaizmom i sovremennost'iu" (stat'ia vtoraia), *Aziia i Afrika Segodnia,* no. 9 (September 1980): 19.

58. Holden and Johns, *House of Saud,* p. 237, and Page, *USSR and Arabia,* p. 80.

59. A. Vasil'ev, "Saudovskaia Araviia mezhdu arkhaizmom i sovremennost'iu" (stat'ia pervaia), *Aziia i Afrika Segodnia,* no. 8 (August 1980): 20-21. See also Holden and Johns, *House of Saud,* p. 237.

60. Holden and Johns, *House of Saud,* pp. 227, 231-233.

61. Mordechai Abir, *Oil, Power and Politics* (London: Frank Cass, 1974), pp. 53-54.

62. Page, *USSR and Arabia,* p. 119, Kelly, *Arabia,* p. 271, *Middle East Contemporary Survey, 1980-81* (New York: Holmes and Meier, 1982), p. 736, and Riyadh Domestic Service in Arabic, April 24, 1983, in *FBIS ME,* April 25, 1983, p. C3.

63. Kelly, *Arabia,* p. 271.

64. Aden *Sawt al-Tali'ah,* 14 October, July 4, 5, 1973, in JPRS 60197, *Translations on the Near East,* no. 1039 (October 30, 1973): 65-71; Fred Halliday, *Arabia without Sultans,* (Harmondsworth, Middlesex: Penguin Books, 1974), pp. 67-69, and Kelly, *Arabia,* pp. 270-271.

65. Abir, *Oil, Power and Politics,* p. 54, and A. M. Vasil'ev, *Istoriia Saudovskoi Aravii (1745-1973)* (Moscow: Nauka, 1982), p. 421. See also A. I. Iakovlev, *Saudovskaia Araviia i zapad* (Moscow: Nauka, 1982), p. 87.

66. Aryeh Y. Yodfat, *The Soviet Union and the Arabian Peninsula* (London: Croom Helm; New York: St. Martin's Press, 1983), pp. 99-100, Richard F. Starr, "Checklist of Communist Parties in 1983," *Problems of Communism* 33, 2 (March April 1984): 43, and Mahdi Habib, "The Ability to Overcome Difficulties," *World Marxist Review,* no. 1 (January 1985): 37-41.

An unnamed SACP official said that the Party cooperates with another leftist group known as the Arab Socialist Labor Party; "In Confrontation with Reaction," pp. 37-38.

67. See, for example, Moscow Radio Peace and Progress in English, May 15, 1972, in *FBIS SU,* May 16, 1972, pp. B2-B3.

68. The Soviets apparently did not even announce the existence of the Party until the year following its formation; Moscow Radio Peace and Progress, October 1, 1976, in *FBIS SU,* October 4, 1976, p. F7.

69. Yodfat, *Soviet Union,* p. 133.

70. See, for example, Moscow in Persian, January 30, 1981, in *FBIS SU*, February 5, 1981, p. H1; and Moscow TASS in English, February 23, 1983, in *FBIS SU*, February 24, 1983, pp. H3-H4.

71. Vasil'ev, "Saudovskaia Araviia" (stat'ia vtoraia), p. 19.

72. Moscow Radio Peace and Progress, December 4, 1979, in *FBIS SU*, December 5, 1979, p. H9; *Middle East Contemporary Survey, 1980–81*, pp. 733-734; and "Saudi Arabia," in *FBIS ME*, September 26, 1983, p. ii.

There is a Saudi opposition group based in Tehran called the Islamic Revolutionary Organization of the Arabian Peninsula. It has apparently had no more success inside the Kingdom than any other opposition movement.

73. For an account of the seizure of the mosque and the ideas and goals of the group that seized it, see Holden and Johns, *House of Saud*, ch. 25. The entire operation appears to have been internally based and did not involve émigré opposition groups. One such group, the UPAP, did claim responsibility for the move. After this announcement its leader, Nasser Said, was abducted from Beirut on December 17, 1979, and was perhaps brought to Riyadh (according to ibid., p. 532).

For Soviet commentary on the rebels, see Moscow World Service in English, November 25, 1979, in *FBIS SU*, November 26, 1979, p. H4; "Napadenie na mechet'," *Izvestiia*, November 28, 1979, p. 4; Moscow Domestic Service in Russian, December 5, 1979, in *FBIS SU*, December 6, 1979, p. H6; and Moscow Domestic Service in Russian, December 18, 1979, in *FBIS SU*, December 19, 1979 p. H3.

74. Riyadh SNA in Arabic, December 20, 1979, in *FBIS ME*, December 20, 1979, p. C3.

75. Oddly enough, though, this appeal was broadcast in Mandarin; Moscow in Mandarin, December 28, 1981, in *FBIS SU*, December 31, 1981, pp. H6-H7.

76. Yodfat, *Soviet Union*, pp. 16-21, 61-67, 86-93.

77. Ibid., pp. 21-23, 67-71, 75-86.

78. Ibid., pp. 120-131, and Zalmay Khalizad, "Islamic Iran: Soviet Dilemma," *Problems of Communism* 33, 1 (January–February 1984): 15.

79. Khalizad, "Islamic Iran" p. 16.

80. Quandt, *Saudi Arabia in the 1980s*, p. 21.

81. Yodfat, *Soviet Union*, p. 132. Yodfat also claimed that Soviet arms were delivered to North Yemen and then transported from there overland across Saudi Arabia to Iraq (p. 132). Since the roads from the YAR into Saudi Arabia are very poor and the arms could be delivered to Iraq more easily from Red Sea ports farther to the north, such as Aqaba in Jordan, this claim does not seem credible.

82. Riyadh SPA in Arabic, December 13, 1980, in *FBIS ME*, December 15, 1980, p. C2.

It was also reported in June 1983 that King Fahd sent a message to Andropov with regard to the Iran-Iraq war; Dusko Doder, "Saudi King Reportedly Sends Note to Andropov," *The Washington Post*, June 7, 1983, p. A12.

83. *Middle East Contemporary Survey, 1979–80*, p. 62.

84. On Soviet foreign policy toward the Arab-Israeli conflict, see Freedman, *Soviet Policy;* on Saudi Arabia's views and involvement in it, see A. I. Dawisha, "Saudi Arabia and the Arab-Israeli Conflict: The Ups and Downs of Pragmatic Moderation," *International Journal* 38, 4 (Autumn 1983): 674-689.

85. Tunis Domestic Service in Arabic, April 12, 1974, in *FBIS ME,* April 12, 1974, p. C1.

86. Jidda *Al-Bilad,* July 25, 1971, p. 2, in *FBIS ME,* August 2, 1971, p. B4; and Jidda *'Ukaz,* September 30, 1978, p. 1, in *FBIS ME,* October 4, 1978, pp. C4-C5.

87. Jidda *'Ukaz,* January 3, 1979, p. 1, in *FBIS ME,* January 12, 1979, p. C2.

88. Kuwait *As-Siyasah,* April 26, 1981, p. 17, in *FBIS ME,* May 1, 1981, pp. C1-C2; and Riyadh *Al-Jazirah,* December 14, 1982, p. 2, in *FBIS ME,* December 21, 1982, pp. C3-C4.

89. Riyadh *Al-Jazirah,* September 13, 1982, p. 3, in *FBIS ME,* September 15, 1982, pp. C1-C2; and Riyadh SPA in Arabic, April 2, 1983, in *FBIS ME,* April 4, 1983, p. C6.

90. Dmitry Volsky, "King Faisal's 'Holy War'," *New Times,* no. 5 (February 1973): 26-27; Moscow in Arabic, February 20, 1973, in *FBIS SU,* February 21, 1973, pp. B6-B7; Moscow Radio Peace and Progress, April 4, 1974, in *FBIS SU,* April 5, 1974, pp. F6-F7; Moscow in Arabic, September 13, 1974, in *FBIS SU,* September 19, 1974, pp. F7-F9; Moscow TASS in English, December 16, 1974, in *FBIS SU,* December 16, 1974, p. F9; and A. Kapralov, "Vtiagivaiut v al'ians," *Izvestiia,* April 28, 1981, p. 4.

91. Moscow Radio Peace and Progress in English, December 17, 1972, in *FBIS SU,* December 18, 1972, pp. B3-B4; and Y. Tsaplin, "Teamed Up," *New Times,* no. 48 (November 1976): 23.

92. Moscow Radio Peace and Progress, October 20, 1981, in *FBIS SU,* October 20, 1981, in *FBIS SU,* October 21, 1981, pp. H7-H8; and Moscow Radio Peace and Progress in Arabic, October 26, 1981, in *FBIS SU,* October 29, 1981, p. H7. On the Fahd Plan, see Dawisha, "Saudi Arabia," pp. 681-682.

93. Moscow in Arabic, November 5, 1981, in *FBIS SU,* November 6, 1981, p. H1; Riyadh SPA in English, November 7, 1981, in *FBIS ME,* November 9, 1981, p. C3; and Riyadh SPA in English, November 16, 1981, in *FBIS ME,* November 17, 1981, p. C4.

94. Dawisha, "Saudi Arabia," pp. 684-686, and Moscow in Arabic, September 22, 1982, in *FBIS SU,* September 23, 1982, pp. H11-H12.

95. Riyadh SPA in English, December 2, 1982, in *FBIS ME,* December 3, 1982, pp. C1-C2.

96. Jidda *'Ukaz,* January 15, 1983, p. 3, in *FBIS ME,* January 20, 1983, pp. C1-C3.

97. The one "confrontation state" that is still closely allied to Moscow is Syria, but the Saudis insist that Damascus is not a Soviet puppet. U.S. attempts to isolate Syria have induced Damascus to turn toward Moscow in the Saudi view. Eric Rouleau, "Espoirs de réconciliation au Liban," *Le Monde,* October 30–31, 1983, pp. 1, 5, and Katz, "Saudis Deny Rumors," p. 14.

98. Moscow Radio Peace and Progress, July 11, 1981, in *FBIS SU,* July 13, 1981, p. H1; and Moscow TASS in English, November 10, 1981, in *FBIS SU,* November 10, 1981, p. H1.

99. Kudriavtsev, "Politika dezorientatsii." In this article, the United States was seen as about to seize Iran's Kharg Island to obtain a base for an invasion of Saudi

Arabia. The author also implied that the U.S. arms paid for by Saudi Arabia and sent to North Yemen the previous year might be used by the YAR against the Saudis.

100. A. Vasil'ev, "Fakely persidskogo zaliva," *Pravda,* May 31, 1974, p. 4.

101. Riyadh Domestic Service in Arabic, April 19, 1984, in *FBIS ME,* April 20, 1984, p. C1.

102. Riyadh SPA in Arabic, December 13, 1980, in *FBIS ME,* December 15, 1980, p. C3; and Riyadh Domestic Service in Arabic, December 22, 1980, in *FBIS ME,* December 23, 1980, pp. C1-C2.

The Brezhnev Persian Gulf peace proposals also called for all countries to respect the nonaligned status of the Gulf states and for these states not to be drawn into military groupings including the nuclear powers; for all countries to respect the right of Gulf states to their natural resources; and for there to be no hindrance to freedom of trade between the Gulf and all other countries. Freedman, *Soviet Policy,* pp. 397-398.

103. Page, *USSR and Arabia,* pp. 33, 51, 53, 55-56, 118.

104. Moscow in Arabic, November 28, 1973, in *FBIS SU,* November 29, 1973, pp. F2-F3; Moscow Radio Peace and Progress in Arabic, June 11, 1974, in *FBIS SU,* June 12, 1974, p. F6; and Moscow in Arabic, December 4, 1974, in *FBIS SU,* December 5, 1974, pp. F1-F2.

105. Moscow Radio Peace and Progress in English, March 14, 1972, in *FBIS SU,* March 15, 1972, pp. B5-B6; Moscow in Arabic, May 16, 1972, in *FBIS SU,* May 17, 1972, pp. B5-B6; and Moscow in Arabic, September 4, 1973, in *FBIS SU,* September 6, 1973, pp. F13-F14.

106. M. Fyodorov, "Oil—The Arabs' Weapon," *New Times,* no. 50 (December 1973): 14-15; Moscow in Arabic, December 11, 1973, in *FBIS SU,* December 12, 1973, p. F2; Moscow in Arabic, December 25, 1973, in *FBIS SU,* December 28, 1973, pp. F8-F9; Moscow Radio Peace and Progress in English, February 5, 1974, in *FBIS SU,* February 6, 1974, pp. F2-F3; and Moscow in Arabic, March 11, 1974, in *FBIS SU,* March 12, 1974, p. F2.

107. Moscow TASS in English, January 10, 1980, in *FBIS SU,* January 11, 1980 p. H3.

108. Moscow in Arabic, November 11, 1974, in *FBIS SU,* November 15, 1974, pp. F2-F3; Moscow Radio Peace and Progress in Arabic, June 14, 1976, in *FBIS SU,* June 15, 1976, p. F4; Moscow in Arabic, December 20, 1976, in *FBIS SU,* December 21, 1976, p. F1; Moscow in Arabic, January 18, 1977, in *FBIS SU,* January 19, 1977, p. F3; Moscow TASS in English, July 4, 1977, in *FBIS SU,* July 6, 1977, p. F2; and Moscow in Arabic, August 25, 1981, in *FBIS SU,* August 26, 1981, p. H2.

109. Marshall I. Goldman, "The Soviet Union," in *The Oil Crisis,* ed. Raymond Vernon (New York: W. W. Norton, 1976), p. 138, and David Wilson, *Soviet Oil and Gas to 1990* (Cambridge, Mass.: Abt Books, 1982), p. 170.

110. "Report on Oil Reserves," *The New York Times,* June 3, 1983, p. D9.

111. This is what several young Saudis have told me. They say they do not want to see a one-man dictatorship like the other Arab "republics" replace the Saudi monarchy. Many Saudis seem to hope for some sort of constitutional monarchy, but there are some who wish to see the monarchy overthrown altogether.

CHAPTER 5: KUWAIT, THE UNITED ARAB EMIRATES, BAHRAIN, AND QATAR

1. *The Middle East and North Africa 1982-83* (London: Europa Publications, 1982), pp. 535-536; J. B. Kelly, *Arabia, the Gulf and the West* (New York: Basic Books, 1980), pp. 169-170; and George Lenczowski, *The Middle East in World Affairs*, 4th ed. (Ithaca and London: Cornell University Press, 1980), pp. 660-661.

2. *Middle East and North Africa 1982-83*, pp. 536, 539-540, and Lenczowski, *Middle East*, pp. 662, 665-666.

3. Kelly, *Arabia*, p. 276. King Ghazi of Iraq had also unsuccessfully attempted to claim Kuwait in 1938-39.

4. *Keesing's Contemporary Archives*, June 17-24, 1961, p. 18159, July 8-15, 1961, pp. 18187-90, October 7-14, 1961, p. 18355, August 18-25, 1962, p. 18934, and Kelly, *Arabia*, pp. 276-277.

5. Kelly, *Arabia*, pp. 281-284, and *Keesing's Contemporary Archives*, June 17-24, 1961, p. 18159, and August 18-24, 1975, p. 27285.

6. *Middle East Contemporary Survey, 1976-77* (New York: Holmes and Meier, 1978), pp. 345-346.

7. *Keesing's Contemporary Archives*, June 4, 1982, p. 31523, and *Middle East Contemporary Survey, 1980-81* (New York: Holmes and Meier, 1982), p. 480.

8. "Keeping out of It," *The Economist*, June 23, 1984, pp. 45-46.

9. *Keesing's Contemporary Archives*, August 18-24, 1975, p. 27285.

10. *Middle East Contemporary Survey, 1980-81*, p. 480.

11. Dubai *Khaleej Times*, January 11, 1984, p. 3, in *FBIS ME*, January 12 1984, p. C1.

12. Fred Halliday, *Arabia without Sultans* (Harmondsworth, Middlesex: Penguin Books, 1974), p. 434, and Lenczowski, Middle East, pp. 664-665.

13. *Middle East Contemporary Survey, 1980-81*, p. 474; Kuwait KUNA in Arabic, February 21, 1985, in *FBIS ME*, February 21, 1985, p. C2; Kuwait *Arab Times*, February 23, 1985, p. 1, in *FBIS ME*, February 25, 1985, p. C1; and "A Better Vote," *The Economist*, March 2, 1985, pp. 41-42.

14. Lenczowski, *Middle East*, pp. 661-664.

15. Stephen Page, *The USSR and Arabia: The Development of Soviet Policies and Attitudes towards the Countries of the Arabian Peninsula, 1955-1970* (London: Central Asian Research Centre, 1971), pp. 61-62, and Charles B. McLane, *Soviet-Third World Relations*, vol. 1, *Soviet-Middle East Relations* (London: Central Asian Research Centre, 1973), p. 70.

16. Page, *USSR and Arabia*, p. 62.

17. Ibid., p. 81, and McLane, *Soviet-Third World Relations*, p. 70.

18. Cited in Page, *USSR and Arabia*, p. 81.

19. Ibid.

20. Ibid., p. 120, and McLane, *Soviet-Third World Relations*, pp. 70-71.

21. Moscow TASS in English, March 10, 1973, in *FBIS SU*, March 20, 1973, pp. B10-B11; Moscow in Arabic, March 11, 1974, in *FBIS SU*, March 13, 1973,

pp. B9-B10; and Moscow Domestic Service in Russian, March 13, 1973, in *FBIS SU,* March 16, 1973, p. B12.

22. Anne M. Kelly, "The Soviet Naval Presence during the Iraq-Kuwaiti Border Dispute: March–April 1973," Center for Naval Analyses Professional Paper no. 122, June 1974, p. A-2; and Moscow TASS in English, March 21, 1973, in *FBIS SU,* March 21, 1973, p. B1.

23. Anne M. Kelly, "Soviet Naval Presence" pp. 5-6.

24. Kuwait *Ar-Ra'y al-'Amm,* March 25, 1973, p. 1, in *FBIS ME,* April 4, 1973, p. B2; Kuwait *Ar-Ra'y al-'Amm,* March 26, 1973, p. 1, in *FBIS ME,* April 6, 1973, pp. B1-B2; and Paris AFP in English, April 5, 1973, in *FBIS ME,* April 5, 1973, p. B1.

25. "Border Incident," *New Times,* no. 14 (April 1973): 7.

26. Moscow TASS in English, July 24, 1973, in *FBIS SU,* July 25, 1973, p. B8; and "Nikolaiu Podgornomu," *Pravda,* November 14, 1973, p. 4.

27. Cairo MENA in Arabic, January 31, 1974, in *FBIS ME,* January 31, 1974, p. B4.

28. Kuwait *As-Siyasah,* February 11, 1975, p. 13, in *FBIS ME,* February 21, 1975, pp. C1-C3; and Kuwait *Ar-Ra'y al-'Amm,* August 19, 1975, p. 1, in *FBIS ME,* August 26, 1975, p. C2.

29. Baghdad Domestic Service in Arabic, October 5, 1975, in *FBIS ME,* October 6, 1975, p. C1; Kuwait *Ar-Ra'y al-'Amm,* March 1, 1976, p. 1, in *FBIS ME,* March 5, 1976, p. C2; and Cairo MENA in Arabic, June 25, 1976, in *FBIS ME,* June 28, 1976, p. C1.

30. Doha QNA in Arabic, December 5, 1976, in *FBIS ME,* December 6, 1976, p. C1; Central Intelligence Agency, *Communist Aid to the Less Developed Countries of the Free World, 1976,* ER 77-10296 (Washington, D.C.: CIA, August 1977), p. 33; and CIA, *Communist Aid to Less Developed Countries of the Free World, 1977,* ER 78-10478U (Washington, D.C.: CIA, November 1978), p. 34.

31. "Iraq-Kuwait," *New Times,* no. 31 (July 1977), p. 15.

32. International Institute for Strategic Studies, *The Military Balance, 1980–1981* (London: IISS, 1981), p. 103.

33. *Middle East Contemporary Survey, 1980–81,* p. 482.

34. At least publicly. The CIA stated that there were five military technicians from the USSR and Eastern Europe in Kuwait in 1979, but none were there in 1981 according to the State Department. Yet even if there have been Soviet advisers in Kuwait, their numbers have been extremely low. Central Intelligence Agency, *Communist Aid Activities in Non-Communist Less Developed Countries, 1979 and 1954–79,* ER 80-10318U (Washington, D.C.: CIA, October 1980), p. 15, and U.S. Department of State, *Soviet and East European Aid to the Third World, 1981* (Washington, D.C.: U.S. GPO, February 1983), p. 14.

For Kuwaiti denials that Soviet military advisers had arrived, see Riyadh SNA in Arabic, April 12, 1978, in *FBIS ME,* April 13, 1978, p. C1; and Cairo MENA in Arabic, August 28, 1978, in *FBIS ME,* August 29, 1978, p. C1.

35. According to ACDA, over the years 1976–80 Kuwait bought arms worth $390 million from the United States, $220 million from the United Kingdom, and

$130 million from France. Since 1981, Kuwait has purchased additional arms worth over $1,237 million from the United States, $309 million from France, $114 million from the United Kingdom, and until 1984 nothing from the USSR. U.S. Arms Control and Disarmament Agency, *World Military Expenditures and Arms Transfers, 1971–1980* (Washington, D.C.: U.S. GPO, March 1983), p. 119; International Institute for Strategic Studies, *Military Balance, 1981–82*, p. 115; ibid., 1982–83, p. 120; ibid., 1983–84, p. 129; ibid., 1984–85, p. 143 and Doha QNA in Arabic, May 22, 1977, in *FBIS ME*, May 23, 1977, p. C1.

36. Rich Atkinson and Fred Hiatt, "Kuwait Asks U.S. to Sell It Stinger Antiplane Missiles," *The Washington Post*, May 31, 1984, pp. A1, A31; "U.S. Proposes Plan for Upgrading of Kuwaiti Defenses" *The Washington Post*, June 16, 1984, p. A20; and David B. Ottaway, "Kuwait Appeals to U.S. for Missiles," *The Washington Post*, June 19, 1984, pp. A1, A13.

37. Rowland Evans and Robert Novak, "Kuwait Finds an Open Door," *The Washington Post*, June 25, 1984, p. A11; *The Wall Street Journal*, July 10, 1984, p. 1; Herbert H. Denton, "Soviets Agree to Sell Major Arms Systems, Missiles to Kuwait," *The Washington Post*, July 13, 1984, pp. A1, A26; Mark N. Katz, "Kuwait Should Get U.S. Missiles," *Newsday*, July 26, 1984, p. 76; "Soviet Arms Experts to Teach Kuwaitis to Use New Weapons," *The Christian Science Monitor*, October 4, 1984, p. 2 ("not more than ten" were reported to be sent from the USSR to Kuwait); and Kuwait KUNA in Arabic, January 14, 1985, in *FBIS ME*, January 14, 1985, p. C2.

38. It fell further to 5.7 million rubles in 1983. Ministerstvo Vneshnei Torgovli, *Vneshniaia torgovlia SSSR, 1922–1981* (Moscow: "Financy i Statistika," 1982), pp. 16-17, and Ministerstvo Vneshnei Torgovli, *Vneshniaia torgovlia SSSR v 1983 g.* (Moscow: "Financy i Statistika," 1984), p. 11.

39. Page, *USSR and Arabia*, p. 119.

40. Ibid., Central Intelligence Agency, *Communist Aid, 1979*, p. 20, and U.S. Department of State, *Soviet Aid*, p. 19.

41. Kuwait *Al-'Anba*, January 15, 1984, p. 17, in *FBIS SU*, January 19, 1984, pp. H1-H3.

42. See, for example, McLane, *Soviet–Third World Relations*, p. 71; Moscow TASS International Service in English, August 30, 1971, in *FBIS SU*, August 31, 1971, p. B4; Moscow in Arabic, June 27, 1974, in *FBIS SU*, June 28, 1974, p. F4; Moscow TASS in English, December 5, 1975, in *FBIS SU*, December 5, 1975, pp. F1-F3; Moscow in Arabic, September 12, 1978, in *FBIS SU*, September 13, 1978, p. F5; and Moscow Domestic Service in Russian, March 16, 1982, in *FBIS SU*, March 17, 1982, p. H1.

43. Page, *USSR and Arabia*, p. 119, and Moscow in Arabic, September 12, 1978 in *FBIS SU*, September 13, 1978, p. F5.

44. Moscow TASS in English, March 23, 1978, in *FBIS SU*, March 24, 1978, p. F2; Moscow in Arabic, November 20, 1979, in *FBIS SU*, November 23, 1979, p. H8; and Kuwait KUNA in Arabic, May 17, 1983, in *FBIS SU*, May 20, 1983, pp. H5-H6.

45. The most important of these visits were made in November 1964 by the

Deputy Prime Minister/Finance Minister (who is currently Amir) and in December 1975 and April 1981 by the Kuwaiti Foreign Minister, Shaykh Sabah al-Ahmad al-Jabir Al Sabah. The Kuwaiti trade, oil, fisheries, and cultural ministers have also visited the USSR on various occasions, as have the Minister of State for Cabinet Affairs, 'Abd al-'Aziz Hussein, and the Undersecretary for Foreign Affairs, Rashid ar-Rashid. The Kuwaiti Defense Minister also visited Moscow in July 1984.

A reigning Amir has not yet visited the USSR, but the current one did visit Hungary, Romania, Bulgaria, and Yugoslavia in September 1980 (and bought state bonds of all four countries). According to *Afrique-Asie,* a secret meeting was held by Soviet Foreign Minister Andrei Gromyko, the Kuwaiti Amir, the Moroccan Foreign Minister, and a PLO official, though the date and place of the meeting were not published. Although there have been several Soviet visitors to Kuwait, none of them has been on as high a level as the Kuwaiti visitors to Moscow. The Kuwaiti press, though, expected Gromyko to visit Kuwait in 1985.

See McLane, *Soviet–Third World Relations,* p. 71; "Sovmestnoe sovetsko-kuveitskoe kommiunike," *Pravda,* April 26, 1981, p. 4; "Druzhestvennaia beseda," *Pravda,* October 21, 1981, p. 4; Doha QNA in Arabic, November 18, 1982, in *FBIS ME,* November 19, 1982, pp. C1-C2; "Obmen mneniiami," *Pravda,* April 7 1983, p. 4; Kuwait KUNA in Arabic, May 14, 1984, in *FBIS SU,* May 16, 1984, p. H1; Kuwait KUNA in Arabic, September 21, 1981, in *FBIS ME,* September 21, 1981, pp. C1-C2; "Les Dirigeants sovietiques aux Arabes: 'Attendez-vous le don du ciel?'" *Afrique-Asie,* November 8–21, 1982, pp. 58-60; Denton, "Soviets Agree," pp. A1, A26; Kuwait KUNA in Arabic, June 21, 1984, in *FBIS ME,* June 21, 1984, p. C1; and Kuwait *Al Qabas,* July 13, 1984, p. 1, in *FBIS ME,* July 16, 1984, p. C1.

46. Page, *USSR and Arabia,* p. 52.

47. Moscow TASS in English, July 23, 1973, in *FBIS SU,* July 25, 1973, p. B8; Moscow in Arabic, August 20, 1974, in *FBIS SU,* August 21, 1974, p. F5; and "Kuwait's Decision," *New Times,* no. 28 (July 1975): 30.

48. L. Smirnova, "Kuwait's Trade Unions," *New Times,* no. 30 (July 1974): 23.

49. Moscow in Arabic, January 22, 1974, in *FBIS SU,* January 24, 1974, p. F5; Moscow TASS in English, August 22, 1974, in *FBIS SU,* August 23, 1974, p. F4; L. Koriavin, "Problemy neftianogo el'dorado," *Izvestiia,* May 7, 1977, p. 4; Moscow TASS in English, March 3, 1978, in *FBIS SU,* March 6, 1978, p. F1; Moscow TASS in English, September 27, 1978, in *FBIS SU,* September 27, 1978, p. F8; V. Kassis, "Kuwait Today," *International Affairs,* no. 10 (October 1978): 111-117; and Vladimir Shelepin, "Island in a Sea of Oil," *New Times,* no. 36 (September 1979): 26-28.

50. A. Vasil'ev, "Chto proiskhodit v Kuveite," *Pravda,* September 1, 1976, p. 5; "K sobytiiam v Kuveite," *Izvestiia,* September 2, 1976, p. 3; and A. Kniazev, "Na vzaimovygodnoi osnove," *Izvestiia,* March 12, 1983, p. 4.

51. See, for example, Kassis, "Kuwait Today," pp. 111-117; Shelepin, "Island," pp. 26-28; Kniazev, "Na vzaimovygodnoi osnove" p. 4; and E. Aleksandrov and A. Filonik, "Tri nedeli v Kuveite," *Aziia i Afrika Segodnia,* no. 9 (September 1980): 37-40.

52. Page, *USSR and Arabia,* p. 52.

53. In interviews in January 1984 at both the Institute for the USA and Canada and the Oriental Institute in Moscow, Soviet scholars denied to me that there even existed a Kuwaiti Communist Party.

54. Moscow in Arabic, December 14, 1972, in *FBIS SU,* December 15, 1972, p. B4. Although certainly leftist, the Kuwait ANM branch was criticized for not being radical enough by South Yemen's National Liberation Front and by PFLOAG (many leaders of both these organizations were ANM members). After a conference in 1969, the more radical groups split with the Kuwaiti ANM. The Kuwaiti ANM's weekly *At-Talia* (like other Kuwaiti newspapers) was suspended on several occasions, and the National Assembly was dissolved in 1976 largely because of the actions of al-Khatib and the other radical members. This group, however, was not revolutionary in that they did not seek to overthrow the government by force. Instead, they sought more power for the legislature, nationalization of all foreign oil companies (which was achieved), and a foreign policy in line with the radical Arabs and less close to the West. According to former Soviet diplomat Vladimir Sakharov, who served in Kuwait in 1971, al-Khatib worked for the KGB, but in an April 1984 interview Dr. al-Khatib denied that either he or his party was ever communist. (He also said there were no opposition parties in Kuwait, since such parties existed only in democracies and Kuwait's democracy was only a modest one.)

See Halliday, *Arabia without Sultans,* p. 462; Vladimir Sakharov, *High Treason* (New York: Ballantine Books, 1980), p. 289; and Kuwait *Arab Times,* April 25, 1984, p. 5, in *FBIS ME,* April 27, 1984, p. C1.

55. Soviet commentary on these events drew mainly on Western media reports; see Moscow TASS in English, December 12, 1983, in *FBIS SU,* December 12, 1983, p. H5; Moscow TASS in English, December 12, 1983, in *FBIS SU,* December 13, 1983, p. H8; Moscow TASS in English, December 12, 1983, in *FBIS SU,* December 13, 1983, pp. H8-H9; and E. Korshunov, "Kto otvetstvenen za vzryvy?" *Izvestiia,* December 14, 1983, p. 1.

56. Kuwait KUNA in Arabic, January 30, 1979, in *FBIS SU,* January 31, 1979, pp. F15-F16.

57. Kuwait *Ar-Ra'y al-'Amm,* July 21, 1975, p. 2, in *FBIS ME,* July 25, 1975, p. C1.

58. Sakharov, *High Treason,* p. 270.

59. On the similarity of Soviet and Kuwaiti views about the Arab-Israeli situation, see "Soviet-Kuwait Talks," *New Times,* no. 50 (December 1975): 16-17; Kuwait KUNA in Arabic, January 5, 1980, in *FBIS ME,* January 8, 1980, p. C1; Kuwait KUNA in English, July 27, 1980, in *FBIS ME,* July 29, 1980, pp. C1-C2; A. Usvatov, "Similarity of Views," *New Times,* no. 18 (May 1981): 13; Kuwait KUNA in English, October 22, 1981, in *FBIS ME,* October 23, 1981, pp. C1-C2; "Zaiavlenie ministra innostrannykh del Kuveita," *Pravda,* August 24, 1982, p. 4; Kuwait KUNA in English, March 5, 1983, in *FBIS ME,* March 7, 1983, p. C1; and Kuwait *Al-Qabas,* March 7, 1984, p. 1, in *FBIS ME,* March 9, 1984, p. C1.

60. Kuwait *Ar-Ra'y al-'Amm,* March 21, 1971, pp. 1-2, in *FBIS ME,* March

25, 1971, p. B1; and Kuwait *Ar-Ra'y al-'Amm,* April 11, 1971, p. 8, in *FBIS ME,* April 20, 1971, pp. B1-B2.

61. Kuwait *Ar-Ra'y al-'Amm,* December 20, 1971, p. 1, in *FBIS ME,* December 30, 1971, p. B1; Kuwait *Ar-Ra'y al-'Amm,* October 28, 1972, pp. 1, 11, in *FBIS ME,* November 10, 1972, p. B7; and Kuwait *Ar-Ra'y al-'Amm,* April 1, 1974, p. 1, in *FBIS ME,* April 5, 1974, pp. C1-C2.

62. Doha QNA in Arabic, June 15, 1982, in *FBIS ME,* June 16, 1982, pp. C1-C2; and Kuwait KUNA in English, October 21, 1982, in *FBIS SU,* October 22, 1982, p. H4.

63. "Soviet Gulf Proposals," in *FBIS ME,* December 11, 1980, p. ii; "Brezhnev Gulf Proposals," in *FBIS ME,* December 12, 1980, p. ii; and Kuwait KUNA in Arabic, December 11, 1980, in *FBIS ME,* December 12, 1980, p. C1.

64. For expressions of these ideas, see Kuwait KUNA in Arabic, February 27, 1979, in *FBIS ME,* March 2, 1979, p. C2; Kuwait KUNA in English, August 24, 1980, in *FBIS ME,* August 25, 1980, p. C1; Jidda *'Ukaz,* March 18, 1981, p. 5, in *FBIS ME,* March 23, 1981, p. C1; Kuwait KUNA in Arabic, March 22, 1981, in *FBIS ME,* March 23, 1981, pp. C1-C2; Riyadh SPA in Arabic, March 28, 1981, in *FBIS ME,* March 30, 1981, p. C1; and Kuwait KUNA in Arabic, April 16, 1984, in *FBIS ME,* April 16, 1984, p. C1.

65. Kuwait KUNA in Arabic, May 3, 1981, in *FBIS ME,* May 4, 1981, pp. C1-C2.

66. Kuwait *Al-Hadaf,* May 7, 1981, p. 7, in *FBIS ME,* May 13, 1981, p. C5.

67. London *Ash-Sharq al-Awsat,* September 17, 1981, pp. 1, 2, in *FBIS ME,* September 21, 1981, p. C1; and Kuwait KUNA in Arabic, September 21, 1981, in *FBIS ME,* September 21, 1981, pp. C1-C2.

68. Page, *USSR and Arabia,* p. 120; Kuwait *Ar-Ra'y al-'Amm,* December 20, 1971, p. 1, in *FBIS ME,* December 30, 1971, p. B1; Amman Domestic Service in Arabic, February 5, 1972, in *FBIS ME,* February 8, 1972, p. B1; Riyadh SNA in Arabic, May 23, 1978, in *FBIS ME,* May 24, 1978, p. C3; and Manama Gulf News Agency in Arabic, June 13, 1978, in *FBIS ME,* June 14, 1978, p. C1.

69. Kuwait KUNA in Arabic, December 29, 1979, in *FBIS ME,* December 31, 1979, pp. C1-C2; Kuwait KUNA in Arabic, January 23, 1980, in *FBIS ME,* January 24, 1980, pp. C2-C3; and Kuwait KUNA in English, April 8, 1980, in *FBIS ME,* April 8, 1980, p. C1.

70. Moscow in Arabic, February 29, 1980, in *FBIS SU,* March 11, 1980, p. H5.

71. Kuwait *Al-Qabas,* November 1, 1981, p. 2, in *FBIS ME,* November 4, 1981, pp. C1-C2.

72. "Report on Oil Reserves," *The New York Times,* June 3, 1983, p. D9.

73. Kuwait's total population in 1980 was 1.35 million. *Middle East and North Africa 1982–83,* p. 535.

74. "Keeping out of It," pp. 45-46.

75. *Middle East and North Africa 1982–83,* pp. 854-855, and Lenczowski, *Middle East,* p. 676.

76. Lenczowski, *Middle East,* p. 676, and *Middle East and North Africa 1982–83,* p. 855.

77. The total area of the UAE is 77,700 square kilometers; Abu Dhabi alone has an area of 67,350 km². The next largest is Dubai (3,900 km²) and the smallest is Ajman (250 km²). *Middle East and North Africa 1982–83*, pp. 857-858, 863.

78. *Keesing's Contemporary Archives*, September 28, 1979, pp. 29847-49, and *Middle East Contemporary Survey, 1978–1979* (New York: Holmes and Meier, 1980), pp. 477-478.

79. Each of the emirates is also represented on the Council of Ministers, but Abu Dhabi and Dubai control the most important posts. Kelly, *Arabia*, p. 204.

80. Ibid., pp. 201-202, Lenczowski, *Middle East*, p. 679, and *Keesing's Contemporary Archives*, August 20-27, 1966, p. 21573.

81. *Keesing's Contemporary Archives*, May 22, 1981, p. 30878, and October 9, 1981, p. 31120.

82. *Middle East and North Africa 1982–83*, pp. 856-857, 863.

83. *Middle East Contemporary Survey, 1976–1977*, p. 763, and *Middle East Contemporary Survey, 1977–1978* (New York: Holmes and Meier, 1979), pp. 455-456.

84. *Keesing's Contemporary Archives*, December 25, 1971–January 1, 1972, pp. 25010-11.

85. *Keesing's Contemporary Archives*, February 19-25, 1973, p. 25740, and *Middle East Contemporary Survey, 1980–1981*, p. 506.

Unlike the outright seizure of the two Tunbs from Ras al-Khaimah, Sharjah "agreed" to the takeover of Abu Musa and then received the right of civil administration, half the oil revenues, and aid from Iran. By 1984, however, Iran had reportedly stopped making payments to Sharjah. Dubai *Khaleej Times*, June 21, 1984, p. 3, in *FBIS ME*, June 22, 1984, p. C4.

86. Kelly, *Arabia*, pp. 210-212.

87. *Middle East Contemporary Survey, 1979–1980* (New York: Holmes and Meier, 1981), p. 432, and *Middle East Contemporary Survey, 1980–81*, p. 505.

88. *Middle East and North Africa 1982–83*, pp. 287, 292.

89. Lenczowski, *Middle East*, pp. 670-671, "Report on Oil Reserves" p. D9.

90. Kelly, *Arabia*, pp. 184-185, *Keesing's Contemporary Archives*, February 4-10, 1974, p. 26340, and September 29–October 5, 1975, p. 27364.

91. *Middle East and North Africa 1982–83*, p. 287.

92. Lenczowski, *Middle East*, p. 671, *Middle East Contemporary Survey, 1978–1979*, pp. 440-441, and *Keesing's Contemporary Archives*, February 26, 1982, pp. 31353-54.

93. *Keesing's Contemporary Archives*, July 1-8, 1972, p. 25348, and September 2, 1977, p. 28538.

94. Kelly, *Arabia*, pp. 185-187, *Middle East and North Africa 1982–83*, pp. 667-669, and *BP Statistical Review of World Energy* (London: British Petroleum Co., June 1984), pp. 2, 5.

95. Kelly, *Arabia*, p. 189, *Middle East and North Africa 1982–83*, p. 667, *Middle East Contemporary Survey, 1976–1977*, pp. 354-355, and *Keesing's Contemporary Archives*, March 13-20, 1971, p. 24500.

96. Kelly, *Arabia*, p. 192, Lenczowski, *Middle East*, p. 675, and *Middle East Contemporary Survey, 1979–1980*, p. 424.

97. G. Drambyants, "Sir William Returns," *New Times,* no. 37 (September 1970): 14-15. See also Page, *USSR and Arabia,* pp. 121-124.

98. Page, *USSR and Arabia,* p. 30.

99. G. Drambyants, "The Gulf Federation," *New Times,* no. 34 (August 1971): 13-14.

100. Aden Domestic Service in Arabic, December 6, 1971, in *FBIS ME,* December 7, 1971, pp. B5-B6; and Moscow TASS International Service in English, December 27, 1971, in *FBIS SU,* December 28, 1971, p. B3.

101. Dubai Domestic Service in Arabic, January 31, 1972, in *FBIS ME,* January 31, 1972, p. B4; Dubai Domestic Service in Arabic, February 15, 1972, in *FBIS ME,* February 16, 1972, pp. B2-B3.

102. Amman Domestic Service in Arabic, April 25, 1972, in *FBIS ME,* April 26, 1972, p. B1; and Damascus MENA in Arabic, March 1, 1973, in *FBIS ME,* March 2, 1973, p. B2.

103. A. Vasil'ev, "Fakely persidskogo zaliva," *Pravda,* May 31, 1974, p. 4.

104. Moscow TASS International Service in English, December 2, 1971, in *FBIS SU,* December 2, 1971, pp. B4-B5.

105. V. Kudryavtsev, "Abu Dhabi Enters the 20th Century," *New Times,* no. 51 (December 1972): 30-31; Moscow in Arabic, January 18, 1977, in *FBIS SU,* January 19, 1977, p. F3; Yuri Tyssovsky, "What Was Once the Pirate Coast," *New Times,* no. 19 (May 1977): 23-25; and V. Vinogradov, "Oruzhie dlia arabskoi reaktsii," *Krasnaia Zvezda,* September 13, 1978, p. 3.

106. V. Vinogradov, "Neftianye emiry persidskogo zaliva," *Krasnaia Zvezda,* August 11, 1978, p. 3.

107. "Emirates' Decisions," *New Times,* no. 21 (May 1975): 13.

108. M. Vasilyev, "What Will the 'Golden Rain' Bring?" *New Times,* no. 50 (December 1979): 24-25.

109. Doha QNA in Arabic, November 5, 1978, in *FBIS ME,* November 7, 1978, pp. C3-C4.

110. Kuwait KUNA in English, March 31, 1982, in *FBIS ME,* March 31, 1982, p. C3.

111. Robin Allen, "UAE: Prospects Improve for East European Exporters," Middle East Economic Digest, September 9, 1983, p. 63.

112. Dubai *Khaleej Times,* June 21, 1984, p. 3, in *FBIS ME,* June 22, 1984, p. C4.

113. *The New York Times,* July 9, 1984, p. A7; and Manama WAKH in Arabic, November 1, 1984, in *FBIS ME,* November 1, 1984, p. C1.

114. The Arab Nationalist Movement and the Ba'th were also active in Bahrain. Page, *USSR and Arabia,* pp. 52, 63.

115. Ibid., pp. 52, 67, 71, 94.

116. Moscow in Arabic, August 16, 1971, in *FBIS SU,* August 17, 1971, p. B1; Moscow TASS International Service in English, August 19, 1971, in *FBIS SU,* August 19, 1971, p. B4; Moscow TASS International Service in English, August 25, 1971, in *FBIS SU,* August 26, 1971, p. B2; Aden ANA in Arabic, August 15 1971, in *FBIS ME,* August 16, 1971, p. B3; Aden ANA in Arabic, August 14, 1971, in *FBIS*

ME, August 17, 1971, p. B2; Cairo MENA in Arabic, August 17, 1971, in *FBIS ME,* August 18, 1971, p. B1; and Baghdad INA in Arabic, December 25, 1971, in *FBIS ME,* December 27, 1971, p. B1.

117. N. Zaborin, "Snova bazy," *Sovetskaia Rossiia,* August 11, 1977, p. 3; Moscow in Arabic, August 29, 1975, in *FBIS SU,* September 3, 1975, pp. F8-F9; and Moscow TASS in English, May 17, 1977, in *FBIS SU,* May 19, 1977, p. F3.

118. Moscow in Arabic, August 14, 1978, in *FBIS SU,* August 15, 1978, pp. F6-F7.

119. Moscow Radio Peace and Progress in Arabic, March 3, 1976, in *FBIS SU,* March 4, 1976, p. F3; Moscow Radio Peace and Progress, February 16, 1980, in *FBIS SU,* February 20, 1980, p. H9; Moscow in Arabic, February 16, 1980, in *FBIS SU,* February 25, 1980, p. H3; Moscow Radio Peace and Progress, February 22, 1980, in *FBIS SU,* February 27, 1980, p. H5; Moscow Radio Peace and Progress in Arabic, January 26, 1981, in *FBIS SU,* January 29, 1981, p. H1; Moscow in Arabic, February 7, 1981, in *FBIS SU,* February 9, 1981, p. H2; Moscow in Persian, March 6, 1981, in *FBIS SU—Proceedings of the 26th CPSU Congress,* 9:30; Moscow Radio Peace and Progress, January 4, 1983, in *FBIS SU,* January 6, 1983, pp. H4-H5; and Moscow Radio Peace and Progress in Arabic, December 22, 1983, in *FBIS SU,* December 23, 1983, pp. H4-H5.

120. Moscow in Arabic, March 16, 1981, in *FBIS SU,* March 18, 1981, p. H2. The Popular Front (or People's Front) was apparently founded in 1973.

121. Moscow Radio Peace and Progress, February 20, 1982, in *FBIS SU,* February 23, 1982, p. H4.

122. Page, *USSR and Arabia,* pp. 52, 83.

123. "Qatar Declares Independence," *New Times,* no. 37 (September 1971): 9; Moscow Domestic Service in Russian, May 23, 1972, in *FBIS SU,* May 24, 1972, pp. B4-B5; and V. Kudryavtsev, "Independent Qatar," *New Times,* no. 30 (July 1972): 30-31.

Saudi Arabia and Bahrain do not have diplomatic relations with any communist country. Qatar apparently has relations with one, Czechoslovakia, though the Czech embassy is resident in Kuwait.

124. Vinogradov, "Oruzhie dlia arabskoi reaktsii," p. 3.

125. Moscow in Arabic, February 6, 1981, in *FBIS SU,* February 9, 1981, p. H4; V. Peresada, "Po opasnomu ruslu," *Pravda,* February 10, 1981, p. 5; Moscow TASS in English, May 27, 1981, in *FBIS SU,* May 28, 1981, p. H8; and Moscow Radio Peace and Progress, November 12, 1981, in *FBIS SU,* November 13, 1981, pp. H4-H5.

126. Moscow in Arabic, March 23, 1982, in *FBIS SU,* March 24, 1982, pp. H2-H3; Moscow TASS in English, November 11, 1982, in *FBIS SU,* November 12, 1982, p. H1; Moscow TASS in English, February 21, 1983, in *FBIS SU,* February 22, 1983, p. H7; Moscow TASS in English, October 16, 1983, in *FBIS SU,* October 25, 1983, p. H6; and Moscow TASS in English, November 7, 1983, in *FBIS SU,* November 8, 1983, p. H3.

127. "Irano-Irakskii konflikt," *Pravda,* June 18, 1984, p. 5; and Moscow International Service in Arabic, June 21, 1984, in *FBIS SU,* June 22, 1984, pp. H2-H3.

128. Doha QNA in Arabic, December 30, 1979, in *FBIS ME,* December 31, 1979, p. C8; Doha QNA in Arabic, December 30, 1979, in *FBIS ME,* December 31, 1979, p. C1; Doha QNA in Arabic, December 30, 1979, in *FBIS ME,* December 31, 1979, p. C5; Doha QNA in Arabic, May 22, 1980, in *FBIS ME,* May 23, 1980, p. C6; Manama Gulf News Agency in Arabic, June 1, 1980, in *FBIS ME,* June 2, 1980, p. C1; and Manama Gulf News Agency in Arabic, June 15, 1980, in *FBIS ME,* June 16, 1980, p. C1.

In June 1981, UAE President Shaykh Zayid criticized Western statements about what the Soviets were doing in Afghanistan, but later he denied that he had condoned the Soviet invasion. "Interviu prezidenta OAE," *Krasnaia Zvezda,* June 7, 1981, p. 3; and Abu Dhabi Emirates News Agency in Arabic, June 8, 1981, in *FBIS ME,* June 9, 1981, p. C5.

129. On these treaties, see "Saudi Arabia," in *FBIS ME,* February 22, 1982, p. ii, and "Gulf Affairs," in *FBIS ME,* February 24, 1982, p. ii.

CONCLUSION

1. According to a recent Rand Corporation study, "the PDRY retains the potential to support revolutionaries of either kind [leftist or Islamic fundamentalist] on the Arabian peninsula." Nowhere in this study, though, does the author show any link between the PDRY and Islamic fundamentalism. Nor does she acknowledge that Islamic fundamentalists may prove a threat to the leftist government in Aden as well as the conservative ones in the GCC. Laurie Mylroie, "Politics and the Soviet Presence in the People's Democratic Republic of Yemen: Internal Vulnerabilities and Regional Challenges," N-2052-AF (Santa Monica, Calif.: Rand Corporation, December 1983), p. v.

2. Ibid., pp. 66-67.

Bibliography

Abir, Mordechai. *Oil, Power and Politics.* London: Frank Cass, 1974.

"Aggression in South Arabia." *New Times,* no. 21 (May 1972): 11, 13.

Akehurst, John. *We Won a War: The Campaign in Oman 1965–1975.* London: Michael Russell, 1982.

Akhmedov, A. "Katar: Vek nyneshnii i vek minuvshii." *Aziia i Afrika Segodnia,* no. 4 (1979): 40–42.

Al-Ebraheem, Hassn A. *Kuwait: A Political Study.* Kuwait: Kuwait University, 1975.

Aleksandrov, E., and Filonik, A. "Tri nedeli v Kuveite." *Aziia i Afrika Segodnia,* no. 9 (September 1980): 37–40.

Aleksandrov, I. A. *Narodnaia demokraticheskaia respublika Iemen.* Moscow: Nauka, 1976.

Aleksandrov, S. "Oman: Bor'ba prodolzhaetsia." *Aziia i Afrika Segodnia,* no. 6 (1978): 20–21.

Alexandrov, V. "Dynamic Progress." *New Times,* no. 42 (October 1976): 15.

Al'-Khameri, Abdalla. "NDRI: Istoricheskoe znachenie 'ispravitel'nogo dvizheniia.'" *Aziia i Afrika Segodnia,* no. 6 (1979): 30–32.

Allen, Robin. "U.A.E.: Prospects Improve for East European Exporters." *Middle East Economic Digest,* September 9, 1983, 63.

Al-Rashid, Ibrahim, ed. *Documents of the History of Saudi Arabia.* Salisbury, N.C.: Documentary Publications, 1976.

Andreasian, R. "Arabskaia neft': Slagaemye fenomena." *Aziia i Afrika Segodnia,* nos. 10 and 11 (1982): 16–19, 14–17.

Anichkin, O. "Vmeshatel'stvo pentagona." *Izvestiia,* March 18, 1979, 5.

Atkinson, Rich, and Hiatt, Fred. "Kuwait Asks U.S. to Sell It Stinger Antiplane Missiles." *The Washington Post,* May 31, 1984, A1, A31.

Baldry, John. "Soviet Relations with Saudi Arabia and the Yemen 1917–1938." *Middle Eastern Studies* 20, 1 (January 1984): 53–80.

Barns, William Fleming. "Conflict and Commitment: The Case of the Yemens." Alexandria, Va.: Defense Technical Information Center, March 1980.

Behbehani, Hashim S. H. *China's Foreign Policy in the Arab World, 1955–75: Three Case Studies.* London: Kegan Paul International, 1981.

Beliaev, Igor'. "Kto zhe ugrozhaet Saudovskoi Aravii?" *Literaturnaia Gazeta,* July 9, 1980, 14.

———. "Saudovskaia Aravia: Chto zhe dal'she?" *Literaturnaia Gazeta,* January 31, 1979, 14.

Bell, J. Bowyer. *South Arabia: Violence and Revolt.* Conflict Studies, no. 40. London: Institute for the Study of Conflict, November 1973.

———. "Southern Yemen: Two Years of Independence." *The World Today* 26, 2 (February 1970): 76–82.

Bidwell, Robin. *The Two Yemens.* Singapore: Longman/Westview, 1983.

Binder, Leonard. "United States Policy and the Middle East: Toward a Pax Saudiana." *Current History* 81, 1 (January 1982): 1–4, 40–42, 48.

Bissell, Richard E. "Soviet Use of Proxies in the Third World: The Case of Yemen." *Soviet Studies* 30, 1 (January 1978): 87–106.

Bodianskii, V. L. *Bakhrein.* Moscow: Izdatel'stvo Vostochnoi Literatury, 1962.

———. *Sovremennyi Bakhrein.* Moscow: Nauka, 1976.

———. *Sovremennyi Kuveit.* Moscow: Nauka, 1971.

Bodianskii, V. L.; Gerasimov, O.; and Medvedko, L. *Kniazhestva persidskogo zaliva.* Moscow: Mysl', 1970.

Bodianskii, V. L., and Lazarev, M. S. *Saudovskaia Araviia posle Sauda.* Moscow: Nauka, 1967.

"Border Incident." *New Times,* no. 14 (April 1973): 7.

BP Statistical Review of World Oil. London: British Petroleum Co., annual.

Brezhnev, L. "Tovarishchu Ali Naseru Mukhammedu." *Pravda,* April 23, 1980, 1.

———. "Tovarishchu Ali Naseru Mukhammedu." *Pravda,* May 1, 1980, 1.

Bujra, Abdalla S. *The Politics of Stratification: A Study of Political Change in a South Arabian Town.* Oxford: Oxford University Press, 1971.

Burns, John F. "TASS Says U.S. Acts in Persian Gulf Imperil Peace." *The New York Times,* March 8, 1984, A4.

Caesar, Terry. "Outside the Inside of Saudi Arabia." *The Yale Review,* 73, 3–4 (Spring–Summer 1984): 457–480, 622–640.

"Calling Iran's Bluff—for a While." *The Economist,* February 25, 1984, 64.

Campbell, John C. "Soviet Strategy in the Middle East." *American-Arab Affairs,* no. 8 (Spring 1984): 74–82.

Central Intelligence Agency. *Communist Aid Activities in Non-Communist Less Developed Countries 1978.* ER 79-10412U. Washington, D.C.: CIA, September 1979.

———. *Communist Aid Activities in Non-Communist Less Developed Countries, 1979 and 1954–79.* ER 80-10318U. Washington, D.C.: CIA, October 1980.

———. *Communist Aid to Less Developed Countries of the Free World, 1977.* ER 78-10478U. Washington, D.C.: CIA, November 1978.

———. *Communist Aid to the Less Developed Countries of the Free World, 1976.* ER 77-10296. Washington, D.C.: CIA, August 1977.

———. *Handbook of Economic Statistics, 1984.* CPAS 84-10002. Washington, D.C.: CIA, September 1984.

———. *The International Energy Situation: Outlook to 1985.* ER 77-10240U. Washington, D.C.: CIA, April 1977.

———. *Prospects for Soviet Oil Production.* ER 77-10270. Washington, D.C.: CIA, April 1977.

———. *Prospects for Soviet Oil Production: A Supplemental Analysis.* ER 77-10425. Washington, D.C.: CIA, July 1977.

Chistiakov, A. "NDRI: Stanovlenie natsional'noi ekonomiki." *Aziia i Afrika Segodnia,* no. 11 (1979): 17–19.

Clements, F. A. *Oman: The Reborn Land.* London and New York: Longman, 1980.

Cline, Kenneth. "North Yemen Oil Find May Enliven Politics." *The Christian Science Monitor,* October 4, 1984, 11.

Copper, John F., and Papp, Daniel S., eds. *Communist Nations' Military Assistance.* Boulder, Colo.: Westview Press, 1983.

Creekman, Lt. Cmdr. Charles T., Jr. "Sino-Soviet Competition in the Yemens." *U.S. Naval War College Review* 32, 4 (July–August 1979): 73–82.

Dawisha, A. I. "Intervention in the Yemen: An Analysis of Egyptian Perceptions and Policies." *The Middle East Journal* 29, 1 (Winter 1975): 47–63.

———. "Saudi Arabia and the Arab-Israeli Conflict: The Ups and Downs of Pragmatic Moderation." *International Journal* 38, 4 (Autumn 1983): 674–689.

Denton, Herbert H. "PLO Evacuees in North Yemen Miss Delights of City." *The Washington Post,* January 10, 1984, A12.

———. "Soviets Agree to Sell Major Arms Systems, Missiles to Kuwait." *The Washington Post,* July 13, 1984, A1, A26.

"Les Dirigeants sovietiques aux Arabes: 'Attendez-vous le don du ciel?'" *Afrique-Asie,* November 8–21, 1982, 58–60.

Dixon, Michael J. "The Soviet Union and the Middle East." Report No. 83-229 S. Washington, D.C.: Congressional Research Service, December 12, 1983.

Documents of the National Struggle in Oman and the Arabian Gulf. London: Gulf Committee, 1974.

Doder, Dusko. "Saudi King Reportedly Sends Note to Andropov." *The Washington Post,* June 7, 1983, A12.

———. "Soviets, N. Yemen Sign Treaty." *The Washington Post,* October 10, 1984, A19.

Drambiants, G. G. "The Gulf Federation." *New Times,* no. 34 (August 1971): 13–14.

———. *Persidskii zaliv bez romantiki.* Moscow: Mezhdunarodnye Otnosheniia, 1968.

———. "Sir William Returns." *New Times,* no. 37 (September 1970): 14–15.

"Druzheskaia vstrecha." *Pravda,* September 30, 1983, 1.

"Druzhestvennaia beseda." *Pravda,* October 21, 1981, 4.

Dunn, Michael C. "Soviet Interests in the Arabian Peninsula: The Aden Pact and Other Paper Tigers." *American-Arab Affairs,* no. 8 (Spring 1984): 92–98.

Eickelman, Dale F. "Kings and People: Oman's State Consultative Council." *The Middle East Journal* 38, 1 (Winter 1984): 51–71.

"Emirates' Decisions." *New Times,* no. 21 (May 1975): 13.

Esemov, Rakhim. "Preobrazhennyi krai." *Pravda,* July 8, 1979, 4.

Evans, Lt. Colonel De Lacy. *On the Designs of Russia.* London: John Murray, 1828.

Evans, Rowland, and Novak, Robert. "Kuwait Finds an Open Door." *The Washington Post,* June 25, 1984, A11.

Farley, Jonathan. "The Gulf War and the Littoral States." *The World Today* 40, 7 (July 1984): 269–276.

Fedorov, V. "V soiuze s reaktsiei." *Krasnaia Zvezda,* January 26, 1979, 3.

Feoktistov, A. "Saudi Arabia and the Arab World." *International Affairs*, no. 7 (July 1977): 101–107.

Fiennes, Ranulph. *Where Soldiers Fear to Tread*. London: Hodder and Stoughton, 1975.

Filippov, A. "Patrioty nanosiat udary." *Pravda*, April 6, 1976, 5.

"For the Record." *The Washington Post*, May 23, 1983, A22.

Freedman, Robert O. *Soviet Policy toward the Middle East since 1970*. 3d ed. New York: Praeger, 1982.

Fyodorov, M. "Oil—The Arabs' Weapon." *New Times*, no. 50 (December 1973): 14–15.

Gainullina, I. L., and Isaev, V. A. "Vliianie neftedollarov na razvitie arabskikh stran i Irana." *Narody Azii i Afriki*, no. 3 (1977): 153–164.

Garthoff, Raymond L. *Soviet Military Policy: A Historical Analysis*. New York: Frederick A. Praeger, 1966.

Gavin, R. J. *Aden under British Rule, 1839–1967*. New York: Barnes and Noble, 1975.

Gavrilov, Iu., and Vinogradov, V. "Dofar: Bitva za svobodu." *Krasnaia Zvezda*, November 2, 1975, 3.

Geivandov, Konstantin. "Eskalatsiia 'diplomatii kanonerok.'" *Izvestiia*, November 18, 1983, 5.

Genin, I. A. *Iemen*. Moscow: Izdatel'stvo geograficheskoi literatury, 1953.

Gerasimov, O. G. *Iemenskaia revoliutsiia, 1962–1975 gg*. Moscow: Nauka, 1979.
———. *Oman*. Moscow: Mysl', 1975.

Glukhov, Iu. "Opasnaia sdelka." *Pravda*, February 12, 1977, 5.

Goldman, Marshall I. "The Soviet Union." In *The Oil Crisis*, ed. Raymond Vernon. New York: W. W. Norton, 1976.

Gol'ts, A. "Greiut ruki." *Krasnaia Zvezda*, October 21, 1983, 3.

Golubovskaia, E. K. *Revoliutsiia 1962 g. v Iemene*. Moscow: Nauka, 1971.

Grigoryev, V. "People's Democratic Republic of Yemen." *International Affairs*, no. 5 (May 1977): 144–146.

Gueyras, Jean. "La 'guerre civile oubliée.'" *Le Monde*, November 18, 1981, 7.

"L'Unité entre les deux Yemens n'est pas une entreprise utopique nous declare M. Salem Saleh Mohamed." *Le Monde*, May 7, 1982, 6.

Guldescu, Stanko. "Yemen: The War and the Haradh Conference." *Review of Politics* 28, 3 (July 1966): 319–331.

Gusarov, V. I. *Aden*. Moscow: Nauka, 1981.

Gus'kov, A. S. *Natsional'nyi front demokraticheskogo Iemena 1963–1975 gg*. Moscow: Nauka, 1979.

Gvoydev, Yuri. "Democratic Yemen: Problems and Aims." *New Times*, no. 48 (November 1972): 14–15.

Gwertzman, Bernard. "Shultz Says Iran Won't Be Allowed to Blackmail U.S." *The New York Times*, October 18, 1983, A1, A12.

Halliday, Fred. *Arabia without Sultans*. Harmondsworth, Middlesex: Penguin Books, 1974.
———. "Economic Decline in Oman: PFLO's New Political Strategy." *MERIP Reports*, no. 68 (May 1978): 18–21.

———. *Soviet Policy in the Arc of Crisis*. Washington, D.C.: Institute for Policy Studies, 1981.

Harvey, Nigel. "New Stability Emerges—but for How Long?" *Middle East Economic Digest*, November 5, 1982, 24, 27.

Helms, Christine Moss. *The Cohesion of Saudi Arabia: Evolution of Political Identity*. Baltimore: Johns Hopkins University Press, 1981.

Hewett, Ed A. *Energy Economics and Foreign Policy in the Soviet Union*. Washington, D.C.: Brookings Institution, 1984.

Holden, David, and Johns, Richard. *The House of Saud: The Rise and Rule of the Most Powerful Dynasty in the Arab World*. New York: Holt, Rinehart and Winston, 1981.

Hosmer, Stephen T., and Wolfe, Thomas W. *Soviet Policy and Practice toward Third World Conflicts*. Lexington, Mass.: Lexington/D. C. Heath, 1983.

Iakovlev, A. I. "Saudovskaia Araviia i ARAMKO." *Narody Azii i Afriki*, no. 2 (1979): 108–117.

———. *Saudovskaia Araviia i zapad*. Moscow: Nauka, 1982.

"In Confrontation with Reaction." *World Marxist Review*, 26, 4 (April 1983): 37–38.

International Bank for Reconstruction and Development. *People's Democratic Republic of Yemen: A Review of Economic and Social Development*. Washington, D.C.: World Bank, 1979.

———. *Yemen Arab Republic: Development of a Traditional Economy*. Washington, D.C.: World Bank, 1979.

International Institute for Strategic Studies. *The Military Balance*. London: IISS, annual.

———. *Security in the Persian Gulf*. 4 vols. Montclair, N.J.: Allanheld, Osmun, 1981 and 1982.

"Interviu prezidenta OAE." *Krasnaia Zvezda*, June 7, 1981, 3.

Ioffe, A. E. "Nachal'nyi etap vzaimootnoshenii Sovetskogo Soiuza s arabskimi i afrikanskimi stranami (1923–1932)." *Narody Azii i Afriki*, no. 6 (1965): 57–66.

"Irano-Irakskii konflikt." *Pravda*, June 18, 1984, 5.

"Iraq-Kuwait." *New Times*, no. 31 (July 1977): 15.

Isaev, V. A. "Vyvoz arabskogo kapitala v razvivaiushchiesia strany." *Narody Azii i Afriki*, no. 4 (1977): 119–126.

Jeapes, Colonel Tony. *SAS: Operation Oman*. London: William Kimber, 1980.

Jelavich, Barbara. *A Century of Russian Foreign Policy 1814–1914*. Philadelphia: J. B. Lippincott, 1964.

Johnston, Charles. *The View from Steamer Point*. London: Cox and Wyman, 1964.

"K namechennoi tseli." *Pravda*, October 14, 1980, 4.

"K sobytiiam v Kuveite." *Izvestiia*, September 2, 1976, 3.

Kapitonov, K. "Nepokorennyi Dofar." *Izvestiia*, January 10, 1973, 2.

Kapralov, A. "Vtiagivaiut v al'ians." *Izvestiia*, April 28, 1981, 4.

Kassis, V. B. *Bakhrein*. Moscow: Mysl', 1974.

———. "Kuwait Today." *International Affairs*, no. 10 (October 1978): 111–117.

Katz, Mark N. "Hard-liners Gaining Clout in S. Yemen." *The Christian Science Monitor*, October 4, 1984, 11.

———. "Kuwait Should Get U.S. Missiles." *Newsday,* July 26, 1984, 76.

———. "North Yemen between East and West." *American-Arab Affairs,* no. 8 (Spring 1984): 99–107.

———. "Oman Security Gets Boost in Soviet-Urged Moderation." *The Christian Science Monitor,* January 18, 1983, 6.

———. "Sanaa and the Soviets." *Problems of Communism* 33, 1 (January February 1984): 21–34.

———. "Saudis Deny Rumors They Plan to Establish Ties with USSR." *The Christian Science Monitor,* May 9, 1984, 14.

———. "The Soviet-Cuban Connection." *International Security* 8, 1 (Summer 1983): 88–112.

———. "The Superpowers and the Gulf War." *The Christian Science Monitor,* July 12, 1984, 16.

———. *The Third World in Soviet Military Thought.* Baltimore: Johns Hopkins University Press, 1982.

———. "War-Torn Dhofar . . . Only 39 Rebels Remain." *The Christian Science Monitor,* January 18, 1983, 6.

Kauppi, Mark V., and Nation, R. Craig, eds. *The Soviet Union and the Middle East in the 1980s: Opportunities, Constraints, and Dilemmas.* Lexington, Mass.: Lexington/D. C. Heath, 1983.

"Keeping out of It." *The Economist,* June 23, 1984, 45–46.

Kelly, Anne M. "The Soviet Naval Presence during the Iraq-Kuwaiti Border Dispute: March–April 1973." *Center for Naval Analyses Professional Paper* no. 122, June 1974.

Kelly, J. B. *Arabia, the Gulf and the West.* New York: Basic Books, 1980.

Khaled, Seif Sail'. "Revolutsiia: Istoki, zadachi, sversheniia." *Aziia i Afrika Segodnia,* no. 10 (1983): 20–23.

Khalizad, Zalmay. "Islamic Iran: Soviet Dilemma." *Problems of Communism* 33, 1 (January–February 1984): 1–20.

Khrustalev, M. A. "Sotsial'naia struktura sovremennogo saudovskogo obshchestva." *Narody Azii i Afriki,* no. 4 (1973): 27–35.

Kirkham, Norman. "Yemen to Get MIGs." *The Sunday Telegraph,* March 5, 1972, 2.

Kniazev, A. "Na vzaimovygodnoi osnove." *Izvestiia,* March 12, 1983, 4.

Korff, Baron S. A. *Russia's Foreign Relations during the Last Half Century.* New York: Macmillan, 1922.

Koriavin, L. "Problemy neftianogo el'dorado." *Izvestiia,* May 7, 1977, 4.

Korshunov, E. "Kto otvetstvenen za vzryvy?" *Izvestiia,* December 14, 1983, 1.

Kostiner, Joseph. "Arab Radical Politics: Al-Qawmiyyun al-Arab and the Marxists in the Turmoil of South Yemen, 1963-1967." *Middle East Studies* 17, 4 (October 1981): 454–476.

Kotlov, L. N. *Iemenskaia arabskaia respublika.* Moscow: Nauka, 1971.

Krakhmalov, S. P. *Iemenskaia arabskaia respublika i ee vooruzhennye sily.* Moscow: Voenizdat, 1977.

Kudriavtsev, V. "Abu Dhabi Enters the 20th Century." *New Times,* no. 51 (December 1972): 30–31.

———. "Independent Qatar." *New Times,* no. 30 (July 1972): 30-31.

———. "Politika dezorientatsii." *Izvestiia,* April 6, 1980, 5.

———. "Teni nad krasnym morem." *Izvestiia,* April 16, 1977, 4.

Kudryavtsev, A. "Looking for a New Prop." *New Times,* no. 11 (March 1979): 12.

"Kuwait's Decision." *New Times,* no. 28 (July 1975): 30.

Landen, Robert Geran. *Oman since 1856: Disruptive Modernization in a Traditional Arab Society.* Princeton: Princeton University Press, 1967.

Lee, Christopher D. "Soviet and Chinese Interests in Southern Arabia." *Mizan* 13, 1 (August 1971): 35-47.

Lee, Gary. "Soviet Oil Output Shows a Decline." *The Washington Post,* April 3, 1985, A1, A14.

Lenczowski, George. *The Middle East in World Affairs.* 4th ed. Ithaca and London: Cornell University Press, 1980.

Leont'ev, A., and Vinogradov, V. "Reshimost' naroda." *Krasnaia Zvezda,* January 13, 1974, 3.

Little, Tom. *South Arabia: Arena of Conflict.* New York: Praeger, 1968.

Lutskevich, V. A. "Sotsial'no-ekonomicheskie problemy Ob"edinennykh Arabskikh Emiratov." *Narody Azii i Afriki,* no. 6 (1982): 68-74.

McHale, T. R. "A Prospect of Saudi Arabia." *International Affairs,* 56, 4 (Autumn 1980): 622-647.

McLane, Charles B. *Soviet-Third World Relations.* Vol. 1. *Soviet Middle East Relations.* London: Central Asian Research Centre, 1973.

McNaugher, Thomas L. "Balancing Soviet Power in the Persian Gulf." *Brookings Review,* 1,4 (Summer 1983): 20-24.

Macro, Eric. *Yemen and the Western World since 1571.* New York: Frederick A. Praeger, 1968.

Maksimov, S. L. "Mezhdunarodnyi simposium neft' i sotsial'no-ekonomicheskaia differentsiatsia na arabskom vostoke." *Narody Azii i Afriki,* no. 4: 144-149.

Malone, Joseph J. "America and the Arabian Peninsula: The First Two Hundred Years." *The Middle East Journal* 30, 3 (Summer 1976): 406-424.

———. "The Yemen Arab Republic's 'Game of Nations.'" *The World Today* 27,12 (December 1971): 541-548.

Martin, Paul. "N. Yemen Premier Threatens to Resign If No Political Solution Is Found to Conflict with the South." *The Times,* October 23, 1972, 5.

Matthews, Roger. "Strong Protection for the Oil Lanes." *Financial Times,* January 13, 1983, viii.

Medvedko, L. I. *Vetry peremen v persidskom zalive.* Moscow: Nauka, 1973.

Melikhov, I. A. *Oman mezhdu proshlym i nastoiashchim.* Moscow: Znanie, 1979.

The Middle East and North Africa 1982-83. London: Europa Publications, 1982.

Middle East Contemporary Survey. New York: Holmes and Meier, annual.

Mikhailov, A. "Intrigi vokrug demokraticheskogo Iemena." *Pravda,* August 1, 1972, 5.

Mikhin, V. "Ob"edinennye Arabskie Emiraty." *Aziia i Afrika Segodnia,* no. 4 (1980): 41-43.

———. "Omanskie 'Pravdoiskateli.'" *Sovetskaia Rossia,* July 8, 1983, 5.

———. "Pod dudku Vashingtona." *Sel'skaia Zhizn',* April 26, 1983, 3.

"Milestone in Yemeni History." *New Times,* no. 40 (October 1972): 16–17.

Ministerstvo Vneshnei Torgovli. *Vneshniaia torgovlia SSSR, 1922–1981.* Moscow: "Financy i Statistika" 1982.

———. *Vneshniaia torgovlia SSSR v 1982 g.* Moscow: "Financy i Statistika" 1983.

———. *Vneshniaia torgovlia SSSR v 1983 g.* Moscow: "Financy i Statistika" 1984.

Mironov, L. "Pentagon na Masire." *Krasnaia Zvezda,* January 6, 1977, 3.

Mirsky, Georgi. "The Proletariat and National Liberation." *New Times,* no. 18 (May 1964): 6–9.

Morgan, Dan. "U.S. Expedites N. Yemen Arms; Saudis Cautious." *The Washington Post,* March 10, 1979, A1, A11.

Morison, D. L. "Soviet Interest in Middle East Oil." *Mizan* 13, 1 (August 1971): 30–34.

Morsy, Abdullah Muhammad. *The United Arab Emirates: A Modern History.* London: Croom Helm; New York: Barnes and Noble, 1978.

Murav'ev, V. "S dal'nim pritselom." *Krasnaia Zvezda,* July 9, 1983, 5.

Mylroie, Laurie. "Politics and the Soviet Presence in the People's Democratic Republic of Yemen: Internal Vulnerabilities and Regional Challenges." N-2052-AF. Santa Monica, Calif.: Rand Corporation, December 1983.

"Napadenie na mechet'." *Izvestiia,* November 28, 1979, 4.

"Narod Omana oderzhit pobedu." *Izvestiia,* October 10, 1963, 2.

Naumkin, V. "Southern Yemen: The Road to Progress." *International Affairs,* no. 1 (January 1978): 64–69.

"Nikolaiu Podgornomu." *Pravda,* November 14, 1973, 4.

Noreng, Oysten. *Oil Politics in the 1980s: Patterns of International Cooperation.* New York: McGraw-Hill, 1978.

"North Yemen." *New Times,* no. 2 (January 1979): 7.

"North Yemen: The Answer Lies in the Soil." *The Economist,* May 15, 1982, 87–88.

Novik, Nimrod. *On the Shores of Bab al-Mandab: Soviet Diplomacy and Regional Dynamics.* Philadelphia: Foreign Policy Research Institute, 1979.

Nurthen, William Augustine. "Soviet Strategy in the Red Sea Basin." Alexandria, Va.: Defense Technical Information Center, March 1980.

Nyrop, Richard F., et al. *Area Handbook for the Yemens.* Washington, D.C.: U.S. Government Printing Office, 1977.

O'Ballance, Edgar. *The War in the Yemen.* London: Faber and Faber, 1971.

"Obmen mneniiami." *Pravda,* April 7, 1983, 4.

"Oil Found in North Yemen." *Financial Times,* July 12, 1984, 2.

O'Neill, Bard E.; Heaton, William R.; and Alberts, Donald J., eds. *Insurgency in the Modern World.* Boulder, Colo.: Westview Press, 1980.

Oney, Ernest. "The Iranian Intervention in Oman, 1973–1979." External research paper published by the U.S. Department of State, Bureau of Intelligence and Research, Office of Long Range Assessments and Research, September 1981.

Onis, Juan de. "Southern Yemen Cites Soviet Support." *The New York Times,* October 7, 1972, 12.

"Otnosheniia normalizuiutsia." *Pravda,* November 20, 1982, 4.

Ottaway, David B. "Kuwait Appeals to U.S. for Missiles." *The Washington Post,* June 19, 1984, A1, A13.

———. "North Yemen's War: Sanaa Turns to Soviets for Military Aid." *The Washington Post,* April 21, 1982, A1, A19.

"Otvlekaiushchii manevr." *Pravda,* July 31, 1978, 5.

Owen, R. P. "Developments in the Sultanate of Muscat and Oman." *The World Today* 26, 9 (September 1970): 379–383.

Ozoling, V. "Neft' i dollary arabiiskikh monarkii." *Aziia i Afrika Segodnia,* no. 3 (1982): 35–37.

Page, Stephen. "Moscow and the Arabian Peninsula." *American-Arab Affairs,* no. 8 (Spring 1984): 83–91.

———. "Moscow and the Persian Gulf Countries, 1967–1970." *Mizan* 13, 2 (October 1971): 72–88.

———. *The USSR and Arabia: The Development of Soviet Policies and Attitudes towards the Countries of the Arabian Peninsula, 1955–1970.* London: Central Asian Research Centre, 1971.

Paget, Julian. *Last Post: Aden, 1964–1967.* London: Faber and Faber, 1969.

Peresada, V. "Nagnetaiut napriazhennost'." *Pravda,* February 17, 1981, 5.

———. "Po opasnomu ruslu." *Pravda,* February 10, 1981, 5.

———. "Sbrasyvaia gruz proshlogo." *Pravda,* October 26, 1981, 6.

———. "Vovse ne beskorystno." *Pravda,* January 20, 1980, 5.

Perkins, Major General K. "Oman 1975: The Year of Decision." *RUSI Journal* 124, 1 (March 1979): 38–45.

Perminov, P. "Gorizonty respubliki." *Izvestiia,* October 29, 1982, 5.

———. "Problems and Policies." *New Times,* no. 44 (October 1981): 24–25.

Peterson, J. E. *Conflict in the Yemens and Superpower Involvement.* Occasional Papers Series. Washington, D.C.: Georgetown University Center for Contemporary Arab Studies, December 1981.

———. *Oman in the Twentieth Century: Political Foundations of an Emerging State.* London: Croom Helm; New York: Barnes and Noble, 1978.

———. "Tribes and Politics in Eastern Arabia." *The Middle East Journal* 31, 3 (Summer 1977): 297–312.

———. *Yemen: The Search for a Modern State.* Baltimore: Johns Hopkins University Press, 1982.

———. "The Yemen Arab Republic and the Politics of Balance." *Asian Affairs* 12, 3 (October 1981): 254–266.

Piotrovskaia, I. L. *Strany araviiskogo poluostrova: Neft', financy, razvitie.* Moscow: Nauka, 1981.

Piotrovskii, M. B. *Predanie o khimiaritskom tsare As'ade al-Kamile.* Moscow: Nauka, 1977.

"Podpisan protokol." *Pravda,* December 11, 1982, 4.

The Policy of the Soviet Union in the Arab World. Moscow: Progress Publishers, 1975.

"President's News Conference on Foreign and Domestic Issues." *The New York Times,* February 23, 1984, A12.

263

"Pribytie delegatsii." *Krasnaiia Zvezda,* April 8, 1978, 1.

Price, David Lynn. "Moscow and the Persian Gulf." *Problems of Communism* 28, 2 (March–April 1979): 1–13.

———. *Oman: Insurgency and Development. Conflict Studies,* no. 53. London: Institute for the Study of Conflict, January 1975.

Primakov, A. "Voennaia sila na sluzhbe neftianoi diplomatii Vashingtona." *Aziia i Afrika Segodnia,* no. 12 (1980): 15–17.

Primakov, E. *Strany Aravii i kolonializm.* Moscow: Politizdat, 1956.

Proshin, N. I. *Saudovskaia Arabiia.* Moscow: Nauka, 1964.

"Qatar Declares Independence." *New Times,* no. 37 (September 1971): 9.

Quandt, William B. *Saudi Arabia in the 1980s: Foreign Policy, Security, and Oil.* Washington, D.C.: Brookings Institution, 1981.

———. *Saudi Arabia's Oil Policy.* Washington, D.C.: Brookings Institution, 1982.

Quarterly Economic Review of Bahrain, Qatar, Oman, the Yemens. London: Economist Intelligence Unit, quarterly.

Rambaud, Alfred. *The Expansion of Russia: Problems of the East and Problems of the Far East.* New York: Scott-Tharo, 1904.

"Report on Oil Reserves." *The New York Times,* June 3, 1983, D9.

The Revolution Is Alive: The Liberation Struggle in Oman. n.p.: KROAG, 1979.

Richey, Warren. "North Yemen: Land of Donkeys and Camels Learns to Cope with Toyotas, Radios . . . and Canned Peas." *The Christian Science Monitor,* January 14, 1983, 12–13.

Ro'i, Yaacov. *From Encroachment to Involvement: A Documentary Study of Soviet Policy in the Middle East, 1945–1973.* New York: John Wiley, 1974.

Rouleau, Eric. "Le Chef du gouvernement de Sanaa accuse le régime d'Aden de fomenter la guerre civile à l'intérieur du pays." *Le Monde,* May 7, 1982, 6.

———. "Espoirs de réconciliation au Liban." *Le Monde,* October 30 31, 1983, 1, 5.

Rubinstein, Alvin Z. "The Soviet Union and the Arabian Peninsula." *The World Today* 35, 11 (November 1979): 442–452.

Russell, David A. "South Yemen: From Colonialism to Communism." Unpublished manuscript, August 1, 1981.

Ryder, Vincent. "Move to Reduce Russian Influence." *The Daily Telegraph,* December 1, 1975, 4.

"S rabochim vizitom." *Pravda,* September 28, 1983, 1.

Sakharov, Vladimir. *High Treason.* New York: Ballantine Books, 1980.

"Saudi Envoy Hosts Dinner for Dobrynin." *Arab Times,* April 15, 1984, 1.

Schmidt, Dana Adams. *Yemen: The Unknown War.* New York: Holt, Rinehart and Winston, 1968.

Sergeev, A. "V bor'be za svobodu." *Krasnaia Zvezda,* April 10, 1975, 3.

Shelepin, Vladimir. "Island in a Sea of Oil." *New Times,* no. 36 (September 1979): 26–28.

Shichor, Yitzhak. *The Middle East in China's Foreign Policy, 1949–1977.* Cambridge: Cambridge University Press, 1979.

Shin, A. "Avangard iemenskoi revoliutsii." *Aziia i Afrika Segodnia,* no. 1 (1979): 18–20.

———. "Etapy revoliutsii." *Aziia i Afrika Segodnia,* no. 11 (1977): 36–38.

Shvakov, A. V. *Probuzhdenie Aravii.* Moscow: Mezhdunarodnye Otnosheniia, 1969.

Skeet, Ian. *Muscat and Oman: The End of an Era.* London: Faber and Faber, 1974.

Smirnova, L. "Kuwait's Trade Unions." *New Times,* no. 30 (July 1974): 23.

Smolansky, Bettie M., and Smolansky, Oles M. "The Sino-Soviet Interaction in the Middle East." In *The Sino-Soviet Conflict: A Global Perspective,* ed. Herbert J. Ellison. Seattle and London: University of Washington Press, 1982.

"Soviet Arms Experts to Teach Kuwaitis to Use New Weapons." *The Christian Science Monitor,* October 4, 1984, 2.

The Soviet Attitude toward the N.L.F. and FLOSY. Background Brief no. 83. [U.S. Foreign Broadcast Information Service], 1968.

"Soviet Grip on South Yemen Tightened." *The Daily Telegraph,* April 30, 1981, 4.

"Soviet-Kuwait Talks." *New Times,* no. 50 (December 1975): 16–17.

"Sovmestnoe kommiunike." *Pravda,* May 31, 1980, 1, 4.

"Sovmestnoe kommiunike o vizite v NDRI predsedatelia soveta ministrov SSSR A. N. Kosygina." *Izvestiia,* September 19, 1979, 1, 4.

"Sovmestnoe sovetsko-kuveitskoe kommiunike." *Pravda,* April 26, 1981, 4.

Starr, Richard F. "Checklist of Communist Parties in 1983." *Problems of Communism* 33, 2 (March–April 1984): 41–51.

Steele, Jonathan. *Soviet Power: The Kremlin's Foreign Policy—Brezhnev to Andropov.* New York: Simon and Schuster, 1983.

Stepanov, A. "Plemena iemenskoi arabskoi respubliki." *Aziia i Afrika Segodnia,* no. 12 (1974): 41–43.

———. "The Sana Assassination." *New Times,* no. 43 (October 1977): 14–15.

Stookey, Robert W., ed. *The Arabian Peninsula: Zone of Ferment.* Stanford: Hoover Institution Press, 1984.

———. "Social Structure and Politics in the Yemen Arab Republic." *The Middle East Journal* 28, 3–4 (Summer–Autumn 1974): 248–260, 409–418.

———. *South Yemen: A Marxist Republic in Arabia.* Boulder, Colo.: Westview Press; London: Croom Helm, 1982.

———. *Yemen: The Politics of the Yemen Arab Republic.* Boulder, Colo.: Westview Press, 1978.

Sumner, B. H. *Tsardom and Imperialism in the Far East and Middle East, 1880–1914.* n.p.: Anchor Books, 1968 (originally published 1940).

"Tainaia voina." *Pravda,* January 5, 1976, 4.

Townsend, John. *Oman: The Making of a Modern State.* New York: St. Martin's Press, 1977.

Trevaskis, Kennedy. *Shades of Amber.* London: Hutchinson, 1968.

Tsaplin, V. "Teamed Up." *New Times,* no. 48 (November 1976): 23.

Tumanovich, N. N. *Evropeiskie derzhavy v persidskom zalive v 16–19 vv.* Moscow: Nauka, 1982.

Tyssovskii, Iu. "Sluga trekh gospod." *Izvestiia,* May 30, 1979, 5.

———. "What Was Once the Pirate Coast." *New Times,* no. 19 (May 1977): 23–25.

The USSR and the Middle East: Problems of Peace and Security. Moscow: Novosti, 1972.

U.S. Arms Control and Disarmament Agency. *World Military Expenditures and Arms Transfers 1964–1973.* Washington, D.C.: U.S. Government Printing Office, 1975.

———. *World Military Expenditures and Arms Transfers 1968–1977.* Washington, D.C.: U.S. Government Printing Office, 1979.

———. *World Military Expenditures and Arms Transfers 1971–1980.* Washington, D.C.: U.S. Government Printing Office, 1983.

———. *World Military Expenditures and Arms Transfers 1972–1982.* Washington, D.C.: U.S. Government Printing Office, 1984.

U.S. Congress, House Committee on Foreign Affairs, Subcommittee on Europe and the Middle East. *Proposed Arms Transfers to the Yemen Arab Republic.* 96th Congress, 1st session. Washington, D.C.: U.S. Government Printing Office 1979.

———. *U.S. Interests in, and Policies toward, the Persian Gulf.* 96th Congress, 2d session. Washington, D.C.: U.S. Government Printing Office, 1980.

U.S. Congress, Joint Economic Committee, Subcommittee on International Trade, Finance, and Security Economics. *Allocation of Resources in the Soviet Union and China—1981.* 97th Congress, 1st session. Washington, D.C.: U.S. Government Printing Office, 1982.

U.S. Congress, Senate Committee on Foreign Relations, Subcommittee on Near Eastern and South Asian Affairs. *U.S. Security Interests and Policies in Southwest Asia.* 96th Congress, 2d session. Washington, D.C.: U.S. Government Printing Office, 1980.

U.S. Department of Commerce, Bureau of the Census. *Statistical Abstract of the United States, 1982–83.* Washington, D.C.: U.S. Government Printing Office, 1982.

U.S. Department of State, Bureau of Intelligence and Research. *Soviet and East European Aid to the Third World, 1981.* DOS Pub. 9345. Washington, D.C.: U.S. Government Printing Office, February 1983.

"U.S. Proposes Plan for Upgrading of Kuwaiti Defenses." *The Washington Post,* June 16, 1984, A20.

Usvatov, A. "Provocation." *New Times,* no. 28 (July 1978): 16–17.

———. "Similarity of Views." *New Times,* no. 18 (May 1981): 13.

Val'kov, L. V. "Saudovskaia Araviia: Vnutrennee polozhenie i vneshniaia politika." *Narody Azii i Afriki,* no. 6 (1975): 40–49.

Val'kova, L., and Kotlov, L. *Iuzhnyi Iemen.* Moscow: Mysl', 1973.

Van Hollen, Christopher. "North Yemen: A Dangerous Pentagonal Game." *The Washington Quarterly* 5, 3 (Summer 1982): 137–142.

Vasil'ev, A. "Araviiskii tupik Londona." *Pravda,* August 7, 1970, 5.

———. "Buntuiushchie gory Dofara." *Pravda,* September 29, 1969, 4.

———. "Chto proiskhodit v Kuveite." *Pravda,* September 1, 1976, 5.

———. "Fakely persidskogo zaliva." *Pravda,* May 31, 1974, 4.

———. *Istoriia Saudovskoi Aravii (1745–1973).* Moscow: Nauka, 1982.

——. "'My—ne raby.'" *Pravda*, October 12, 1969, 4.

——. "Nekotorye osobennosti sotsial'no-politicheskoi struktury Saudovskoi Aravii (20-30-e gody XXv.)." *Narody Azii i Afriki*, no. 5 (1980): 52–64.

——. "Partizanskimi tropami Dofara." *Pravda*, October 4, 1969, 4.

——. "Saudovskaia Araviia mezhdu arkhaizmom i sovremennost'iu." *Aziia i Afrika Segodnia*, nos. 8–9 (August–September 1980): 19–21, 17–21.

——. "Visiting South Yemen." *New Times*, no. 30 (July 1970): 26–29.

——. "What Will the 'Golden Rain' Bring?" *New Times*, no. 50 (December 1979): 24–25.

Vasil'ev, A., and Peresada, V. "Opasnye zamysly." *Pravda*, November 4, 1975, 5.

Viktorov, G. "Kuwait." *International Affairs*, no. 5 (May 1977): 142–143.

Vinogradov, V. "Nagnetaiut napriazhennost'." *Krasnaia Zvezda*, April 18, 1979, 3.

——. "Neftianye emiry persidskogo zaliva." *Krasnaia Zvezda*, August 11, 1978, 3.

——. "Oruzhie dlia arabskoi reaktsii." *Krasnaia Zvezda*, September 13, 1978, 3.

——. "Platsdarmy dlia interventsii." *Krasnaia Zvezda*, February 12, 1981, 3.

Vinogradov, V., and Chursanov, V. "Arabskii vostok v planakh imperializma." *Krasnaia Zvezda*, July 30, 1978, 3.

"Vizit delegatsii." *Izvestiia*, May 1, 1979, 5.

Volsky, Dmitry. "The Fall of Sultan Said." *New Times*, no. 32 (August 1970): 26–27.

——. "King Faisal's 'Holy War.'" *New Times*, no. 5 (February 1973): 26–27.

Wenner, Manfred W. *Modern Yemen, 1918-1966*. Baltimore: Johns Hopkins Press, 1967.

Wiles, Peter, ed. *The New Communist Third World: An Essay in Political Economy*. New York: St. Martin's Press, 1982.

Wilson, David. *Soviet Oil and Gas to 1990*. Cambridge, Mass.: Abt Books, 1982.

Winder, R. Bayly. *Saudi Arabia in the Nineteenth Century*. London: Macmillan; New York: St. Martin's Press, 1965.

Wood, Mark. "Soviets Cite Problems in Siberian Oil Output." *The Washington Post*, May 28, 1984, E2-E3.

Yodfat, A., and Abir, M. *In the Direction of the Persian Gulf: The Soviet Union and the Persian Gulf*. London: Frank Cass, 1977.

Yodfat, Aryeh Y. *The Soviet Union and the Arabian Peninsula*. London: Croom Helm; New York: St. Martin's Press, 1983.

Zaborin, N. "Snova bazy." *Sovetskaia Rossiia*, August 11, 1977, 3.

"Zaiavlenie ministra innostrannykh del Kuveita." *Pravda*, August 24, 1982, 4.

"Zaiavlenie natsional'nogo fronta severnogo Iemena." *Krasnaia Zvezda*, October 27, 1977, 3.

"Zaiavlenie TASS." *Krasnaia Zvezda*, March 8, 1984, 3.

Zgersky, Dmitry. "Oman's 'Open Door.'" *New Times*, no. 44 (October 1982): 14–15.

Index

U.S. Department of State, 84, 218n.78, 246n.34; and 1979 Yemeni war, 36, 38
USS *Constellation,* 37
USSR. *See* Union of Soviet Socialist Republics

Vance, Cyrus, 205n.103
Vasil'ev, A. M., 114, 199n.3
Vietnam, 10, 70, 192
Voice of Free South Yemen, 76–77
Voice of the Free Sons of the Yemeni South, 98
Voice of the PFLO, 233n.65

Wadiah, 76–77
Wadi al-Kalim, 109
Wahabism, 127, 129, 134, 178
Warbah Island, 159–60
Washington Post, 41
Al-Watan (Kuwait), 41
Watts, Lt. Gen. John, 237n.99
Wazaiyyah, 36
al-Wazir, 'Abdallah, 18
West Bank, 148
Western Europe, 53, 103, 191; oil imports, 3–4, 8, 126
Western Protectorate, 66–67, 69–70
West Germany, 50, 84, 97
Wilson, David, 6

Wolfe, Thomas W., 44, 84, 209n.156, 218n.74
World Federation of Trade Unions, 166
World Peace Council, 231n.43

Yaaribah tribe, 105
Yahya bin Muhammad Hamid ad-Din, 5, 17–18, 65, 129, 132
Yemen Arab Republic. *See* North Yemen
Yemeni Revolutionary Resistance Fighters, 32
Yemeni Socialist Party (YSP), 43, 73, 92–93, 97, 209n.149, 224nn.118, 127, 225n.133
Yemen People's Unity Party (YPUP), 43, 209n.149
Yodfat, Aryeh, 148, 242n.81
Young Kuwaiti movement, 166
YPUP. *See* Yemen People's Unity Party
YSP. *See* Yemeni Socialist Party
Yugoslavia, 117, 225n.132, 248n.45

Zaidis: in North Yemen, 15–16, 17, 22, 23, 26, 32, 39, 82, 203n.67; and South Yemen, 63
Zanzibar, 106–7
Zayid bin Sultan Al Nuhayan, 173–74, 178–79, 254n.128
Zinjibar Congress, 71, 91

ABOUT THE AUTHOR

Mark N. Katz is a specialist on Soviet foreign and military policy toward the Third World. He is currently a research associate at the Kennan Institute—a component of the Woodrow Wilson International Center for Scholars at the Smithsonian Institution in Washington, D.C. His work on this book was supported by grants from the Rockefeller Foundation and from the Kennan Institute. He is author of *The Third World in Soviet Military Thought,* also from Johns Hopkins.

THE JOHNS HOPKINS UNIVERSITY PRESS

Russia & Arabia

This book was composed in Times Roman text and Franklin Gothic Condensed display by BG Composition, Inc., from a design by Martha Farlow. It was printed on 50-lb Glatfelter Offset by Thomson-Shore, Inc., and bound in Kivar.